Lecture Notes in Artificial Intelli

Subseries of Lecture Notes in Computer Science

LNAI Series Editors

Randy Goebel
University of Alberta, Edmonton, Canada
Yuzuru Tanaka
Hokkaido University, Sapporo, Japan
Wolfgang Wahlster
DFKI and Saarland University, Saarbrücken, Germany

LNAI Founding Series Editor

Joerg Siekmann
DFKI and Saarland University, Saarbrücken, Germany

Michael Fisher   Leon van der Torre
Mehdi Dastani   Guido Governatori (Eds.)

Computational Logic in Multi-Agent Systems

13th International Workshop, CLIMA XIII
Montpellier, France, August 27-28, 2012
Proceedings

Springer

Series Editors

Randy Goebel, University of Alberta, Edmonton, Canada
Jörg Siekmann, University of Saarland, Saarbrücken, Germany
Wolfgang Wahlster, DFKI and University of Saarland, Saarbrücken, Germany

Volume Editors

Michael Fisher
University of Liverpool, UK
E-mail: mfisher@liverpool.ac.uk

Leon van der Torre
University of Luxembourg
E-mail: leon.vandertorre@uni.lu

Mehdi Dastani
Utrecht University, The Netherlands
E-mail: m.m.dastani@uu.nl

Guido Governatori
NICTA, Queensland Research Laboratory
St. Lucia, QLD, Australia
E-mail: guido@governatori.net

ISSN 0302-9743   e-ISSN 1611-3349
ISBN 978-3-642-32896-1   e-ISBN 978-3-642-32897-8
DOI 10.1007/978-3-642-32897-8
Springer Heidelberg Dordrecht London New York

Library of Congress Control Number: 2012945036

CR Subject Classification (1998): I.2.11, F.4.1, D.2, D.3.1-2, I.2.4, F.3

LNCS Sublibrary: SL 7 – Artificial Intelligence

Typesetting: Camera-ready by author, data conversion by Scientific Publishing Services, Chennai, India

Printed on acid-free paper

Springer is part of Springer Science+Business Media (www.springer.com)

Preface

These are the proceedings of the 13th International Workshop on Computational Logic in Multi-Agent Systems (CLIMA-XIII), held during August 27–28, 2012 in Montpelier, co-located with ECAI.

The CLIMA workshops provide a forum for discussing techniques, based on computational logic, for representing, programming, and reasoning about agents and multi-agent systems in a formal way. CLIMA has been successful over a number of years, and further details of previous events can be found at http://centria.di.fct.unl.pt/~clima.

Multi-Agent Systems contain autonomous computational entities perceiving their environment and acting upon it in order to achieve their goals. They integrate many technologies and concepts from Artificial Intelligence and Computer Science, as well as from other disciplines. The agent paradigm has been used for several domains in which it is crucial to be able to describe, concisely and clearly, the precise behaviours of the agents involved, such as search engines, autonomous vehicles, recommendation systems, educational support, robotics, e-procurement, simulation and routing, electronic commerce and trade.

Computational Logic provides a well-defined, general, and rigorous framework for studying the syntax, semantics, and procedures for the various tasks in individual agents, as well as the interactions between, and integration among, agents in multi-agent systems. It also provides tools, techniques, and standards for implementations and environments, for linking specifications to implementations, and for the verification of properties of individual agents, multi-agent systems, and their implementations.

Thus, it is this combination of *computational logic* approaches to *multi-agent systems* that is the primary focus of the CLIMA workshop series. This particular edition was held as a workshop associated with the European Conference on Artificial Intelligence in Montpelier, France, during August 2012.

We received 27 submissions, each of which was then reviewed by three Program Committee members. These proceedings comprise the 11 regular papers selected, as well as contributions from the three invited speakers:

- Dov Gabbay — "Bipolar Argumentation Frames and Contrary to Duty Obligations, Preliminary Report" (full paper)
- Gerhard Lakemeyer — "Multi-agent Only-Knowing" (abstract only)
- Emiliano Lorini — "Logics for Reasoning About Agents' Attitudes in Strategic Contexts" (abstract only)

The contribution of Isaac Pinyol, entitled "A Time-Situated Meta-Logic for Characterizing Goal-Processing Bounded Agents," provides a logical framework for characterising the reasoning of goal-processing bounded agents, based on a "time-situated meta-logic," in which goals and beliefs are primitive attitudes evaluated at specific moments in time.

In "Distributed Defeasible Speculative Reasoning in Ambient Environment," Ho-Pun Lam, Guido Governatori, Ken Satoh, and Hiroshi Hosobe describe how "speculative computation" can allow agents to postulate solutions in unknown environments and provide a formal semantics for such an approach. This is particularly useful in complex, open, and error-prone environments where communications delay, or even failure, is common.

In their paper "A Formal Semantics for Agent (Re)Organization," Frank Dignum and Virginia Dignum tackle the complex problem of large-scale agent interactions. Agent organizations are multi-agent systems that are adaptbale and dynamic, and that can place restrictions on the agents involved through social order mechanisms. This work provides a "Logic for Agent Organization" that can be used to reason about a range of properties within such systems.

Work by Dimitar Guelev and Catalin Dima, described in "Epistemic ATL with Perfect Recall, Past and Strategy Contexts," involves an extension to epistemic ATL with perfect recall, past, and distributed knowledge by strategy contexts and demonstrate the strong completeness of a Hilbert-style proof system for a fragment.

Matei Popovici describes a new modeling method in "Using Evolution Graphs for Describing Topology-Aware Prediction Models in Large Clusters." The author defines and studies the complexity of the model checking problem for the language, and the relation between the language and Computation Tree Logic.

The contribution of Isabelle Mirbel and Serena Villata, with title "Enhancing Goal-Based Requirements Consistency: An Argumentation-Based Approach," proposes an approach to detecting consistent sets of goal-based requirements and to maintaining their consistency over time. Their approach relies on meta-argumentation, allowing one to detect the conflicts among elements called arguments.

In "A Game Theoretic Approach for Optimal Network Topologies in Opportunistic Networks," Nils Bulling, Michael Koester, and Matei Popovici introduce a formal description of an opportunistic network and of optimal communication topologies. They determine the complexity of associated verification and synthesis problems of network topologies.

The work of Martin Homola, Matthias Knorr, Joao Leite, and Martin Slota, described in "MKNF Knowledge Bases in Multi-Context Systems," investigates the relationship between Multi-Context Systems and Hybrid MKNF Knowledge Bases. It is shown that Hybrid MKNF Knowledge Bases can be used as particular contexts in Multi-Context Systems, and transformations from the former into the latter are provided.

The contribution of Ben Wright, Enrico Pontelli, and Tran Cao Son, entitled "Implementing Reversible Processes in Multi-agent Action Languages Using Answer Set Planning," presents an implementation of an action language in answer set programming. Processes are used to execute delayed effects for actions, and processes can be reversed or canceled.

In "Full Hybrid mu-Calculus, Its Bisimulation Invariance and Application to Argumentation," Cristian Gratie, Adina Magda Florea, and John-Jules Meyer show that full hybrid mu-calculus cannot describe the preferred argumentation semantics.

Finally, in "A Numerical Approach to the Merging of Argumentation Networks," Dov Gabbay and Odinaldo Rodrigues consider an augmented network containing the arguments and attacks of all networks to be merged. The combined weighted network is then used to define a system of equations from which the overall strength of the arguments is calculated.

We thank all the authors of submissions for CLIMA-XIII for sending their papers and the authors of accepted papers for revising their contributions to be included in these proceedings. We are very grateful to the members of the CLIMA-XIII Program Committee and the additional reviewers. Their service ensured the high quality of the accepted papers.

June 2012

Michael Fisher
Leon van der Torre
Mehdi Dastani
Guido Governatori

Organization

Program Committee

Natasha Alechina	University of Nottingham
Jose Julio Alferes	Universidade Nova de Lisboa
Alexander Artikis	NCSR "Demokritos"
Lacramioara Astefanoaei	CWI
Francesco Belardinelli	Imperial College London
Antonis Bikakis	University College London
Guido Boella	University of Turin
Rafael H. Bordini	Federal University of Rio Grande do Sul
Gerhard Brewka	Leipzig University
Nils Bulling	Clausthal University of Technology
Stefania Costantini	Università di L'Aquila
Mehdi Dastani	Utrecht University
Marina De Vos	University of Bath
Louise Dennis	University of Liverpool
Juergen Dix	Clausthal University of Technology
Jenny Eriksson Lundström	Uppsala University
Michael Fisher	University of Liverpool
Chiara Ghidini	FBK-irst
Aditya Ghose	University of Wollongong
Guido Governatori	NICTA
Davide Grossi	University of Liverpool
Hisashi Hayashi	Toshiba
Koen Hindriks	Delft University of Technology
Katsumi Inoue	NII
Wojtek Jamroga	University of Luxembourg
Jérôme Lang	LAMSADE
Joao Leite	Universidade Nova de Lisboa
Brian Logan	University of Nottingham
Emiliano Lorini	IRIT
Viviana Mascardi	Università degli Studi di Genova
John-Jules Meyer	Utrecht University
Jan Odelstad	University of Gävle
Mehmet Orgun	Macquarie University
Maurice Pagnucco	The University of New South Wales
Gabriella Pigozzi	Université Paris-Dauphine
Enrico Pontelli	New Mexico State University
R. Ramanujam	Institute of Mathematical Sciences, Chennai

Antonino Rotolo	CIRSFID, University of Bologna
Fariba Sadri	Imperial College London
Chiaki Sakama	Wakayama University
Ken Satoh	National Institute of Informatics and Sokendai
Tran Cao Son	New Mexico State University
Bas Steunebrink	IDSIA
Michael Thielscher	The University of New South Wales
Nicolas Troquard	Laboratory of Applied Ontology
Paolo Turrini	University of Luxembourg
Wiebe van der Hoek	University of Liverpool
Leon van der Torre	University of Luxembourg
M. Birna Van Riemsdijk	TU Delft
Wamberto Vasconcelos	University of Aberdeen
Srdjan Vesic	University of Luxembourg
Emil Weydert	University of Luxembourg
Thomas Ågotnes	University of Bergen

Additional Reviewers

Banerjee, Mohua
Hjelmblom, Magnus
Li, Tingting

Sano, Katsuhiko
Shams, Zohreh

Table of Contents

Bipolar Argumentation Frames and Contrary to Duty Obligations, Preliminary Report*

Dov Gabbay[1,2,3]

[1] Bar Ilan Univ., Israel
[2] King's College London
[3] Univ. Luxembourg
dov.gabbay@kcl.ac.uk

Abstract. In my papers [2,7], I modelled the Chisholm paradox and generally Chisholm like sequences of contrary to duty obligations by using Reactive Kripke models [4]. Reactive Kripke frames have two types of arrows: ordinary single arrows $x \to y$ indicating accessibility relations and double arrows of the form $(u \to v) \twoheadrightarrow (x \to y)$, indicating reactive connections. In the frames where the ordering is a tree, as it is in the models for contrary to duty obligations, the double arrow $(u \to v) \twoheadrightarrow (x \to y)$ can be uniquely represented by $v \twoheadrightarrow y$. We thus get a bipolar network where we interpret $\to$ as support and $\twoheadrightarrow$ as attack. Of course the same reactive graph can be manipulated in the Deontic way [2], when we read it as modelling contrary to duty obligations and it can be manipulated in the argumentation way [1,3], when viewed as a bipolar network. The question arises, can we find a family of tree like graphs, (which do not sacrifice generality neither in the contrary to duty area nor in the bipolar argumentation area) for which the Deontic and the argumentation manipulations are the same. This paper shows that this is possible, and thus establishes a connection between the contrary to duty area and the bipolar argumentation area. Note the following:

1. This connection with bipolar argumentation frames is made possible because of the modelling of contrary to duty obligation using reactive Kripke models. The connection between Reactivity and Bipolarity is more easy to see.
2. The way the game is played in each area is different. So we have here a wide scope for interaction and exchange of ideas between argumentation and normative reasoning. These include:
   (a) Deontic like modelling and axiomatisations for bipolar argumentation
   (b) argumentation semantics for contrary to duty paradoxes which can especially handle contrary to duty loops (a subject hardly mentioned in the contrary to duty literature)[1]
   (c) The equational approach to contrary to duty, imported from the equational approach to argumentation [8]

---

* I am grateful to M. Caminada, L. van der Torre and S. Villata for valuable comments. Research done under THE ISRAEL SCIENCE FOUNDATION Grant No 1321/10: Integrating Logic and Network reasoning.

[1] There is however the Moebius Example of Makinson [15]. The example is formulated in the context of input -output logic but would give rise to the following contrary to duty loop:

$$a \to Ox; x \to Oy; y \to O\neg a.$$

See Example 6 below.

M. Fisher et al. (Eds.): CLIMA XIII 2012, LNAI 7486, pp. 1–24, 2012.
© Springer-Verlag Berlin Heidelberg 2012

> (d) The fact that bipolar frames can be instantiated as contrary to duty obligation might shed some light on the polarised debate in the argumentation community on how to instantiate argumentation networks, see [5].
> (e) Settle quesions of how to model (what is) support in argumentation
> 3. Doing Modal Logic in Bipolar Argumentation Theory (compare with [6]).

This paper shows a connection between deontic contrary to duty obligations [2,7] and bipolar argumentation networks [1,3]. We need to give a short introduction to each area.

1 Cayrol and Lagasquie-Schiex's Bipolar Argumentation Framework

In this section we summarize the definitions of bipolar argumentation frameworks with the terminology used by Cayrol and Lagasquie-Schiex [3].

Definition 1 (Bipolar argumentation framework BAF). *A bipolar argumentation framework* $(A, \rightarrow, \twoheadrightarrow)$ *consists of a finite set* A *called arguments and two binary relations on* A *called attack and support respectively.*

Definition 2 (Conflict free). *Given an argumentation framework* $AF = (A, \twoheadrightarrow)$ *a set* $C \subseteq A$ *is conflict free, denoted as* $cf(C)$, *iff there do not exists* $\alpha, \beta \in C$ *such that* $\alpha \twoheadrightarrow \beta$.

The union of elementary coalitions in [3] is defined as follows:

Definition 3 (Elementary coalitions). *An elementary coalition of BAF is a subset* $EC = \{a_1, \dots, a_n\}$ *of* A *such that*

1. *there exists a permutation* $\{i_1, \dots, i_n\}$ *of* $\{1, \dots, n\}$ *such that the sequence of support* $a_i \rightarrow a_{i_1} \rightarrow a_{i_n}$ *holds;*
2. $cf(EC)$;
3. *EC is maximal (with respect to* $\subseteq$) *among the subsets of* A *satisfying (1) and (2).*

EC denotes the set of elementary coalitions of BAF and $ECAF = (EC(A), c\text{-attacks})$ is the elementary coaltion framework associated with BAF. Cayrol and Lagasqie-Schiex define a conflict relation on $EC(A)$ as follows:

Definition 4 (c-attacks relation). *Let* EC_1 *and* EC_2 *be two elementary coalitions of BAF.* EC_1 *c-attacks* EC_2 *if and only if there exists an argument* a_1 *in* EC_1 *and an argument* a_2 *in* EC_2 *such that* $a_1 \twoheadrightarrow a_2$.

Remark 1. Extensions can now be defined in the Dung traditional manner on ECAF. We get sets of coalitions on A. Our interest stops at this point. However [3] continued to the next definition 5.

Definition 5 (Acceptability semantics).

- *S is a ecp-extention of BAF if and only if there exists* $\{EC_1, \dots, EC_p\}$ *a preferred extension of ECAF such that* $S = EC_1 \cup \dots \cup EC_p$.

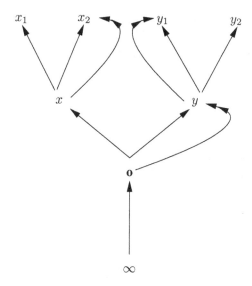

Fig. 1.

- S is an *ecs-extension of BAF if and only if there exists $\{EC_1, \ldots, EC_p\}$ a stable extension of $ECAF$ such that $S = EC_1 \cup \ldots \cup EC_p$.*
- S is a *ecg-extension of BAF if and only if there exists $\{EC_1, \ldots, EC_p\}$ a grounded extension of $ECAF$ such that $S = EC_1 \cup \ldots \cup EC_p$.*

Example 1. Consider the bipolar network of Figure 1. We shall see later that Figure 1 arises from the modelling of the Chisholm paradox and so we have good reason for choosing it here.

Fig. 2.

Note that we allow nodes to both attack and support other nodes at the same time. This is allowed in [3].[2]

---

[2] If the reader is uncomfortable with this we can add auxiliary points and the problem disappears. We can replace any occurrence of Figure 2 by Figure 3.

Since the bipolar semantics deals with coalitions, and $W_{x,y}$ is between x and y, it will appear in any coalition containing x and y and there will be no technical consequences to using Figure 2 instead of Figure 3.

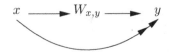

Fig. 3.

The maximal support paths of Figure 1 are

$$\beta = (\infty, \mathbf{o}, y, y_2)$$
$$\alpha = (\infty, \mathbf{o}, y, y_1)$$
$$\delta = (\infty, \mathbf{o}, x, x_2)$$
$$\gamma = (\infty, \mathbf{o}, x, x_1)$$

The maximal coalitions according to Definition 3 are

$$\{\infty, \mathbf{o}, x, x_1\}, \{y, y_2\}.$$

The attack relation among coalitions is Figure 4.

$$\gamma = \{\infty, \mathbf{o}, x, x_1\} \quad \beta' = \{y, y_2\}$$

Fig. 4.

Thus the extension is $\{\gamma, \beta'\}$ since they don't attack each other.

If we want to proceed according to Definition 5, we get the extension for 1 to be $\gamma \cup \beta = \{\infty, \mathbf{o}, x, x_1, y, y_2\}$.

Note that if we compute the extensions for 1 directly, we get the same set, $\{\infty, \mathbf{o}, x, x_1, y, y_2\}$.

Note that the reason we cannot take the maximal paths $\alpha, \beta, \gamma, \delta$ as our "coalition" network elements is that α, β and δ are not conflict free, and Definition 3 requires conflict freeness. If we ignore the conflict free restriction we can consider the network with $\alpha, \beta, \gamma, \delta$.

The attack relation among the paths is as in Figure 5.

Example 2. Another example from [1] is Figure 6

The coalitions are as in Figure 7. The extension of Figure 7 is $\{(d), (e)\}$. and according to Definition 5, this yields the extension $\{d, e\}$ for Figure 6. The $\{d, e\}$ extension is not correct according to Dung. Paper [1] offers a remedy.[3] We are not interested in that in the current paper. For the purpose of comparison with contrary to duty obligations it is sufficient for us to stop at the step where we got extensions for Figure 7.

Note that we prefer to take a modified form of Figure 6. Namely, Figure 8. We add a new node ∞ and add $\infty \to x$, to any x such that there is no y with $y \to x$, i.e. to all $\to$ minimal xs.

---

[3] In [1] we extend the notion of attack. If a supports b and c attacks b we consider a as being under attack as well. See Remark 3 below.

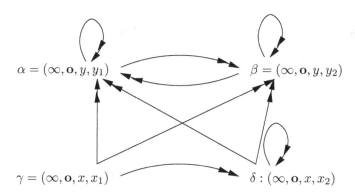

Fig. 5.

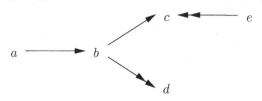

Fig. 6.

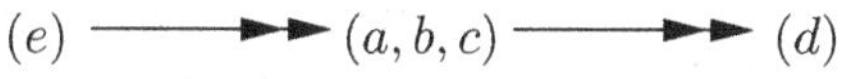

$$(e) \longrightarrow (a, b, c) \longrightarrow (d)$$

Fig. 7.

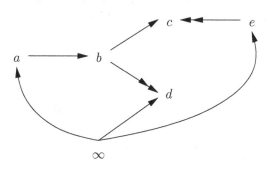

Fig. 8.

This helps the bipolar network to be similar to models of contrary to duty obligations.

Definition 6. *Let* $(S, \to, \twoheadrightarrow)$ *be a bipolar network. Let* ∞ *be a new point. Define* $S' = S \cup \{\infty\}$ *and extend* $\to$ *on* S' *as follows.*
For any $x \in S$ *such that for no* $y \in S$ *do we have that* $y \to x$ *holds, let* $\infty \to x$ *be added.*
We call $(S', \to, \twoheadrightarrow)$ *the deontic friendly extension of* $(S, \to, \twoheadrightarrow)$.

Proposition 1. *The mapping*

$$(\infty, x_1, \ldots, x_n) \leftrightarrow (x_1, \ldots, x_n)$$

between the coalitions in S' *to coalitions in* S *is an isomorphism of the coalition graph of* S *(as in Definition 4) and the coalition graph of* S'.

Proof. Obvious.

2 Reactive Semantics for Contrary to Duty Obligations

We now very quickly present the problems of contrary to duty paradoxes and outline our reactive models for their solution.

Consider the following set of obligations, known as the Chisholm set. Notation: $p = $ go, $q = $ tell.

1. It is obligatory to go and help your friend.
2. If you go, you ought to tell him you are coming.
3. If you do not go, you ought to tell him you are not going.
4. Fact: you do not go.

A proper modelling of these clauses requires that these clauses be indepedent and consistent. Standard deontic logic **SDL** cannot do the job and in our papers [2,7] we offer a reactive variant of **SDL**. **SDL** is the modal logic **K** with the operator O and the additional axiom $\neg O \bot$. The English statements (1)–(4) are formalised (at best) as (1a), (2b), (3a), (4a) below. If read as wffs of **SDL** they are still problematic, but if modelled by reactive frames like Figure 9, we avoid difficulties and have a solution, see [2,7].

Let us take the translation into **SDL** (1a), (2b), (3a), (4a).

(1a) Op
(2b) $p \to Oq$
(3a) $\neg p \to O\neg q$
(4a) $\neg p$

The problem with this translation when taken as wffs of **SDL** is that (4a) implies logically (2b). We lose independence.

Let us look at Figure 9, which gives a graphical representation of the linguistic clauses (1a), (2b), (3a), and (4a).

Figure 9 expresses exactly the same as the lingusitic clauses. However, it is clear that this is a different representation and we can see from the figure at which node each of these clauses is associated with.

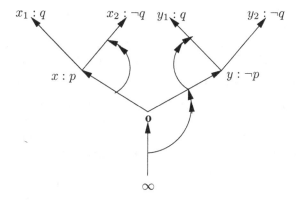

Fig. 9. Representation of the Chisholm set

(1a) is associated with node **o**
(2b) is associated with node x
(3a) is associated with node y
(4a) is associated with node y

Before we explain how we understand Figure 9, let us compare it, purely as a graph, with Figure 1. First note that since the $\rightarrow$ part of this figure is a tree, we can represent the double arrows

$$(\infty \rightarrow \mathbf{o}) \twoheadrightarrow (\mathbf{o} \rightarrow y)$$

$$(\mathbf{o} \rightarrow y) \twoheadrightarrow (y \rightarrow y_1)$$

$$(\mathbf{o} \rightarrow x) \twoheadrightarrow (x \rightarrow x_2)$$

respectively by

$$\mathbf{o} \twoheadrightarrow y$$

$$y \twoheadrightarrow y_1$$

$$x \twoheadrightarrow x_2$$

This can be done because each point in the tree (except ∞) has a unique $\rightarrow$ predecessor, and so we can identify any $u \rightarrow v$ by v alone.

If we do this indentification we see that Figure 9 becomes Figure 1.

This is good, however, in bipolar argumentation we read and do extensions with the figure while in deontic logic we read contrary to duty obligations from the figure. Are these two "readings" related?[4] Let me tell you first the deontic reading and then we compare the way we read the figure. Our deontic reading is as follows. ∞ is our starting

---

[4] Note that this is a key question. If what we do with the basic figure is different then there is no relation between the approaches. This point will arise also in Remark 2 when we compare our approach with other papers, for example with paper [12].

point. We go to node **o** (say office), where our obligations begin. Obligation 1 says we ought to go and help.

This means we need to travel to node x. This is why we have the double arrow from $(\infty \to \mathbf{o})$ to $(\mathbf{o} \to y)$. Double arrows in the reactive semantics post a warning sign

"Do not pass through this arc"

If we indeed go through $\mathbf{o} \to x$, we need to continue to point x_1 and so another double arrow $(\mathbf{o} \to x) \twoheadrightarrow (x \to x_2)$ tells our traveller not to go through $x \to x_2$. Similarly if we ignore the warning sign on the arc $\mathbf{o} \to y$ and go across it to y, then the contrary to duty says do not go to y_1, do go to y_2. It put a warning sign on $y \to y_1$. This is done by the double arrow $(\mathbf{o} \to y) \twoheadrightarrow (y \to y_1)$.

Our deontic perception of Figure 9 and its equivalent (as a graph only) Figure 1 is that we walk along maximal paths following the arrows.

So let us ask ourselves, what are the possible paths? These are

$$\beta = (\infty, \mathbf{o}, y, y_2)$$

$$\alpha = (\infty, \mathbf{o}, y, y_1)$$

$$\delta = (\infty, \mathbf{o}, x, x_2)$$

$$\gamma = (\infty, \mathbf{o}, x, x_1)$$

The facts in the contrary to duty set, is information about the path we actually took. The full information is a maximal path, and partial information is a family of (possible) paths. In our example the fact is that he went to node y but we do not know whether he continued to y_1 or to y_2. So the possible paths are α and β.

The $\twoheadrightarrow$ are the attacks. We can perceive them as attacks in the contrary to duty deontic case because they represent instructions to block some paths. This is their function.[5]

Now we ask, if we walk according to all obligations and obey all double arrows (obey all signs which say **do not pass**), which paths are Kosher and OK?

By looking at the figure, we see it is

$$(\infty, \mathbf{o}, x, x_1)$$

Here we obey all our obligations. We are really good.

It can also be (y, y_2) if we obey the contrary to duty. Having violated the Ox and gone to y, we no longer commit violations and obey $y \to Oy_2$.

Now we ask, doing the bipolar extensions according to [3], as in Definition 5, what do we get? The answer is $\{\infty, \mathbf{o}, x, x_1\}$, and $\{y, y_2\}$.

So we are getting all the paths in which we are somewhat obedient.

We now get a suggested correspondence as follows:

---

[5] The idea of nodes or arrows attacking other arrows was introduced in [4] and gave rise to the notion of Reactive Kripke Semantics, which was widely applied. In our papers [11] and its expanded version [10], these ideas were used in argumentation. See also [9] for details and discussions. [19,24] independently considered this idea. See also [1]. In our paper [2] we used reactive arrows to model contrary to duty obligations, and this use allows for the connection between argumentation and normative systems. A detailed general overview and priorities on second and higher levels attacks can be found in my forthcoming book [25].

Support = possible path connection
Attack = Obligation
Extensions = sets of maximal paths without violation

We shall see later in Example 5, that we recommend to change the notion of attack in bipolar argumentation and take paths instead of sets as our elements. This would be our message to [3].[6]

Example 3. Let us look at Figure 8 from the deontic contrary to duty point of view. First we comment that the family of examples (paradoxes) of contrary to duty sets is limited and this graph (given in [1] as an example to discuss the adequacy of [3]) does not fit any known deontic example. However, we do have an interpretation for it. We have in Figure 8 several options for paths beginning at ∞ and we would like to offer a maximal package of paths for the righteous people to follow, without any risk of violations. Looked at the figure in this way we want extensions in the sense of Definition 5 for paths. The answer is

$$\{(\infty, d), (\infty, e)\}$$

Note that is is meaningless for the deontic case to look at $\{d, e\}$ as suggested in Definition 5, as an extension of the points graph. We want only coalition extensions.

3 New Ideas Arising from the Connection between Argumentation and Deontic Logic

The previous two sections presented the connections between bipolar networks and contrary to duty obligations. This section will describe new ideas arising from these connections. We discuss

1. Bipolar argumentation semantics for contrary to duty (looping) obligations
2. The equational approach to contrary to duty
3. New path semantics for bipolar argumentation networks

We now know how to turn every reactive tree frame into a bipolar system, and hence get argumentation semantics for contrary to duty sets. Let us get some mileage out of this correspondence. In [7] there is a loop example whose semantics was left as an open problem. Can we make use of our new insight?

Example 4 (Loop). Consider the following 3-loop.

1. $\neg x \rightarrow$ Obligatory y
2. $\neg y \rightarrow$ Obligatory z
3. $\neg z \rightarrow$ Obligatory x.

We cannot build a tree graph for it. We have a loop.

---

[6] The reader familiar with Abstract Dialectical frameworks of Brewka and Woltran [23] will recall that they claim in their paper, that they do better analysis of support than [3]. Our aim here is not to do better than [3] but to show the interaction of BAF with Deontic reasoning. By the way, we use in Remark 3 the notion of disjunctive attacks, introduced in [17], to model multiple support. The logical machinery of Abstract Dialectical Framework is implicit in [17], as recognised by Brewka and Woltran in their paper. This means that they are also capable of doing what we are doing in Remark 3.

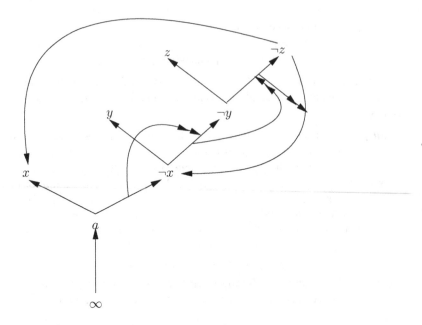

Fig. 10. 3-level loop

The coalitions in this case are

$$\{\infty, a, x\}$$
$$\{\infty, a, \neg x, y\}$$

These are the only conflict free coalitions in Figure 10 and are therefore the bipolar extensions according to Definition 4 and Remark 1.[7]

We now check the maximal path point of view for Figure 10.

---

[7] The perceptive reader will note that Figure 10 is not a kosher figure of bipolar network as defined by Cayrol and Lagasquie-Schiex's in Definition 1. The attack arrows do not emanate from nodes but from arcs. Such attacks were never considered in the argumentation networks, except in [11] and [10]. The attacks arrows also terminate in arcs. The idea of attacking arcs was also first introduced in [11] and was followed up, sometimes independently, in the literature. Note that Figure 10 is not a tree and so we cannot convert it to an equivalent figure with double arrows emanating from nodes and terminating at nodes. We can and should, however, generalise the notion of bipolar argumentation networks by saying that attacks should emanate from support arrows, and terminate at other support arrows, using the rationale that when we support an argument , part of our support strategy is to initiate attacks on other arguments and their supports. We shall later develop these concepts. Meanwhile let us execute the obvious steps for Figure 10.

The finite paths are as follows:

$$\alpha = (\infty, a, x)$$
$$\beta = (\infty, a, \neg x, y)$$
$$\gamma = (\infty, a, \neg x, \neg y)$$
$$\delta = (\infty, a, \neg x, \neg y, \neg z, x)$$
$$w = (\neg y, \neg z, \neg x)$$

Then we loop into the infinite number of sequences

$$\zeta_n = \alpha(w)^n(y)$$
$$\eta_n = \alpha(w)^n(\neg y, z)$$
$$\rho_n = \alpha(w)^n(\neg y, \neg z, x).$$
$$n = 1, 2, 3, \ldots$$

The path attack relation is as follows:

1. α attacks nobody
2. $\beta \twoheadrightarrow$ all except α, β
3. All nodes except α, β attack each other.

Clearly the extension there for the path network is: $\{\alpha, \beta\}$.

These are also the righteous paths with no violations, and they correspond to the bipolar extensions.

Example 5 (Gabbay's first proposal for the concept of bipolar network). This example imports concepts from contrary to duty oblgations into bipolar argumentation. Consider the network of Figure 11. This represents the contrary to duty

1. You ought to either work or rest
2. If you work you ought to rest
3. If you rest you ought to work.

What these rules say is that you ought to start working or get yourself ready by resting, and then alternate between work and rest.

The paths here are

$$\Pi_1 = (\infty, \mathbf{o}, W, R, W, R, \ldots)$$
$$\Pi_2 = (\infty, \mathbf{o}, R, W, R, W, \ldots)$$

According to the bipolar definitions, Definitions 3 and 4 we take subsets as maximal conflict free coalitions and the attack relation is done element-wise. So there is only one coalition $\{\infty, \mathbf{o}\}$. This does not mean much in our context.

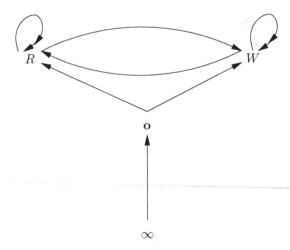

Fig. 11.

This example shows a sharp difference between the path approach and the coalition bipolar approach. We did have good correspondence between the two approaches when the graphs were trees (Examples 1 and 2 and the analysis of Figure 9).

The correspondence still worked even in the looping example 4, but not for Figure 11. We need now to recommend changes in the abstract machinery of Definitions 1–4.

This is our message of change to C. Cayrol and M. C. Lagasquie-Schiex's bipolar concept.

The following table, Table 1 outlines the differences, which is then followed by a discussion.

We assume in this table that we have as given a bipolar graph $(S, \rightarrow, \twoheadrightarrow)$.

Table 1.

Concept	Cayrol and Lagasquie-Schiex	Gabbay
Path	A sequence $(x_1, \ldots, x_n)$ such that $x_1 \rightarrow x_2 \rightarrow \ldots \rightarrow x_n$ holds	same
conflict free path	For no $x, y, \in \{x_1, \ldots, x_n\}$ do we have $x \twoheadrightarrow y$	For no $1 \leq i \leq n - 1$ do we have $x_i \twoheadrightarrow x_{i+1}$
Attack between paths	$(x_1, \ldots, x_n)$ attacks $(y_1, \ldots, y_k)$ if for some x_i and y_j we have $x_i \twoheadrightarrow y_j$ '	$(x_1, \ldots, x_n)$ attacks $(y_1, \ldots, y_k)$ if for some $r < \min(k, n)$ we have $x_r \twoheadrightarrow y_{r+1}$.
Coalition	Maximal conflict free set which is a path (Definition 3)	Maximal Gabbay conflict free path.

According to Gabbay's path semantics, the paths Π_1 and Π_2 are conflict free each and do not attack each other. They are the two violation free courses of action for the contrary to duty Figure 11. So we get the right result here.[8]

Example 6 (Makinson Moebius example). Consider the loop

1. $a \rightarrow Ox$
2. $x \rightarrow Oy$
3. $y \rightarrow O\neg a$

Figure 12 draws this set

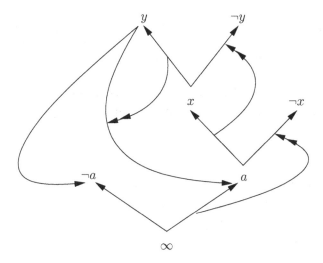

Fig. 12.

The only coalition or path coalition which is not self attacking in Figure 12 is $(\infty, a, x, , \neg a)$. Neither Cayrol and Lagasquie-Schiex (Definition 4) nor Gabbay (Example 7) is bothered by the fact that we have both a and $\neg a$ in this coalition because there is no formal attack $a \twoheadrightarrow \neg a$ or $\neg a \twoheadrightarrow a$ n the Figure. One must not criticise Cayrol and Lagasquie-Schiex for not requiring that $a \twoheadrightarrow \neg a$ an $\neg a \twoheadrightarrow a$ because "$\neg$" is not assumed in the language.

In the case of Gabbay the definition is in terms of paths and although we pass through node a we do follow instructions and end up at $\neg a$. So Gabbay would not need to stipulate $a \twoheadrightarrow \neg a$ and $\neg a \twoheadrightarrow a$.

Example 7 (The equational approach to contrary to duty obligations). We can import more from argumentation to deontic logic. We can import the equational approach. See [8].

Consider Figure 13.

---

[8] Note that sequences can be proofs and so we may be able to deliver an abstract bipolar network in between the abstract Dung networks and the fully instantiated ASPIC networks.

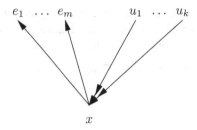

Fig. 13.

x is attacked by $u_1, \ldots, u_k$ and is supporting $e_1, \ldots, e_m$. The equations are:

$$Eq_{max} : x = 1 - \max\{u_1, \ldots, u_k, 1 - e_1, \ldots, 1 - e_m\}$$
$$Eq_{inverse} : x = e_1 \times \ldots \times m \times (1 - u_1) \times \ldots \times (1 - u_k).$$

Let us check the equations for the Chisholm paradox in Figure 1.

Note that the figure has the node **o** to distinguish it from the numeral 0. We use Eq_{max}:

1. $\infty = \mathbf{o}$
2. $\mathbf{o} = 1 - \max\{1 - y, 1 - x\}$
3. $y = 1 - \max\{1 - y_2, \mathbf{o}, 1 - y_1\}$
4. $x = 1 - \max\{1 - x_1, 1 - x_2\}$
5. $x_1 = y_2 = 1$
6. $y_1 = 1 - y$
7. $x_2 = 1 - x$

Solving the equations we get:

From (6) and (3) we get

8. $y = 1 - \max\{y, \mathbf{o}, 1 - y_2\}$

From (7), (5) and (4) we get

9. $x = 1 - x = \frac{1}{2}$

From (7) and (9) we get

10. $x_2 = x = \frac{1}{2}$

From (8), (5), (9) and (2) we get

11. $y = 1 - \max\{y, 1 - y\}$ and hence $y = \frac{1}{2}$

We compare with equation 2 and get that the solution is

$$y = \mathbf{o} = \frac{1}{2}$$

This will solve the equations.

We get

$$\infty = \mathbf{o} = x = y = x_2 = y_1 = \frac{1}{2}$$

and

$$x_1 = y_2 = 1.$$

The result we got is not yet satisfactory. We hope for a solution

$$\infty = \mathbf{o} = x = x_1 = 1$$

which gives the correct

$$(\infty, \mathbf{o}, x, x_1)$$

path (no violations on this path) and all the other paths have 0 in them. Instead we got a lot of $\frac{1}{2}$ values. However, we can still continue, because $\frac{1}{2}$ means undecided.

Indeed, in Figure 1 we have three loops with $\frac{1}{2}$ = undecided values. These are (the loop is that a node both supports and attacks the other node).

$$L_1 = \{x, x_2\}, L_2 = \{\mathbf{o}, y\} \text{ and } L_3 = \{y, y_1\}$$

We can use loop busting methods to break these loops, see [9] and get

$x = 1, x_2 = 0$, for L_1
$\mathbf{o} = 1, y = 0$, for L_2
$y_1 = 1, y = 0$, for L_3

We now have the solution we want!

Let us use the equational approach for this example in a different way and compare. Let us look at Figure 5. This is the coalitions attack figure used to compute the bipolar extension. The winning extension was $\{(\infty, \mathbf{o}, x, x_1)\}$.

Let us give values 1 to all nodes in this winning extension and 0 to all other nodes. Did we get the same result as before? The answer is yes.

We can follow this method in general. Start with a bipolar argumentation network. Obtain the extensions as in Remark 1 and then form the set S as in Definition 5.

Now give numerical value 1 to members of S and 0 to other nodes.

We now want to define a bipolar argumentation network associated with a general arbitrary set of contrary to duty obligations. Such obligations have the form $x \rightarrow$ Obligatory y, which we can also write as (x, y) or the form Obligatory z, which we can also write as $(\top, z)$.

We look at all the atomic letters $x, y, z, \ldots$ and their negations $\neg x, \neg y, \neg z, \ldots$ and take these as our nodes in the bipolar argumentation network, together with the additional node ∞.

We let $x \rightarrow y$ and $x \rightarrow \neg y$ be support arrows in the network whenever (x, y) is in the contrary to duty set. We also let the attack $x \twoheadrightarrow \neg y$ be in the network if (x, y) is in the set and $x \twoheadrightarrow y$ be in the network if $(x, \neg y)$ is in the contrary to duty set. If x is $\top$ we use ∞ instead of x. This is basically the idea. We now give the definition.

Definition 7 (Bipolar argumentation semantics for a general contrary to duty set)

1. *Let Q be a set of atomic letters and let*

$$Q^{\pm} = Q \cup \{-x | x \in Q\} \cup \{\top\}.$$

A set $\mathbb{C}$ of pairs of the form (x, y) where $x, y \in Q^{\pm}$ and $y \neq \top$ is called a contrary to duty obligations set. We can write $(x, y) \in \mathbb{C}$ in a linguistic semi-formal language as $x \to$ Obligatory y. If $x = \top$, we can write Obligatory y.

2. *Let $\mathbb{C}$ be a contrary to duty obligations set. We define a bipolar arugmentation network $(S, \to, \twoheadrightarrow)$ as follows. Let Q_0 be the set of all $y \in Q$ such that y or $\neg y$ appear in $\mathbb{C}$.*
   Let

$$S = Q_0 \cup \{\neg y | y \in Q_0\} \cup \{\infty\}.$$

   We define $\to$ and $\twoheadrightarrow$ on S as follows

   (a) *Let $\infty \to x$ and $\infty \to -x$ hold whenever $(\top, x)$ or $(\top, \neg x)$ are in $\mathbb{C}$ for $x \in Q_0$.*

   (b) *Let $\infty \to x$ hold whenever (x, y) is in $\mathbb{C}$ and there is no z such that (z, x) is in $\mathbb{C}$.*

   (c) *Let $x \to y$ and $x \to -y$ hold, whenever either (x, y) or $(x, -y)$ are in $\mathbb{C}$ for $y \in Q_0$.*

   (d) *Let $x \twoheadrightarrow y$ hold whenever $(x, -y)$ is in $\mathbb{C}$ for $y \in Q_0$, and let $x \twoheadrightarrow -y$ hold whenever (x, y) is in $\mathbb{C}$ for $y \in Q_0$.[9]*

3. *A complete fact is a maximal path of the form $(\infty, x_1, \dots, x_n, \dots)$, such that $\infty \to x_1$ holds and for all i, $x_i \to x_{i+1}$ holds. A fact is a set of complete facts.*

4. *The path semantics outlined in Definition 5 would give us bipolar path argumentation semantics for contrary to duty obligations.[10]*

Example 8 (Chisolm set). Let us use Definition 7 on the Chisholm set

1. $\top \to$ Obligatory g
2. $g \to$ Obligatory t
3. $\neg g \to$ Obligatory $\neg t$
4. $\neg g$

Figure 14 describes this set, according to Definition 7.

Figure 14 should be compared with Figure 9. They are essentially the same. The latter is the unfolding of the former, with an additional intermediary point **o**. The complete facts are paths in Figure 14. These are:

$$(\infty, g, t), (\infty, g, \neg t), (\infty, \neg g, t), (\infty, \neg g, \neg t).$$

The fact g corresponds to the set of two paths

$$\{(\infty, g, t), (\infty, g, \neg t)\}.$$

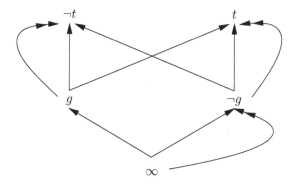

Fig. 14.

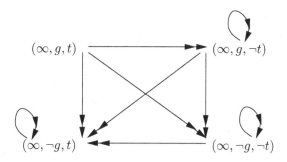

Fig. 15.

Figure 15 shows the path coalitions and the attacks among them.

Obviously there is exactly one winning coalition, namely (∞, g, t).

Remark 2 (Comparison with [12]). We take this opportunity to compare our analysis of the Chisholm set in Example 8, with example 6 of [12]. In [12], Tosatto, Boella, Torre and Villata use input-output logic to model abstract normative systems. Example 6 and Figure 6 in their paper addesses the Chisholm set. Our Figure 16 reproduces their Figure 6.

The arrows are input-output connections.

In Figure 6 of [12] they use a for our g and $\top$ for our ∞. Their representation of facts (i.e. $\neg g$) is a set A of nodes. Their choice is $A = \{\infty, \neg g\}$. They apply a variety of input-output operations to A (called deontic operations) to obtain families of sets $\odot_i A$, where $\odot_i$ is one of twelve possible operations.

---

[9] Note that we defined attacks from node to node and not from arc to arc, as remarked in footnote 7. We adopt the view that the contrary to duty obligation $x \to Oy$ actually means that once you are at x you should continue to y and this obligation is independent of how (by what route) you got to x.

[10] This definition should be compared with Definition 2 of [12].

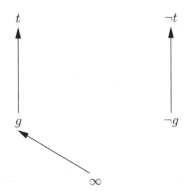

Fig. 16.

Let us consider their operation $\odot_3$. We have

$$\odot_3(\{\infty, \neg g\}) = \{\neg t\}.$$

My understanding of this in terms of our representation is that $\odot_3$ says if you go down the path $(\infty, \neg g)$ it is recommended by the norms that you continue to $\{\neg t\}$.

So in general for a set of nodes A, the operations $\odot_i(A)$ are various recommendations of where else to "continue". The approach in [12] is essentially proof theoretic whereas our approach is essentially semantic. The two approaches of course can be combined and benefit one another to obtain better tools for modelling. We shall pursue this in the expanded version of this paper. We note in passing that the Chisholm set has a temporal aspect to it, the tell comes before go. Our approach can represent the temporal order by using Figure 17 instead of Figure 14.[11] The approach of [12] cannot be modified so easily.

We need to systematically compare the two approaches, and this we shall do in the full expanded version of this paper.

Definition 8 (Gabbay's second proposal for the concept of bipolar network)

1. *Let $\mathcal{A} = (A, \to, \twoheadrightarrow)$ be a bipolar network as in Definition 1. We define the notion of tree coalitions as follows:*
   A subset TC of A is a tree coalition iff the following holds
   (a) TC is conflict free
   (b) If $x \in TC$ and $y \to x$ holds then $y \in TC$
   (c) Let $\to_*$ be the transitive closure of $\to$. Then if $x, y \in TC$ then for some $z, y \to_*$
   z and $x \to_* z$ hold.

---

[11] See paper [2], where temporal sequences are addressed. Note that we would need to change the notion of attack as defined in Table 1. We would need to adopt Cayrol and Lagasquie-Schiex's definition and let:

$(x_1, \ldots, x_n)$ attacks $(y_1, \ldots, y_k)$ if for some r, j we have that $x_r \twoheadrightarrow y_j$.

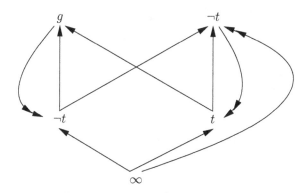

Fig. 17.

2. *Let S be the set of all tree coalitions. Define a notion of attack on S by letting $TC_1 \twoheadrightarrow TC_2$ iff for some $x \in TC_1$ and $y \in TC_2$ we have $x \twoheadrightarrow y$ holds. Then $\mathcal{T A} = (S, \twoheadrightarrow)$ is a traditional Dung argumentation network. It is the derived network of $\mathcal{A}$.*

Example 9 (Proof theory example). We can give a proof theory interpretation to the concepts defined in Definition 8.

Let Q be a set of atoms q and their negations $\neg q$. Construct formulas of the form φ, where

$$\varphi = (\alpha_1 \Rightarrow (\alpha_2 \Rightarrow \ldots \Rightarrow (\alpha_n \Rightarrow \beta)\ldots))$$

where $\Rightarrow$ is logical implication, and $\alpha_i, \beta \in Q$.

Let A be the set of all such formulas. Define $\rightarrow$ (support) on A by letting

$$\varphi_1 \rightarrow \varphi, \psi \rightarrow \varphi$$

where ψ is

$$\psi = (\alpha_2 \Rightarrow (\alpha_3 \Rightarrow \ldots (\alpha_n \Rightarrow \beta)\ldots))$$

and φ is as above.

Define $x \twoheadrightarrow y$, for $x, y \in A$ iff x and y are inconsistent together, i.e. can prove in the logic $\neg q$ and q.

Consider $\mathcal{A} = (A, \rightarrow, \twoheadrightarrow)$ and consider $\mathcal{T A}$. The latter is an abstract argumentation network which can be instantiated in the ASPIC [16] sense. In fact it was built that way.

Thus in fact we can offer a notion of abstract instantiation which is still abstract and is an intermediate concept between the Dung and the ASPIC concepts.

A tree bipolar argumentation network $\mathcal{A}$ is an instantiation of an argumentation network $\mathcal{B}$ if we have $\mathcal{B} = \mathcal{T A}$.

Remark 3. Note that Figures 6 and 7 fall under Definition 8 and the problem that $\{d, e\}$ is not a valid extension of the network of Figure 6 still exists. We need to offer a solution.

Our solution is similar to the solution of [1]. We need to consider the situation in Figure 18.

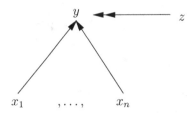

Fig. 18.

If we understand $x_1, \ldots, x_n$ as the essential assumptions for proving y then a successful attack of z on y must reflect an attack on at least one of the supportive x_i, because we understand the support illustrated in Figure 18 as $\bigwedge_i x_i \vdash y$.

This is a disjunctive attack of z on $\{x_1, \ldots, x_n\}$.

Disjunctive attacks were considered in [17], where we used the notation of Figure 19.

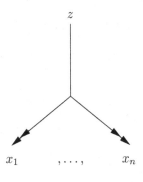

Fig. 19.

Disjunctive attacks can be realised in ordinary argumentation networks by adding new variables and replacing the structure of Figure 19 by the structure of Figure 20.

Thus the original $\mathcal{A} = (A, \to, \twoheadrightarrow)$ can be reduced to a $(B, \twoheadrightarrow)$ with additional new nodes. See [17].

Example 10 (Support only). We illustrate our methods by applying them to an example given to us by Martin Caminada. Let $x =$ rent an appartment and thus have an address, $z =$ open a bank account.

It is the case that you need x to achieve z and you need z to achieve x. We thus have the mutual support situation of Figure 21.

According to our theory in Remark 3, Figure 21 is equivalent to Figure 22, which contains auxiliary points

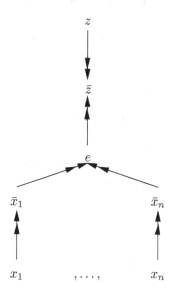

Fig. 20.

Fig. 21.

Fig. 22.

We can also write directly equations for Figure 21, as proposed in Example 7:

$$x = 1 - \max(1 - z) = z$$
$$z = 1 - \max(1 - x) = x.$$

Note the following:

1. Common sense requires a solution of two extensions, either both x and z are in or both x and z are out.
2. the equational approach, as well as the situation in Figure 22, do give such two solutions: ϕ and $\{x, z\}$. The coalition approach of Caryol and Lagasquie-Schiex (Definition 5) give only one extension, namely $\{x, z\}$.

Example 11. Consider Figure 23

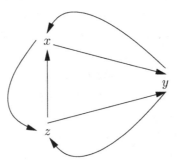

Fig. 23.

Here, any two nodes support the third. The equations are as follows:

$$x = 1 - \max(1 - y, y - z)$$
$$y = 1 - \max(1 - x, 1 - z)$$
$$z = 1 - \max(1 - x, 1 - y)$$

There are two solutions: $x = y = z = 1$ and $x = y = z = 0$. So there are two extensions $\{x, y, z\}$ and ϕ. As it should be!

4   Conclusion

In this position paper, we took the concept of bipolar abstract argumentation network and modified it a bit. This change enabled us to connect to contrary to duty obligations and give them argumentation semantics (using Gabbay's reactive modelling of contrary to duty). We were also able to extend our equational approach to bipolar argumentation as well as offer instantiations for abstract argumentation in the ASPIC spirit, by using a proof theoretic interpretation of support.

The connection with input-output logic allows us to give argumentation semantics for input-output logic, and more interestingly, equational semantics.

We shall address the above in the full version of this paper.

References

1. Boella, G., Gabbay, D., van der Torre, L., Villata, S.: Support in abstract argumentation. In: Baroni, P., Cerutti, F., Giacomin, M., Simari, G. (eds.) Computational models of Argument, COMMA 2010, pp. 111–122. IOS Press (2010); Expanded version of this paper is to appear in special issue, AMAI (2012)
2. Gabbay, D.: Temporal Deontic Logic for the Generalised Chisholm Set of Contrary to Duty Obligations. In: Broersen, J. (ed.) DEON 2012. LNCS (LNAI), vol. 7393, pp. 91–107. Springer, Heidelberg (2012)
3. Cayrol, C., Lagasquie-Schiex, M.-C.: Coalitions of arguments: A tool for handling bipolar argumentation frameworks. Int. J. Intell. Syst. 25(1), 83–109 (2010)
4. Gabbay, D.M.: Introducing Reactive Kripke Semantics and Arc Accessibility. In: Avron, A., Dershowitz, N., Rabinovich, A. (eds.) Trakhtenbrot/Festschrift. LNCS, vol. 4800, pp. 292–341. Springer, Berlin (2008); Earlier version published in Proceeding of CombLog04 (http://www.cs.math.ist.utl.pt/comblog04/); Carnielli, W., Dionesio, F.M., Mateus, P. (eds.) Centre of Logic and Computation University of Lisbon, pp 7–20 (2004), ftp://logica.cle.unicamp.br/pub/e-prints/comblog04/gabbay.pdf; Also published as a book report, by CLC: Centre for Logic and Computation, Instituto Superior Technico, Lisbon 1 (2004) ISBN 972-99289-0-8
5. Modgil, S., Prakken, H.: A General Account of Argumentation with Preferences, http://www.dcs.kcl.ac.uk/staff/smodgil/GAP.pdf
6. Grossi, D.: Doing Argumentation Theory in Modal Logic, http://www.illc.uva.nl/Research/Reports/PP-2009-24.text.pdf
7. Gabbay, D.: Reactive Kripke Models and Contrary-to-duty Obligations Expanded version. original version (2008); Revised 2012 into two parts: Part A Semantics, to appear in Journal of Applied Logic; Part B Proof Theory, to be submitted to Journal of Applied Logic
8. Gabbay, D.: The equational approach to argumentation. Argumentation and Computation 3(2-3) (to appear in special issue 2012)
9. Gabbay, D.: The equational approach to CF2 semantics. In: Proceedings of COMMA 2012. IOS press (short version to appear 2012)
10. Barringer, H., Gabbay, D., Woods, J.: Temporal, Numerical and Metalevel Dynamics in Argumentation Networks. Argumentation and Computation 3(2-3) (to appear, 2012)
11. Barringer, H., Gabbay, D.M., Woods, J.: Temporal Dynamics of Support and Attack Networks: From Argumentation to Zoology. In: Hutter, D., Stephan, W. (eds.) Mechanizing Mathematical Reasoning. LNCS (LNAI), vol. 2605, pp. 59–98. Springer, Heidelberg (2005)
12. Tosatto, S.C., Boella, G., van der Torre, L., Villata, S.: Abstract Normative Systems: Semantics and Proof Theory. In: KR 2012 (2012)
13. Makinson, D., van der Torre, L.: Constrains for input/output logics. Journal of Philosophical Logic 30, 155–185 (2001)
14. Bochman, A.: Explanatory Nonmonotonic Reasoning. Advances in Logic. World Scientific (2005)
15. Makinson, D.: On a fundamental problem of deontic logic. In: McNamara, P., Prakken, H. (eds.) Norms, Logics and Information Systems, pp. 29–54. IOS Press (1999)

16. Prakken, H.: An abstract framework for argumentation with structured arguments. Arguement and Computation 1(2), 93–124 (2010)
17. Gabbay, D.: Fibring argumentation frames. Studia Logica 93(2-3), 231–295 (2009)
18. Gabbay, D.: Semantics for higher level attacks in extended argumentation frames Part 1: Overview. Studia Logica 93, 355–379 (2009)
19. Baroni, P., Cerutti, F., Giacomin, M., Guida, G.: Encompassing Attacks to Attacks in Abstract Argumentation Frameworks. In: Sossai, C., Chemello, G. (eds.) ECSQARU 2009. LNCS, vol. 5590, pp. 83–94. Springer, Heidelberg (2009)
20. Boella, G., Gabbay, D.M., van der Torre, L., Villata, S.: Meta-argumentation modelling I: Methodology and techniques. Studia Logica 93(2-3), 297–355 (2009)
21. Boella, G., van der Torre, L., Villata, S.: Social Viewpoints for Arguing about Coalitions. In: Bui, T.D., Ho, T.V., Ha, Q.T. (eds.) PRIMA 2008. LNCS (LNAI), vol. 5357, pp. 66–77. Springer, Heidelberg (2008)
22. Boella, G., van der Torre, L., Villata, S.: On the acceptability of meta-arguments. In: Proc. of the 2009 IEEE/WIC/ACM International Conference on Intelligent Agent Technology, IAT 2009, pp. 259–262. IEEE (2009)
23. Brewka, G., Woltran, S.: Abstract dialectical frameworks. In: Proc. of the 20th International Conference on the Principles of Knowledge Representation and Reasoning (KR 2010), pp. 102–111 (2010)
24. Modgil, S., Bench-Capon, T.J.M.: Integrating object and meta-level value based argumentation. In: Besnard, P., Doutre, S., Hunter, A. (eds.) COMMA. Frontiers in Artificial Intelligence and Applications, vol. 172, pp. 240–251. IOS Press (2008)
25. Gabbay, D.: Meta-Logical Investigations in Argumentation Networks. Research Monograph. Springer (forthcoming 2012)

Multi-agent Only-Knowing

Gerhard Lakemeyer

Department of Computer Science V
Aachen University of Technology
D-52056 Aachen, Germany
gerhard@informatik.rwth-aachen.de

Abstract. Levesque introduced the notion of only-knowing to precisely capture the beliefs of a knowledge base. He also showed how only-knowing can be used to formalize non-monotonic reasoning within a monotonic logic. Despite its appeal, all attempts to extend only-knowing to the many-agent case have undesirable properties. A belief model by Halpern and Lakemeyer, for instance, appeals to proof-theoretic constructs in the semantics and needs to axiomatize validity as part of the logic. It is also not clear how to generalize their ideas to the first-order case. In this talk, I present a new account of multi-agent only-knowing which, for the first time, has a natural possible-world semantics for a quantified language with equality. An axiom system for the propositional fragment will also be discussed.

This is joint work with Vaishak Belle.

M. Fisher et al. (Eds.): CLIMA XIII 2012, LNAI 7486, p. 25, 2012.
© Springer-Verlag Berlin Heidelberg 2012

Logics for Reasoning about Agents' Attitudes in Strategic Contexts

Emiliano Lorini

IRIT, LILaC Team, Université Paul Sabatier
31062 Toulouse Cedex 9, France
Emiliano.Lorini@irit.fr

Abstract. Logics, especially modal logics, have been widely used in the past to model the properties of autonomous agents and multi-agent systems (MAS). Different variants of epistemic logics, dynamic epistemic logics, logics of preferences and intention have been proposed whose aim is to describe both the static and the dynamic properties of agents' mental attitudes. Furthermore, there are logics of collective attitudes including common knowledge and common belief, joint intention and collective acceptance. Finally, several logical systems for reasoning about actions and capabilities of agents and groups of agents have been proposed such as Coalition Logic, STIT logic and ATL. The concepts formalized in these logics are mainly inspired by game theory and social choice theory. In this talk I will present some recent works on the logical formalization of agents' attitudes, both individual and collective, in strategic contexts. The logics I will present support reasoning about different concepts such as group preference, graded belief, disposition to believe, certain belief, robust belief, common certainty and common robust belief. I will show how these logics can be applied to game theory by providing a formal analysis of the epistemic conditions of different solution concepts such as Nash equilibrium, iterated strong dominance, iterated weak dominance and social-welfare equilibrium. In the last part of my talk (time permitting) I may discuss some open issues and challenges in the area of logical modelling of agents' attitudes such as the issue of representing strategic emotions (e.g., regret and guilt), as well as the problem of relaxing the assumption of logical omniscience in order to represent both the static and the dynamic properties of explicit beliefs and explicit common beliefs and in order to distinguish them from implicit beliefs and implicit common beliefs.

M. Fisher et al. (Eds.): CLIMA XIII 2012, LNAI 7486, p. 26, 2012.
© Springer-Verlag Berlin Heidelberg 2012

A Time-Situated Meta-logic for Characterizing Goal-Processing Bounded Agents

Isaac Pinyol

ASCAMM, Tehcnology Center, PlastiaSite S.A.
Cerdanyola del Valles, Barcelona, Spain
ipinyol@ascamm.com

Abstract. In this paper, we present a logical framework to characterize the reasoning of goal-processing bounded agents. This reasoning is characterized by the particular role of beliefs in goal activation and maintenance. The logical framework is defined as a time-situated meta-logic, where only goals and beliefs exist as primitive attitudes and hold for a given instant of time. The meta-logic is composed of a hierarchy of three many-sorted first-order languages, and a set of axioms and axioms schemata that compile a first-order theory, describing the reasoning of the agent, i.e., the interplay between beliefs, goals and belief-supporting sets. We also show how the time-situated nature of the logic provides protection against inconsistencies, proving that the meta-logic is consistent for all underlying languages.

1 Introduction

A future trend for the formalization of rational agents is the development of logical frameworks for analyzing and predicting the internal reasoning process of the agents. The work presented here represents a step in this direction.

Our formalism is inspired by the work of Castelfranchi and Paglieri [1] regarding the role of beliefs in goal dynamics. They point out that goals are the only necessary motivational attitudes for modeling cognitive agents, and that goals are not static but follow an on-going process of stages that goes from the mere activation of goals to an executive stage, which is necessary for present-directed intentions. Moreover, the authors argue that each stage of the goal processing is supported by a concrete set of beliefs that must hold to keep the goal at the current stage (so called belief-supporting sets).

These beliefs and goals dynamics differ considerably from the classical Belief-Desire-Intention (BDI) formalism, where motivational attitudes are modeled by a set of desires and intentions, and where semantics are usually given by a Kripke possible-worlds structure. Also, the transition between desires and intentions is usually not clear, and the role of beliefs in this interplay is not deeply considered. In contrast, Castelfranchi and Paglieri's conceptualization proposes that desires and intentions are, in fact, the same attitude (goal) at different stages, and each stage requires the proper activation of beliefs or goals.

M. Fisher et al. (Eds.): CLIMA XIII 2012, LNAI 7486, pp. 27–42, 2012.
© Springer-Verlag Berlin Heidelberg 2012

In order to explore the reasoning of these kind of cognitive agents (BG agents from now on) we develop a logical framework to model the evolution of beliefs and goals through time. Beliefs and goals evolve depending on new observations, and each can be falsified (or deactivated) if their supporting set of beliefs is invalid. We define it as a meta-logic built over a hierarchy of many-sorted first-order languages where time is present explicitly in all predicates at a meta-level. Several features arise in our logical formalization:

1. Only goals and beliefs are considered as primitive attitudes of the agents. This is in tune with the descriptive model of intentional agents by Castelfranchi and Paglieri [1], Cohen and Levesque [2] and many other researchers who consider that intentions are, in fact, a mental state composed of other simpler mental attitudes. See for instance some recent work by computational argumentation theorists [3,4]. However, it does contradict other research which considers intentions as primitive attitudes, like Bratman [5], Rao and Georgeff [6,7] and in general, all BDI formalisms.
2. Belief and goal revision (or change thereof) is treated as part of the normal reasoning process of agents. The time situated formalism permits that beliefs and goals need not to hold forever.
3. Belief-supporting sets are explicitly represented for both beliefs and goals. Even when they are not primitive attitudes of the agents, we consider special predicates at the meta-level to control the validity of belief-supporting sets.
4. The meta-theory defined to describe the reasoning process is always consistent. This is important since even when at the agent level, agents can fall into inconsistencies, at the meta-level the time-situated nature of the logic offers protection against inconsistencies.

In the following section we define the logic, in section 3 we discuss the basic semantics. In section 5 we place an example, and finally, in section 6 we state the current state-of-the-art and conclude the analysis in section 7.

2   Logic Definition

In this section we define the meta-logic that designers of agents will use to characterize the reasoning process of goal-processing bounded agents. Firstly, we define the language L_{BG} to express beliefs and goals of the agents, and later, the axioms and axioms schemata to define a theory over L_{BG}. This theory describes the exact reasoning process of the agents.

In general, agents observe and interact with the environment, activating and deactivating goals accordingly. We leave for future work the incorporation of third-party communications as a source for belief creation. We consider the reasoning of the agents as an on-going process. This idea captures the notion of goal-processing that several authors have pointed out (for instance [1]).

To define L_{BG}, we use the approach described in [8,9] where first-order languages are structured as a hierarchy. A different approach that also uses hierarchies of languages is the one taken by [10], that could be used alternatively. These works suggest that first-order logic is enough to define consistent theories of propositional attitudes for rational agents. In these papers, formulas φ from a certain propositional language A can be *embedded* into another language B as constants for the language, usually written as $\lceil \varphi \rceil$. For instance, we can have a language that describes possible weather events in cities: $Rain(Barcelona)$, $Sunny(Rome) \wedge Sunny(Berlin)$, and another language can talk about these events in terms of date/time:

$$Forecast(10/11/2010, \lceil Rain(Barcelona) \rceil)$$

2.1 The Syntax of L_{BG}

We define three languages: The first one, denoted by L_{basic}, is the object language, a classical propositional language that contains the symbols needed by the agents for writing statements about the application domain[1]. It is not time-situated. The second language, denoted by L_{Ag}, is the language of the agents and is a first-order many-sorted language. It contains the necessary symbols to write sentences about the knowledge and current goals of the agents regarding the application domain captured by L_{basic} in a given instant of time. Finally, L_{BG}, is the language that designers of the system may use to write sentences about the reasoning process of the agents. It is also a first-order many-sorted language and includes the necessary symbols to characterize the reasoning process of the agents. Formally:

Definition 1. L_{basic} *is a non-sorted propositional language that talks about the application domain. It is constructed with the standard syntax of propositional logic and includes the symbols* $\neg$, $\wedge$, $\vee$ *and* $\rightarrow$. $\mathcal{F}(L_{basic})$ *is the set of valid formulas from* L_{basic}.

Definition 2. L_{Ag} *is a first-order many-sorted language and contains the following sorts:*

- S_T: *the sort representing time instants.*
- S_F: *the sort representing formulas from* L_{basic} *and from* L_{Ag} *itself.*

We use different letters for variables of different sorts:

- $t, t_1, t_2, \ldots$ *for variables of sort* S_T
- $x, x_1, x_2, \ldots$ *for variables of sort* S_F

$\mathcal{F}(L_{Ag})$ *is the set of syntactically valid formulas of* L_{Ag}*, which contains* $\mathcal{F}(L_{basic})$ *and the formulas obtained by the standard syntax of first-order logic, that includes the predicate symbols and constants that will be defined below. Constants and predicate symbols of* L_{Ag} *are identified by their sorts. The sort* S_T *is defined as in [8], and contains the constant* 0 *(starting time), the unary predicate* $Now(S_T)$ *and the successor unary function symbol* $+ : S_T \rightarrow S_T$. *The application of* $n \in \mathbb{N}$ *times the operator* $+$ *over the constant* 0 *will be written as* n. *For instance,* 3 *will stand for* $0 + ++$.

The sort S_F *represents the formulas that can participate in the predicates. It includes the entire set* $\mathcal{F}(L_{Ag})$ *minus the quantified formulas. Only those that can be inside a*

---

[1] Alternatively, L_{basic} could be a first-order language. This would imply though a more complex notation for L_{BG}, that is outside the objective of this paper. We refer to [8] for such development.

first-order predicate will be present in S_F. Also, S_F includes a corresponding set of constant symbols C_{Ag} that is constructed simultaneously and recursively. The set C_{Ag} contains constants of the form $\lceil \sigma \rceil$, where $\sigma \in \mathcal{F}_{Ag}$. It is important to remark that the symbols $x, x_1, x_2, \ldots$ are for variables of sort S_F in general, while the symbols $\lceil \varphi \rceil$ are constants of the sort S_F that denote formulas of $\mathcal{F}(L_{Ag})$.

Now we specify the predicate symbols corresponding to various sorts. In the notation introduced below, the predicate symbol B, for instance, is written $B(S_T, S_F)$. This means that B is a predicate symbol of arity 2, with first argument in S_T and second argument in S_F. The language L_{Ag} contains the following predicate symbols:

- $B(S_T, S_F)$ - Belief predicate: It represents the knowledge of the agent at a given time. For instance,

$$B(3, \lceil rain(Barcelona) \rceil)$$

indicates intuitively that the agent believes at time 3 that it rains in Barcelona.
- $G(S_T, S_F)$ - Goal predicate: It represents a goal of the agent at a given time. For instance,

$$G(5, \lceil run\_away(home) \rceil)$$

indicates that at time 5, the agent holds a goal to run away from home.

Definition 3. L_{BG} is a first-order many-sorted language that contains the same sorts, constant symbols and predicate symbols as L_{Ag}, and includes two new predicate symbols:

- $F_b(S_T, S_F, S_F)$ - Belief-supporting belief: It represents a supporting set of beliefs that hold in a given time. For instance,

$$F_b(3, \lceil live(Paris) \rceil, \lceil live(France) \rceil)$$

indicates that at time 3, the formula $live(France)$ holds because $live(Paris)$ also holds. This predicate is at a meta-level for the agents because it is used to control possible inconsistencies at the agent level. Also, it indicates that the former is a sufficient condition for the latter formula.
- $F_g(S_T, S_F, S_F)$ - Belief supporting goal: It represents a belief that supports the existence of a goal. For instance,

$$F_g(3, \lceil fire(home) \rceil, \lceil run\_away(home) \rceil)$$

indicates that at time 3, the goal of $run\_away(home)$ is supported by the belief that $fire(home)$.

Also, L_{BG} contains various function symbols that allow us to deal with parts of the agents' formulas and to express the reasoning of the agents. The functions applied to the sort S_F are one unary function $neg : S_F \to S_F$ for the negation of formulas, and the binary functions $con : S_F \times S_F \to S_F$ for conjunctions and $imp : S_F \times S_F \to S_F$ for implications.

For instance, if $\lceil \varphi \rceil, \lceil \phi \rceil \in C_{Ag}$ then $imp(\lceil \varphi \rceil, \lceil \phi \rceil)$ is interpreted as $\lceil \varphi \to \phi \rceil$, $con(\lceil \varphi \rceil, \lceil \phi \rceil)$ as $\lceil \varphi \wedge \phi \rceil$, and $neg(\lceil \phi \rceil)$ as $\lceil \neg \phi \rceil$. The expression $or(x, y)$ stands for $\neg(con(\neg(x), \neg(y)))$. At first sight, all these functions can be regarded as purely syntactic transformations, but they are important in our construction because they allow us to write sentences that talk about parts of the formulas.

2.2 Axioms of L_{BG}

The semantics of L_{BG} is the usual for a first-order many-sorted language. In this section we have presented only a few definitions and notation. A detailed introduction to the syntax and semantics of first-order many-sorted logics can be found in [11].

Here we define a theory Γ over L_{BG}, i.e., the axioms that agents use to reason. The theory contains the minimal formulas to describe the behavior of the predicates introduced above. Remark that we are not giving an axiomatization of the logic, but only a set of axioms for a theory (a set of sentences in this first-order language closed under the logical consequence relation). For that reason we do not need to introduce inference rules. We assume that the deductive system is given (for instance, as defined in [11]).

A1 - Time Knowledge: The agent is always aware of the current time.

$$\forall t B(t, now(t))$$

A2 - Modus Ponens: Agents use modus ponens to deduce formulas in the belief context. We assume that implication is in fact, default implications.

$$\forall t x_1 x_2 B(t, imp(x_1, x_2)) \wedge B(t, x_1)$$
$$\wedge \neg \exists x_3 (B(t, x_3) \wedge x_2 = neg(x_3))$$
$$\rightarrow B(t+, x_2) \wedge F_b(t+, x_1, x_2)$$
$$\wedge F_b(t+, imp(x_1, x_2), x_2)$$

A3 - Conjunction: Agents use conjunction rules for beliefs, but not for goals.

$$\forall t x_1 x_2 B(t, x_1) \wedge B(t, x_2)$$
$$\rightarrow B(t+, con(x_1, x_2)) \wedge F_b(t+, x_1, con(x_1, x_2))$$
$$\wedge F_b(t+, x_2, con(x_1, x_2))$$

A4a, A4b, A4c, A4d - Detachment: Agents use detachment when reasoning about beliefs and goals

A4a- $\forall t x_1 x_2 B(t, con(x_1, x_2))$
$\rightarrow B(t+, x_1) \wedge B(t+, x_2)$

A4b - $\forall t x_1 x_2 G(t, con(x_1, x_2))$
$\rightarrow G(t+, x_1) \wedge G(t+, x_2)$

A4c - $\forall t x_1 x_2 F_b(t, x_3, con(x_1, x_2))$
$\rightarrow F_b(t+, x_3, x_1) \wedge F_b(t+, x_3, x_2)$

A4d - $\forall t x_1 x_2 F_g(t, x_3, con(x_1, x_2))$
$\rightarrow F_g(t+, x_3, x_1) \wedge F_g(t+, x_3, x_2)$

A5a, A5b - Inheritance of Beliefs and Goals: These axioms describe the inheritance rules of predicates B and G. Beliefs are inherited only when they do not present contradictions. Goals are only inherited when their belief-supporting set holds. Axiom A5a states that a belief will be inherited to the next time step only if there exists a supporting belief and all of the beliefs hold. We include the condition $x_2 \neq now(t_2)$ to deal with beliefs that come directly from observations (see axiom A8). Due to space limitation, we are only placing the case of quantified positive atoms, although it should be an axiom for each possible combination of positive and negative quantified atoms. For instance, axiom A5a considers for both x_1 and x_2, only the formulas that do not start with a negation ($neg(\cdot)$), but we should include an axiom for the case where only x_1 starts with neg, another where only x_2 starts with neg and a last one where both x_1 and x_2 start with neg. We must do this because in our logic, an agent might believe a but not necessary $neg(neg(a))$. This situation is the same for the axiom A5b.

$$A5a - \forall t x_1 B(t, x_1) \wedge \neg \exists x_2 t_2((F_b(t, x_2, x_1)$$
$$\wedge x_2 \neq now(t_2) \wedge (\neg B(t, x_2) \vee B(t, neg(x_2))))$$
$$\wedge \exists x_4 (F_b(t, x_4, x_1)) \wedge \neg B(t, neg(x_4))$$
$$\wedge \forall x_3 (x_1 \neq neg(x_3) \wedge x_2 \neq neg(x_3)))$$
$$\rightarrow B(t+, x_1)$$

$$A5b - \forall t x_1 G(t, x_1) \wedge \neg \exists x_2((F_g(t, x_2, x_1)$$
$$\wedge (\neg B(t, x_2) \vee B(t, neg(x_2))))$$
$$\wedge \forall x_3 (x_1 \neq neg(x_3) \wedge x_2 \neq neg(x_3)))$$
$$\rightarrow G(t+, x_1)$$

A6a, A6b, A6c - Inheritance of Belief-Supporting Sets of Beliefs: The inheritance of predicates F_b ensures the inheritance of supporting sets that do not present contradictions. We consider the special case of beliefs that are supported directly by observations (A6a and A6b): The intuitive idea says that if at time t the observation A is acquired, and at instant time q (where $t < q$. We assume that the operator $<$ is defined as a first-order predicate) the observation $\neg A$ is acquired, the latter will be the valid one, meaning that the former will not be inherited to the next time unit. In this case, A6a deals with positive atoms while A6b with negative. Regarding axiom A6c, we only place the case for positive atoms but like for axiom A5a, each combination should have a different axiom.

$$A6a - \forall t_1 t_2 x_1 F_b(t_1, now(t_2), x_1)$$
$$\wedge \neg \exists t_3 F_b(t_1, now(t_3), neg(x_1))$$
$$\wedge t_1 < t_3 \wedge \forall x_3 x_1 \neq neg(x_3)$$
$$\rightarrow F_b(t_1+, not(t_2), x_1)$$

$$A6b - \forall t_1 t_2 x_1 F_b(t_1, now(t_2), neg(x_1))$$
$$\wedge \neg \exists t_3 F_b(t_1, now(t_3), x_1)$$
$$\wedge t_1 < t_3 \wedge \forall x_3 x_1 \neq neg(x_3)$$
$$\rightarrow F_b(t_1+, now(t_2), neg(x_1))$$

A6c- $\forall t x_1 x_2 F_b(t, x_2, x_1) \wedge \neg B(t, neg(x_2))$
$\wedge \neg B(t, neg(x_1)) \wedge \forall x_3 x_2 \neq now(x_3)$
$\rightarrow F_b(t+, x_2, x_1)$

A7 - Inheritance of Belief-Supporting Sets of Goals: As well, the inheritance of predicates F_g ensures the inheritance of supporting sets that do not present contradictions while the goal is still active. Again, we only place the axiom for positive x_1 and x_2 but all the combinations should be placed in different axioms (see axiom A5a).

$$\forall t x_1 x_2 F_g(t, x_2, x_1) \wedge \neg B(t, neg(x_2)) \wedge G(t, x_1)$$
$$\wedge \forall x_3 (x_1 \neq neg(x_3) \wedge x_2 \neq neg(x_3))$$
$$\rightarrow F_g(t+, x_2, x_1)$$

A8 - Observation to Knowledge: This axiom states that agents will know in one time step what they observe. The predicate F_b that we include in the consequent serves to control possible inconsistencies.

$$\forall t x Obs(t, x) \rightarrow B(t+, x) \wedge F_b(t+, now(t), x)$$

A9 - Goal Activation: This set of axioms describe the activation of goals from beliefs. Of course, they are domain dependent, but should follow the below structure. Both $\lceil \alpha \rceil$ and $\lceil \beta \rceil$ cannot contain variables nor quantifiers since they belong to S_F. Thus, the set of axioms A9 determine the link between the belief $\lceil \alpha \rceil$ and the goal $\lceil \beta \rceil$.

$$\forall t B(t, \lceil \alpha \rceil) \rightarrow G(t+, \lceil \beta \rceil) \wedge F_g(t+, \lceil \alpha \rceil, \lceil \beta \rceil)$$

A10 - Observations: The observations that the agent has at each time. For each $i \in S_T$, the agent can have $j \in I\!N$ different observations:

$$Obs(i, \lceil \alpha_{ij} \rceil)$$

AEQ - Equality Predicates: We must introduce equality predicates for terms: For all formulas $\varphi, \phi \in \mathcal{F}(L_{Ag})$ and $t \in S_t$ the theory contains the following: $neg(\lceil \varphi \rceil) = \lceil \neg \varphi \rceil$, $imp(\lceil \varphi \rceil, \lceil \phi \rceil) = \lceil \varphi \rightarrow \phi \rceil$, $con(\lceil \varphi \rceil, \lceil \phi \rceil) = \lceil \varphi \wedge \phi \rceil$ and $now(t) = \lceil Now(t) \rceil$.

Notice that AEQ defines equality predicates, not the predicates themselves. We omit the axiom for sort S_t regarding time treatment, they should be a variation of Peano's axioms for natural numbers.

3 Consistency

In this section we show that the set of axioms presented above defines a first-order theory (say Γ) that is consistent. We do it by showing that the theory has, at least, a model that contains a set of positive atoms that exist in the model. Such model represents the reasoning process that the agent follows to deduce belief predicates. Following the same approach as used in [9] and [8], we consider only models that contain ground terms of the language, i.e. Herbrand models.

Theorem 1. *The theory Γ has a minimal model $\mathcal{M}$ for any underlying language L_{BG}.*

Proof. To prove it, we construct $\mathcal{M}$ by induction following a *stratification* construction of the model. The main idea is to add the minimal number of atoms that accomplish the axioms, starting from the atoms that must be present in all the models at time 0, i.e. equality predicates, observations at time '0' ($Obs(0, \lceil \alpha \rceil)$), the knowledge of time 0 ($B(0, now(0))$) and any special relevant axiom, and continuing by induction over time. Similar to the construction of models used in logical programming, the strata k ($k \geq 1$) of the model will include all the generated atoms that require at least k time steps to be created. In the induction step we assume that $\mathcal{M}$ already contains the atoms until the time k. The generation of the atoms of time $k+1$ is done by applying any relevant axiom to the atoms already in $\mathcal{M}$, following a simple priority relationship between atoms in the Herbrand Universe: we give priority to atoms whose time parameter is higher.

The *application* of axioms in the induction step implies to add the minimal number of atoms that satisfy each axiom. We do not show the details on how each axiom creates and adds new atoms. However, we illustrate it with the axiom A5b (inheritance of goals). Let us assume that the following atom is already in the model in the strata k: $G(k, \lceil \alpha \rceil)$ but there does not exist any x such that $F_g(k, x, \lceil \alpha \rceil)$ and $B(k, neg(x))$. Then, to preserve the consistency and accomplish the axiom we could either add to the model the atom $G(k+, \lceil \alpha \rceil)$, or invent an x to add the respective F_g and B predicates. However, since according to our priority relation, the former formulas has priority over the latter formulas, the atom $G(k+, \lceil \alpha \rceil)$ would belong to $\mathcal{M}$. The construction is possible because all axioms are atoms, quantified atoms, or implications where consequent formulas have higher time components than antecedent formulas.

This result is important because it establishes that the theory Γ is always consistent for any underlaying language L_{BG}. The reason relies on the fact that we are defining a meta-theory that has protection over possible inconsistencies found at the agent level. Surely through observations, agents can fall into inconsistencies. However, our meta-logic offers a stratified time where not all formulas are available at the same time, providing still a useful theory even when inconsistencies occur. For instance, formulas $B(t, x)$ and $B(t, neg(x))$ can coexists in the meta-theory, but they will not appear at time $t+$.

Another important consequence of Theorem 1 is that the construction of the minimal model $\mathcal{M}$ illustrates the reasoning process of the agent. Hence, adding a set of observations and the relevant axioms for goal activation, we can build a model one period at a time and determine at a given time k, the active goals, the beliefs of the agent and the current structure of belief-supporting sets, both for beliefs and goals.

4   Comments on Complexity Issues

Regarding complexity issues, we must recall that our theory is a first-order theory, and therefore, semi-decidable. This means that we cannot guarantee for any arbitrary formula ϕ that we have an answer for the question *can the formula ϕ be deduced from the theory Γ defined in Section 2? ($\Gamma \vdash \phi$?).* We cannot guarantee in general any lower degree of complexity.

Nevertheless, we are dealing with bounded agents under a time-situated formalism, which allows for new properties. We start with a simple definition regarding the predicates generated until a given instant of time:

Definition 4. *Let Γ be a first-order theory as defined in section 2, and a time $t \in S_T$ we define $\mathcal{G}(\Gamma, t)$ as the set of all predicates of the form $B(\cdot)$, $F_b(\cdot)$, $F_g(\cdot)$ or $G(\cdot)$ that hold at time t.*

The following proposition holds:

Proposition 1. *Given a predicate $\varphi \in \mathcal{F}(L_{BG})$ of the form $B(\cdot)$, $F_b(\cdot)$, $F_g(\cdot)$ or $G(\cdot)$ without free variables, and a time $t \in S_T$, determining whether $\varphi \in \mathcal{G}(\Gamma, t)$ is decidable.*

Proof. The proof is obvious, since as shown in section 3 we can construct all atoms that belong to the minimal model at each time step. Then it is a matter of generating all possible predicates following the construction of section 3, stopping at time t and checking whether ϕ is present in the resulting set.

In general, dealing with first-order logic restricts us to provide complexities lower than NP-complete in the case of the proposition above. However, this is not a critical issue in our analysis, since the purpose of our framework is for offline simulations and analysis for agent systems' architects instead of online execution of agents.

We acknowledge that this is a very preliminary analysis and that further development is needed.

5   An Example

5.1   Initial Knowledge

We want to illustrate the reasoning process of a BG agent with a simple example. The scenario we propose is a simplification of the reasoning that winery farmers used to perform years ago to deal with the dilemma of harvesting the grapes later to obtain a higher sugar yield, or earlier to avoid the heavy rain that often hits the middle and south of Europe during the last weeks of summer and beginning of autumn.

Experienced farmers would observe the sky at sunset and the way birds were flying. When the sunset was orange/red and the birds were flying low, the farmers' experience led them to forecast heavy rains during the week. In that case, they would organize a group of people to harvest grapes as soon as possible. To model the situation, we use the following pieces of information:

Proposition	Acronym
$\lceil pick\_grapes\_on\_time \rceil$	$pgot$
$\lceil pick\_grapes\_right\_now \rceil$	$pgrn$
$\lceil birds\_fly\_down \rceil$	bfd
$\lceil red\_sky \rceil$	rs
$\lceil prevision\_rain\_week \rceil$	prw
$\lceil rain \rceil$	$rain$

The activation of goals is performed by axiom A9. In this example we define two possible goals. On one hand, the farmer will have the goal of picking the grapes as soon as possible when he believes that it will rain during the week, and it is not yet raining. On the other hand, if there is no such prevision, the farmer will wait until the grapes are completely right:

$$A9a - \forall t B(t, con(prw, neg(rain)))$$
$$\rightarrow G(t+, pgrn)$$
$$\wedge F_g(t+, con(prw, neg(rain)), pgrn)$$

$$A9b - \forall t B(t, con(neg(prw), neg(rain)))$$
$$\rightarrow G(t+, pgot)$$ The knowledge at time 0 corresponds to
$$\wedge F_g(t+, con(neg(prw), neg(rain)), pgot)$$

observations regarding the state of the world, including known implications that belong to L_{basic} language. In our example, we have the following statements (Axiom A10):

$(1) Obs(0, imp(con(bfl, rs), prw))$
$(2) Obs(0, imp(neg(bfl), neg(prw)))$
$(3) Obs(0, imp(neg(rs), neg(prw)))$
$(4) Obs(0, bfl)$
$(5) Obs(0, rs)$
$(6) Obs(0, neg(rain))$

For instance, observation 1 indicates that when birds fly low and a red sky is observed at sunset, heavy rain is expected during the week. Observations 2 and 3 say that if this is not the case, there is not such prediction. Observations 4 to 6 represent the current state of affairs that are observed at the starting point of the reasoning.

5.2   Goal Activation

We follow the normal reasoning process and show only the relevant generated predicates. By axiom A8, all observations become beliefs in one unit of time. For instance, from observations 4, 5 and 6, we obtain the following predicates:

(7)$B(1, bfl)$
(8)$F_b(1, now(0), bfl)$
(9)$B(1, rs)$
(10)$F_b(1, now(0), rs)$
(11)$B(1, neg(rain))$
(12)$F_b(1, now(0), neg(rain))$

At time 2, all the previous predicates are inherited, and new beliefs appear. In particular, by axiom A3 (conjunction) and considering beliefs 7 and 9, we obtain:

(13)$B(2, con(bfl, rs))$
(14)$F_b(2, bfl, con(bfl, rs))$
(15)$F_b(2, rs, con(bfl, rs))$

At time 3, all previous predicates are inherited, and new beliefs are generated through axiom A2 (modus ponens). The previous belief in combination with the implication from observation 1, we obtain:

(16)$B(3, prw)$
(17)$F_b(3, con(bfl, rs), prw)$

Again, at time 4, the previous predicates are inherited, and through axiom A3 (conjunction) with beliefs 16 and 11, we obtain:

(18)$B(4, con(prw, neg(rain)))$
(19)$F_b(4, prw, con(prw, neg(rain)))$
(20)$F_b(4, neg(rain), con(prw, neg(rain)))$

It is not until time 5 that the first goal is activated. Again, since no observation is included and no inconsistencies produced, all previous predicated are inherited to time 5. Also, through axiom A9a (goal activation) and from belief 18 the following formulas are generated:

(21)$G(5, pgrn)$
(22)$F_g(5, con(prw, neg(rain)), pgrn)$

At this point, all generated predicates have been inherited to time 5. We remark here that at this time not only the goal holds, but also a whole structure of beliefs supporting the activation of the goal. Following F_g and F_b predicates we could reconstruct the entire reasoning tree of the agent.

5.3 Goal Deactivation

Keeping this structure is important because it allows us to react in consequence when some belief does not hold anymore. Imagine that also at time 5, the agent observes that it is raining:

(23)$Obs(5, rain)$

Thus, at time 6 the agents knows it. Note that at this instant of time the following predicates coexist:

(24)$B(6, rain)$
(25)$F_b(6, now(5), rain)$
(26)$B(6, neg(rain))$
(27)$F_b(6, now(0), neg(rain))$

Predicates 26 and 27 have been inherited from time 1 (predicates 11 and 12). The key point at this time is that the inheritance axiom A6a of F_b predicates prevents predicate 27 to pass at the next time step. At time 7, the following predicates are still active:

(28)$B(7, rain)$
(29)$F_b(7, now(5), rain)$
(30)$B(7, neg(rain))$

Note that at time 7 the belief that it is not raining is still present, since at time 6 the belief still had a belief supporting it. Under these conditions, the inheritance axiom for beliefs prevents to pass predicate 30 to time 8. At this time, the following predicates are still active (we only show the ones relevant for the next inference):

(31)$B(8, con(prw, neg(rain)))$
(32)$F_b(8, prw, con(prw, neg(rain)))$
(33)$F_b(8, neg(rain), con(prw, neg(rain)))$

At time 8, the belief that it is not raining does not hold anymore. Then, inheritance axiom A5a of beliefs prevents to inherit belief 31 to the next time unit, because it exists a predicate F_b that says that the belief

$$B(8, neg(rain))$$

should hold to support the belief 31, but it does not hold at time 8. Then, belief 31 in not passed to time 9. Then at time 9 we have the following active predicates among others:

(34)$G(9, pgrn)$
(35)$F_g(9, con(prw, neg(rain)), pgrn)$

However, by the inheritance axiom of goals A5b, the goal 34 does not pass to time 10, because it exists a predicate F_g that says that to support such a goal, the belief

$$B(9, con(prw, neg(rain)))$$

should hold, and this is not the case because it has not been inherited from time 8.

6   Related Work and Discussion

Several topics are related to the work developed in this paper. We start with the intended meaning of this research, the development of a formal framework for characterizing agents' reasoning. The most well-known formal model of agency follows BDI formalisms, popularized among others, by Bratman [5] and Rao and Georgeff [6,7]. Most BDI approaches use Kripke possible world semantics [12] using the classical KD45 axioms of modal logic for beliefs (or alternatively modal system S5), and a variation of KD systems for both desires and intentions (e.g [13,14,15]). In particular, Rao and Georgeff's BDI model [6] uses branching time structures to model belief-desire-intention accessible worlds. All these models suffer from the logical omniscience for beliefs; thus, they are closed under consequence relationship. Also, the relationship between desires and intentions is not clearly defined, specially how desires become intentions. The main reason is that BDI theorists try to model a snapshot of the mental state, not considering evolution through time.

Our formalism does not use modal logic. Instead, we use a syntactic approach to deal with the equivalent notion of modalities. This is possible because we intend to model bounded agents, and avoid the problem of logical omniscience. Also, we concentrate on the evolution of beliefs and goals through time. Different from BDI formalisms which cannot express time, our framework uses many-sorted first-order logic where time is considered a special sort and appears in the formulas.

Another important difference with BDI formalisms is that we do not consider neither desires nor intentions, but rather use the notion of goal as primitive attitude, as suggested by Castelfranchi and Paglieri [1]. We agree that both desires and intentions are in fact goals at different stages of processing. Our framework allows for such processing because of the time situated nature of the logic.

It is worth mentioning the work of Casali et al. [16,17] and Pinyol et al. [9]. Both works use BDI formalisms to describe their models of agency with multi-context logic [10]. The former's objective is to model graded attitudes, while the latter's is to include reputation information in the reasoning process. Despite that both use the primitive attitude of intention with the corresponding axiomatization (a KD system), intentions are generated from desires and beliefs in both cases. This means that intentions could be described in terms of desires and beliefs [2] and that beliefs play a crucial role in the processing transition between desires and intentions, which is reflected in our formalism and pointed out by [1].

Besides BDI formalisms, our work is closely related to the work developed by Grant et al. in [8]. We follow their basic development to build our logic as a many-sorted first-order logic. Their focus is on the evolution of knowledge through time, and pay a lot of attention to the formalism, since they consider that the object language (the equivalent of our L_{basic}) is a first-order language that includes variables, predicates and quantifiers. Because of that, the development of their logic becomes much more complex. In contrast, we introduce goals as a motivational attitude, and manage belief-

---

[2] We completely agree that intentions, as a mental state of cognitive agents, have emerging properties attached exclusively to them, for instance, the idea of commitment. However, we believe that this does not contradict of not considering them as primitive.

supporting sets. Because of that, our approach handles much better the inconsistencies at the agent level: When two beliefs are contradictory, the *newest* one remains, and the beliefs and goals that depend on the falsified beliefs drop progressively through time. Instead, Grant *et al.* approach *eliminates* the formulas that present contradictions.

Our logic is in fact a meta-logic and therefore, it performs meta-reasoning and non-monotonic reasoning. Regarding this aspect, the artificial intelligence and logic field has developed a large literature (e.g. [18,19]). In this aspect, our work has similarities to computational argumentation. This field aims at managing inconsistencies by analyzing how formulas are justified. This is similar to our notion of belief-supporting sets. For instance, work done by Amgoud *et al.* [4,3] uses argumentation techniques to model practical reasoning. In this work, the authors define intentions as the set of desires of the agent that are not contradictory by themselves, and that the way to achieve them is also not contradictory. This idea is similar to our concept of active goals that are supported by a set of beliefs. The difference is that we consider this process as an on-going process, while Amgoud *et al.* consider the reasoning in a single instant of time. However, it would be interesting to adapt our approach to an internal argumentation process in phases. This can be considered as future work.

Another field that deals with a special kind of non-monotonic reasoning is the field of belief revision. In our logic, belief revision is treated in the same reasoning process, as a belief change rather than theory change. For instance, the classical AGM approaches [20] consider the set of beliefs as part of the theory of the agents, while in our approach the theory remains stable and beliefs and goals are formulas that belong to the model. The main objective of AGM is to eliminate the minimum elements of the theory in order to maintain its consistency. In our approach, we do not eliminate inconsistencies, but adapt the model to them.

7   Conclusions and Future Work

In this paper, we have introduced a new logical framework to characterize goal-processing bounded agents. Its purpose is to provide an analytical tool for agent systems designers for determining when and under which conditions goals and beliefs are activated. The framework is defined as a meta-logic and is built on top of a hierarchy of three languages: L_{basic} is a propositional language to describe the domain of the agents. L_{Ag} is a many-sorted first-order that contains L_{basic} and is the language that agents use to reason about beliefs and goals. Finally, L_{BG} is also a many-sorted first-order language that contains L_{Ag} and is the language that designers of the agents system would use to reason about the reasoning process of the agent.

We provide a set of axioms and axiom schemata to build a theory Γ over the language L_{BG}, and prove that the theory is always consistent because it has a model. This model represents the exact reasoning process of the agents.

We consider the reasoning of the agents as an on-going process through time. Then, *time* is considered a sort in the logic and appears in the formulas. Not all formulas hold all the time. Together with belief-supporting predicates, it permits the implementation of a belief revision procedure (or belief change) that is implicit in the same reasoning process of the agent. The time-situated nature of the framework also provides protection against inconsistencies.

As mentioned in the paper, this formalism is inspired by the work of Castelfranchi and Paglieri [1] where the authors describe a taxonomy of beliefs that participate in the goal processing of cognitive agents. Their main thesis (that we share) is that desires and intentions from the BDI point of view are in fact the same attitude (goals) but at different stages of processing. Our formalism is prepared to handle such processing. However, we have not considered all types of beliefs that Castelfranchi and Paglieri use. We only consider triggering and conditional beliefs (axiom A9) and implement the lack of self-realization beliefs and satisfaction beliefs in the inheritance of goals and belief-supporting structures (axioms A5b and A7). As a future work we plan to include the most relevant types of belief that participate in the goal processing of the agents, for instance, cost beliefs, preference beliefs and means-end beliefs.

We have not dealt with intentions in any form. As we mention though, we believe that intentions are a mental state of the agent composed of a set of goals in an executive stage and set of belief supporting them. We plan to investigate this further, in particular, the notion of commitment and how this affects the dropping of belief-supporting structures.

Also, in a more technical fashion, we want to investigate the relationship between our approach and computational argumentation techniques. In particular, those based on Dung's argumentation framework [21,22] where the internal structure of arguments is not considered, and those based on inference rules, like [23], where the internal structure is as important as the conclusion itself.

In the future extended version of the paper we also plan to consider L_{basic} as a first-order language instead of a propositional language. This will entail the addition of new axioms in the theory to deal with quantified formulas, variables and predicates. An example of such development can be found at [8]. In this case, we expect a much complex formalism, but more expressiveness. Moreover, we envisage changes neither in the consistency of the meta-theory nor the computational complexity.

Acknowledgments. This work was plartially supported by the European project Mold4ProdE (FP7-NMP2-SE-2010-246450), and the Spanish National CENIT project cvREMOD (CEN20091044). Also, we would like to thank the anonymous referees for their valuable suggestions and detailed corrections on the original manuscript.

References

1. Castelfranchi, C., Paglieri, F.: The role of beliefs in goal dynamics: Prolegomena to a constructive theory of intentions. Synthese 155, 237–263 (2007)
2. Cohen, P.R., Levesque, H.J.: Intention is choice with commitment. Artif. Intell. 42, 213–261 (1990)
3. Rahwan, I., Amgoud, L.: An argumentation based approach for practical reasoning. In: AAMAS 2006: Proceedings of the Fifth International Joint Conference on Autonomous Agents and Multiagent Systems, pp. 347–354. ACM, New York (2006)
4. Amgoud, L., Devred, C., Lagasquie-Schiex, M.: Generating possible intentions with constrained argumentation systems. International Journal of Approximate Reasoning (2011) (in press)
5. Bratman, M.: Intentions, Plans and Practical Reasoning. Harvard University Press, Cambridge (1987)

6. Rao, A.S., Georgeff, M.P.: Modeling rational agents within a BDI-architecture. In: Allen, J., Fikes, R., Sandewall, E. (eds.) Proc. of KR 1991, pp. 473–484. Morgan Kaufmann publishers Inc., San Mateo (1991)

7. Rao, A., Georgeff, M.: Bdi agents: From theory to practice. In: Proc. of the First International Conference on Multi-Agent Systems, San Francisco, USA (1995)

8. Grant, J., Kraus, S., Perlis, D.: A logic for characterizing multiple bounded agents. Autonomous Agents and Multi-Agent Systems 3, 351–387 (2000)

9. Pinyol, I., Sabater-Mir, J., Dellunde, P., Paolucci, M.: Reputation-based decisions for logic-based cognitive agents. In: Autonomous Agents and Multi-Agent Systems, vol. 24, pp. 1–42 (2010)

10. Giunchiglia, F., Serafini, L.: Multilanguage hierarchical logic (or: How we can do without modal logics). Journal of AI 65, 29–70 (1994)

11. Enderton, H.B.: A mathematical introduction to logic. Academic Press, New York (1972)

12. Kripke, S.: Semantical analysis of modal logic i: Normal modal propositional calculi. In: Zeitschrift fr Mathematische Logik und Grundlagen der Mathematik, vol. 9, pp. 67–96 (1963)

13. Halpern, J.Y., Moses, Y.: A guide to completeness and complexity for modal logics of knowledge and belief. Artificial Intelligence 54, 275–317 (1992)

14. Halpern, J.Y.: The relationship between knowledge, belief, and certainty. Annals of Mathematics and Artificial Intelligence 4(3-4), 301–322 (1991)

15. Fagin, R., Halpern, J.: Reasoning about knowledge and probability. J. ACM 41(2), 340–367 (1994)

16. Casali, A., Godo, L., Sierra, C.: Graded BDI Models for Agent Architectures. In: Leite, J., Torroni, P. (eds.) CLIMA 2004. LNCS (LNAI), vol. 3487, pp. 126–143. Springer, Heidelberg (2005)

17. Casali, A., Godo, L., Sierra, C.: A logical framework to represent and reason about graded preferences and intentions. In: Proc. of KR 2008, Sydney, Australia (2008)

18. Horvitz, E., Klein, A.: Reasoning, metareasoning, and mathematical truth: Studies of theorem proving under limited resources. In: Proc. of the 11th Conference on Uncertainty and in Artificial Intelligence, pp. 306–314 (1995)

19. Brogi, A., Turini, F.: Metalogic for knowledge representation. In: Proc. of Knowledge Representation and Reasoning, KR 1991, pp. 61–69 (1991)

20. Alchourrn, C.E., Grdenfors, P., Makinson, D.: On the logic of theory change: Partial meet contraction and revision functions. The Journal of Symbolic Logic 50(2), 510–530 (1985)

21. Dung, P.M.: On the acceptability of arguments and its fundamental role in nonmonotonic reasoning, logic programming and n-person games. AI 77(2), 321–358 (1995)

22. Dunne, P., Hunter, A., McBurney, P., Parsons, S., Wooldridge, M.: Inconsistency tolerance in weighted argument systems. In: Proc. of the AAMAS 2009, Budapest, Hungary, pp. 851–858 (2009)

23. Chesevar, C., Simari, G.: Modelling inference in argumentation through labeled deduction: Formalization and logical properties. Logica Universalis 1, 93–124 (2007)

Distributed Defeasible Speculative Reasoning in Ambient Environment

Ho-Pun Lam[1,2], Guido Governatori[2], Ken Satoh[3], and Hiroshi Hosobe[3]

[1] School of Information Technology and Electrical Engineering
The University of Queensland, Brisbane, Australia
[2] NICTA*, Queensland Research Laboratory, Brisbane, Australia
[3] National Institute of Informatics, Tokyo, Japan

Abstract. Speculative Computation is an effective means for solving problems with incomplete information in an open and distributed environment, such as peer-to-peer environment. It allows such a system to compute tentative (and possibly final) solutions using default knowledge about the current environment, or the agent's perception, even if the communications between peers are delayed or broken. However, previous work in speculative reasoning assumed that agents are hierarchically structured, which may not be the case in reality. We propose a more general multi-agents system with no centralized control. Agents in the framework have equivalent functionalities and can collaborate with each other to achieve their common goals. We characterize the framework using the argumentation semantics of defeasible logic, which provides support of speculative reasoning in the presence of conflicting information. We provide an operational model for the framework and present a prototype implementation of the model.

1 Introduction

The study on ambient intelligence and pervasive computing has introduced lots of research challenges in the field of distributed artificial intelligence during the past few years. These are mainly caused by the dynamic and imperfect nature of the environment, and the special characteristics of the entities that process and share the context information available [1].

However, in practice, it is often difficult to guarantee efficient and reliable communications between agents. For example, if an agent was deployed on an unreliable network, such as the Internet, or if an agent requires human interaction, then communications might be largely delayed or even fail. Besides, due to the dynamic (open and restricted) nature of the environment, agents may not know a priori which other entities will be present at a *specific time frame* nor whether they are able to, or willing to, provide the information requested.

Besides, according to [2], most of the ambient intelligence systems are following the classical reasoning approaches and lacking of a reasoning model that can handle cases of *uncertain* (or in some cases *missing*) or *ambiguous* context information.

* NICTA is funded by the Australian Government as represented by the Department of Broadband, Communications and the Digital Economy and the Australian Research Council through the ICT Centre of Excellence program.

M. Fisher et al. (Eds.): CLIMA XIII 2012, LNAI 7486, pp. 43–60, 2012.

To rectify these shortcomings, in this paper, we propose a totally distributed approach for ambient intelligence through *Distributed Defeasible Speculative Reasoning* (DDSR). We model an ambient environment as a Multi-Context System [3,4,5] and ambient agents as *autonomous* logic-based entities. Knowledge possessed by an agent is formalized as a local context theory and associations between the knowledge possessed by other ambient agents using *askable literals*. Inconsistencies and ambiguities in local context theory are handled by the semantics of *Defeasible Logic* (DL); while uncertainties or missing context information, on the other hand, will first be substituted by the default values used in the speculative computation process [6] and will be replaced by the "real" information when they are available.

This paper is organized as follows. Background information about defeasible logic and speculative computation will be presented in Section 2. Section 3 is devoted to the presentation of the DDSR framework that we propose. Section 4 and 5 present the argumentation semantics and operational model of DDSR respectively, followed by a conclusion.

2 Background

2.1 An Informal Introduction to Defeasible Logic

Defeasible logic (DL) [7] is a simple rule-based skeptical approach to non-monotonic reasoning. It is based on a logic programming-like language and is a simple, efficient but flexible formalism capable of dealing with many intuitions of non-monotonic reasoning in a natural and meaningful way [8].

A defeasible theory D is a triple $(F, R, >)$ where F and R are finite sets of facts and rules respectively, and $>$ is an acyclic superiority relation on R. Facts are logical statements describing indisputable facts, represented by (atomic) propositions (i.e. literals). A rule r describes the relation between a set of literals (the antecedent $A(r)$, which can be empty) and a literal (the consequence $C(r)$). DL supports three kinds of rules: *strict rules* $(r : A(r) \rightarrow C(r))$, *defeasible rules* $(r : A(r) \Rightarrow C(r))$ and *defeaters* $(r : A(r) \rightsquigarrow C(r))$. *Strict rules* are rules in the classical sense, the conclusion follows every time the antecedent holds; a *defeasible rule* is allowed to assert its conclusion if there is no contrary evidence to it. *Defeaters* cannot support conclusions but can provide contrary evidence to them. The *superiority relation* describes the relative strength of rules, and is used to obtain a conclusion where there are applicable conflicting rules.

DL is able to distinguish positive conclusions from negative conclusions, that is, literals that can be proved or literals that are refuted. In addition, it is able to determine the strength of conclusions, i.e., whether something is concluded using only strict rules and facts, or whether we have a defeasible conclusion, a conclusion that can be retracted if more evidence is provided. Accordingly, for a literal q we have the following four types of conclusions, called tagged literals: $+\Delta q$ (q is definitely provable), $-\Delta q$ (q is definitely rejected), $+\partial q$ (q is defeasibly provable), and $-\partial q$ (q is defeasibly rejected).

A *proof* (or *derivation*) in DL is a finite sequence $P = (P(1), \ldots, P(n))$ of tagged literals satisfying the proof theory. For example, to prove $+\partial q$[1]:

---

[1] We denote the set of all strict rules by R_s and the set of all strict and defeasible rules by R_{sd}; and name $R[q]$ the rule set in R with head q.

$+\partial$) If $P(n+1) = +\partial q$ then either
    (1) $+\Delta q \in P(1..n)$; or
    (2) (2.1) $\exists r \in R_{sd}[q] \; \forall a \in A(r), +\partial a \in P(1..n)$, and
        (2.2) $-\Delta{\sim}q \in P(1..n)$, and
        (2.3) $\forall s \in R[{\sim}q]$ either
            (2.3.1) $\exists a \in A(s), -\partial a \in P(1..n)$; or
            (2.3.2) $\exists t \in R_{sd}[q]$ such that
                $\forall a \in A(t), +\partial a \in P(1..n)$ and $t > s$.

The above structure enables us to define several variants of DL, such as ambiguity blocking, ambiguity propagation and well-founded semantics [9]. In [10], Governatori et al. describe DL and its variants in argumentation theoretic terms, on which this paper is based.

2.2 Speculative Computation

Speculative computation is an implementation technique that aims at speeding up the execution of programs, by computing piece of information in advance, without being sure whether these computations are actually needed [11]. It is an eager computational approach that can yield improvements over conventional approaches to parallel computing by providing: (i) a means to favor the most promising computation; and (ii) a means to abort computation and reclaim computation resources [6,12].

Speculative computation was first used in *master-slave* multi-agent system (MAS) in [13], which can be realized by exploiting abduction. Their aims are to resolve the incompleteness problem in query answering between agents by using a *default* as tentative answer (which are somehow most likely to be the answers according to the current context), and continues the computation speculatively without much waiting for the response [14].

If the revised information is different from the default or the values that are currently used, the current process will be suspended/preempted and an alternate line of computation will be started. It features the possibility of reusing parts of the computation already done during the phases when answers arrive and answer revision is required, as the *partially* computed suspend process may become active again and resume its computation. Since then the framework has been extended to support more general MAS that are hierarchically structured [14,15,16,17].

3 Defeasible Speculative Reasoning Framework

In this section, we give a formal definition of an MCS (Multi-Context System) which handles Distributed Defeasible Speculative Reasoning (DDSR) with multi-agent belief revision using conventional concepts and notation from logic programming. It is based on the argumentation semantics of DL presented in Governatori et al. [10] with the notion of askable literals and preference among system contexts.

Definition 1. *An MCS $P = \{P_1, \ldots, P_n\}$ is a set of peers where each peer $P_i \in P$ is defined as a tuple $P_i = (id_i, grp_i, C_i, \Psi_i, T_i)$, where:*

- id_i is a unique symbol that identifies the agent P_i within the context, called the *agent identifier* of P_i,
- grp_i is the context groups that P_i is associated with in P,
- $C_i = (V_i, R_i)$ is the context (local) defeasible theory (or the knowldege base) in P_i where V_i is the vocabulary used by P_i and R_i is the set of rules defined in C_i,
- Ψ_i is the set of default hypotheses assumed by P_i,
- T_i is a reputation score table on P.

V_i is a finite set of positive and negative (modalised) literals. A literal is either of the form $p(t)$ (called *local* or *non-askable literal*) or $p(t)@S$ (called *askable* or *foreign literal* in belief), where p is its predicate (name), t is a shorthand for its arguments as a vector of terms $t_1, \ldots, t_n (n \geq 0)$ and S is a context group identifier. We assume that each peer uses a distinct vocabulary.

R_i is a set of rules of the form:

$$r_j^i : a_1^i, a_2^i, \ldots, a_n^i \hookrightarrow a_{n+1}^i$$

where $\hookrightarrow \in \{\rightarrow, \Rightarrow\}$, a_{n+1}^i is a local literal, and each of $a_1^i, \ldots, a_n^i$ is a literal.

Rules that do not contain any askable literals in their bodies are called *local rules* and are interpreted in the classical sense. That is, whenever the literals of the body of the rule are consequences of the local theory, so is the literal in the head of the rule. Local rules with empty body denote factual knowledge.

Rules that contain askable literals in their bodies are called *mapping rules* and are used to express uncertainty that may appear in the environment. They are used to associate local literals with literals from external contexts (*foreign literals*). An askable literal $q@S$ in a mapping rule has two functions:

- It represents a question/query to agents in the context of group S;
- An askable literal in Ψ_i represents a belief of truth value of the literal.
  - If $p(t)@S \in \Psi_i$, the agent assumes that $p(t)@S$ is *true* or *defeasibly provable*.
  - If $\sim p(t)@S \in \Psi_i$, the agent assumes that $p(t)@S$ is *false* or *not defeasibly provable*.
  - Otherwise, the agent will assume that information about the askable literal $p(t)@S$ does not exist and will continue the inference process using the underlying semantics.

Ψ_i is the set the default hypotheses (for askable literals) assumed by P_i, which can be obtained based on the P_i's partial knowledge or as specified by the agent's users, and can be considered as a heuristics used for prioritizing parallel computation by the agent, which may have impact on the performance of the speculative computation [17].

Finally, each peer P_i defines a *reputation score table* $T_i = [\rho_j, \rho_k, \ldots, \rho_n]$ on P and each ρ_j is a name-value pairs (C_m, v) where $C_m \in P$ $(m \neq i)$ is a context that appears in P and v, a numerical value between 0 and 1, is the *reputation score* of C_m w.r.t. C_i, denoted $Rep_{C_i}(C_m)$. It is a quantitative measure of agents' reputation in the environment and can be used to express the confidence in the knowledge that an agent imports from other agents. Besides, it also provides a way to resolve potential conflicts that may arise from the interaction of contexts through their mapping rules. Accordingly, for two agents $P_j, P_k \in P$, P_j is preferred by P_k if $v_j > v_k$, and are equally trustable if $v_j = v_k$.

Definition 2 (Query message). *A query is a triple* $\mathcal{Q} = (id, GS, hist)$ *where id is the agent identifier of the querying agent, GS is a finite set of askable literals, and hist is a sequence of askable literals.*

Given a query, the ambient agents collaboratively compute the answers using their respective knowledge and assumptions on the environment. Each query contains a finite set of askable literals GS to be proven (the goal set) and a history $hist$ which is initialized to the empty sequence. A history is a sequence of askable literals $[l_n, l_{n-1}, \ldots, l_0]$ represents a branch of reasoning initiated by the goal set of the initial query. It is used to avoid cyclic dependencies among askable literals. AID is the agent identifier of the querying agent and is used to return the results back to the agent after computations.

Definition 3 (Reply message). *A reply from an agent for an askable literal $L@CG$ is defined as $Msg = (Sender, Receiver, L@CG, CT)$, where Sender and Receiver are the unique identifiers of the agents that send and receive the message respectively, $L@CG$ is an askable literal, $CT \in \{+\partial, -\partial, cycle, undefined\}$ is a conclusion tag where $+\partial$ and $-\partial$ are as defined in DL,* undefined *if the agent Sender has no information about L and* cycle *if the literals that L relies on depend on each other and form a cycle.*

Definition 4 (Message update). *Let $CurrRep = \{Msg_1, \ldots, Msg_n\}$ be the set of replies received by an agent and $Msg = (Sender, Receiver, L@CG, CT)$ be a message just received by an agent. Then a message update in $CurrRep$ of the receiving agent is defined as:*

$$CurrRep \setminus \{(Sender, Receiver, L@CG, \overline{CT})\} \cup \{(Sender, Receiver, L@CG, CT)\}$$

where $\overline{+\partial} = -\partial$ and $\overline{-\partial} = +\partial$, and cycle *and* undefined *will be handled separately using the underlying reasoning formalism.*

The above definition specifies the message update process that appears in the agents. Here, $CurrRep$ contains the set of most updated replies received from external contexts and will distinguish them according to the context identifier and the context group of the foreign literals. It is used to replace an *outdated* contextual information with an *updated* one sent from the same agent.

Definition 5 (Literal score). *Let $Msg = (aid_j, aid_i, L@CG, CT)$ be a message reply sent from an ambient agent P_j to another agent P_i. The* literal score *of the literal L w.r.t. context C_i, $Rep_{C_i}(L, C_j)$, is equal to the value of $Rep_{C_i}(C_j)$.*

The above definition states that, given a message received by an agent P_i, the literal score of a foreign literal is equal to the reputation score of the context (in T_i) that sent the message.

Example 1 (Context aware mobile phone). Consider the following scenario. Professor A is now having a meeting with his colleagues and has configured his mobile phone to decide whether it should *ring* according to his preferences and context. He has the following preferences: While receiving an incoming call (*call*), the mobile phone should ring if it is operating in normal mode (*mode_normal*). If, however, he is in the middle of a meeting (*meeting*) or giving a lecture (*give_lecture*), then the mobile phone should not ring unless the call is received from an emergency agencies (such as police, ambulance, etc) ($isEmergency$). The local knowledge of Professor A's mobile phone, C_1 is encoded in the following rules:

$$r_1^1 : call_1, mode\_normal_1 \Rightarrow ring_1$$
$$r_2^1 : \qquad\qquad meeting_1 \Rightarrow \neg ring_1$$
$$r_3^1 : \qquad give\_lecture_1 \Rightarrow \neg ring_1$$
$$r_4^1 : \qquad isEmergency_1 \Rightarrow ring_1$$

and

$$r_2^1 > r_1^1 \qquad r_3^1 > r_1^1 \qquad r_4^1 > r_2^1 \qquad r_4^1 > r_3^1$$

In case the mobile phone cannot reach a decision using its local knowledge, it imports knowledge from other ambient agents. For example, to determine whether Professor A is giving a lecture, the mobile phone needs to import knowledge from the university registry service agent, as well as the localization services agents; while to determine whether Profess A is in the middle of a meeting, the mobile phone needs to import knowledge from the room manager.

However, as is commonly appeared in our daily environment, communications between agents may be largely delayed, and in some cases cannot be established. Under these situations, when external information cannot be acquired, in order to avoid any mis-interruption from the mobile phone, Profess A can configure the mobile phone further by assuming that he is in the middle of a meeting (or giving a lecture) while waiting for the replies from external entities.

This example characterizes the types of application in which each ambient agent is aware of the type of knowledge that it receives externally and how to reason when the required external information is missing.

4   Semantics of DDSR

Similar to the construct in [1], the DDSR semantics use arguments of local range, in which conclusions are derived from a single context. Arguments made by external contexts are, at least conceptually, linked by *bridges* (Definition 6) through mapping rules. It is intended to provide an argumentative characterization of DL with notions of distributed information and preference among system context.

Definition 6. *Let* $P = \{P_1, \ldots, P_n\}$ *be an MCS where each peer* $P_i = (id_i, grp_i, C_i, \Psi_i, T_i)$ *and* $C_i = (V_i, R_i)$. *The* Bridges (Φ_P) *of* P *is the set of tuples of the form* $(p_i, C_i, \Psi_i, PT_{p_i})$, *where* $p_i \in V_i$ *and* PT_{p_i} *is the proof tree for literal* p_i *based on the set of local and mapping rules of* C_i *and the set of default hypotheses* Ψ_i.

Definition 7 (Proof Tree). *Let* $P = \{P_1, \ldots, P_m\}$ *be an MCS where each peer* $P_i = (id_i, grp_i, C_i, \Psi_i, T_i)$. *A proof tree* PT_p *of* P *is a tree with nodes labeled by literals such that the root is labeled by p and for every node q:*

- If $q \in V_i$ and $a_1, \ldots, a_n$ label the children of q then
  - If $\forall a_i \in \{a_1, \ldots, a_n\} : a_i \in V_i$ and the set $\{a_1, \ldots, a_n\}$ contains no askable literals, then there is a local rule $r \in C_i$ with body $a_1, \ldots, a_n$ and head q.
  - If $\exists a_j \in \{a_1, \ldots, a_n\}$ such that $a_j \notin V_i$ or is askable, then there is a mapping rule $r \in C_i$ with body $a_1, \ldots, a_n, \ldots, a_n$ and head q.
- If $q \in V_j \neq V_i$ then this is a leaf node of the tree and there is a tuple of the form $(p_i, C_i, \Psi_i, PT_{p_i})$ in Φ_P.
- the arcs in a proof tree are labeled by the rules used to obtained them.

and $\forall q \in \Psi_i$, q is an askable literal in V_i.

Definition 8. An argument *for a literal* p_i *is a tuple* $(p_i, C_i, \Psi_i, PT_{p_i})$ *in* Φ_P.

Definition 9. *Given an MCS* $P = \{P_1, \ldots, P_n\}$, *the set of arguments that can be generated from* P *is denoted by* $Args_P$, *while the set of arguments that can be generated from each peer context* C_i *is denoted by* $Args_{C_i}$. *Consequently,* $Args_P = \bigcup Args_{C_i}$.

Any literal labeling a node of an argument A of a proof tree PT_{p_i} is called a *conclusion* of A. However, when we refer to the conclusion of an argument, we refer to the literal labeling the root of the argument (i.e., p_i).

Definition 10. *A* (proper) subargument *of an argument* A *is a (proper) subtree of the proof tree associated to* A.

Based on the literals used in the proof tree, an argument can be classified into two different types: local argument and mapping argument.

Definition 11. *A* local argument *of context* C_i *is an argument with a proof tree that contains only local literal of* C_i. *If a local argument contains only strict rules, then it is a strict local argument; otherwise it is a defeasible local argument.*

Definition 12. *A* mapping argument *of context* C_i *is an argument with proof tree that contains at least one foreign literal of* C_i.

The derivation of local logical consequences of a context relies only on their local arguments. Actually, the conclusions of all local arguments are just the same as the logical consequences of C_i. However, the derivation of distributed logical consequences is different. It relies on the combination of both the local arguments in $Args_{C_i}$ and mapping arguments in $Args_P$. In this case, we have to consider conflicts that may arise when mapping arguments from external contexts *attack* each other.

As mentioned before, we can resolve the conflicts among mapping arguments by *ranking* them according to the agents' reputations score in T_i, and select the one with the highest value. That is, given three conflicting arguments A_1, A_2, A_3 received from contexts C_1, C_2, C_3 respectively: If $Rep(C_1) < Rep(C_2)$ and $Rep(C_2) < Rep(C_3)$, we should conclude A_3 and falsify both A_1 and A_2. This is equivalent to the *preference ordering* approach employed in [18] such that that context with the highest reputation value dominates the results being concluded.

However, in a collaborative and dynamic environment, justifying mapping arguments based on the preference ordering may not be good enough. Ambient agents in the environment may *not* have enough knowledge to justify whether a particular context has a

stronger evidence for the correctness of her answers, nor do they have enough knowledge about the environment. Besides, we also have to consider situations where the
same foreign literals may receive positive and negative support by mapping arguments
coming from multiple contexts.

Here the role of docility is worth citing. According to Herbert Simon, humans are
docile in the sense that their *fitness* is enhanced by "...the tendency to depend on suggestions, recommendations, persuasion, and information obtained through social channels as a major basis for choice" [19]. In other words, human beings support their limited decision-making capabilities through receiving inputs, data, perceptions from the
social environment [20]. It is the social context that gives human beings the main data
filter to increase their individual fitness.

Put it into our context, due to its limited capabilities, an ambient agent should en-
hance its fitness in the ambient environment by learning or receiving information from
those that surround it. Ambient agents should have their own knowledge and perceptions about the environment, but should also be able to adapt to the norms of the context
in such a way that group collaboration between agents can evolve adaptively. This is
where *belief revision* can be expected to help. It ensures that the information that an
ambient agent received remains applicable and can be constantly *updated* when more
information becomes accessible.

Definition 13 (Argument rank). *Let $CurrRep = \{Msg_1, \ldots, Msg_n\}$ be the set of
most updated messages received by an agent P_i. The argument rank of p_i w.r.t. the context C_i is equal to the sum of all literal scores $Rep_{C_i}(p_i, C_j)$ $(i \neq j)$ of messages that
appear in $CurrRep$ concerning p_i, denoted by $\Sigma_{C_i}(p_i)$.*

It is worth mentioning that numerous mechanisms have been proposed in literature
to evaluate agents' opinion or agents' trust management under distributed environment [21,22,23,24]. The definition above states that in order to leverage individual
agent's reputation as well as the majority of agents' belief within a particular context,
in our framework, we will evaluate an askable literal using the sum of reputation scores
of the agents that support the literal.

4.1   Conflicting Arguments: Attack and Undercut

It is important to note that the definitions of *attack* and *defeat* apply only for local
defeasible and mapping arguments.

Definition 14. *An argument A attacks a defeasible local or mapping argument B at p_i
if p_i is a conclusion of B and $\sim p_i$ is a conclusion of A, and the subargument of B with
conclusion p_i is not a local argument.*

Definition 15. *An argument A defeats a defeasible local or mapping argument B if A
attacks B at p_i, and for the subargument of A, A' with conclusions p_i and the subargument of B, B' with conclusion $\sim p_i$, $\Sigma_{C_i}(p_i) \geq \Sigma_{C_i}(\sim p_i)$.*

To links arguments to the mapping rules that they contain, we introduce the notion of
argumentation line, as follow.

Definition 16. *For a literal p_i in context C_i, an* argumentation line *$AL_{C_i}(p_i)$ is a sequence of arguments in $Args_P$, constructed using the following steps:*

- *In the first step add to $AL_{C_i}(p_i)$ an argument for p_i.*
- *In each next step, for each distinct literal q_j labeling a leaf node of the proof tree of the arguments added in the previous step, add one argument with conclusion q_j from $\Pi_{C_i}(p_i)$ which satisfy the following restriction.*
- *An argument B with conclusion q_j can be added in $AL_{C_i}(p_i)$ only if $AL_{C_i}(p_i)$ does not already contain a different argument D with conclusion q_j.*

For an argument p_i in context C_i with argumentation line $AL_{C_i}(p_i)$, p_i is called the *head argument* of $AL_{C_i}(p_i)$ and its conclusion p_i is also the conclusion of $AL_{C_i}(p_i)$. If the number of steps required to build an argumentation line is finite, then $AL_{C_i}(p_i)$ is also finite. An infinite argumentation line implies that some mapping arguments that p_i relies on in $Args_C$ depend on each other forming a loop. An argument in an infinite argumentation line can participate in *attacks* against counter-arguments but may not be used to *support* the conclusions of their argumentation line.

Definition 17 (Tentative belief state). *Let CR_i be a subset of the askable literals. The* tentative belief state *of P_i w.r.t. C_i and Ψ_i is a set:*

$$\{L|L \in CR_i \text{ and } \sim L \in \Psi_i\} \cup \{L|L \in \Psi_i \text{ and } \sim L \notin CR_i\}$$

and is denoted $\Pi_{C_i}(CR_i, \Psi_i)$.

In an ambient environment, tentative replies from different agents may frequently arrive at the querying agent. The notion of *belief state* for an ambient agent provides a means to (1) substitute mapping arguments which have not yet been confirmed with default hypotheses and start the inferencing process while waiting for the pending replies from external contexts. This is particularly important in our framework as *proactive inferencing* is the key of success for speculative computation. (2) it helps in handling the possibly conflicting mapping arguments that the agent may receive from *multiple* external contexts. Hence, in the definition above, CR_i can be regarded as the current set of beliefs derived based on the latest replies (*CurrRep*) received from the external contexts. In the case where mapping arguments from different contexts attack each other, it is then possible to justify them according to their argument rank (Σ_{C_i}). Therefore, for every foreign literal that appears in C_i, its tentative belief state, $\Pi_{C_i}(CR_i, \Psi_i)$, will be assigned first according to values available in CR_i, or otherwise the values that appear in default hypotheses Ψ_i.

Definition 18. *An argument A is* supported *by a set of arguments S if*

- *every proper subargument of A is in $S \cup \Pi_{C_i}(CR_i, \Psi_i)$, and*
- *there is a finite argumentation line $AL_{C_i}(A)$ with head A such that every arguments in $AL_{C_i}(p_i) \setminus \{A\}$ is in $AL_{C_i}(A)$.*

Despite the similarity of name, this concept is not directly related to support in defeasible logic, nor to supportive arguments/proof trees. It is meant to indicate when an argument may have an active role in proving or preventing the derivation of a conclusion.

Definition 19. *An argument A is* undercut *by a set of arguments S if for every argumentation line $AL_{C_i}(A)$ with head A: there is an argument B, such that B is supported by S, and B defeats a proper argument of A or an argument in $AL_{C_i}(A) \setminus A$.*

4.2 The Status of Arguments

The heart of an argumentation semantics is the notion of *acceptable argument*. Based on this concept it is possible to define *justified arguments* and *justified conclusions* – conclusions that may be drawn even taking conflicts into account.

Definition 20. *An argument A is* acceptable *by a set of arguments S if:*

1. *A is a strict local argument; or*
2. *(a) A is supported by S, and*
   (b) every arguments that defeat A in $Args_P$ is undercut by S.

Intuitively, an argument A is acceptable w.r.t. a set of arguments S if, once we accept S as valid arguments, we feel compelled to accept A as valid.

Based on this concept we proceed to define *justified arguments* and *justified literals*.

Definition 21. *Let P be a multi-context system. We define J_i^P as follows: $J_0^P = \emptyset$ and $J_{i+1}^P = \{a \in Args_P \mid a$ is acceptable w.r.t. $J_i^P\}$.*

The set of *justified arguments* in an MCS P is $JArgs^P = \bigcup_{i=1}^{\infty} J_i^P$. A literal p is justified in P if it is the conclusion of a supportive argument in $JArgs^P$. That is, an argument A is justified means that it resists every reasonable refutation; while a literal is justified if it is a logical consequence of P, from the perspective of P_i.

Finally, we proceed to define the notion of *rejected arguments* and *rejected literals* for the characterization of conclusions that are not derivable in P. Roughly speaking, an argument is rejected by a sets of arguments S and T (defined below) if it has a rejected subargument or it cannot overcome an attack from another argument, which can be thought of as the set of justified arguments from P.

Definition 22. *An argument A is* rejected *by a sets of argument S, T if:*

1. *A is* not *a local strict argument; and*
2. *(a) a proper subargument of A is in T, or*
   (b) A is defeated by an argument supported by S, or
   (c) for every argumentation line $AL_P(A)$ with head A there exists an argument $A' \in AL_P(A) \setminus A$ s.t. either a subargument of A' is in S; or A' is defeated by an argument supported by T,
   where S, T are the sets of arguments supported *and* rejected *by P respectively.*

Based on this we then proceed to define *rejected arguments* and *rejected literals*.

Definition 23. *Let P be a multi-context system and $JArgs^P$ be the set of justified arguments in P. We define R_i^P as follows: $R_0^P = \emptyset$ and $R_{i+1}^P = \{a \in Args_P \mid a$ is rejected by $R_i^P, JArgs^P\}$.*

The set of *rejected arguments* in an MCS P is $RArgs^P = \bigcup_{i=1}^{\infty} R_i^P$. A literal p is rejected in P if there is no argument in $Args_P \setminus RArgs^P$ with conclusion p. That a literal is rejected means that we are able prove that it is not a logical consequence of P, from the perspective of P_i.

5   Operational Model

Proactive reasoning is the key of success for speculative computation. With an external query an agent will compute all answers with a local *inference procedure*, which is based on two phases: a *process reduction* phase and an *answer arrival* phase [12][2]. The former is a normal inference process executed within an ambient agent and is basically the *iff* reduction proposed in [25]. It is a process that determines the set of conclusions to the query received, which are abducible, based on agent's current (tentative) belief state (Definition 17), and new queries are sent out to other ambient agents (according to their agent groups) when askable literals are reduced. After completing the inference process, the (tentative but possibly final) conclusions derived will then return to the querying agent for further processing.

Whenever an answer (either new or revised) arrives, the process reduction phase is interrupted and the answer arrival phase takes over to revises the current computation accordingly. Instead of discarding any completed but outdated computation, i.e., conclusions that are derived using the default hypotheses or an old answer being revised, the revision process is designed based on the principle of reusing it as much as possible [17], which is the major novelty of speculative reasoning. The algorithms present in the following sections are based on a *demand-driven* approach and a *top-down* procedure is employed for speculative computation.

5.1   Preliminary Definitions

Definition 24 (Speculative process). *A* process *is a tuple* $\mathcal{P} = (pid, ps, GS, \Pi, \Theta)$ *where*

- *pid is the unique process identifier,*
- *ps is state of this process,*
- *GS is a set of (askable or non-askable) literals to be proven, or called the* goal set *of the process,*
- *Π is the set of foreign literals, corresponding to the tentative belief state of the agent $\Pi_{C_i}(CR_i, \Psi_i)$ as defined in Definition 17, and*
- *Θ is a set of conclusions derived w.r.t. Π.*

Each *process* in an agent represents an alternative way of computation w.r.t. the set of belief state Π. It is created when a new choice point is encountered, such as case splitting and new/revised answers arrival. There are two kinds of process (*ps*): *active* and *suspended*. A process is active when its belief state is consistent with the set of agent's current belief state; while a suspended process is a process using a belief state which is (partially) contradictory with the current belief state.

---

[2] In [12] the authors are using the term *fact arrival phase* instead of *answer arrival phase*.

For each ambient agent $P_i \in P$, we have the following definition.

Definition 25. *A current belief state* $\Pi_{C_i}(CR_i, \Psi_i)$, *which contains a subset of askable literals in* C_i *w.r.t. the set of beliefs* CR_i *derived based on the latest replies* $(Curr Rep)$ *received from other ambient agents and the default hypotheses* Ψ_i.

To facilitate our discuss on process reduction phase, we have the following definition.

Definition 26. – *A set of already asked queries* AAQ *is a set of queries that have been sent by the agent.*
– *A set of already sent answers* ASA *is a set of askable literals and their conclusions.*
– *An active process set* APS *is a set of active processes.*
– *A suspended process set* SPS *is a set of suspended processes.*

In the algorithm, AAQ is used to avoid asking redundant questions to other agents. ASA is used to accumulate the set of previously computed answers. It is used to avoid sending redundant same answers to querying agents and calculating the same answer redundantly when the same questions already asked by other agents. APS and SPS is used to store the set of active and suspended processes respectively. All AAQ, ASA, APS and SPS are initialized to empty set when an ambient agent starts its operations.

5.2   Process Reduction Phase

The inference procedure is triggered by the reception of a query message $Q = (Sender, GS, hist)$ sent by an agent Sender to agents in the context group. Agents in the context group process the literals in GS and return the results of each literal to Sender. This process is performed only by agents that share with the sender literals in GS. Accordingly, for a literal L the returned result can has one of the following values: (1) $+\partial$; indicates that L is justified in the local context; (2) $-\partial$; indicates that L is rejected locally; (3) *undefined*; indicates the queried agent has no information about L; and (4) *cycle*; indicates that L appears in a cycle under the current environment and cannot be concluded.

In the algorithm we let the local agent be P_i with agent identifier "*Self*" and its associated context group be S; and "*Sender*" be the agent identifier of the agent who issues the query.

The inference procedure proceeds in two steps. In the first step, when a new query arrives, *NewQueryArrival* (Algorithm 1) it determines if any conclusions from the previously computed answers match the goal set (GS). If conclusions are found, then the agent will reply to the *Sender* with the conclusions available; or a new process will be created according to GS and the agent's current belief state $\Pi_{C_i}(CR_i, \Psi_i)$.

In the second step, *ProcessReduction* (Algorithm 2) will iterate on the set of active processes that are consistent with the current agent belief state. If a process is found and the required literals appear in the conclusions set, the conclusions will then be retrieved from the process and return it to the *Sender* directly. (Lines 1 to 3).

Otherwise, the procedure will select a process that is consistent with the agent's current belief set and continues the reduction process iteratively (Lines 5 to 23). For a non-askable literal L, *ProcessReduction* proceeds by determining whether L or its

---

Algorithm 1. Process reduction phase: New query arrival

Algorithm: $NewQueryArrival(\Pi_i, \mathcal{Q})$

Data: Π_i: current belief state of the agent corresponding to $\Pi_{C_i}(CR_i, \Psi_i)$

Data: $\mathcal{Q} = (Sender, GS, hist)$: query received from agent $Sender$

1 **if** $GS = \emptyset$ **then**
2 | **sendReply** $message(Self, Sender, \emptyset, \emptyset)$
3 **else if** *there is a conclusion substitution* Θ *s.t.* $GS \cdot \Theta \in ASA^a$ **then**
4 | **sendReply** $message(Self, Sender, GS, GS \cdot \Theta)$
5 **else**
6 | $APS \leftarrow APS \cup \{(pid_{new}, active, GS, \Pi_i, \epsilon)\}^b$

---

^{a} $GS \cdot \Theta$ is the result of applying assignments of Θ to $\{GS, \overline{GS}\}$ where $\overline{GS}$ is the point-wise complement of each literals in GS.

^{b} ϵ is an empty substitution.

---

negation $\overline{L}$ are consequences of the local rules (Lines 10 to 15). If it is the case, the process continues by adding the set of body literals for rules with conclusion L to the GS. Otherwise a reply indicating that the literal L is *undefined* in the local context will be sent to the agent $Sender$.

Note that, by the answer arrival phase defined below, $\Pi_{C_i}(CR_i, \Psi_i)$ is always consistent. The condition defined in line 17 is used to handle cases when cyclic literals dependencies occur in the external context. That is, when foreign literals in the contexts depend on each other and form a loop, no further query for the same foreign literal (in the same query) will be sent. Instead, the default hypotheses will be used as the ambient agent, in that situation, does not have the ability to determine the true value of the foreign literals under the current environment, which follows the idea used in handling literal-dependencies in the well-founded semantics. However, instead of falsifying the literals using the *failure-by-looping* strategy, here we will use the default hypotheses as the agent's belief state in the computations. Otherwise, the agent will issue a query to agents in context group S', as is indicated by the literal (Lines 19 to 22).

5.3   Answer Arrival Phase

The *answer arrival* phase is triggered by the reception of a reply message $\mathcal{Q} = (Sender, Receiver, L@S, CT)$ sent by the peer $Sender$ to peer $Receiver$ which executes the procedure: it processes the conclusion CT sent back by $Sender$ for the literal L, updates its belief state of the environment w.r.t. $\Pi_{C_i}(CR_i, \Psi_i)$ and consequently adapts its behavior according to the conclusions derived based on its local theory.

AnswerArrival (Algorithm 3) ensures that if a returned answer confirms the agent's current belief, then the computation continue (Lines 5 to 10). If, on the other hand, the revised answer contradicts the agent's current belief, then processes that are inconsistent with the revised answer will be set to the suspended mode and will temporary removed from the active process set; while processes that are consistent with the current belief will be set to the active mode and will be added to the active process set for further process (Lines 11 to 22).

Algorithm 2. Process reduction phase: Iterative step

Algorithm: $ProcessReduction(C_i, \Pi_i, \mathcal{Q})$

Data: $C_i = (V_i, R_i)$: local context theory
Data: Π_i: current belief state of the agent corresponding to $\Pi_{C_i}(CR_i, \Psi_i)$
Data: $\mathcal{Q} = (Sender, GS, hist)$: query received from agent $Sender$

1   **if** $\exists \mathcal{P} = (\_, active, \_, \Pi_i, \Theta) \in APA$ s.t. $L \cdot \Theta \notin ASA$ **then**
2 | $ASA \leftarrow ASA \cup \{L \cdot \Theta\}$
3 | **sendReply** $message(Self, Sender, L, L \cdot \Theta)$
4   **else**
5 | select an active process $\mathcal{P} = (\_, active, GS, \Pi_i, \Theta)$ from APS
6 | $APS' = APS \setminus \{\mathcal{P}\}$
7 | Select a literal L from GS
8 | $GS' = GS \setminus \{L\}$
9 | $AL =$ the set of askable literals in GS
10 | **if** L *is a non-askable literal* **then**
11 | | **if** $R_i[L] = null$ **and** $R_i[\overline{L}] = null$ **then**
12 | | | **sendReply** $message(Self, sender, L, undefined)$
13 | | **else**
14 | | | $APS \leftarrow APS' \cup \{(pid_{new}, active, (body(R) \cup GS')\theta, \Pi_i, \Theta \circ \theta_\Theta) \mid \exists R \in R_i$
15 | | | **and** $\exists$ most general unifier (mgr) θ s.t. $head(R)\theta = \{L, \overline{L}\}\theta\}^a$
16 | **else**   `/* L is an askable literal */`
17 | | **if** $L \in hist$ **then**
18 | | | **sendReply** $message(Self, Sender, L, cycle)$
19 | | **else if** $L \notin AAQ$ **and** $\overline{L} \notin AAQ$ **then**
20 | | | $\mathcal{Q} = message(Self, L, hist \cup \{AL\})$
21 | | | **sendQuery** $\mathcal{Q}$
22 | | | $AAQ \leftarrow AAQ \cup \mathcal{Q}$
23 | | $APS \leftarrow APS' \cup \{(pid_{new}, active, GS', \Pi_i, \Theta)\}$

---

[a] θ_Θ is an assignment for variable in the query and $\circ$ is a composition operator of assignments.

5.4 Correctness

The following propositions summarize the main properties of the DDSR framework[3].

Proposition 1. *For a multi-context system* $P = \{P_1, \ldots, P_n\}$ *where each* $P_i = (id_i, grp_i, C_i, \Delta_i, T_i)$ *is a peer in* P, *the inference process is guaranteed to terminate in finite time returning one of the values:* true, false *and* undefined *as an answer for the queried literal.*   .

Proposition 2. *For a multi-context system* $P = \{P_1, \ldots, P_n\}$ *where each* $P_i = (id_i, grp_i, C_i, \Delta_i, T_i)$ *is a peer in* P, *and a literal* $p_i \in C_i$, *the operational model*

---

[3] Due to the limited space the proof of the above proposition can be found in:
http://spin.nicta.org.au/spindle/docs/
defeasibleSpeculativeReasoningProof.pdf

Algorithm 3. Answer Arrival Phase

Algorithm: $AnswerArrival(CurrRep, \Pi_{C_i}(CR_i, \Psi_i), Msg)$

Data: $CurrRep$: the set of updated reply messages received from external agents

Data: $\Pi_{C_i}(CR_i, \Psi_i)$: the current belief state of the agent

Data: $Msg = (Sender, Self, Q@CG, CT)$: the message received from an external agent

1 update $CurrRep$ w.r.t. the Msg received
2 update CR_i w.r.t. $CurrRep$
3 $\Pi = \Pi_{C_i}(CR_i, \Psi_i)$
4 update $\Pi_{C_i}(CR_i, \Psi_i)$ w.r.t. CR_i and Ψ_i
5 **if** $Q \in \Pi_{C_i}(CR_i, \Psi_i)$ **and** $\sim Q \notin \Pi$ **then**
6 $\quad | \quad L = Q$
7 **else if** $\sim Q \in \Pi_{C_i}(CR_i, \Psi_i)$ **and** $Q \in \Pi$ **then**
8 $\quad | \quad L = \sim Q$
9 **else**
10 $\quad | \quad L = null$

11 **if** $L \neq null$ **then**   /* execute only when a change of literal value appears */
12 $\quad | \quad \Xi = \{(\_, active, \_, \Pi, \_) \in APS \mid \overline{L} \in \Pi\}$
13 $\quad | \quad \Lambda = \{(\_, suspended, \_, \Pi, \_) \in SPS \mid L \in \Pi\}$
14 $\quad | \quad$ **if** $\Lambda = null$ **then**   /* create a new process if no process in the suspended set are consistent with $\Pi_{C_i}(CR_i, \Psi_i)$ */
15 $\quad | \quad\quad | \quad \Lambda = \{(pid_{new}, active, (body(R) \cup GS')\theta, \Pi_{C_i}(CR_i, \Psi_i), \Theta \circ \theta_\Theta) \mid \exists R \in R_i$
16 $\quad | \quad\quad | \quad \quad$ **and** $\exists$ most general unifier (mgr) θ s.t. $head(R)\theta = \{L, \overline{L}\}\theta\}$
17 $\quad | \quad APS \leftarrow APS \setminus \Xi$
18 $\quad | \quad SPS \leftarrow SPS \setminus \Lambda$
19 $\quad | \quad$ change all process state of processes in Ξ to "suspended" and
20 $\quad | \quad \quad$ all process state of processes in Λ to "active".
21 $\quad | \quad APS \leftarrow APS \cup \Lambda$
22 $\quad | \quad SPS \leftarrow SPS \cup \Xi$

---

returns: (a) $CT_{p_i} = +\partial$ iff p_i is justified in P. (b) $CT_{p_i} = -\partial$ iff p_i is rejected in P. (c) $CT_{p_i} = cycle$ iff p_i appears in a cycle such that literals in the cycles are depending on each other. (d) $CT_{p_i} = undefined$ iff p_i is neither justified or rejected in P.

5.5 Implementation

A system prototype, called *Conspire*, has been developed using the operational model proposed in the previous section to support our research in defeasible speculative reasoning. It is built on top of JADE [26] such that agents can run on different host and can exchange information through ACL messages. Agents in the framework maintain their own sets of *beliefs*, *information* about the environment and the *default hypotheses*, and has embedded a defeasible reasoning engine executing the inference procedures. The implementation also covers the *distributed reasoning* approach described in [27]. We have run the "Context-Aware Mobile Phone" example described in [18]. In general, it takes about 90ms for a querying agent to receive the first reply using DDSR; while

120ms or more is needed if distributed reasoning is used (assuming that there is no delay due to communication).

6   Discussion and Conclusions

The idea of speculative computation has been employed in several areas of computer science, from optimistic transaction in database to execution of functional programming and computer architecture. In multi-agent systems, agents in the environment have no idea on whether or when an answer will arrive. Even though we may risk wasted work in the speculative computation, if we allow the agents to sit idle while waiting for the replies and no default were used, then the computation time of the agents are wasted. In either case, the main overhead is the extra computation required to decide, during answer arrival phase, whether the revised answers are consistent with the existing one [17]. Besides, as pointed out in [6], some computations may be more promising than others. As resources of ambient agents are always limited, it is important to use them efficiently. So, speculative reasoning is a compromise approach that prevents agents from idling or expending agents' computation power doing unnecessary computation while waiting for the answers.

Petersen [28] has proposed to solve the reasoning problem in ambient intelligence through case-based reasoning, and has shown how different concepts for reasoning and modeling can be combined. However, as pointed out in [29] his approach may suffer from maintaining the potentially very large case base, which is a risk when running in an on-line manner. Besides, it may not be feasible for an ambient device to store a very high number of cases.

On the other hand, [30] has extended the speculative computation framework with deadline (and resources negotiation), and has shown that their approach can improve the accuracy of speculative computation and reduce the risk of the result. While most of the previous work in speculative computation [14,15,16,17] required agents to be arranged in a hierarchical order such that queries can only be sent from agents in the higher level of the hierarchy to the one in the lower level, our approach *does not* have this requirement. Agents in the ambient environment can continuously gather and update their beliefs with acquired new information and responses to the external environment. This type of approach is related to the *reactive* behavior of intelligent agents, which have been studied by Kowalski and Sadri [31] and Dell'Acqua et al. [32,33] intensively.

In conclusion, the DDSR framework presented here allows agents in ambient environment to efficiently handle inconsistent, incomplete and revisable information returned by other agents. Thanks to the formalism supported by defeasible logic, our model supports (foreign) literals without negation as failure, and hence can be applied in solving many real-life problems.

References

1. Bikakis, A., Antoniou, G.: Contextual Argumentation in Ambient Intelligence. In: Erdem, E., Lin, F., Schaub, T. (eds.) LPNMR 2009. LNCS, vol. 5753, pp. 30–43. Springer, Heidelberg (2009)

2. Bikakis, A., Patkos, T., Antoniou, G., Plexousakis, D.: A Survey of Semantics-Based Approaches for Context Reasoning in Ambient Intelligence. In: Constructing Ambient Intelligence - AmI 2007 Workshops, CCIS 11, pp. 14–23. Springer (2008)
3. Ghidini, C., Giunchiglia, F.: Local Models Semantics, or contextual reasoning=locality+compatibility. Artificial Intelligence 127(2), 221–259 (2001)
4. Giunchiglia, F., Weyhrauch, R.: A Multi-Context Monotonic Axiomatizations of Inessential Non-Monotonicity. In: Nardi, D., Maes, P. (eds.) Meta-level Architectures and Reflection. North-Holland (1988)
5. Giunchiglia, F., Serafini, L.: Multilanguage Hierarchical Logics, or: How we can do without modal logics. Articical Intelligence 65(1), 29–70 (1994)
6. Osborne, R.B.: Speculative Computation in Multilisp. In: Proceedings of the 1990 ACM Conference on LISP and Functional Programming, LFP 1990, pp. 198–208. ACM, New York (1990)
7. Nute, D.: Defeasible logic: Theory, Implementation and Applications. In: Bartenstein, O., Geske, U., Hannebauer, M., Yoshie, O. (eds.) INAP 2001. LNCS (LNAI), vol. 2543, pp. 151–169. Springer, Heidelberg (2003)
8. Antoniou, G.: A Discussion of Some Intuitions of Defeasible Reasoning. In: Vouros, G.A., Panayiotopoulos, T. (eds.) SETN 2004. LNCS (LNAI), vol. 3025, pp. 311–320. Springer, Heidelberg (2004)
9. Antoniou, G., Billington, D., Governatori, G., Maher, M., Rock, A.: A Family of Defeasible Reasoning Logics and its Implementation. In: Proceedings of the European Conference on Artifical Intelligence, ECAI 2000, pp. 459–463 (2000)
10. Governatori, G., Maher, M.J., Antoniou, G., Billington, D.: Argumentation Semantics for Defeasible Logics. Journal of Logic and Computation 14(5), 675–702 (2004)
11. Boudol, G., Petri, G.: A Theory of Speculative Computation. In: Gordon, A.D. (ed.) ESOP 2010. LNCS, vol. 6012, pp. 165–184. Springer, Heidelberg (2010)
12. Satoh, K., Yamamoto, K.: Speculative Computation with Multi-agent Belief Revision. In: Proceedings of the First International Joint Conference on Autonomous Agents and Multiagent Systems: Part 2, AAMAS 2002, pp. 897–904. ACM, New York (2002)
13. Satoh, K., Inoue, K., Iwanuma, K., Sakama, C.: Speculative Computation by Abduction under Incomplete Communication Environments. In: Proceedings of the Fourth International Conference on Multi-Agent Systems, pp. 263–270 (2000)
14. Inoue, K., Iwanuma, K.: Speculative Computation Through Consequence-Finding in Multi-Agent Environments. Annals of Mathematics and Artificial Intelligence 42, 255–291 (2004)
15. Ceberio, M., Hosobe, H., Satoh, K.: Speculative Constraint Processing with Iterative Revision for Disjunctive Answers. In: Toni, F., Torroni, P. (eds.) CLIMA 2005. LNCS (LNAI), vol. 3900, pp. 340–357. Springer, Heidelberg (2006)
16. Hosobe, H., Satoh, K., Ma, J., Russo, A., Broda, K.: Speculative constraint processing for hierarchical agents. AI Commun. 23, 373–388 (2010)
17. Ma, J., Broda, K., Goebel, R., Hosobe, H., Russo, A., Satoh, K.: Speculative Abductive Reasoning for Hierarchical Agent Systems. In: Dix, J., Leite, J., Governatori, G., Jamroga, W. (eds.) CLIMA XI. LNCS, vol. 6245, pp. 49–64. Springer, Heidelberg (2010)
18. Bikakis, A., Antoniou, G.: Contextual Defeasible Logic and Its Application to Ambient Intelligence. IEEE Transactions on Systems, Man and Cybernetics, Part A: Systems and Humans 41(4), 705–716 (2011)
19. Simon, H.A.: Altruism and Economics. American Economic Review 83(2), 157–161 (1993)
20. Secchi, D.: A Theory of Docile Society: The Role of Altruism in Human Behavior. Journal of Academy of Business and Economics 7(2), 146–160 (2007)
21. Pusey, B., Maitland, C., Tapia, A., Yen, J.: A Survey of Trust Models in Agent Applications. In: Proceedings of the North American Association for Computational Social and Organizational Sciences (NAACSOS), Atlanta, Georgia, June 7-9 (2007)

22. Wang, Y., Vassileva, J.: Toward trust and reputation based web service selection: A survey. International Transactions on Systems Science and Applications 3(2), 118–132 (2007)
23. Sherwood, R., Lee, S., Bhattacharjee, B.: Cooperative peer groups in NICE. Computer Networks 50(4), 523–544 (2006); Management in Peer-to-Peer Systems
24. Xiong, L., Liu, L.: Building Trust in Decentralized Peer-to-Peer Electronic Communities. In: Proc. 5th Int'l Conf. Electronic Commerce Research, ICECR-5 (2002)
25. Kowalski, R.A., Toni, F., Wetzel, G.: Executing suspended logic programs. Fundamenta Informaticae - Special issue on Foundations of Constraint Programming 34, 203–224 (1998)
26. JADE: Java Agent Development Framework (2003), http://jade.tilab.com/
27. Adjiman, P., Chatalic, P., Goasdouè, F., Rousset, M.C., Simon, L.: Distributed Reasoning in a Peer-to-Peer Setting: Application to the Semantic Web. Journal of Artificial Intelligence Research 25, 269–314 (2006)
28. Kofod-Petersen, A., Aamodt, A.: Contextualised Ambient Intelligence Through Case-Based Reasoning. In: Roth-Berghofer, T.R., Göker, M.H., Güvenir, H.A. (eds.) ECCBR 2006. LNCS (LNAI), vol. 4106, pp. 211–225. Springer, Heidelberg (2006)
29. Kofod-Petersen, A.: Challenges in case-based reasoning for context awareness in ambient intelligent systems. In: Minor, M. (ed.) 8th European Conference on Case-Based Reasoning, Workshop Proceedings, pp. 287–299 (2006)
30. Wang, L., Huang, H., Chai, Y.: Speculative Computation with Deadline and Its Resource Negotiation under Time Constraints. In: Proceedings of the IEEE/WIC/ACM International Conference on Intelligent Agent Technology, IAT 2004, pp. 353–356. IEEE Computer Society, Washington, DC (2004)
31. Kowalski, R., Sadri, F.: From logic programming towards multiagent systems. Annals of Mathematics and Artificial Intelligence 25, 391–419 (1999)
32. Dell'Acqua, P., Sadri, F., Toni, F.: Combining Introspection and Communication with Rationality and Reactivity in Agents. In: Dix, J., Fariñas del Cerro, L., Furbach, U. (eds.) JELIA 1998. LNCS (LNAI), vol. 1489, pp. 17–32. Springer, Heidelberg (1998)
33. Dell'Acqua, P., Moniz Pereira, L.: Enabling Agents to Update their Knowledge and to Prefer. In: Brazdil, P.B., Jorge, A.M. (eds.) EPIA 2001. LNCS (LNAI), vol. 2258, pp. 183–190. Springer, Heidelberg (2001)

A Formal Semantics for Agent (Re)Organization

Frank Dignum[1] and Virginia Dignum[2]

[1] Utrecht University - Dept of Information and Computing Sciences,
The Netherlands
F.P.M.Dignum@uu.nl
[2] Delft University of Technology - Dept. Technology, Policy and Management,
The Netherlands
m.v.dignum@tudelft.nl

Abstract. Agent organizations can be seen as a set of entities regulated by mechanisms of social order and created by more or less autonomous actors to achieve common goals. Just like agents, organizations should also be able to adapt themselves to changing environments. In order to develop a theory on how this reorganization should be performed we need a formal framework in which organizations, organizational performance and the reorganization itself can be described. In this paper, we present a formal description of reorganization actions in LAO (Logic for Agent Organization). We show how this formalization can support the preservation of some nice properties of organizations while it can also be used to reason about which reorganization is needed to achieve some basic organizational properties.

1 Introduction

Multi-Agent System (MAS) researchers increasingly realize that the specification of an organization for a MAS helps coordinating the agents' autonomous behavior [13]. Often, concepts and ideas from Organization Theory (OT) are used to better understand agent organizations and to design more efficient and flexible distributed systems [19,5,9]. However, OT concepts tend to be not very formal in a computational perspective, which makes it difficult when moving from using OT as a paradigm towards the definition of precise organizational concepts for the formalization of MAS organizations. Furthermore, even within the area of OT, definitions, views and classifications are not always commonly accepted. This has lead to several attempts by MAS researchers to formalize (parts of) aspects of organizations using several types of modal logics. We base our work in this paper on one of those, the multi-modal logic LAO for agent organizations [7].

Give the dynamics of environments, agent organizations might become unable to achieve their goals when the environment changes too much. Thus models for agent organizations must also be able to describe how organizations can adapt to their changing environments. We therefore aim to extend LAO to support the specification of a *formal* model for the study of reorganizations. In this paper,

M. Fisher et al. (Eds.): CLIMA XIII 2012, LNAI 7486, pp. 61–76, 2012.

we are especially interested how we can make sure that reorganizations preserve some properties of organizations. E.g. when agents leave, will the organization still have all capabilities minimally needed to achieve its objectives? In order to answer this type of questions the specification of the reorganization itself also needs to be formal such that we can reason very precise about the changes and the differences in the organization before and after the reorganization.

Of course it is also important to reason about *when* an organization should reorganize and what is the most *optimal* reorganization for each situation. Because answering these questions properly would need much more space than available here we will suffice with a short discussion at the end of the paper about these aspects.

This paper is organized as follows. In section 2 we describe the main properties of organizations that we would like to preserve or re-establish when reorganizing. It also serves as a very short and informal introduction of LAO. In section 3 formalisms for handling change of organizations are incorporated and we sketch some proof that the reorganization operators preserve some basic organizational properties. Section 4 discusses the issue of deciding on reorganization. Related work is presented in section 5. Finally, section 6 presents our conclusions and directions for future work.

2   Modeling Organizations

The multi-modal logic LAO has been proposed to formally describe agent organizations in [7]. This section provides a short overview of the elements of LAO that are needed to formally describe reorganization. Due to lack of space, this is not a complete account of LAO, but is meant to give a background for the reorganization operators in the next section. We refer to [7] for all details and full semantics of LAO.

2.1   LAO Logic

The semantics of LAO is a conservative extension of ATL (Alternating-time Temporal Logic) as used for instance in [21] to describe cooperative actions between agents. It is given by a Kripke structure which is extended with a semantic description of organizational structures. An organization is a tuple $O_i = (As_i, R_i, rea_i, \leq_i, D_i, Obj_i, K_i)$, where As_i is the set of agents in the organization, R_i is the set of roles of the organization, rea_i indicates which agents play which role, $\leq_i$ indicates the power structure of the organization, D_i indicates which is the desired state of the organization, Obj_i indicates which role needs to realize a certain objective of the organization and K_i indicates the knowledge present in the organization. An organization is *well-defined* iff $D_i(w) \subseteq \bigcup_{r \in R_i} Obj_i(r, w)$, i.e. for all desired objectives of the organization there is a role in charge of reaching that objective.

Central to the LAO logic is the notion of action for agents, groups of agents and agents playing roles. Most logics of action start by defining the modal operator E for direct, successful action, and introduce the other operators, for capability, ability, attempt or indirect action, based on the definition of E. This results in axioms such as $E_a\varphi \rightarrow C_a\varphi$, informally meaning that if a sees to it that φ then a is (cap)able of φ. From a realistic perspective, such a definition is pretty uninteresting. The interesting issue is, given one's capabilities, to determine under which circumstances one can reach a certain state of affairs. That is, to determine in which situations it can be said that $C_a\varphi$ leads to $E_a\varphi$. For instance, if agent a is capable of achieving φ and also responsible and no other agent is interfering then agent a will actually achieve φ.

Our approach is thus to start with the definition of agent capability and use this definition to progressively introduce the definitions for ability, attempt and activity. We furthermore use a semantic definition of the modal operators instead of the usual axiomatic definition.

Intuitively, the ability of an agent to realize a state of affairs φ in a world w, depends not only on the capabilities of the agent but also on the status of that world. Therefore, we define the ability of a, $G_a\varphi$ to represent the case in which the agent has not only the potential capability to establish φ but is currently in a state in which it has influence over some of the possible transitions that lead to a state where φ holds. Thus the agent also has an actual possibility to use its capability. The attempt by agent a to realize φ is represented by $H_a\varphi$. We say that an agent attempts to realize φ if φ holds after all states that can be reached by a transition that is influenced by a. In our definition of attempt, an attempt only fails in case another agent interferes and tries achieve something which prevents φ to be achieved. So, we do not consider that the environment might just prevent φ to be achieved with some probability. We also assume an agent only attempts to achieve things it is capable of achieving (which does not necessarily mean the agent *knows* it is capable of achieving them). In the special case in which all next possible states from a given state are influenced by an agent a, we say that a is *in-control* in w, represented by IC_a. Finally, the *stit* operator, $E_a\varphi$ ('agent a sees to it that φ) represents the result of successful action (that is, φ holds in all worlds following the current one). This notion of agent activity is based on that introduced by Pörn [17] to represent the externally *'observable'* consequences of an action instead of the action itself, and as such abstracts from internal motivations of the agents. *Stit* can be seen as an abstract representation of the family of all possible actions that result in φ.

Formally, the language $\mathcal{L}_O$ for LAO is an extension of the language $\mathcal{L}$ describing CTL* (Computation Tree Logic with quantifiers over paths and temporal operators). This language is extended with operators for capabilities (C), abilities (G), attempts (H) and successful attempts (E) for (groups of) agents as well as for (groups of) agents playing roles in an organization. Again, we refer to [7] for the description of the semantics, which would take to much space to incorporate in this paper.

Besides these core operators, LAO includes an operator, I_r, indicating which role in the organization has the *initiative* to achieve an objective of that organization (and thus is responsible that this objective is achieved). Finally, the predicates $member(a, o_i)$, $role(r, o_i)$, $play(a, r, o_i)$, $dep(o_i, r, q)$, $know(o_i, q)$, $incharge(o_i, r, q)$, $desire(o_i, q)$ are used self-reflexively in the language to describe organizational aspects. Here o_i is a constant that is interpreted in the semantics as the identifier of an organization tuple (indicated by O_i). In a similar way, we will use a (indicating an agent) and r (indicating a role) both in the syntax and semantics. Formally they are two different constants connected by the interpretation function. However, since this mapping is trivial and would lead to even more convoluted formulas we opted to use the same notation for both and thus indicate the mapping of the constants through their notation.

Definition 1. *Given an organization* $O_i = (As_i, R_i, rea_i, \leq_i, D_i, Obj_i, K_i)$:

1. $\varphi \in \mathcal{L} \Rightarrow \varphi \in \mathcal{L}_\mathcal{O}$
2. $a \in As_i, \varphi \in \mathcal{L}_\mathcal{O} \Rightarrow C_a\varphi, G_a\varphi, H_a\varphi, E_a\varphi, \in \mathcal{L}_\mathcal{O}$
3. $Z \subseteq As_i, \varphi \in \mathcal{L}_\mathcal{O} \Rightarrow C_Z\varphi, G_Z\varphi, H_Z\varphi, E_Z\varphi \in \mathcal{L}_\mathcal{O}$
4. $a \in As_i, r \in R_i, \varphi \in \mathcal{L}_\mathcal{O} \Rightarrow C_{ar}\varphi, G_{ar}\varphi, H_{ar}\varphi, E_{ar}\varphi \in \mathcal{L}_\mathcal{O}$
5. $a \in As_i, r, q \in R_i, \varphi \in \mathcal{L}_\mathcal{O} \Rightarrow member(a, o_i), role(r, o_i), play(a, r, o_i),$
   $dep(o_i, r, q), incharge(o_i, r, q), know(o_i, \varphi), desire(o_i, \varphi) \in \mathcal{L}_\mathcal{O}$
6. $r \in R_i, Z \subseteq R_i, \varphi \in \mathcal{L}_\mathcal{O} \Rightarrow I_r\varphi, I_Z\varphi \in \mathcal{L}_\mathcal{O}$

In this definition $_{ar}$ indicates role enactment, e.g., $C_{ar}\varphi$ stands for the fact that φ is part of the capabilities of role r enacted by agent a. One might argue that the above modalities could be defined in terms of agents acting and playing a role. E.g. $E_{ar}\varphi \equiv E_a\varphi \wedge play(a, r, o_i)$. However, agents can play more than one role at the same time and sometimes it is important to determine that an agent performs an action enacting a particular role, which would be impossible using the equivalence just given. Organizational knowledge is seen merely as a label marking facts that are explicitly known by the organization. That is, LAO does not provide epistemic capabilities in order to reason about knowledge, rather than asserting the fact that something is known. This is done to keep the logic as simple as possible and to avoid combinations of the epistemic modality with other modalities (for the moment).

An organization is said to be *capable* of achieving φ if there is a subset of agents in that organization that has the capability to achieve φ. Formally:

Definition 2 (Organization Capability). *Given a model* M_O, *a world* $w \in W$ *and organization* O_i *organizational capability* C_{o_i} *is defined as:*
$M_O, w \models C_{o_i}\varphi$ *iff* $\exists Z \subseteq As_i(w) : M_O, w \models C_Z\varphi$

Of course, whether an organization actually is able to achieve φ also depends on whether the task of achieving this goal arrives at the agents that are capable of achieving it. It is thus required to describe that the initiative to achieve φ lays with a certain role in the organization and that there are agents playing that role that have the capabilities to achieve φ or that they have the capability to delegate the achievement to agents that have the capability. I.e. if a role is responsible for some activity then the agents playing that role have to initiate some action towards that activity. On the other hand, the organization assumes that the agents playing the role will eventually do something about the activity that the role is responsible for.

The predicate *incharge* represents the organizational fact that a certain role is in charge (has the initiative) of accomplishing a certain state and the operator, I_r, such that $I_r \varphi$ indicates that r has the initiative to achieve φ. This means that an agent playing r should perform some action to achieve φ. The following relation between *incharge* and I_r is assumed:

$$\models incharge(o_i, r, \varphi) \rightarrow I_r \varphi \tag{1}$$

Delegation of tasks is defined as the capability to put an agent, or group, in charge for that task (through the roles they play). In an organization, the power of delegation is associated with structural dependencies, through which some agents are capable of delegating their tasks to other agents.

Definition 3 (Power of delegation). *Given an organization O_i in a model M_O, $O_i = (As_i, R_i, rea_i, \leq_i, D_i, Obj_i, K_i)$, the power of delegation for φ between two roles $r, q \in R_i(w)$ is defined as the following constraint in the model:*
if $M_O, w \models dep(o_i, r, q) \wedge incharge(o_i, r, \varphi) \wedge play(a, r, o_i)$
then $M_O, w \models C_{ar} incharge(o_i, q, \varphi)$

Note that, in LAO, agents are taken to be autonomous and free to decide on whether or not to comply to organizational expectations based on their own reasons. As such, the above considerations can be seen as a kind of necessary conditions for organizational behavior.

2.2 Organization Properties

Given the above definitions, a number of properties for organizational structures are defined. For all of these properties it should be borne in mind that the actual realization of objectives of an organization depend on the actions of the agents populating the organization at a given moment. The properties that are defined in this section pertain to the organizational structures only. They indicate that if the structure has some property in potential the agents populating the organization could always achieve some desired state. Whether the organization will actually achieve this state depends on the autonomous decisions of the agents. Since we do not assume anything about the agents internal mechanism we can also not guarantee a certain outcome except that if an agent is responsible to achieve a certain state and is capable to achieve it, it will eventually attempt to achieve the state.

A *well-defined organization* is one where there is someone in charge for each of the organizational objectives.

Definition 4 (Well-Defined Organization). $O_i = (As_i, R_i, rea_i, \leq_i, D_i, Obj_i, K_i)$, *in a model M_O, is a* well-defined organization *(indicated as $WD(o_i)$) if it satisfies the following requirement:*

$$\begin{aligned} M_O, w &\models WD(o_i) \textbf{ iff} \\ M_O, w &\models desire(o_i, \varphi) \rightarrow \exists r : (role(r, o_i) \wedge I_r \varphi) \end{aligned} \tag{2}$$

An organization is (potentially) *successful* if the organization also has the capabilities to achieve each objective. This does not mean that an organization will always achieve all it's objectives. Rather it means that the organization does contain enough capabilities to reach the objectives and that there is some role in charge (responsible) to reach each objective. Thus the organization potentially can reach it's objectives if the attempts of the agents trying to achieve them succeed. Formally,

Definition 5 (Successful Organization). $O_i = (As_i, R_i, rea_i, \leq_i, D_i, Obj_i, K_i)$, in a model M_O, is a successful organization *(denoted by $SU(o_i)$) if it satisfies the following requirement:*

$$M_O, w \models SU(o_i) \textbf{ iff}$$
$$M_O, w \models desire(o_i, \varphi) \rightarrow C_{o_i}\varphi \wedge \exists r : (role(r, o_i) \wedge I_r\varphi) \tag{3}$$

A *good organization* is such that if the organization has the capability to achieve φ and there is a group of roles in the organization responsible for realizing it, then the roles having the initiative to realize φ have a chain of delegation to roles that are played by agents in As_i that are actually capable of achieving it. Note that it is possible that $Z = U$. Formally:

Definition 6 (Good Organization). $O_i = (As_i, R_i, rea_i, \leq_i, D_i, Obj_i, K_i)$, *in a model M_O, is a good organization (denoted by $GO(o_i)$) if it satisfies the following requirement:*

$$M_O, w \models GO(o_i) \textbf{ iff}$$
$$\text{if } M_O, w \models (C_{o_i}\varphi \wedge I_Z\varphi) \text{ then } (\exists U \subseteq R_i(w) \tag{4}$$
$$\text{and } M_O, w \models dep(o_i, Z, U) \wedge C_V\varphi)$$

where $Z, U \subseteq R_i(w)$ represent a group of roles in O_i and V is defined as the set of agents playing one of the roles of the set U.

From this definition, it immediately follows that in *Good organizations* if there is a role in charge of a given state of affairs, then eventually the state will be attempted (of course, the success of such attempt is dependent on possible external interferences). I.e.:

$$I_r\varphi \rightarrow \Diamond H_{o_i}\varphi \tag{5}$$

Definition 7 (Effective Organization). $O_i = (As_i, R_i, rea_i, \leq_i, D_i, Obj_i, K_i)$, *in a model M_O, is an effective organization (denoted by $EF(o_i)$) if it satisfies the following requirement:*

$$M_O, w \models EF(o_i) \textbf{ iff}$$
$$M_O, w \models (I_r\varphi \wedge (\neg C_r\varphi) \wedge dep(o_i, r, Q) \wedge$$
$$\exists b, q : q \in Q \wedge play(b, q, o_i) \wedge know(o_i, C_{bq}\varphi)) \rightarrow \tag{6}$$
$$(\exists a : play(a, r, o_i) \wedge E_{ar}incharge(o_i, q', \varphi) \wedge q' \in Q \wedge$$
$$\exists b' : play(b', q', o_i) \wedge know(o_i, C_{b'q'}\varphi))$$

This states that if a role r has the initiative to achieve φ but none of the agents playing role r is capable, but it is known that there is at least one agent b playing a subordinate role q that has the capability to achieve φ then some agent a playing role r will delegate the responsibility to a subordinate role q' that has an agent capable of achieving φ. Thus a hands responsibility of tasks to those agents of which it is known that they can achieve them (if it cannot achieve them itself). (Note that the complex formula is needed, because there might be several agents capable of achieving φ and it is delegated to only one of them.) So, in an effective organization the structure has means of delegating each achievable objective to the roles that are capable of achieving it.

Related to the notion of a good organization is the idea that agents should supervise each other's work. I.e. if role r is in charge that agent b attempts to achieve a certain objective then role r becomes responsible for that objective again if b fails in his attempt. For instance, when a project leader delegates the task of implementing a module of the system to a certain person and that person fails to implement the module (maybe because he becomes ill) then the project leader should take back the task and give it to someone else (or do it himself).

Definition 8 (Responsible Organization). *Given $O_i = (As_i, R_i, rea_i, \leq_i , D_i, Obj_i, K_i)$, in a model M_O, and group of roles $Z \subseteq R_i(w)$, and a group of agents $V \subseteq As_i(w)$ playing the role $r \in R_i(w)$ and $r \leq Z$, O_i is an responsible organization (denoted by $RES(o_i)$) if it satisfies the following requirement:*

$$M_O, w \models RES(o_i) \text{ iff}$$
$$M_O, w \models E_Z incharge(o_i, r, \varphi) \wedge X(H_{Vr}\varphi \rightarrow X(\varphi \vee I_Z\varphi)). \tag{7}$$

The definition states that if Z has delegated φ to agents playing role r and the set of agents V attempt to realize φ then either they manage to realize φ become true, or the roles Z get back the initiative to realize φ again. I.e. the set of roles Z stay responsible to realize φ after delegation and failure by the role(s) to which they delegate the objective to.

3   Organizational Change

Changes in the environment lead to alterations in the effectiveness of the organization and therefore to consider the consequences of that change to the organization's effectiveness and efficiency. On the other hand, organizations are active entities, capable not only of adapting to the environment but also of changing that environment. This means that, to a certain degree, organizations are able of altering environment conditions to meet their aims and requirements. As such, reorganization requires an (explicit) action resulting in the modification of some organizational characteristics. In terms of the formal model of organizations introduced in the previous section, changes are represented as (temporal) transitions between two different worlds.

Organizations will try to identify the optimal design with respect to their environment, and will choose a change strategy that they believe will improve their current situation. Intuitively, reorganization activities aim at aligning the set of desires D_i with the scope of control of the agents in the organization C_{o_i}, such that $D_i \varphi \to C_{o_i} \varphi$. Reorganization requires both the ability to represent and evaluate organizational performance, and the ability to represent reorganization activities. This section focuses on the ability to represent reorganization activities. In section 4 we discuss the representation and evaluation of the performance of an organization.

In human organizations, internal reorganization strategies take different forms, such as hiring new personnel, downsizing, training or reassigning tasks or personnel [3]. Organizations can also decide to modify their mission or objectives[1]. Because organizations aim at making certain states of affairs to be the case, and only agents can bring affairs to be, it is important for the organization to make sure it 'employs' and organizes an adequate set of agents such that the combined action of those agents has the potentiality to bring about the desired state of affairs D_i. The dependency relation $\leq_i$ between roles must allow for the desired states to be achieved, that is, dependencies must be sufficient for initiative to be passed to the appropriate agents, that is, the agents that have the necessary capabilities. If that is not the case, the organization should take the steps needed to decide and implement reorganization, such that the resulting organization O_i' is indeed able to realize its objectives D_i'. In practice, reorganization activities can be classified in six groups[2]:

- **Staffing** (*staff⁺*, *staff⁻*): Changes on the set of agents: adding new agents, or deleting agents from the set. Corresponding to personnel activities in human organizations (hiring, firing and training).
- **Restaffing** (*enact*, *deact*, *move*): Assigning agents to different roles within the organization. This can be promotions, demotions or reorganizations in human organizations.
- **Structuring** (*position⁺*, *position⁻*, *struct⁺*, *struct⁻*): Changes on the organization structure. These can be changing roles and/or dependencies between the roles. Corresponding to changes in composition of departments or positions in human organizations.
- **Strategy** (*strateg⁺*, *strateg⁻*): Changes on the objectives of the organization: adding or deleting desired states. Corresponding to strategic (or second-order) changes in human organizations: modifications on the organization mission, vision, or charter.
- **Duty** (*duty⁺*, *duty⁻*): Changes the initiatives in the organization: adding or deleting *incharge* relations. Corresponds to duty assignment in human relations.
- **Learn** (*learn⁺*, *learn⁻*): Changes the knowledge of the organization: adding or deleting *know* predicates. Corresponds to the change of experiences, knowledge and learning in human organizations.

---

[1] External types of reorganization, such as mergers and takeovers are outside the scope of this paper.

[2] This is an abstraction from types of reorganization used in management science [1].

The formal definition of these reorganization activities is as follows:

Definition 9 (Reorganization Operations). *Given an organization $O_i = (As_i, R_i, rea_i, \leq_i, D_i, Obj_i, K_i)$, in a model M_O, the reorganization operations over O_i in M_O are:*

1. $w \models staff^+(o_i, a, U)$ iff $w \models \neg member(a, o_i) \wedge \mathcal{X}(member(a, o_i) \wedge$
   $\forall r \in U : play(a, r, o_i) \wedge \forall \varphi : C_{ar}\varphi \rightarrow know(o_i, C_{ar}\varphi))$, where $U \subseteq R_i(w)$
2. $w \models staff^-(o_i, a)$ iff
   $w \models member(a, o_i) \wedge \mathcal{X}(\neg member(a, o_i) \wedge \neg \exists r \in R_i : play(a, r, o_i))$,
3. $w \models enact(o_i, a, r)$ iff $w \models \neg play(a, r, o_i) \wedge \mathcal{X}(member(o_i, a) \wedge play(a, r, o_i))$
4. $w \models deact(o_i, a, r)$ iff $w \models play(a, r, o_i) \wedge \mathcal{X}\neg play(a, r, o_i)$,
5. $w \models move(o_i, a, r, q)$ iff
   $w \models play(a, r, o_i) \wedge \neg play(a, q, o_i) \wedge \mathcal{X}(play(a, q, o_i) \wedge \neg play(a, r, o_i))$
6. $w \models position^+(o_i, r)$ iff $w \models \neg role(r, o_i) \wedge \mathcal{X}role(r, o_i)$
7. $w \models position^-(o_i, r)$ iff $w \models role(r, o_i) \wedge \neg \exists a \in As_i : play(a, r, o_i) \wedge$
   $\neg \exists q \in R_i : (dep(q, r, o_i) \vee dep(r, q, o_i)) \wedge \mathcal{X}\neg role(r, o_i)$,
8. $w \models struct^+(o_i, (r \leq q))$ iff $w \models role(r, o_i) \wedge role(q, o_i) \wedge \mathcal{X}dep(o_i, r, q)$,
9. $w \models struct^-(o_i, (r \leq q))$ iff $w \models role(r, o_i) \wedge role(q, o_i) \wedge \mathcal{X}\neg dep(o_i, r, q)$,
10. For $d : \neg(d \wedge D) \rightarrow \perp$, $w \models strateg^+(o_i, d)$ iff $w \models \mathcal{X}desire(o_i, d)$
11. $w \models strateg^-(o_i, d)$ iff $w \models \mathcal{X}\neg desire(o_i, d)$
12. $w \models duty^+(o_i, r, \varphi)$ iff $w \models \mathcal{X}incharge(o_i, r, \varphi)$
13. $w \models duty^-(o_i, r, \varphi)$ iff $w \models \mathcal{X}\neg incharge(o_i, r, \varphi)$
14. $w \models learn^+(o_i, \varphi)$ iff $w \models \mathcal{X}know(o_i, \varphi)$
15. $w \models learn^-(o_i, \varphi)$ iff $w \models \mathcal{X}\neg know(o_i, \varphi)$

This definition gives a very simple description of the updates. The only operation having some extensive checking is the removal of a role from the organization. This can only be done if no agent plays that role and the role is not dependent on or from any other role. The consequence of this precondition is that before removing a role an organization first has to let all agents deact that role and remove the dependencies between the role and other roles. Similar treatment must be further developed for other types of organization update, in particular for strategic reorganization operations.

The above updates do not guarantee the conservation of properties of organizations as described in section 2.2. E.g. if an agent is fired from the organization, the organization might loose some essential capability and change from a successful organization into an unsuccessful organization. In order to prevent these unwanted consequences of reorganization, a number of properties must be defined that make a reorganization update safe (i.e. property preserving).

Definition 10 (Safe Reorganization). *For a semantic model M_O, given an organization $O_i = (As_i, R_i, rea_i, \leq_i, D_i, Obj_i, K_i)$, the reorganization operations over O_i in M_O are safe if the following properties hold:*

1. $\models I_r\varphi \wedge staff^-(o_i, a) \rightarrow \mathcal{X}I_r\varphi$
2. $\models C_Z\varphi \wedge staff^-(o_i, a) \rightarrow \mathcal{X}C_Z\varphi$

3. $\models (I_r\varphi \land (\forall a : play(a, r, o_i) \to \neg C_{ar}\varphi) \land \textit{staff}^-(O_i, a)) \to \neg E_{ar}\textit{incharge}$
(o_i, q, φ)
4. $\models I_r\varphi \land \textit{deact}(o_i, a, r) \to \mathcal{X}I_r\varphi$
5. $\models C_Z\varphi \land \textit{deact}(o_i, a, r) \to \mathcal{X}C_Z\varphi$
6. $\models (I_r\varphi \land (\forall a : play(a, r, o_i) \to \neg C_{ar}\varphi) \land \textit{deact}(o_i, a, r)) \to \neg E_{ar}\textit{incharge}$
(o_i, q, φ)
7. $\models I_r\varphi \land \textit{move}(o_i, a, r, q) \to \mathcal{X}(I_r\varphi \lor I_q)$
8. $\models C_Z\varphi \land \textit{move}(o_i, a, r, q) \to \mathcal{X}C_Z\varphi$
9. $\models (I_r\varphi \land (\forall a : play(a, r, o_i) \to \neg C_{ar}\varphi) \land \textit{move}(o_i, a, r, q)) \to \neg E_{ar}\textit{incharge}$
(o_i, t, φ)
10. $\models (C_{o_i}\varphi \land I_r\varphi \land \textit{struct}^-(o_i, (r \le q)) \land \exists U \subseteq R_i(w) :$
$(dep(o_i, r, U) \land C_U\varphi) \to \mathcal{X}(\exists W \subseteq R_i(w) : (dep(o_i, r, W) \land C_W\varphi))$
11. $\models \textit{strateg}^+(o_i, \varphi) \to \mathcal{X}(C_{o_i}\varphi \land \exists r : (role(r, o_i) \land I_r\varphi))$
12. $\models C_{o_i}\varphi \land \textit{duty}^+(o_i, r, \varphi) \to \mathcal{X}\exists U \subseteq R_i(w) : (dep(o_i, r, U) \land C_U\varphi)$
13. $\models (\textit{duty}^+(o_i, r, \varphi) \land (\forall a : play(a, r, o_i) \to \neg C_{ar}\varphi) \land dep(o_i, r, q) \land play(b, q, o_i) \land$
$know(C_{bq}\varphi)) \to \mathcal{X}(\exists a : play(a, r, o_i) \land E_{ar}\textit{incharge}(o_i, q, \varphi))$
14. $\models \textit{desire}(o_i, \varphi) \to \exists r : (role(r, o_i) \land I_r\varphi) \land \textit{duty}^-(o_i, t, \psi)$
$\to \mathcal{X}(\textit{desire}(o_i, \varphi) \to \exists r : (role(r, o_i) \land I_r\varphi))$
15. $\models I_r \land (\forall a : play(a, r, o_i) \to \neg C_{ar}\varphi) \land dep(o_i, r, q) \land play(b, q, o_i) \land \textit{learn}^+(o_i, \varphi))$
$\to \mathcal{X}(\exists a : play(a, r, o_i) \land E_{ar}\textit{incharge}(o_i, q, \varphi))$

The first 9 properties all make sure that when an agent leaves a role, the agents that remain playing that role are still having enough capabilities, etc. and the agent leaving was not the one that was needed to delegate the achievement of a desire of the organization. The properties for agents moving between roles are a bit conservative. It might be that an agent fulfilling a different role has the same (or more) capabilities in its new role. However, this is not guaranteed. So, we assume it is not the case and defined the properties against this worst case scenario.

One might assume that some restrictions are needed on the removal of roles, because they function in many definitions. However, because roles can only be removed when no agent is playing the role anymore and it is not linked to other roles, none of the definitions is affected. (When a role r can be removed we have that for all φ $w \models \neg I_r\varphi$). Whenever a dependency between roles is removed we make sure that alternative dependency paths exist along which tasks can be delegated if needed.

When duties or desires are added we have to make sure that these new duties and desires can be handled in the same way by the organization as existing ones. This is exactly what is ensured by the restrictions on the $\textit{duty}^+$ and the $\textit{strateg}^+$ operators. When duties are discharged we have to make sure that all desires of the organization are still being pursued by the roles. And finally if the organization knows about a new capability of an agent fulfilling a role, this knowledge is used to ensure an effective delegation.

Most of the properties above ensure that when a reorganization operator takes out an element of the organization, what is left of the organization still complies to the definition of a well-defined, successful, good and effective organization.

Given the above definitions of safe reorganization operators it is now actually possible to prove that an organization that is well-defined, good, successful or effective remains so after applying a safe reorganization operator:

Theorem 1. *Given $O_i = (As_i, R_i, rea_i, \leq_i, D_i, Obj_i, K_i)$ and a semantic model M_O, a safe reorganization Reorg, is such that:*

$$M_O, w \models WD(o_i) \wedge Reorg \rightarrow \mathcal{X}WD(o_i)$$
$$M_O, w \models SU(o_i) \wedge Reorg \rightarrow \mathcal{X}SU(o_i)$$
$$M_O, w \models GO(o_i) \wedge Reorg \rightarrow \mathcal{X}GO(o_i)$$
$$M_O, w \models EF(o_i) \wedge Reorg \rightarrow \mathcal{X}EF(o_i)$$
$$M_O, w \models RES(o_i) \wedge Reorg \rightarrow \mathcal{X}RES(o_i)$$

Proof
For a formal proof we would have to show that for each combination of organization type and safe reorganization operator the above holds. However, because the properties of the safe reorganization operators are defined in order to preserve the properties the proofs are rather trivial and we will just sketch the proof for the first combination. I.e. $M_O, w \models WD(o_i) \wedge staff^-(o_i, a) \rightarrow \mathcal{X}WD(o_i)$.

In order to proof this we thus have to show that: $M_O, w \models (desire(o_i, \varphi) \rightarrow \exists r : (role(r, o_i) \wedge I_r\varphi)) \wedge staff^-(o_i, a) \rightarrow \mathcal{X}(desire(o_i, \varphi) \rightarrow \exists r : (role(r, o_i) \wedge I_r\varphi))$ Because $staff^-(o_i, a)$ does not change anything on the desires or the roles of the organization, the only thing that could invalidate the above formula is that: $M_O, w \models I_r\varphi \wedge \neg \mathcal{X}(I_r\varphi)$. But because $staff^-(o_i, a)$ is safe we have that: $M_O, w \models I_r\varphi \rightarrow \mathcal{X}(I_r\varphi)$ and thus: $M_O, w \models WD(o_i) \wedge staff^-(o_i, a) \rightarrow \mathcal{X}WD(o_i)$
All other cases can be proven in similar ways and more or less follow directly from the defined properties for safe reorganization operators. $\square$

4   Deciding about Change

In this paper, reorganization refers both to *endogenous* reorganization, that is, the reorganization is a result of an activity by the agents themselves (run-time), and to *exogenous* reorganization, in which reorganization is achieved by activity outside of the system, for example by the designer (off-line). Given that reorganization operations are just propositions in the language $\mathcal{L}_\mathcal{O}$, in the *endogenous* case, agents or groups can control these propositions (i.e. see to it that a certain reorganization issue is the case). That is, agent or group x is such that $C_x\rho$ where ρ is one of the reorganization results specified above. For example, the fact that agent a is able to hire agent b for the organization is represented by $C_a staff^+(o_i, b)$. Thus in that case:

$$staff^+(o_i, a, U) \equiv \exists x : member(o_i, x) \wedge \\ \forall r \in U : E_x(member(o_i, a) \wedge play(a, r, o_i)) \tag{8}$$

The other reorganization operations could be tied to individual agents or roles in a similar way. Using these properties we can recursively indicate e.g. that a certain role is responsible for adding a new agent to the organization and which agents might be capable of firing agents from the organization. Thus we could also formally reorganize on these properties and in the other hand should make sure that these properties are preserved (e.g. the only agent that can fire agents from the organization should not be able to fire itself).

An explicit, planned, reorganization strategy must take into account the current performance and determine which characteristics of the organization should be modified in order to achieve a better performance. The idea behind reorganization strategies, is that one should be able to evaluate the utility of the current state of affairs (that is, what happens if nothing changes), and the utility of future states of affairs that can be obtained by performing reorganization actions. The choice is then to choose the future with the highest utility. However, this utility should not be measured over one future state but over a whole interval, because the organization is meant to provide some stability in a changing world an only should reorganize occasionally and not with every small change in the environment. Instruments are needed to determine the current and future performance of the organization over time, and also calculate the cost of reorganization. In the following section we show through an example how this can be done and how LAO is used in this case.

4.1   Case Study

In this section, we present a simple case study to demonstrate the applicability of LAO to a realistic domain. We have chosen to use the RoboSoccer [14] example previously described by another research group using a different framework to discuss the applicability of LAO to the formalization and analysis of different systems.

Based on [14], we consider a RoboSoccer team of 5 robots, together with agents representing the coach that can change the composition of the team, the monitor that determines which is the (next) objective of the team based on observation of the environment, and (re)organization designers that are able to determine which team composition is appropriate to achieve a given objective. We furthermore assume that each soccer player can have 3 different behaviors: keep, attack or defend. For our study, we define five generalist soccer player robots p_i, which have 3 different capabilities, $\forall i = 1, ..., 5 : C_{p_i} attack \wedge C_{p_i} defend \wedge C_{p_i} keep$, and a coach agent c with the capability of defining playing strategies, $C_c strategy$. We also define a specialist attacker robot, $pele$, with capability $C_{pele} attack$. The initial RoboSoccer organization O_s is then represented in LAO by:

$$O_s^0 = (As_s^0, R_s^0, rea_s^0, \leq_s^0, D_s^0, Obj_s^0, K_s^0), \text{ where}$$

1. $As_s^0 = \{c, pele, p_1, p_2, p_3, p_4, p_5\}$, with capabilities as above.
2. $R_s^0 = \{coach, keeper, defender, attacker\}$, such that
   $C_{coach} strategy$, and $C_{keeper} keep, C_{defender} defend, C_{attacker} attack$.
3. $rea_s^0 = \{(c, coach)\}$
4. $\leq_s^0 = \{coach \leq_{O_s} keeper, coach \leq_{O_s} defender, coach \leq_{O_s} attacker\}$
5. $D_s^0 = \{not - loose\}$

6. $Obj_s^0(coach) = \{not\text{-}loose\}$
7. $K_s^0 \supseteq \{k_s^01, k_s^02, k_s^03, k_s^04, k_s^05, k_s^06, k_s^07, k_s^08, k_s^09\}$, where
$k_s^01 = know(O_s^0, (not\text{-}loose \leftarrow (win \vee draw)))$,
$k_s^02 = know(O_s^0, (win \leftarrow (score \wedge defense)))$,
$k_s^03 = know(O_s^0, (draw \leftarrow (defense)))$,
$k_s^04 = know(O_s^0, ((goalsfor \geq goalsagainst) \rightarrow defense))$,
$k_s^05 = know(O_s^0, ((goalsfor < goalsagainst) \rightarrow score))$,
$k_s^06 = know(O_s^0, (goalsfor = goalsagainst = 0))$,
$k_s^07 = know(O_s^0, (score \leftarrow (\#attacker \geq 3 \wedge \#defender = 1 \wedge \#keeper = 1)))$,
$k_s^08 = know(O_s^0, (defend \leftarrow \#defender \geq 2 \wedge \#keeper = 1))$
$k_s^09 = know(O_s^0, (\forall i = 1, ..., 5 : C_{p_i} attack \wedge C_{p_i} defend \wedge C_{p_i} keeper))$
$k_s^010 = know(O_s^0, (C_{pele} attack))$

Note that the capabilities of roles indicated above specify the requirements needed for agents enacting those roles. E.g. only agents with capability *attack* can play the *attacker* role. Furthermore, we take large liberty in the specification of knowledge, where e.g. $(\#attacker = 3)$ means $|\{a|plays(a, attacker, O_s)\}| = 3$. I.e. that three agents enact the *attacker* role. In this organizational setting, the coach is in charge of achieving the organization's objective, *not-loose*. For simplicity sake, we also omit from the specification above utility-related knowledge, including the fact that a win is better than a draw, but on the other hand, a draw can be achieved with the generalist agents, while the chances of scoring increase if the forward specialist is used, who is more costly than the other agents.

For the organization O_s^0 we have that $M_O, w_0 \models WD(O_s^0) \wedge GO(O_s^0) \wedge SU(O_s^0)$. I.e. it is well-defined, good and successful, which can be easily checked from the definitions 4, 6, 5. Moreover, it can be proven that $M_O, w_0 \models EF(O_s^0)$. I.e. O_s^0 is efficient (see definition 7) as it has knowledge about the capabilities of its agents.

A possible strategy for the coach is then to start the game with the generalist agents, that can play both attacker and defender reasonably well, and later on, if the team is loosing, change the organization to include the specialist forward player. The initial instantiation is thus:

$s_{1_a}: E_{coach} desire(O_s^1, score)$
$s_{1_b}: E_{coach}(enact(O_s^1, p_1, attacker))$
$s_{1_c}: E_{coach}(enact(O_s^1, p_1, defender))$
$s_{1_b}: E_{coach}(enact(O_s^1, p_2, attacker))$
$s_{1_d}: E_{coach}(enact(O_s^1, p_2, defender))$
$s_{1_b}: E_{coach}(enact(O_s^1, p_3, attacker))$
$s_{1_b}: E_{coach}(enact(O_s^1, p_3, defender))$
$s_{1_e}: E_{coach}(enact(O_s^1, p_4, defender))$
$s_{1_f}: E_{coach}(enact(O_s^1, p_5, keeper))$

This organization is in state of playing both not-loose strategies known to the organization. However, it has lower performance than an organization where *pele* is enacting the role of *attacker*. This is because intuitively generalists (having many capabilities) have lower performance than specialists (mastering one capability very well). So, if the team is loosing, the coach may decide to bring *pele* into the team. This is formally described as follows:

$$s_{t_a}: learn^-(O_s^t, k_s^0 6)$$
$$s_{t_b}: learn^+(O_s^t, (goalsfor < goalsagainst))$$
$$s_{t_c}: E_{coach}(deact(O_s^1, p_1, attacker$$
$$s_{t_c}: E_{coach}(deact(O_s^1, p_1, defender$$
$$s_{t_d}: E_{coach}(enact(O_s^1, pele, attacker))$$

Of course, the above example is extremely simplified. However, it shows that many organizational aspects can be modeled, that we can now prove a number of interesting properties about the organizations and also how reorganizations can be described.

5   Related Work

Several approaches have already been presented to investigate the complexity of reasoning and analysis of multi-agent systems. Formal methods for MAS have a logical basis, typically based on dynamic, temporal and/or deontic logics [21,18,10]. However, their treatment of organizational concepts is in most cases very basic. The approach that comes most close to the one described in this paper is based on ATL. In these logics an operator is defined that expresses that a coalition of agents controls a formula. I.e. $\ll C \gg \phi$ means that the coalition C can achieve ϕ no matter what the agents outside C do. It is a kind of ensured achievement. However, in order to be able to ensure this in a consistent way [21] assume a complete division of agent capabilities and total control over the domain. This means that all basic propositions can be controlled by exactly one agent. Although this provides a nice logical system it is not very realistic as usually a proposition can be controlled by more than one agent. Given that LAO is a conservative extension of these logics, it allows to express the possible interference of the agents starting with basic propositions. The work presented by Santos et.al. in [18] also uses attempts to achieve situations and therefore is, in this respect, closer to LAO than ATL. However, their work lacks temporal issues. Therefore it is not possible to reason about the difference that an action makes on the world. E.g. LAO, $\neg\phi \wedge E_a\phi$ states that ϕ is false, but agent a will make it true. In a *stit* logic without temporal aspects it holds that $E_a\phi \to \phi$ and thus the formula above would be inconsistent.

Besides the formal, logical approaches towards organizational description and analysis there are also engineering frameworks. Such approaches provide sound representation languages that include many realistic organizational concepts, but have often a limited formal semantic basis, which makes analysis and comparison difficult [13,16,20].

6   Conclusions

Dynamic reorganization of agent systems is needed in order to enable systems to enforce or adapt to changes in the environment. This issue has been discussed by many researchers and several domain-oriented solutions have been proposed. However, such solutions often lack a formal basis. This prohibited the development of theories about reorganization and it prevented comparison or adaptation to other domains or situations. In this paper we presented an attempt at a formal model for reorganization concepts based on LAO, [7]. Although the language itself seems very rich, it actually is only a relative small extension to that of CTL*. This addition allows LAO to express not only abilities and achievements of (role enacting) agents, but also their *attempts* to achieve a state. Thus LAO provides a uniform framework in which these different concepts can be expressed and combined. We have described a number of desirable properties of organizations and how these can be expressed in the LAO formalism. Subsequently we have shown how our reorganization operators preserve these properties of organizations. The current model is based on the notions of controllability, *stit*, attempt and initiative. In the language presented in this paper we did distinguish between the role (or position) in an organization and the actual agent performing that role. However, we assumed that agents playing a role will always attempt to fulfill the objectives of that role. In reality agents might make different choices depending on their other commitments and preferences. This could be reflected through the incorporation of the theory presented in [6] in the current framework. This also allows for the introduction of mental notions such as knowledge and belief in the framework.

We already did work and will extend this in future work on the reorganization mechanism itself and decision making. The operations described in this paper enable the description of the reorganization of an agent organization. However, this does not answer the issue of deciding about when, what, who and how to reorganize. How do organizations reach the decision to reorganize? What should then be reorganized? When should one reorganize? Is there one agent or role responsible to make the decision or is it a democratic process? We refer to [8,12,4,15] for some related work on this topic.

Finally, we will extend the model to include deontic concepts based on work on norms in organizations given in [11,2]. This will be important in order to ensure that organizations can (and will) fulfill certain norms after reorganization.

References

1. http://www.eurofound.europa.eu/areas/industrialrelations/dictionary/definitions/RESTRUCTURING.htm
2. Aldewereld, H.: Autonomy vs. Conformity: an Institutional Perspective on Norms and Protocols. SIKS Dissertation Series 2007-10. Utrecht University, PhD Thesis (2007)
3. Carley, K., Svoboda, D.: Modeling organizational adaptation as a simulated annealing process. Sociological Methods & Research 25(1), 138–168 (1996)
4. Cholvy, L., Garion, C., Saurel, C.: Ability in a multi-agent context: A model in the situation calculus. In: Toni, F., Torroni, P. (eds.) CLIMA VI 2005. LNCS (LNAI), vol. 3900, pp. 23–36. Springer, Heidelberg (2006)

5. Cohen, M.: Artificial intelligence and the dynamic performance of organization designs. In: March, J., Weissinger-Baylon, R. (eds.) Ambiguity and Command: Organizational Perspectives on Military Decision Making, Pitman, pp. 53–71 (1986)
6. Dastani, M., Dignum, V., Dignum, F.: Role assignment in open agent societies. In: AAMAS 2003. ACM Press (July 2003)
7. Dignum, V., Dignum, F.: A logic of agent organizations. Logic Journal of the IGPL 20(1), 283–316 (2012)
8. Dignum, V., Dignum, F., Sonenberg, L.: Towards dynamic organization of agent societies. In: Vouros, G. (ed.) Workshop on Coordination in Emergent Agent Societies, ECAI 2004, pp. 70–78 (2004)
9. Fox, M.: An organizational view of distributed systems. Transactions on Systems, Man, and Cybernetics 11(1), 70–80 (1981)
10. Governatori, G., Gelati, J., Rotolo, A., Sartor, G.: Actions, institutions, powers. preliminary notes. In: Lindemann, G., et al. (eds.) RASTA 2002. Mitteilung, vol. 318, pp. 131–147. Fachbereich Informatik, Universitt Hamburg (2002)
11. Grossi, D.: Designing Invisible Handcuffs. Formal investigations in Institutions and Organizations for Multi-agent Systems. SIKS Dissertation Series 2007-16. Utrecht University, PhD Thesis (2007)
12. Grossi, D., Royakkers, L., Dignum, F.: Organizational structure and responsibility, an analysis in a dynamic logic of organized collective agency. Journal of AI and Law 15, 223–249 (2007)
13. Hübner, J., Sichman, J., Boissier, O.: S-moise+: A middleware for developing organised multi-agent systems. In: Boissier, O., Padget, J., Dignum, V., Lindemann, G., Matson, E., Ossowski, S., Sichman, J.S., Vázquez-Salceda, J. (eds.) ANIREM 2005 and OOOP 2005. LNCS (LNAI), vol. 3913, pp. 64–78. Springer, Heidelberg (2006)
14. Hübner, J.F., Sichman, J.S., Boissier, O.: Using the Moise+ for a Cooperative Framework of MAS Reorganisation. In: Bazzan, A.L.C., Labidi, S. (eds.) SBIA 2004. LNCS (LNAI), vol. 3171, pp. 506–515. Springer, Heidelberg (2004)
15. Matson, E., DeLoach, S.A.: Formal transition in agent organizations. In: IEEE International Conference on Knowledge Intensive Multiagent Systems, KIMAS 2005 (2005)
16. McCallum, M., Vasconcelos, W., Norman, T.: Verification and Analysis of Organisational Change. In: Boissier, O., Padget, J., Dignum, V., Lindemann, G., Matson, E., Ossowski, S., Sichman, J.S., Vázquez-Salceda, J. (eds.) ANIREM 2005 and OOOP 2005. LNCS (LNAI), vol. 3913, pp. 48–63. Springer, Heidelberg (2006)
17. Pörn, I.: Some basic concepts of action. In: Stenlund, S. (ed.) Logical Theory and Semantical Analisys. Reidel (1974)
18. Santos, F., Jones, A., Carmo, J.: Action concepts for describing organised interaction. In: Sprague Jr., R.A. (ed.) Proc. HICCS, vol. V, pp. 373–382. IEEE Computer Society Press (1997)
19. So, Y., Durfee, E.: Designing organizations for computational agents. In: Carley, K., Pritula, M.J., Gasser, L. (eds.) Simulating Organizations, pp. 47–64 (1998)
20. van den Broek, E., Jonker, C., Sharpanskykh, A., Treur, J., Yolum, P.: Formal Modeling and Analysis of Organizations. In: Boissier, O., Padget, J., Dignum, V., Lindemann, G., Matson, E., Ossowski, S., Sichman, J.S., Vázquez-Salceda, J. (eds.) ANIREM 2005 and OOOP 2005. LNCS (LNAI), vol. 3913, pp. 18–34. Springer, Heidelberg (2006)
21. Wooldridge, M., van der Hoek, W.: On the logic of cooperation and propositional control. Artificial Intelligence 24(1-2), 81–119 (2005)

Epistemic *ATL* with Perfect Recall, Past and Strategy Contexts

Dimitar P. Guelev[1] and Catalin Dima[2]

[1] Institute of Mathematics and Informatics, Bulgarian Academy of Sciences
gelevdp@math.bas.bg
[2] Laboratory of Algorithms, Complexity and Logic, Université Paris Est-Créteil
France
dima@univ-paris12.fr

Abstract. We propose an extension to epistemic *ATL* with perfect recall, past, and distributed knowledge by strategy contexts and demonstrate the strong completeness of a Hilbert-style proof system for its (.U.)-free subset.

Introduction

Alternating time temporal logic (*ATL*, [2,3]) was introduced as a reasoning tool for the analysis of strategic abilities of coalitions in extensive multiplayer games with temporal winning conditions. Systems of *ATL* in the literature vary on their restrictions on the players' information on the game state, which may be either *complete* or *incomplete* (*imperfect*), and the players' ability to keep full record of the past, which is known as *perfect recall* [11,17].

The informal reading of the basic game-theoretic (cooperation) construct $\langle\langle \Gamma \rangle\rangle\varphi$ of *ATL* is *the members of coalition Γ can cooperate to enforce temporal condition φ regardless of the actions of the rest of the players*. Every player is either committed to the objective φ, or free to obstruct it. This restriction is overcome in *Strategy Logic* (*SL*, [6]), where propositional *LTL* language is combined with a predicate language interpreted over a domain of strategies to enable flexible quantification over strategies. *LTL* formulas are evaluated at the unique paths which are determined by dedicated parameter lists of strategies. For instance, assuming just two players 1 and 2, $\langle\langle 1 \rangle\rangle(p\mathsf{U}q)$ translates into the *SL* formula $\exists x \forall y (p\mathsf{U}q)(x,y)$, where (x,y) indicates evaluating $(p\mathsf{U}q)$ at the path determined by 1 and 2 following strategies x and y, respectively. This translation is not invertible in general and *ATL* is not *expressively complete* wrt *SL*. Some practically interesting properties which cannot be written in *ATL* for this reason are given in [5]. To enable the expression of such properties, *ATL* was extended by *strategy contexts* in various ways [20,5,15,21]. Strategy contexts are assignments of strategies to some of the players which the rest of the players can safely assume to be followed. All of the works [20,15,21] are about strategy contexts in *ATL* with complete information. To facilitate reasoning about games with incomplete information, *ATL* was extended with epistemic operators [18,11]. Such combinations can be viewed as extending temporal logics of

M. Fisher et al. (Eds.): CLIMA XIII 2012, LNAI 7486, pp. 77–93, 2012.

knowledge (cf. e.g [7]) in the way ATL extends computational tree logic CTL. A study of the system of epistemic linear- and branching-time *temporal* logics (without the game-theoretic modalities) which arise from the various possible choices can be found in [19,10].

In this work we embark on the study of an extension of epistemic ATL with perfect recall and past by strategy contexts. Our extension to the language of ATL is different from those in [15,21] but brings the same expressive power for the case of complete information. The language extension we chose has facilitated upgrading our axiomatic system for epistemic ATL with perfect recall from [9] to include strategy contexts by making only the obvious changes. Following [9], the semantics in this paper is based on the variant from [13,14] of *interpreted systems*, which are known from the study of knowledge-based programs [7]. The main result in the paper is the completeness of our proof system for the "basic" subset of epistemic ATL with past, perfect recall and strategy contexts. This subset excludes the iterative constructs $\langle\!\langle \Gamma \rangle\!\rangle(.U.)$, $\langle\!\langle \Gamma \rangle\!\rangle\diamond$ and $\langle\!\langle \Gamma \rangle\!\rangle\square$, but includes the past operators $\ominus$ and $(.S.)$, and following [9] again, the operator D_Γ of *distributed* knowledge. The future subset of the system can be viewed as an extension of Coalition Logic [16] as well. The system is compact. This enabled us to prove *strong* completeness, i.e., that an arbitrary consistent set of formulas is also satisfiable. The proof system includes axioms for temporal logic (cf. e.g. [12]), epistemic modal logic with distributed knowledge (cf. e.g. [7]), appropriately revised ATL-specific axioms and rules from the axiomatization of ATL with complete information in [8] and from the extension of ATL by strategy contexts proposed in [20], and some axioms from our previous work [9].

Structure of the Paper. After preliminaries on interpreted systems we introduce our logic. We briefly review the related logics from [20,15,21] and give a satisfaction preserving translation between our proposed logic and that from [15]. In the subsequent sections we present our proof system for the basic subset of the logic and demonstrate its completeness.

1   Preliminaries

In this paper we define ATL_{iR}^{DPC} on *interpreted systems*. An *interpreted system* is defined with respect to some given finite set $\Sigma = \{1, \ldots, N\}$ of *players*, and a set of *propositional variables* (*atomic propositions*) AP. There is also an *environment* $e \notin \Sigma$. In the sequel we write Σ_e for $\Sigma \cup \{e\}$.

Definition 1 (interpreted systems). *An* interpreted system *for Σ and AP is a tuple of the form $\langle\langle L_i : i \in \Sigma_e\rangle, I, \langle Act_i : i \in \Sigma_e\rangle, t, V\rangle$ where:*

L_i, $i \in \Sigma_e$, *are nonempty sets of* local states; L_Γ *stands for* $\prod_{i\in\Gamma} L_i$, $\Gamma \subseteq \Sigma_e$;

$I \subseteq L_{\Sigma_e}$ *is a nonempty set of* initial global states;
Act_i, $i \in \Sigma_e$, *are nonempty sets of* actions; Act_Γ *stands for* $\prod_{i\in\Gamma} Act_i$;

$t : L_{\Sigma_e} \times Act_{\Sigma_e} \to L_{\Sigma_e}$ *is a transition* function;
$V \subseteq L_{\Sigma_e} \times AP$ *is a* valuation *of the atomic propositions.*

The elements of L_{Σ_e} are called global states. *For every $i \in \Sigma_e$ and $l', l'' \in L_{\Sigma_e}$ such that $l'_i = l''_i$ and $l'_e = l''_e$ the function t is required to satisfy $(t(l', a))_i = (t(l'', a))_i$.*

In the literature, interpreted systems also have a *protocol* $P_i : L_i \to \mathcal{P}(Act_i)$ for every $i \in \Sigma_e$. $P_i(l)$ is the set of actions which are available to i at local state l. We assume the same sets of actions to be available to agents at all states for the sake of simplicity. For the rest of the paper in our working definitions we assume the considered interpreted system IS to be clear from the context and its components to be named as above.

Definition 2 (global runs). *Given an $n \le \omega$, $r = l^0 a^0 l^1 a^1 \ldots \in L_{\Sigma_e} (Act_{\Sigma_e} L_{\Sigma_e})^n$ is a* run *of length $|r| = n$, if $l^0 \in I$ and $l^{j+1} = t(l^j, a^j)$ for all $j < n$. We denote the set of all runs of length n by $R^n(IS)$. We denote $\bigcup_{k<n} R^k(IS)$ and $\bigcup_{k \le n} R^n(IS)$ by $R^{<n}(IS)$ and $R^{\le n}(IS)$, respectively. We write $R^{fin}(IS)$ and $R(IS)$ for $R^{<\omega}(IS)$ and $R^{\le\omega}(IS)$, respectively.*

Given $m, k < \omega$ such that $m \le k \le |r|$, we write $r[m..k]$ for $l^m a^m \ldots a^{k-1} l^k$. We write $R[m..k]$ for $\{r[m..k] : r \in R\}$ in case the lengths of the runs in $R \subset R(IS)$ are at least k.

Runs of length $n < \omega$ are indeed sequences of $2n + 1$ states and actions.

Definition 3 (local states, local runs and indiscernibility of runs). *Given an $l \in L$ and $\Gamma \subseteq \Sigma_e$, we write l_Γ for $\langle l_i : i \in \Gamma \rangle$; $a_\Gamma \in Act_\Gamma$ is defined similarly for $a \in Act_{\Sigma_e}$, and indeed for $a \in Act_\Delta$ with arbitrary Δ such that $\Gamma \subseteq \Delta \subseteq \Sigma_e$. Sometimes we write l_Γ (a_Γ) just in order to emphasize that the index set of l (a) is Γ. Given $r = l^0 a^0 \ldots \in R(IS)$, we write $r_\Gamma = l^0_\Gamma a^0_\Gamma \ldots$ for the corresponding local run of Γ. Given $r', r'' \in R(IS)$ and $n \le |r'|, |r''|$, we write $r' \sim^n_\Gamma r''$ if $r'_\Gamma[0..n] = r''_\Gamma[0..n]$ and $r' \sim_\Gamma r''$ for the conjunction of $r' \sim^{|r'|}_\Gamma r''$ and $|r'| = |r''|$.*

Obviously $\sim^n_\Gamma$ and $\sim_\Gamma$ are equivalence relations on $R(IS)$. We denote $\{r' \in R(IS) : r' \sim_\Gamma r\}$ by $[r]_\Gamma$. Sequences of the form $r_\emptyset$ consist of $\langle \rangle$s and $[r]_\emptyset$ is the class of all runs of length $|r|$.

Definition 4 (joins of vectors of actions). *Given two vectors $a_i = \langle a_{i,j} : j \in \Gamma_i \rangle$, $i = 1, 2$, such that $\Gamma_1, \Gamma_2 \subseteq \Sigma_e$ and $\Gamma_1 \cap \Gamma_2 = \emptyset$, we write $a_1 \cup a_2$ for the vector indexed by $\Gamma_1 \cup \Gamma_2$ with action $(a_1 \cup a_2)_j$ being either $a_{1,j}$ or $a_{2,j}$, depending on whether $j \in \Gamma_1$ or $j \in \Gamma_2$.*

Definition 5 (strategies and outcomes). *A* strategy *for $i \in \Sigma_e$ is a function of type $\{r_i : r \in R^{fin}(IS)\} \to Act_i$. We write $S(\Gamma)$ for the set of the vectors of strategies with one strategy for every member of Γ in them. We apply the notation introduced for vectors of actions in Definitions 3 and 4 to vectors of strategies as well. Given $s \in S(\Gamma)$ and $r \in R^{fin}(IS)$, we write* out(r, s) *for the set*

$$\{r' = l^0 a^0 \ldots \in R^\omega(IS) : r'[0..|r|] = r, a^j_i = s_i(r_{\{i\}}[0..j]) \text{ for all } i \in \Gamma, j \ge |r|\}$$

of the possible outcomes *of* r *when* Γ *follow* s *from time* $|r|$ *on. Given an* $X \subset R^{fin}(IS)$, *we write* $\mathrm{out}(X, s)$ *for* $\bigcup\limits_{r \in X} \mathrm{out}(r, s)$.

Definition 6 (indiscernibility of strategy vector sequences). *Given* s', $s'' \in S(\Sigma_e)$, *we write* $s' \sim_\Gamma s''$ *if* $s'_\Gamma = s''_\Gamma$. *Given two sequences* $s' = s'^0 \ldots s'^n$, $s'' = s''^0 \ldots s''^n \in (S(\Sigma_e))^{n+1}$, *we write* $s' \sim_\Gamma s''$ *if* $s'^k \sim_\Gamma s''^k$ *for* $k = 0, \ldots, n$.

Definition 7 (strategy revision). *Given* $\Gamma \subseteq \Sigma_e$, $s', s'' \in S(\Gamma)$, *and an* $n < \omega$, *we write* $s' \triangle^n s''$ *for the vector of strategies which is defined by the case distinction:*

$$(s' \triangle^n s'')_i(r) = \begin{cases} s'_i(r_{\{i\}}), & \text{if } |r| < n; \\ s''_i(r_{\{i\}}), & \text{if } |r| \geq n. \end{cases}$$

Definition 8 (consistency of strategy vector sequences). *A sequence* $s = s^0, \ldots, s^n \in S(\Sigma_e)^{n+1}$ *is consistent, if* $s^k(r) = s^{k+1}(r)$ *for all* $r \in R^{<k}(IS)$ *and all* $k < n$.

In words, s is consistent, if, for $k > 0$, s^{k+1} returns the same vectors of actions as s^k for runs of length up to $k - 1$. The reason to require $s^{k-1}(r) = s^k(r)$ only if $|r| \leq k - 1$ is that, according to the definition of $\models$ in ATL_{iR}^{DPC} below, for $|r| \geq k$, the values of $s^k(r)$ represent the context strategies to be followed from step k on and these strategies are subject to revision.

2   Epistemic *ATL* with Perfect Recall, Past and Strategy Contexts (ATL_{iR}^{DPC})

ATL_{iR}^{DPC} has an additional parameter Δ to its game-theoretic operator to designate the set of the players whose behaviour is assumed to be as described in the strategy context. As it becomes clear below, having a cooperation modality with such a parameter facilitates the use of appropriate variants of the axioms and rules for ATL_{iR}^{DP} from [9]. In Section 3 we explain that this form of the cooperation modality has the same expressive power as (an appropriately defined incomplete-information variant of) the cooperation modalities from [15].

Definition 9 (syntax). *Here follows a BNF for the syntax of formulas in* ATL_{iR}^{DPC} *and the intended informal reading of the connectives:*

$\varphi, \psi ::= \perp \mid p \mid (\varphi \Rightarrow \psi) \mid$ *logical falsehood, atomic proposition, implication*

$\qquad \ominus \varphi \qquad\qquad \mid \varphi$ *one step ago*

$\qquad (\varphi S \psi) \qquad\quad \mid \psi$ *either now, or some time ago*
$\qquad\qquad\qquad\qquad\quad$ *and* φ *has been true ever since* ψ *held last;*

$\qquad \mathsf{D}_\Gamma \varphi \qquad\qquad \mid \Gamma$ *know* φ;

$\qquad \langle\!\langle \Gamma \mid \Delta \rangle\!\rangle \circ \varphi \quad \mid \Gamma$ *can enforce* φ *in one step, provided that* Δ *follow their current strategies;*

$\qquad \langle\!\langle \Gamma \mid \Delta \rangle\!\rangle (\varphi U \psi) \mid \Gamma$ *can enforce reaching a* ψ-*state along a path of* φ-*states, provided that* Δ *follow their current strategies;*

$\qquad [\![\Gamma \mid \Delta]\!](\varphi U \psi) \mid \Gamma$ *cannot prevent reaching a* ψ-*state along a path of* φ-*states,   unless* Δ *give up their current strategies.*

$\langle\!\langle \Gamma \mid \Delta \rangle\!\rangle$ *and* $[\![\Gamma \mid \Delta]\!]$ *are well-formed only if* $\Gamma \cap \Delta = \emptyset$. *We write* $\mathrm{Var}(\varphi)$ *for the set of the atomic propositions which occur in* φ.

Note that we do not introduce dedicated notation for *individual* knowledge. Below it becomes clear that K_i can be written as $\mathsf{D}_{\{i\}}$.

Definition 10 (modelling relation of ATL_{iR}^{DPC}). *The relation $IS, s, r \models \varphi$ is defined for $r \in R^{fin}(IS)$, a consistent strategy vector sequence $s = s^0, \ldots, s^{|r|} \in S(\Sigma_e)^{|r|+1}$, and formulas φ, by the clauses:*

$IS, s, r \not\models \bot;$

$IS, s, l^0 a^0 \ldots a^{n-1} l^n \models p$ *iff* $V(l^n, p)$ *for atomic propositions p;*

$IS, s, r \models \varphi \Rightarrow \psi$ $\qquad$ *iff either* $IS, s, r \not\models \varphi$ *or* $IS, s, r \models \psi$;

$IS, s, r \models \mathsf{D}_\Gamma \varphi$ $\qquad$ *iff* $(\forall r' \in [r]_\Gamma)(s' \in S(\Sigma_e))(s' \sim_\Gamma s \text{ implies } IS, s', r' \models \varphi)$;

$IS, s, r \models \langle\!\langle \Gamma \mid \Delta \rangle\!\rangle \theta$ $\qquad$ *iff*
$\quad (\exists s' \in S(\Gamma))(\forall s'' \in S(\Sigma_e \setminus (\Gamma \cup \Delta)))(\forall s''' \in S(\Sigma_e)^{|r|})(\forall r' \in \mathrm{out}([r]_{\Gamma \cup \Delta}, s' \cup s_\Delta^{|r|}))$
$\qquad\qquad (s''' \sim_{\Gamma \cup \Delta} s \text{ implies } IS, s''' \cdot (s'''^{|r|} \Delta^{|r|}(s' \cup s_\Delta^{|r|} \cup s'')), r', |r| \models \theta);$

$IS, s, r \models [\![\Gamma \mid \Delta]\!]\theta$ $\qquad$ *iff* $IS, s, r \not\models \langle\!\langle \Gamma \mid \Delta \rangle\!\rangle \neg\theta;$

$IS, s, r \models \ominus\varphi$ $\qquad$ *iff* $|r| > 0$ *and* $IS, s[0..|r|-1], r[0..|r|-1] \models \varphi;$

$IS, s, r \models (\varphi \mathsf{S} \psi)$ $\qquad$ *iff* $(\exists k \leq |r|) \left(\begin{array}{l} IS, s[0..n-k], r[0..n-k] \models \psi \text{ and} \\ (\forall u < k) IS, s[0..n-u], r[0..n-u] \models \varphi \end{array} \right).$

In the clauses for $\langle\!\langle \Gamma \mid \Delta \rangle\!\rangle \theta$ and $[\![\Gamma \mid \Delta]\!]\theta$ above, θ stands for a possibly negated $\circ\varphi$ or $(\varphi \mathsf{U} \psi)$. We use an auxiliary form of $\models$ to define the satisfaction of θ, which, being an LTL formula, takes an infinite run and a position in it to interpret. Given an $r \in R^\omega(IS)$ and a $k < \omega$,

$$IS, s, r, k \models \circ\varphi \qquad \textit{iff } IS, s, r[0..k+1] \models \varphi;$$
$$IS, s, r, k \models (\varphi \mathsf{U} \psi) \textit{ iff } (\exists m) \left(\begin{array}{l} IS, s, r[0..k+m] \models \psi \text{ and} \\ (\forall n < m) IS, s, r[0..k+n] \models \varphi \end{array} \right);$$
$$IS, s, r, k \models \neg\theta \qquad \textit{iff } IS, s, r, k \not\models \theta.$$

Validity of formulas in an entire interpreted system and on the class of all interpreted systems, that is, in the logic ATL_{iR}^{DPC}, is defined as satisfaction at all 0-length runs in the considered interpreted system, and at all the 0-length runs in all interpreted systems, respectively.

In the definition of $\models$, we use *sequences* of strategy vectors and not simply strategy vectors as the strategy context, in order to enable the interpretation of the past operators $\ominus$ and $(.\mathsf{S}.)$. This complication of the form of $\models$ is inevitable because the interpretation of $\langle\!\langle \Gamma \mid \Delta \rangle\!\rangle\circ$ allows the strategy context to be revised, and it is necessary to be able to revert to contexts from before such revisions for the correct interpretation of the past operators. The semantics of the future subset of ATL_{iR}^{DPC} can be defined with s being just a vector of strategies in

$\models$. Then the satisfaction condition for $IS, s, r \models \langle\!\langle \Gamma \mid \Delta \rangle\!\rangle \theta$ can be given the following simpler form:

$$(\exists s' \in S(\Gamma))(\forall s'' \in S(\Sigma_e \setminus (\Gamma \cup \Delta)))(\forall s''' \in S(\Sigma_e))(\forall r' \in \text{out}([r]_{\Gamma \cup \Delta}, s' \cup s_\Delta))$$
$$(s''' \sim_{\Gamma \cup \Delta} s \text{ implies } IS, s''' \triangle^{|r|}(s' \cup s_\Delta \cup s''), r', |r| \models \theta)$$

Abbreviations. $\top, \neg, \vee, \wedge$ and $\Leftrightarrow$ are used to abbreviate formulas written with $\bot$ and $\Rightarrow$ in the common way. The abbreviations below are specific to ATL and other temporal and epistemic logics:

$$\mathsf{I} \rightleftharpoons \neg \ominus \top \qquad \boxminus \varphi \rightleftharpoons \neg \diamondminus \neg \varphi \qquad [\![\Gamma \mid \Delta]\!] \circ \varphi \rightleftharpoons \neg \langle\!\langle \Gamma \mid \Delta \rangle\!\rangle \circ \neg \varphi.$$
$$\diamondminus \varphi \rightleftharpoons (\top S \varphi) \qquad \mathsf{P}_\Gamma \varphi \rightleftharpoons \neg \mathsf{D}_\Gamma \neg \varphi$$

3 Related Work

Next we give a brief account of the systems ATL_{sc}, $BSIL$ and $ATLES$ from [15,21,20], respectively. An extension of ATL^* by strategy contexts can be found in [1] too, where the authors focus mainly on modelling issues, and not technical results. We show that ATL_{sc} from [15] admits a satisfaction preserving translation into ATL_{iR}^{DPC}. ATL_{sc}, $BSIL$ and $ATLES$ were originally introduced for alternating transition systems and concurrent game structures. To assert the semantical compatibility with ATL_{iR}^{DPC} and, for the sake of brevity, we spell out their semantics on interpreted systems. Unlike ATL_{iR}^{DPC}, all these systems have complete information semantics. However, complete information can be straightforwardly modelled in interpreted systems by assigning the same local state space $L_1 = \ldots = L_N = L_e$ to each $i \in \Sigma_e$ and restricting the reachable states to be in the diagonal of $L_1 \times \ldots \times L_N \times L_e$.

ATL **with strategy contexts** (ATL_{sc}, [15]) has *state formulas* φ and *path formulas* ψ. Their syntax can be given by the BNFs

$$\varphi ::= \bot \mid p \mid (\varphi \Rightarrow \varphi) \mid \langle \cdot \Gamma \cdot \rangle \psi \mid \rangle \Gamma \langle \varphi \qquad \text{and} \qquad \psi ::= \neg \psi \mid \circ \varphi \mid (\varphi U \varphi)$$

Satisfaction has the form $IS, \rho, r \models \varphi$ with $r \in R^{fin}(IS)$ for state formulas and $IS, \rho, r \models \psi$ with $r \in R^\omega(IS)$ for path formulas. In both cases $\Delta \subseteq \Sigma$ and $\rho \in S(\Delta)$. The clauses about $\models$ for the ATL_{sc}-specific operators are as follows:

$IS, \rho, r \models \langle \cdot \Gamma \cdot \rangle \psi$ iff $(\exists s \in S(\Gamma))(\forall r' \in \text{out}(r, \rho_{\text{dom}\rho \setminus \Gamma} \cup s))IS, \rho_{\text{dom}\rho \setminus \Gamma} \cup s, r' \models \varphi$;

$IS, \rho, r \models \rangle \Gamma \langle \varphi$ iff $IS, \rho_{\text{dom}\rho \setminus \Gamma}, r \models \varphi$.

Thanks to the presence of strategy contexts and the possibility to combine $\langle \cdot \cdot \rangle$ with $\neg$ in ATL_{sc}, ATL_{sc} and ATL_{sc}^*, where path formulas can have arbitrary combinations of boolean connectives, have the same expressive power.

The translation t_Δ below, maps from ATL_{sc} state formulas to ATL_{iR}^{DPC} formulas. The auxiliary parameter $\Delta \subseteq \Sigma$ is the domain of the reference context.

For the sake of brevity $(\cdot\cdot)$ stands for either $[\cdot]$ or $\langle\cdot\cdot\rangle$ in the translation clauses. The meaning of $((.))$ is similar, wrt $\langle\!\langle .|.\rangle\!\rangle$.

$$t_\Delta(\bot) \rightleftharpoons \bot, \qquad t_\Delta(p) \rightleftharpoons p, \qquad t_\Delta(\varphi_1 \Rightarrow \varphi_2) \rightleftharpoons t_\Delta(\varphi_1) \Rightarrow t_\Delta(\varphi_2)$$
$$t_\Delta(\langle\cdot\Gamma\rangle\neg\psi) \rightleftharpoons \neg t_\Delta([\cdot\Gamma]\psi), \qquad t_\Delta([\cdot\Gamma]\neg\psi) \rightleftharpoons \neg t_\Delta(\langle\cdot\Gamma\rangle\psi)$$
$$t_\Delta((\cdot\Gamma\cdot)\circ\varphi) \rightleftharpoons ((\Gamma\mid\Delta\setminus\Gamma))\circ t_{\Gamma\cup\Delta}(\varphi)$$
$$t_\Delta((\cdot\Gamma\cdot)(\varphi_1\mathsf{U}\varphi_2)) \rightleftharpoons ((\Gamma\mid\Delta\setminus\Gamma))(t_{\Gamma\cup\Delta}(\varphi_1)\mathsf{U}t_{\Gamma\cup\Delta}(\varphi_2))$$
$$t_\Delta(\langle\rangle\Gamma\langle\varphi\mid\Delta) \rightleftharpoons t_{\Delta\setminus\Gamma}(\varphi)$$

An induction on the construction of formulas shows that, for any ATL_{sc} state formula φ, $IS, \rho, r \models_{ATL_{sc}} \varphi$ is equivalent to $IS, s, r \models_{ATL_{iR}^{DPC}} t_{\mathrm{dom}\rho}(\varphi)$ where s stands for any sequence of strategy vectors that is consistent with r and features ρ as the strategy assignment to the members of $\mathrm{dom}\rho$ in its last member. The translation can be inverted on the future subset of ATL_{iR}^{DPC}:

$$t^{-1}(\langle\!\langle\Gamma\mid\Delta\rangle\!\rangle\varphi) \rightleftharpoons \rangle\Sigma\setminus\Delta\langle\ \langle\cdot\Gamma\cdot\rangle t^{-1}(\varphi).$$

Basic strategy-interaction logic (*BSIL*, **[21]**) language includes *state* formulas φ, *path* formulas ψ and *tree* formulas θ:

$$\varphi ::= \bot \mid p \mid (\varphi \Rightarrow \varphi) \mid \langle\Gamma\rangle\theta \mid \langle\Gamma\rangle\psi$$
$$\theta ::= \bot \mid (\theta \Rightarrow \theta) \mid \langle+\Gamma\rangle\theta \mid \langle+\Gamma\rangle\psi$$
$$\psi ::= \circ\varphi \mid (\varphi\mathsf{U}\varphi) \mid (\varphi\mathsf{W}\varphi)$$

The modelling relation has the form $IS, \rho, l \models \varphi$ for state and tree φ, and $IS, \rho, r \models \psi$ for path ψ, where l is a (global) state, $r \in R^\omega(IS)$, and ρ is a strategic context. The clauses for $\langle\Gamma\rangle$ and $\langle+\Gamma\rangle$ with a path argument formula ψ are as follows:

$$IS, \rho, l \models \langle\Gamma\rangle\psi \quad \text{iff} \quad (\exists s \in S(\Gamma))(\forall r \in \mathrm{out}(l,s))IS, s, r \models \psi;$$
$$IS, \rho, l \models \langle+\Gamma\rangle\psi \quad \text{iff} \quad (\exists s \in S(\Gamma))(\forall r \in \mathrm{out}(l, \rho_{\mathrm{dom}\rho\setminus\Gamma}\cup s))IS, \rho_{\mathrm{dom}\rho\setminus\Gamma}\cup s, r \models \psi$$

The clauses for tree argument formulas are similar. *BSIL* admits a translation into an appropriate *-extension of ATL_{iR}^{DPC}.

ATL with explicit strategies (*ATLES*, **[20]**) extends the syntax of $\langle\!\langle .\rangle\!\rangle$ by subscripting it with mappings ρ of subsets of Σ to finite syntactical descriptions of strategies called *strategy terms*. In our notation, ρ denote elements of $S(\mathrm{dom}\rho)$ and the clause about $\models$ for $\langle\!\langle\Gamma\rangle\!\rangle_\rho\circ$ is:

$$IS, r \models \langle\!\langle\Gamma\rangle\!\rangle_\rho\circ\varphi \text{ iff } (\exists s \in S(\Gamma\setminus\mathrm{dom}\rho))(\forall r' \in \mathrm{out}(r, s\cup\rho))IS, r'[0..|r|+1] \models \varphi.$$

The clauses for $\langle\!\langle\Gamma\rangle\!\rangle_\rho(\varphi\mathsf{U}\psi)$ and $\langle\!\langle\Gamma\rangle\!\rangle_\rho\Box\varphi$ follow the same pattern. Unlike ATL_{sc}, *BSIL* and ATL_{iR}^{DPC}, an *ATLES* formula may have several (freely occurring) fixed strategy context terms for each player. There appears to be no obvious way to reconcile this with the semantics of the other systems.

4   A Proof System for Basic ATL_{iR}^{DPC}

Basic ATL_{iR}^{DPC} is the subset of ATL_{iR}^{DPC} without $\langle\!\langle . \mid . \rangle\!\rangle(.U.)$ and $[\![. \mid .]\!](.U.)$:

$$\varphi, \psi ::= \bot \mid p \mid (\varphi \Rightarrow \psi) \mid \ominus\varphi \mid (\varphi S \psi) \mid D_\Gamma\varphi \mid \langle\!\langle \Gamma \mid \Delta \rangle\!\rangle \circ \varphi$$

Along with all propositional tautologies and the rule *Modus Ponens* (MP), our system includes the following axioms and rules:

The epistemic operator D.

$(\mathbf{K_D})$	$D_\Gamma(\varphi \Rightarrow \psi) \Rightarrow (D_\Gamma\varphi \Rightarrow D_\Gamma\psi)$	$(\mathbf{T_D})$	$D_\Gamma\psi \Rightarrow \psi$
$(\mathbf{4_D})$	$D_\Gamma\psi \Rightarrow D_\Gamma D_\Gamma\psi$	$(\mathbf{5_D})$	$\neg D_\Gamma\psi \Rightarrow D_\Gamma\neg D_\Gamma\psi$
$(Mono_D)$	$D_\Gamma\psi \Rightarrow D_{\Gamma\cup\Delta}\psi$	(N_D)	$\dfrac{\varphi}{D_\Gamma\varphi}$

$$(INT_D) \quad \frac{(D_{\Gamma\setminus\Delta}(p \Rightarrow \varphi) \wedge D_\Delta(\neg p \Rightarrow \varphi)) \Rightarrow \psi}{D_{\Gamma\cup\Delta}\varphi \Rightarrow \psi}$$

The past modalities $\ominus$ *and* $(.S.)$

$(\mathbf{K_\ominus})$	$\ominus(\varphi \Rightarrow \psi) \Rightarrow (\ominus\varphi \Rightarrow \ominus\psi)$	$(\ominus\bot)$	$\neg\ominus\bot$
$(FP_{(.S.)})$	$(\varphi S \psi) \Leftrightarrow \psi \vee (\varphi \wedge \ominus(\varphi S \psi))$	$(Fun_\ominus)$	$\ominus\neg\varphi \Rightarrow \neg\ominus\varphi$
$(Mono_\ominus)$	$\dfrac{\varphi \Rightarrow \psi}{\ominus\varphi \Rightarrow \ominus\psi}$	$(N_\boxminus)$	$\dfrac{\varphi}{\boxminus\varphi}$

General ATL axioms and rules

$(\langle\!\langle . \mid . \rangle\!\rangle \circ \bot)$ $\neg\langle\!\langle \Gamma \mid \Delta \rangle\!\rangle \circ \bot$

$(\langle\!\langle . \mid . \rangle\!\rangle \circ \top)$ $\langle\!\langle \Gamma \mid \Delta \rangle\!\rangle \circ \top$

(S) $\langle\!\langle \Gamma' \setminus \Gamma'' \mid \Delta' \rangle\!\rangle \circ \varphi \wedge \langle\!\langle \Gamma'' \mid \Delta'' \rangle\!\rangle \circ \psi \Rightarrow \langle\!\langle \Gamma' \cup \Gamma'' \mid \Delta' \cup \Delta'' \rangle\!\rangle \circ (\varphi \wedge \psi)$

$$(INT_{\langle\!\langle . \mid . \rangle\!\rangle\circ}) \quad \frac{\langle\!\langle \Gamma' \setminus \Gamma'' \mid \Delta' \rangle\!\rangle \circ (p \Rightarrow \varphi) \wedge \langle\!\langle \Gamma'' \mid \Delta'' \rangle\!\rangle \circ (\neg p \Rightarrow \varphi) \Rightarrow \psi}{\langle\!\langle \Gamma' \cup \Gamma'' \mid \Delta' \cup \Delta'' \rangle\!\rangle \circ \varphi \Rightarrow \psi}$$

$$(Mono_{\langle\!\langle . \mid . \rangle\!\rangle\circ}) \quad \frac{\varphi \Rightarrow \psi}{\langle\!\langle \Gamma \mid \Delta \rangle\!\rangle \circ \varphi \Rightarrow \langle\!\langle \Gamma \mid \Delta \rangle\!\rangle \circ \psi}$$

Committed versus neutral players (See Lemma 1 from [20].)

(WHW) $\langle\!\langle \Gamma \mid \Psi \cup \Delta \rangle\!\rangle \circ \varphi \Rightarrow \langle\!\langle \Gamma \cup \Psi \mid \Delta \rangle\!\rangle \circ \varphi$

Interactions between $\ominus$, $(.S.)$, $\langle\!\langle . \mid . \rangle\!\rangle\circ$ *and* D.

$(D_\circ)$ $\langle\!\langle \Gamma \mid \Delta \rangle\!\rangle \circ \varphi \Leftrightarrow D_{\Gamma\cup\Delta}\langle\!\langle \Gamma \mid \Delta \rangle\!\rangle \circ \varphi$

 $\langle\!\langle \Gamma \mid \Delta \rangle\!\rangle \circ \varphi \Leftrightarrow \langle\!\langle \Gamma \mid \Delta \rangle\!\rangle \circ D_{\Gamma\cup\Delta}\varphi$

(PR) $\ominus D_\Gamma\varphi \Rightarrow D_\Gamma\ominus\varphi$

$(\langle\!\langle . \mid . \rangle\!\rangle \circ \ominus)$ $\langle\!\langle \Gamma \mid \Delta \rangle\!\rangle \circ (\ominus\varphi \wedge \psi) \Leftrightarrow D_{\Gamma\cup\Delta}\varphi \wedge \langle\!\langle \Gamma \mid \Delta \rangle\!\rangle \circ \psi$

 $\ominus\langle\!\langle \emptyset \mid \Delta \rangle\!\rangle \circ \varphi \Rightarrow \langle\!\langle \emptyset \mid \Delta \rangle\!\rangle \circ \ominus\varphi$

(D_I) $D_\Gamma I \vee D_\Gamma \neg I$

The rules $INT_{\langle\langle .|.\rangle\rangle\circ}$ and INT_{D} require $p \notin \mathrm{Var}(\varphi) \cup \mathrm{Var}(\psi)$. Note that instances of S are well-formed only if $(\Gamma' \cup \Gamma'') \cap (\Delta' \cup \Delta'') = \emptyset$.

5   Completeness of the Proof System

We fix the vocabulary AP for the rest of this section and denote the set of all the basic ATL_{iR}^{DPC} formulas built using variables from AP by $\mathbf{L}$. We write $\Phi \vdash_{MP} \varphi$ for the derivability of φ from the premises Φ, the theorems of ATL_{iR}^{DPC} and MP as the only proof rule.

Auxiliary Propositional Variables and Formulas. Given $\Gamma \subseteq \Sigma$ and $i \in \Sigma$, we write $\Gamma^{<i}$ for the set $\Gamma \cap \{1,\ldots,i-1\}$. Given the formulas $\mathsf{D}_\Gamma \psi$ and $\langle\langle \Gamma \mid \Delta \rangle\rangle \circ \psi$, we introduce the auxiliary variables $q_{i,\mathsf{D}_\Gamma \psi}$, $i \in \Gamma^{<\max \Gamma}$, and $q_{i,\langle\langle \Gamma \mid \Delta \rangle\rangle \circ \psi}$, $i \in (\Gamma \cup \Delta)^{<\max(\Gamma \cup \Delta)}$ and use them to construct the formulas

$$p_{i,\mathsf{D}_\Gamma \psi} \rightleftharpoons q_{i,\mathsf{D}_\Gamma \psi} \wedge \bigwedge_{j \in \Gamma^{<i}} \neg q_{j,\mathsf{D}_\Gamma \psi}, \ i \in \Gamma^{<\max \Gamma}, \text{ and } p_{\max \Gamma, \mathsf{D}_\Gamma \psi} \rightleftharpoons \bigwedge_{j \in \Gamma^{<\max \Gamma}} \neg q_{j,\mathsf{D}_\Gamma \psi}.$$

Obviously these formulas satisfy $\vdash \bigvee_{i \in \Gamma} p_{i,\mathsf{D}_\Gamma \psi}$ and $\vdash \neg(p_{i,\mathsf{D}_\Gamma \psi} \wedge p_{j,\mathsf{D}_\Gamma \psi})$ for $i \neq j$. We put $p_{\max \Gamma, \mathsf{D}_\Gamma \psi} \rightleftharpoons \top$ in case $|\Gamma \cup \Delta| = 1$. We use $p_{i,\mathsf{D}_\Gamma \psi}$ to construct the formulas

$$\mathsf{D}_{i,\Gamma} \psi \rightleftharpoons \mathsf{D}_i(p_{i,\mathsf{D}_\Gamma \psi} \Rightarrow \psi), \ i \in \Gamma.$$

The formulas $p_{i,\langle\langle \Gamma \mid \Delta \rangle\rangle \circ \psi}$, $i \in \Gamma \cup \Delta$, are written similarly in terms of the variables $q_{i,\langle\langle \Gamma \mid \Delta \rangle\rangle \circ \psi}$, $i \in (\Gamma \cup \Delta)^{<\max(\Gamma \cup \Delta)}$. We use $p_{i,\langle\langle \Gamma \mid \Delta \rangle\rangle \circ \psi}$ to construct the formulas

$$\langle\langle i, \Gamma \mid \Delta \rangle\rangle \circ \psi \rightleftharpoons \begin{cases} \langle\langle i \mid \emptyset \rangle\rangle \circ (p_{i,\langle\langle \Gamma \mid \Delta \rangle\rangle \circ \psi} \Rightarrow \psi), \text{ for } i \in \Gamma; \\ \langle\langle \emptyset \mid i \rangle\rangle \circ (p_{i,\langle\langle \Gamma \mid \Delta \rangle\rangle \circ \psi} \Rightarrow \psi), \text{ for } i \in \Delta. \end{cases}$$

Given a set of formulas x written in AP, we write $\bar{x}$ for the set

$$x \cup \{\mathsf{D}_{i,\Gamma} \psi : i \in \Gamma, \mathsf{D}_\Gamma \psi \in x\} \cup \{\langle\langle i, \Gamma \mid \Delta \rangle\rangle \circ \psi : \langle\langle \Gamma \mid \Delta \rangle\rangle \circ \psi \in x, i \in \Gamma \cup \Delta\}.$$

Lemma 1. *Let x be a consistent set of formulas written in AP. Then $\bar{x}$ is consistent too.*

The proof of this lemma is similar to that of Lemma 12 from [9] and involves the rules INT_{D} and $INT_{\langle\langle .|.\rangle\rangle\circ}$.

Lemma 2 (customized Lindenbaum lemma). *Let $\prec$ be a well-ordering of $\mathbf{L}$ and let x be a consistent subset of $\mathbf{L}$. Then there exists a consistent set $x' \supseteq x$ which is maximal in $\mathbf{L}$ and is such that for any initial interval $\Phi \subset \mathbf{L}$ of $\langle \mathbf{L}, \prec \rangle$ the consistency of $x \cup \Phi$ entails $\Phi \subseteq x'$.*

Proof. We construct the ascending (transfinite) sequence x_φ, $\varphi \in \mathbf{L}$, of consistent subsets of $\mathbf{L}$ indexed by the elements of $\mathbf{L}$ by induction on the well-ordering $\prec$. Let φ_0 be the least element of $\mathbf{L}$. Then x_{φ_0} is $x \cup \{\varphi_0\}$ in case $x \cup \{\varphi_0\}$ is consistent; otherwise it is just x. Similarly, for all non-limit φ, given that φ' is the successor of φ in $\prec$, $x_{\varphi'}$ is $x_\varphi \cup \{\varphi'\}$ in case $x_\varphi \cup \{\varphi'\}$ is consistent and x_φ otherwise. For limit φ, $x_\varphi = \bigcup_{\psi \prec \varphi} \varphi_\psi$. A direct check shows that $x' = \bigcup_{\varphi \in \mathbf{L}}$ has the desired property.

In the sequel, given x and a well-ordering a of $\mathbf{L}$, we denote a fixed maximal consistent set (MCS) with the above property by $x + a$.

Next we build a interpreted system $IS = \langle\langle L_i : i \in \Sigma_e\rangle, I, \langle Act_i \in \Sigma_e\rangle, t, V\rangle$ for basic ATL_{iR}^{DPC} which is canonical in the sense adopted in modal logic.

Definition 11 (global states, local states). *Let W to be the set of all the maximal consistent sets of formulas in the vocabulary AP. Given $w \in W$ and $\Gamma \subseteq \Sigma$, we put*

$$D_\Gamma(w) = \{\varphi : \mathsf{D}_\Gamma\varphi \in \overline{w}\}, \; L_i = \{D_{\{i\}}(w) : w \in W\} \text{ for } i \in \Sigma, \text{ and } L_e = W.$$

Given $w \in W$, we write l_w for the state $\langle D_{\{1\}}(w), \ldots, D_{\{N\}}(w), w\rangle$. Below it becomes clear that all reachable states in IS have this form. We work with the MCS w instead of the respective tuples l_w wherever this is more convenient. Note that the environment component of l_w is w itself.

Definition 12 (valuation and initial states). *We put $V(w, p) \leftrightarrow p \in w$ and $I = \{l_w : w \in W, \mathsf{I} \in w\}$.*

Definition 13 (indiscernibility of states in terms of MCS). *Given $\Gamma \subseteq \Sigma_e$, two states $w, v \in W$ are Γ-similar, written $w \sim_\Gamma v$, if $D_\Gamma(w) = D_\Gamma(v)$.*

The following lemma shows that $w \sim_\Gamma v$ is equivalent to $l_w \sim_\Gamma l_v$ in the sense of Definition 3.

Lemma 3 (Γ-similarity in terms of Γ's distributed knowledge). *Let $w, v \in W$, $\Gamma \subseteq \Sigma$. Then $w \sim_\Gamma v$ iff $D_{\{i\}}(w) = D_{\{i\}}(v)$ for all $i \in \Gamma$.*

Proof. ($\leftarrow$): Let $w \sim_\Gamma v$ and $\mathsf{D}_\Gamma\varphi \in D_\Gamma(w)$. Then $\mathsf{D}_{i,\Gamma}\varphi \in \overline{w}$ for every $i \in \Gamma$. Then, by 4_D and $Mono_\mathsf{D}$, $\mathsf{D}_\Gamma\mathsf{D}_{i,\Gamma}\varphi \in \overline{v}$ for every $i \in \Gamma$ too. Now **S5** reasoning and $\vdash \bigvee_{i\in\Gamma} p_{i,\mathsf{D}_\Gamma\varphi}$ entail $\bigwedge_{i\in\Gamma} \mathsf{D}_{i,\Gamma} \Rightarrow \mathsf{D}_\Gamma\varphi$. Hence $\mathsf{D}_\Gamma\varphi \in D_\Gamma(v)$.
($\rightarrow$): Let $\mathsf{D}_i\varphi \in \overline{w}$. Then, by **S5** reasoning, $\overline{w} \vdash_{MP} \mathsf{D}_\Gamma\mathsf{D}_i\varphi$, whence, by $D_\Gamma(w) = D_\Gamma(v)$, $\overline{v} \vdash_{MP} \mathsf{D}_\Gamma\mathsf{D}_i\varphi$ and, finally $\mathsf{D}_i\varphi \in \overline{v}$. Hence $D_{\{i\}}(w) \subseteq D_{\{i\}}(v)$.
   The symmetrical inclusions are proved similarly.

Definition 14 (actions). *An action for player $i \in \Sigma$ is either the symbol d or a tuple of the form $\langle\Phi, \Gamma, \Delta\rangle$ such that $\Gamma, \Delta \subseteq \Sigma$ are disjoint, $i \in \Gamma$, and Φ is a consistent set of formulas. An environment action is a well-ordering of $\mathbf{L}$.*

Player action $\langle\Phi, \Gamma, \Delta\rangle$ is represents the player's contribution to achieving all the objectives from Φ simultaneously as a member of Γ, provided that Δ act as described in the context. Action d indicates choosing to follow the strategy from the context. Allowing infinite sets Φ of objectives in actions is necessary because MCS may contain infinitely many formulas of the form $\langle\langle\emptyset \mid \Delta\rangle\rangle \circ \varphi$.

Definition 15 (the past of a state). *Given a $w \in W$, we write Θ_w for the set $\{\ominus\theta : \theta \in w\}$.*

The formulas from Θ_w hold at states which can be reached from l_w in one step. Environment actions complement the construction of successor states. Let x consist of the formulas to be satisfied due to the player actions performed at state l_w. Then environment action a_e comlements $x \cup \Theta_w$ to an MCS description of the successor state $(x \cup \Theta_w) + a_e$. Lemma 2 entails that any MCS $x' \supseteq x \cup \Theta_w$ has the form $(x \cup \Theta_w) + a_e$ for some appropriate a_e.

Definition 16 (effectiveness of coalitions). *Let $a \in Act_{\Sigma_e}$ and $w \in W$. We write Δ_a for the set $\{i \in \Sigma : a_i = \mathsf{d}\}$. Coalition $\Gamma \subseteq \Sigma$ is effective in a wrt w, if*

(1) $\Gamma \subseteq \Sigma \setminus \Delta_a$, $\Delta \subseteq \Delta_a$;

assuming that $a_i = \langle \Phi_i, \Gamma_i, \Delta_i \rangle$, $i \in \Gamma$,

(2) $\Gamma = \Gamma_i$ for all $i \in \Gamma$;

(3) $\langle\!\langle \Gamma_i \mid \Delta_i \rangle\!\rangle \circ \bigwedge \Phi' \in w$ for all finite $\Phi' \subseteq \Phi_i$;

(4) $\Delta_i = \Delta_j$ for all $i, j \in \Gamma$.

Coalition Γ is effective in state w, iff its objectives are achievable in w. Different coalitions which are effective in the same state cannot overlap.

Definition 17 ($\bar{a}_w$). *Let the coalitions which are effective in $a \in Act_{\Sigma_e}$ wrt $w \in W$ be $\Gamma_1, \ldots, \Gamma_k$. Let $\Upsilon = \Gamma_1 \cup \ldots \cup \Gamma_k$. We define $\bar{a}_w \in Act_{\Sigma_e}$ by the clause*

$$\bar{a}_{w,i} = \begin{cases} a_e, & \text{if } i = e; \\ \langle \Phi_i, \Gamma_i, \Delta_i \rangle, & \text{if } i \in \Upsilon; \\ \langle \{\psi : \langle\!\langle \emptyset \mid i \rangle\!\rangle \circ \psi \in \overline{w}\}, \{i\}, \emptyset \rangle, & \text{if } i \in \Delta_a; \\ \langle \emptyset, \{i\}, \emptyset \rangle, & \text{otherwise.} \end{cases}$$

The vector of actions $\bar{a}_w$ is a revision of a according to the plausibility of the actions from a in w. In $\bar{a}_w$, players i who participate in effective coalitions are described as acting to achieve the common objective of their coalitions; players who follow their respective strategies from the context are described as acting to achieve whatever consequences these actions have according to w, and players who neither participate in effective coalitions, nor follow the context strategies, are described as acting in singleton coalitions $\{i\}$ to achieve nothing. Consequently, all the coalitions in $\bar{a}_w$ are effective wrt w:

Lemma 4 (effectiveness of coalitions in $\bar{a}_w$). *Assuming the notation from Definition 17, if $i \in \Sigma$ and $\bar{a}_{w,i} = \langle \Phi, \Gamma, \Delta \rangle$, then $\langle\!\langle \Gamma \mid \Delta \rangle\!\rangle \circ \bigwedge \Phi' \in w$ for all finite $\Phi' \subset \Phi$.*

Proof. The lemma follows immediately for $i \in \Upsilon$ and $i \in \Sigma \setminus (\Upsilon \cup \Delta_a)$. Players $i \in \Delta_a$ appear in the singleton coalitions $\{i\}$ in $\bar{a}_w$, and we have $\langle\!\langle \emptyset \mid i \rangle\!\rangle \circ \bigwedge \Phi' \in w$ for all finite $\Phi' \subset \Phi$. By Axiom WHW this entails $\langle\!\langle i \mid \emptyset \rangle\!\rangle \circ \bigwedge \Phi' \in w$.

As it becomes clear below, a and $\bar{a}_w$ cause the same transitions from w. The notation $\bar{a}_w$ is introduced to avoid lengthy explanations about treating the various sorts of actions separately.

Definition 18 (transition function). *Let $w \in W$, $a \in Act_{\Sigma_e}$ and $\bar{a}_w = \langle\langle \Phi_i, \Gamma_i, \Delta_i \rangle : i \in \Sigma \rangle \cup \langle a_e \rangle$. Then $t(l_w, a) = l_v$ where $v = \left(\bigcup_{i \in \Sigma} \Phi_i \cup \Theta_w \right) + a_e$,* *i.e., v is the extension of the set of all the objectives which can be simultaneously achieved by the coalitions which are effective in a wrt w and the formulas which describe l_w's past, to an MCS by a_e, as in Lemma 2.*

The definition of t above relies on the fact that $\bigcup_{i \in \Sigma} \Phi_i \cup \Theta_w$ is consistent. To realise that, assume the contrary. Then there exist some finite $\Phi' \subseteq \bigcup_{i \in \Sigma} \Phi_i$ and $\Theta' \subset w$ such that $\vdash \bigwedge \Phi' \Rightarrow \ominus \neg \bigwedge \Theta'$. By the monotonicity of $\langle\!\langle \Sigma \mid \emptyset \rangle\!\rangle \circ$ and Axiom $\langle\!\langle . \mid . \rangle\!\rangle \circ \ominus$, this entails $\vdash \langle\!\langle \Sigma \mid \emptyset \rangle\!\rangle \circ \bigwedge \Phi' \Rightarrow \mathsf{D}_\Sigma \neg \bigwedge \Theta'$. By Axioms S and WHW, $\vdash \bigwedge_{i \in \Sigma} \langle\!\langle \Gamma_i \mid \Delta_i \rangle\!\rangle \circ \bigwedge(\Phi_i \cap \Phi') \Rightarrow \langle\!\langle \Sigma \mid \emptyset \rangle\!\rangle \circ \bigwedge \Phi'$. Hence $\vdash \bigwedge_{i \in \Sigma} \langle\!\langle \Gamma_i \mid \Delta_i \rangle\!\rangle \circ \bigwedge(\Phi_i \cap \Phi') \Rightarrow \mathsf{D}_\Sigma \neg \bigwedge \Theta'$, which is a contradiction because $\Theta' \subset w$ and, by Lemma 4, $\langle\!\langle \Gamma_i \mid \Delta_i \rangle\!\rangle \circ \bigwedge(\Phi_i \cap \Phi') \in w$ for all $i \in \Sigma$. We define t only on states of the form l_w. The set of these states contains I and is closed under t. Hence the definition of t on other states is irrelevant.

Definitions 11, 12, 14 and 18 give a complete description of the interpreted system IS. Below we prove that if $r \in R^{fin}(IS)$ and $s \in S(\Sigma_e)^{n+1}$ is consistent with s, then, for any $\varphi \in \mathbf{L}$, $IS, s, r \models \varphi$ iff $\varphi \in w$ where l_w is the last state of r.

Definition 19 (extracting strategic context from MCS). *Given a $w \in R^0(IS)$, we define $a_w \in Act_\Sigma$ by putting $a_{w,i} = \langle \{\varphi : \langle\!\langle \emptyset | i \rangle\!\rangle \circ \varphi \in \overline{w}\}, \{i\}, \emptyset \rangle$. We define the vector of strategies $s_{IS} \in S(\Sigma)$ by putting, given an arbitrary $r = w^0 a^0 \dots a^{|r|-1} w^{|r|} \in R^{fin}(IS)$, $s_{IS}(r) = a_{w^{|r|}}$.*

The strategies s_{IS} are built according to the working of the transition function along runs in which the players act as described in the context. They are memoryless, i.e., determined by the last state of the argument run. Note that we extract strategic context from $\overline{w}$, which contains the explicit descriptions $\langle\!\langle i, \Gamma \mid \Delta \rangle\!\rangle \circ \psi$ of the contribution of individual coalition members $i \in \Gamma$ to the achievement of goals of their respective coalitions Γ. According to our definition, local runs are sequences of the form

$$r_i = D_{\{i\}}(w^0) a_i^0 D_{\{i\}}(w^1) a_i^1 \dots a_i^{k-1} D_{\{i\}}(w^k) \dots .$$

To realise that the strategies $s_{IS,i}$ are determined from the local run of player i, note that $\langle\!\langle \emptyset | \{i\} \rangle\!\rangle \circ \varphi \in \overline{w}$ is equivalent to $\langle\!\langle \emptyset | \{i\} \rangle\!\rangle \circ \varphi \in \overline{v}$ for v such that $D_{\{i\}}(v) = D_{\{i\}}(w)$ due to the Axioms $\mathsf{D}_\circ$.

Definition 20 (consistency between runs and strategy vector sequences). *Let $n < \omega$. Run $r = w^0 a^0 \dots a^{n-1} w^n \in R^n(IS)$ and strategy vector sequence $s = s^0, \dots, s^n \in (S(\Sigma_e))^{n+1}$ are consistent, if s is consistent (in the sense of Definition 8) and $a^k = s^n(r[0..k])$, $k = 0, \dots, n-1$.*

Note that the restrictions on s^k which follow from the consistency between r and s for $k < n$ are implied by the consistency of s as a sequence of strategy vectors.

The following lemma states that if $w \in W$ and $D_\Gamma(w)$ is consistent with some arbitrary formula φ, then indeed $D_\Gamma(w) \vdash_{MP} \mathsf{P}_\Gamma \varphi$.

Lemma 5. *Let $\Gamma \subseteq \Sigma$, $w \in W$, $\varphi \in \mathbf{L}$ and let w be consistent with φ. Then $D_\Gamma(w) \vdash_{MP} \mathsf{P}_\Gamma \varphi$.*

Proof. Since w is maximal consistent, either $\mathsf{P}_\Gamma \varphi \in w$ or $\mathsf{D}_\Gamma \neg \varphi \in w$. The latter is impossible as it would entail $D_\Gamma(w) \vdash_{MP} \neg \varphi$. By **S5** reasoning, $\mathsf{P}_\Gamma \varphi \in w$ entails $\mathsf{D}_\Gamma \mathsf{P}_\Gamma \varphi \in w$. The latter formula appears in $D_\Gamma(w)$ as well. Hence, by **S5** reasoning again, $D_\Gamma(w) \vdash_{MP} \mathsf{P}_\Gamma \varphi$.

Lemma 6. *Let* $w, v \in W$, $\Gamma \subseteq \Sigma$ *and* $D_\Gamma(w) \subseteq D_\Gamma(v)$. *Then* $D_\Gamma(w) = D_\Gamma(v)$.

Proof. Let $\varphi \in \mathbf{L}$ be such that $\mathsf{D}_\Gamma \varphi \notin w$. Then $\mathsf{D}_\Gamma \mathsf{P}_\Gamma \neg \varphi \in w$ by Lemma 5 and **S5** reasoning. By $D_\Gamma(w) \subseteq D_\Gamma(v)$, this entails $\mathsf{P}_\Gamma \neg \varphi \in v$. Hence $\mathsf{D}_\Gamma \varphi \notin v$.

The following lemmata are the parts of the inductive proof of the Truth Lemma below (Theorem 1) about the various ATL_{iR}^{DPC} modalities.

Lemma 7 (P_Γ). *Let* $n < \omega$, $r = w^0 a^0 \ldots a^{n-1} w^n \in R^n(IS)$, *let* $s = s^0, \ldots, s^n \in (S(\Sigma_e))^{n+1}$ *be consistent with* r. *Let* Φ *be a set of formulas such that* $\mathsf{P}_\Gamma \bigwedge \Phi' \in w^n$ *for all finite* $\Phi' \subseteq \Phi$. *Then there exist an* $r' = v^0 b^0 \ldots b^{n-1} v^n \in R^{fin}(IS)$ *and a sequence* $s' = s'^0, \ldots, s'^n \in (S(\Sigma_e))^{n+1}$ *such that* s' *is consistent with* r', $r' \sim_\Gamma r$, $s' \sim_\Gamma s$, *and* $\Phi \subseteq v^n$.

Proof. Induction on n. If $r \in R^0(IS)$, then $\mathsf{I} \in w^0$ and, by **S5** reasoning and D_I, $\mathsf{P}_\Gamma(\mathsf{I} \wedge \bigwedge \Phi') \in w^0$ for all finite $\Phi' \subseteq \Phi$. By **S5** reasoning this entails that $\Phi \cup \{\mathsf{I}\} \cup \{\mathsf{D}_\Gamma \psi : \mathsf{D}_\Gamma \psi \in w^0\}$ is consistent. Now Lemma 6 entails that we can choose v^0 to be any MCS which contains the latter set and put $s'^0 = s_{IS}$.

Next we prove the lemma for $|r| = n+1$ assuming that it holds for $|r| = n$. Let $\Theta = \{\theta : D_\Gamma(w^{n+1}) \cup \Phi \vdash_{MP} \ominus \theta\}$. Assume that $D_\Gamma(w^n) \cup \Theta$ is inconsistent for the sake of contradiction. Then there exist some finite $D' \subset D_\Gamma(w^n)$ and $\Theta' \subset \Theta$ such that $\vdash \mathsf{D}_\Gamma \ominus \bigwedge D' \Rightarrow \ominus \neg \bigwedge \Theta'$. By Axiom PR, $\mathsf{D}_\Gamma \ominus \bigwedge D' \in D_\Gamma(w^{n+1})$. Hence $\neg \bigwedge \Theta' \in \Theta$, which entails that $D_\Gamma(w^{n+1}) \cup \Phi$ is inconsistent. This means that there exists a finite $\Phi' \subseteq \Phi$ such that $D_\Gamma(w^{n+1}) \vdash_{MP} \mathsf{D}_\Gamma \neg \bigwedge \Phi'$, which is a contradiction. Hence $D_\Gamma(w^n) \cup \Theta$ is consistent, and consequently, because of the closedness of Θ under conjunction, $\{\mathsf{P}_\Gamma \bigwedge \Theta' : \Theta' \subset_{fin} \Theta\} \subset w^n$.

By the inductive hypothesis, there exist an $r'' = v^0 b^0 \ldots b^{n-1} v^n \in R^{fin}(IS)$ and a sequence $s'' = s''^0, \ldots, s''^n \in (S(\Sigma_e))^{n+1}$ such that s'' is consistent with r'', $r'' \sim_\Gamma r[0..n]$, $s'' \sim_\Gamma s[0..n]$, and $\Theta \subseteq v^n$. Next we define $s'^n s'^{n+1} \in S(\Sigma_e)$ so that $s' = s''[0..n-1] \cdot s'^n$, s'^{n+1} is consistent with $r' = r'' b^n v^{n+1} \in R^{n+1}(IS)$ where $b^n = s'^n(r'')$, $v^{n+1} = t(v^n, b^n)$, $s' \sim_\Gamma s$, $D_\Gamma(v^{n+1}) = D_\Gamma(w^{n+1})$ and $\Phi \subseteq v^{n+1}$. Given $g \in R^{fin}(IS)$, we put

$$
s'^n_i(g) = \begin{cases}
s'^{n-1}_i(g), & \text{if } |g| < n, \text{ for all } i \in \Sigma_e, \\
s^n_i(g) & \text{if } |g| = n, \text{ and } i \in \Gamma, \\
\langle i, \emptyset, \{i\}, \emptyset \rangle & \text{if } |g| = n, \text{ and } i \in \Sigma \setminus \Gamma, \\
\text{any well-ordering of } \mathbf{L} \text{ in which} \\
\quad D_\Gamma(w^{n+1}) \cup \Phi \text{ forms an initial interval,} & \text{if } |g| = n, \text{ and } i = e, \\
s_{IS,i}(g), & \text{if } |g| \geq n.
\end{cases}
$$

For s'^{n+1} we put $s'^{n+1}(g) = \begin{cases} s''^n(g), & \text{if } |g| < n+1, \\ s_{IS}(g), & \text{if } |g| \geq n+1. \end{cases}$

By construction, s' is consistent (as a sequence of strategy vectors), $s' \sim_\Gamma s$, and s' is consistent with r''. We need to prove that $\mathsf{D}_\Gamma(v^{n+1}) = \mathsf{D}_\Gamma(w^{n+1})$ and $\Phi \subseteq v^{n+1}$. Note that, by **S5**-reasoning, $\mathsf{D}_\Gamma(w^{n+1}) \subset v^{n+1}n$ entails $\mathsf{D}_\Gamma(w^{n+1}) = \mathsf{D}_\Gamma(v^{n+1})$. This is so, because w^{n+1} is a MCS, whence, if $\mathsf{D}_\Gamma\psi \in v^{n+1} \setminus w^{n+1}$, then, $\mathsf{D}_\Gamma\neg\mathsf{D}_\Gamma\psi \in w^{n+1}$ follows by negative introspection from $\neg\mathsf{D}_\Gamma\psi \in w^{n+1}$. The latter entails $\mathsf{D}_\Gamma\neg\mathsf{D}_\Gamma\psi \in v^{n+1}$, which, by **T**, entails $\neg\mathsf{D}_\Gamma\psi \in v^{n+1}$, and this would contradict the consistency of v^{n+1}. Hence we only need to prove that $\Phi \subseteq v^{n+1}$. By the definition of the transition function t, this would follow from the consistency of $\bigcup_{i \in \Gamma} \Phi_i \cup \{\ominus\theta : \theta \in v^n\} \cup \mathsf{D}_\Gamma(w^{n+1}) \cup \Phi$ where Φ_i are the sets of formulas occurring in $\bar{b}^n_{v^n, \Gamma}$. This boils down to the consistency of $\{\ominus\theta : \theta \in v^n\} \cup \mathsf{D}_\Gamma(w^{n+1}) \cup \Phi$, because $v^n \sim_\Gamma w^n$ entails that a^n has the same effective $\Gamma_i \subseteq \Gamma$ wrt w as b^n wrt v^n, and therefore Φ_i, $i \in \Gamma$, are the same in $\bar{a}^n_{w^n, \Gamma}$. Hence, by the definition of $w^{n+1} = t(w^n, a^n)$ and $\mathsf{D}_\circ$, $\psi \in \bigcup_{i \in \Gamma} \Phi_i$ is equivalent to $\mathsf{D}_\Gamma\psi \in \mathsf{D}_\Gamma(w^{n+1})$. Now let us assume that $\{\ominus\theta : \theta \in v^n\} \cup \mathsf{D}_\Gamma(w^{n+1}) \cup \Phi$ is inconsistent for the sake of contradiction. Then there exist some finitely many $\theta_1, \ldots, \theta_k \in v^n$ such that $\mathsf{D}_\Gamma(w^{n+1}) \cup \Phi \vdash_{MP} \circ\neg(\theta_1 \wedge \ldots \wedge \theta_k)$. This is impossible by the choice of v^n to be a superset of $\Theta = \{\theta : \mathsf{D}_\Gamma(w^{n+1}) \cup \Phi \vdash_{MP} \ominus\theta\}$.

Lemma 8 (D_Γ). *Let $n < \omega$, $r, r' \in R^n(IS)$. Let $r = w^0 a^0 \ldots a^{n-1} w^n$ and $r' = v^0 b^0 \ldots b^{n-1} v^n$. Then $r' \sim_\Gamma r$ implies $\varphi \in v^n$.*

Proof. By the definition of $r' \sim_\Gamma r$, $\mathsf{D}_\Gamma\varphi \in \mathsf{D}_\Gamma(w^n) = \mathsf{D}_\Gamma(v^n) \subseteq v^n$, whence $\varphi \in v^n$ follows by T_D.

Lemma 9 ($\langle\!\langle . \mid . \rangle\!\rangle\circ$). *Let $w \in W$, $\Psi \subset \mathbf{L}$ and $\langle\!\langle \Gamma \mid \Delta \rangle\!\rangle \circ \bigwedge \Psi' \in w$ for all finite $\Psi' \subseteq \Psi$. Let $a'_\Gamma = \langle\langle\{p_{i, \langle\!\langle\Gamma\mid\Delta\rangle\!\rangle\circ\Psi'} \Rightarrow \bigwedge\Psi' : \Psi' \subseteq_{fin} \Psi\}, \{i\}, \emptyset\rangle : i \in \Gamma\rangle$ Then $\Psi \subseteq t(w, a'_\Gamma \cup a_{w,\Delta} \cup a''_{\Sigma_e\setminus(\Gamma\cup\Delta)})$, where $a_{w,\Delta}$ is the restriction of a_w as introduced in Definition 19, for all $a''_{\Sigma_e\setminus(\Gamma\cup\Delta)} \in Act_{\Sigma_e\setminus(\Gamma\cup\Delta)}$.*

Proof. Obviously Γ is effective in $a'_\Gamma \cup a_{w,\Delta} \cup a''_{\Sigma\setminus(\Gamma\cup\Delta)}$ wrt w.

Lemma 10 ($[\![. \mid .]\!]\circ$). *Let $n < \omega$, $r = w^0 a^0 \ldots a^{n-1} w^n \in R^n(IS)$, $\Gamma, \Delta \subseteq \Sigma$, $\Gamma \cap \Delta = \emptyset$. Let $s = s^0, \ldots, s^n \in (S(\Sigma_e))^{n+1}$ be consistent with r. Let $g_\Gamma \in Act_\Gamma$ be such that $\psi \in t(v^n, g_\Gamma \cup s'^n(v^n)_\Delta \cup g'_{\Sigma_e\setminus(\Gamma\cup\Delta)})$ for all $r' = v^0 b^0 \ldots b^{n-1} v^n \in R^n(IS)$ such that $r' \sim_{\Gamma\cup\Delta} r$, all $s' \in (S(\Sigma_e))^{n+1}$ which are consistent with r' and satisfy $s' \sim_{\Gamma\cup\Delta} s$, and all $g'_{\Sigma_e\setminus(\Gamma\cup\Delta)} \in Act_{\Sigma_e\setminus(\Gamma\cup\Delta)}$. Then $\langle\!\langle \Gamma \mid \Delta \rangle\!\rangle \circ \psi \in w^n$.*

Proof. Consider an r' as in the lemma. Let $g'_i = \langle\emptyset, \{i\}, \emptyset\rangle$ for $i \in \Sigma\setminus(\Gamma\cup\Delta)$, Let $a = g_\Gamma \cup s'^n(v^n)_\Delta \cup g'_{\Sigma\setminus(\Gamma\cup\Delta)} \cup g'_e$. Let Φ be the union of all the sets of formulas in $\bar{a}_{w^n}$, i.e., the actions of the coalitions which are effective in a wrt w^n and, consequently, wrt any v^n which is $\Gamma \cup \Delta$-similar to w^n. Then, by the definition of t, $t(v^n, a) = (\Phi \cup \Theta_{v^n}) + g'_e$. Assume that the least element of g'_e is $\neg\psi$. Then, since $\psi \in t(v^n, a)$ and by the construction of $(\Phi \cup \Theta_{v^n}) + g'_e$, $\Phi \cup \Theta_{v^n} \vdash_{MP} \psi$. By compactness, there exists a finite $\Theta'_{v^n} \subset \Theta_{v^n}$ such that $\Phi \vdash_{MP} \bigwedge \Theta_{v^n} \Rightarrow \psi$. Let $\Theta'_{v^n} = \{\ominus\theta_1, \ldots, \ominus\theta_k\}$. Then $\bigwedge \Theta'_{v^n}$ is equivalent to $\ominus(\theta_1 \wedge \ldots \wedge \theta_k)$. The latter formula is in Θ_{v^n}. Hence, for every v^n which is the last state of an r' as described in the lemma, there exists a $\xi \in \mathbf{L}$ such that $\ominus\xi \in \Theta_v^n$ and $\Phi \vdash_{MP} \ominus\xi \Rightarrow \psi$. Let

$$\varXi^n = \{\xi \in \mathbf{L} : \Phi \vdash_{MP} \ominus\xi \Rightarrow \psi, \ominus\xi \in \Theta_{v^n} \text{ for some } v^n \in W \text{ such that}$$
$$\text{there exists an } r' \in R(IS), r' \sim_{\Gamma \cup \Delta} r \text{ with } v^n \text{ as its last state}\}.$$

A direct check shows that $\varXi^n$ is closed under disjunction. Assume that $\{\neg\xi : \xi \in \varXi^n\} \cup D_{\Gamma \cup \Delta}(w^n)$ is consistent for the sake of contradiction. Then, by Lemma 5, $D_{\Gamma \cup \Delta}(w^n) \vdash_{MP} \mathsf{P}_{\Gamma \cup \Delta} \neg\xi$ for every $\xi \in \varXi^n$.

Since $\varXi^n$ is closed under disjunction, we can conclude that $D_{\Gamma \cup \Delta}(w^n) \vdash_{MP}$ $\mathsf{P}_{\Gamma \cup \Delta} \bigwedge_{\xi \in \varXi^{n\prime}} \neg\xi$ for any finite $\varXi^{n\prime} \subset \varXi^n$. By Lemma 7, this entails that there exist an $r' \sim_{\Gamma \cup \Delta} r$ and an $s' \sim_{\Gamma \cup \Delta} s$ such that s' is consistent with r' and $\{\neg\xi : \xi \in \varXi^n\} \subseteq v^n$ where v^n is the last state of r'. This contradicts the consistency of v^n since, as we established above, for every v^n with the specified properties, there exists a $\xi \in \varXi^n$ such that $\xi \in v^n$ as well. Hence $\{\neg\xi : \xi \in \varXi^{n\prime}\} \cup D_{\Gamma \cup \Delta}(w^n)$ is inconsistent. By compactness, this entails that there exists $D_{\Gamma \cup \Delta}(w^n) \vdash_{MP} \bigvee \varXi^{n\prime}$ for some finite $\varXi^{n\prime} \subset \varXi^n$. Now, having in mind that $\Phi \vdash_{MP} \ominus\xi \Rightarrow \psi$ for each of the ξs in $\varXi^{n\prime}$, we can conclude that $\Phi \cup \{\ominus\delta : \delta \in D_{\Gamma \cup \Delta}(w^n)\} \vdash_{MP} \psi$. Hence there exist some finite $\Phi' \subseteq \Phi$ and $D' \subset D_{\Gamma \cup \Delta}(w^n)$ such that $\vdash \bigwedge \Phi' \wedge \ominus \bigwedge D' \Rightarrow \psi$. By the monotonicity of $\langle\!\langle \Gamma \mid \Delta \rangle\!\rangle \circ$, $\vdash \langle\!\langle \Gamma \mid \Delta \rangle\!\rangle \circ (\bigwedge \Phi' \wedge \ominus \bigwedge D') \Rightarrow \langle\!\langle \Gamma \mid \Delta \rangle\!\rangle \circ \psi$. Now, by Axiom $\langle\!\langle . \mid . \rangle\!\rangle \circ \ominus$, the latter entails $\vdash \langle\!\langle \Gamma \mid \Delta \rangle\!\rangle \circ (\bigwedge \Phi') \wedge D_{\Gamma \cup \Delta} \bigwedge D' \Rightarrow \langle\!\langle \Gamma \mid \Delta \rangle\!\rangle \circ \psi$. For any v^n as in the lemma, the definition of Φ entails $\langle\!\langle \Gamma \mid \Delta \rangle\!\rangle \circ (\bigwedge \Phi') \in v^n$, and $D' \subset D_{\Gamma \cup \Delta}(w^n) = D_{\Gamma \cup \Delta}(v^n)$ entails $\bigwedge D' \in v^n$. Hence, finally, $\langle\!\langle \Gamma \mid \Delta \rangle\!\rangle \circ \psi \in v^n$ as well.

Lemma 11 ($\ominus$ and (.S.)). *Let n, $r \in R^n(IS)$ and $s \in (S(\Sigma_e))^{n+1}$ be as in the previous lemmata. Then, $\circ^n\mathsf{I} \in w^n$ and, for any two formulas $\varphi, \psi \in \mathbf{L}$, $\ominus\varphi \in w^n$ iff $n > 0$ and $\varphi \in w^{n-1}$, and $(\varphi \mathsf{S} \psi) \in w^n$ iff there exists a $k \leq n$ such that $\psi \in w^k$ and $\varphi \in w^{k+1}, \ldots, w^n$.*

We omit the proof of this lemma as it contains nothing specific to ATL_{iR}^{DPC}. We only note that the fact $\circ^n\mathsf{I} \in w^n$ guarantees that the presence of (.S.) does not affect the compactness of the system, despite that (.S.) is an iterative operator.

Theorem 1 (truth lemma). *Let $n < \omega$, $r \in R^n(IS)$, $r = w^0 a^0 \ldots a^{n-1} w^n$, and let $s \in S(\Sigma_e)^{n+1}$ be consistent with r. Then $IS, r \models \varphi$ iff $\varphi \in w^n$.*

Proof. Induction on the construction of φ. The cases of φ being $\bot$, an atomic proposition, or an implication, are trivial, and we skip them. For φ of the forms $D_\Gamma \psi$, $\langle\!\langle \Gamma \mid \Delta \rangle\!\rangle \circ \psi$ and $\ominus\psi$ and $(\psi \mathsf{S} \chi)$ the theorem follows from Lemmata 8 and 7, 9 and 10 and Lemma 11, respectively.

Corollary 1 (strong completeness for basic ATL_{iR}^{DPC}). *Let x be a consistent subset of $\mathbf{L}$ and let $\mathsf{I} \in x$. Then there exists an initial state $l \in I$ and a vector of strategies $s \in S(\Sigma_e)$ such that $IS, s, l \models \varphi$ for all $\varphi \in x$.*

Proof. Let w be any MCS such that $x \subseteq w$. Then Theorem 1 entails that $IS, s_{IS}, l_w \models \varphi$ for all $\varphi \in w$.

Concluding Remarks and Future Work

We have shown that extending the game-theoretic operator $\langle\!\langle .\rangle\!\rangle$ of ATL_{iR}^{DP} by a second coalition parameter to denote players who act according to the strategic context, we obtain a language for epistemic ATL with strategic contexts which admits an axiom system that is a straightforward revision of the system for ATL_{iR}^{DP} from our work [9]. So far we have established the completeness of that system for a subset of ATL_{iR}^{DP} with strategy contexts which lacks the combinations of $\langle\!\langle .\rangle\!\rangle$ with the iterative future temporal operator $(.U.)$ and its derivatives $\Diamond$ and $\Box$. Taking advantage of the compactness of this subset, we have obtained a strong completeness theorem. We have established the semantical compatibility between our proposed system and the systems of ATL with strategy contexts and complete information from the literature, especially [5,15]. We intend to further investigate the axiomatizability of ATL_{iR}^{DPC}, seeking to establish weak completeness theorems and the decidability of validity of bigger subsets.

Akcnowledgements. Dimitar P. Guelev did part of the work on this paper while visiting LACL, Université Paris Est-Créteil, in January 2012 and was supported by the EQINOCS research project ANR ANR 11 BS02 004 03 [4] and Bulgarian National Science Fund Grant DID02/32/2009.

References

1. Ågotnes, T., Goranko, V., Jamroga, W.: Strategic Commitment and Release in Logics for Multi-Agent Systems (Extended Abstract). Technical report IfI-08-01, TU Clausthal (May 2008); Ågotnes, T., Goranko, V., Jamroga, W.: Strategic Commitment and Release in Logics for Multi-Agent Systems (Extended Abstract). In: Bonanno, G., Löwe, B., van der Hoek, W. (eds.) Logic and the Foundations of Game and Decision Theory. LNCS, vol. 6006, Springer, Heidelberg (2010)
2. Alur, R., Henzinger, T., Kupferman, O.: Alternating-time Temporal Logic. In: Proceedings of FCS 1997, pp. 100–109 (1997)
3. Alur, R., Henzinger, T., Kupferman, O.: Alternating-time temporal logic. Journal of the ACM 49(5), 1–42 (2002)
4. Asarin, E.: EQINOCS Research Project ANR 11 BS02 004 03, http://www.liafa.univ-paris-diderot.fr/~eqinocs/
5. Brihaye, T., Da Costa, A., Laroussinie, F., Markey, N.: ATL with Strategy Contexts and Bounded Memory. In: Artemov, S., Nerode, A. (eds.) LFCS 2009. LNCS, vol. 5407, pp. 92–106. Springer, Heidelberg (2008)
6. Chatterjee, K., Henzinger, T.A., Piterman, N.: Strategy logic. Information and Computation 208(6), 677–693 (2010)
7. Fagin, R., Halpern, J., Moses, Y., Vardi, M.: Reasoning about Knowledge. MIT Press (1995)
8. Goranko, V., van Drimmelen, G.: Decidability and Complete Axiomatization of the Alternating-time Temporal Logic. Theoretical Computer Science 353(1-3), 93–117 (2006)
9. Guelev, D.P., Dima, C., Enea, C.: An Alternating-time Temporal Logic with Knowledge, Perfect Recall and Past: Axiomatisation and Model-checking. Journal of Applied Non-Classical Logics 21(1), 93–131 (2011)

10. Halpern, J., van der Meyden, R., Vardi, M.: Complete Axiomatizations for Reasoning about Knowledge and Time. SIAM Journal on Computing 33(3), 674–703 (2004)
11. Jamroga, W., van der Hoek, W.: Agents That Know How to Play. Fundamenta Informaticae 63(2-3), 185–219 (2004)
12. Lichtenstein, O., Pnueli, A.: Propositional temporal logics: decidability and completeness. Logic Journal of the IGPL 8(1), 55–85 (2000)
13. Lomuscio, A., Raimondi, F.: Model checking knowledge, strategies, and games in multi-agent systems. In: Proceedings of AAMAS 2006, pp. 161–168. ACM Press (2006)
14. Lomuscio, A., Raimondi, F.: The Complexity of Model Checking Concurrent Programs Against CTLK Specifications. In: Baldoni, M., Endriss, U. (eds.) DALT 2006. LNCS (LNAI), vol. 4327, pp. 29–42. Springer, Heidelberg (2006)
15. Lopes, A.D.C., Laroussinie, F., Markey, N.: ATL with strategy contexts: Expressiveness and model checking. In: FSTTCS. LIPIcs, vol. 8, pp. 120–132 (2010)
16. Pauly, M.: A modal logic for coalitional power in games. Journal of Logic and Computation 12(1), 149–166 (2002)
17. Schobbens, P.Y.: Alternating-time logic with imperfect recall. ENTCS 85(2), 82–93 (2004); Proceedings of LCMAS 2003
18. van der Hoek, W., Wooldridge, M.: Cooperation, Knowledge and Time: Alternating-time Temporal Epistemic Logic and Its Applications. Studia Logica 75, 125–157 (2003)
19. van der Meyden, R., Wong, K.-S.: Complete Axiomatizations for Reasoning about Knowledge and Branching Time. Studia Logica 75(1), 93–123 (2003)
20. Walther, D., van der Hoek, W., Wooldridge, M.: Alternating-time Temporal Logic with Explicit Strategies. In: Samet, D. (ed.) TARK, pp. 269–278. ACM Press (2007)
21. Wang, F., Huang, C.-H., Yu, F.: A Temporal Logic for the Interaction of Strategies. In: Katoen, J.-P., König, B. (eds.) CONCUR 2011 – Concurrency Theory. LNCS, vol. 6901, pp. 466–481. Springer, Heidelberg (2011)

Using Evolution Graphs for Describing Topology-Aware Prediction Models in Large Clusters

Matei Popovici

POLITEHNICA University of Bucharest
Splaiul Independentei nr. 313, Bucharest, Romania, Postal Code 060042
matei.popovici@cs.pub.ro

Abstract. We present and formally investigate a modelling method suitable for describing events and time-dependent properties and for performing possibly complex reasoning tasks regarding the evolution of dynamic domains. Our proposal consists of a distinguished data structure called evolution graph, and a logical language ($L_\mathcal{H}$) used for identifying temporal patterns in evolution graphs. First, we define and study the complexity of the model checking problem for our language. We then investigate the relation between our language and the well-known Computation Tree Logic (CTL), both in terms of complexity and expressive power. Finally, we apply our method for solving a well-known problem from High Performance Computing (HPC): the extraction of topology information from event logs produced by supercomputers.

Keywords: temporal knowledge representation, temporal logic, high-performance computing.

1 Introduction

The world of high performance computing (HPC) is preparing for the exascale era, and according to recent studies [10,16], 20% or more of the computing capacity in a large system is wasted due to failures and recoveries. An alternative approach to classical fault tolerance that might optimize this process is failure avoidance, where the occurrence of a fault is predicted and preventive measures are taken. For this, monitoring systems require a reliable prediction method to give information on what will be generated by the system and at what location. To the best of our knowledge, all other log analysis methods in the literature [23,14,18,11,12] propose theoretical models and algorithms for detecting, predicting or characterizing events, without studying the impact of their methods on large-scale HPC systems such as Blue Gene.

In order to develop a sound and robust prediction system and to fully characterize its performance, a suitable modelling method is required. The success of such a method relies on: (i) the ability to describe events and time-dependent properties of systems with possibly non-deterministic behaviour, and (ii) to perform complex reasoning tasks about the temporal relations between such events and properties.

M. Fisher et al. (Eds.): CLIMA XIII 2012, LNAI 7486, pp. 94–109, 2012.
© Springer-Verlag Berlin Heidelberg 2012

In this paper, we introduce a new modelling method for reasoning about time-dependent properties. Based on it, we extract the topology of large-scale machines after investigating the log files generated by such systems. In our approach, a domain's history is recorded by a distinguished structure called *evolution graph*. It consists of: (i) **action nodes** which model instantaneous stimuli that occur at fixed moments of time, and affect the current state of the domain, (ii) **hypernodes** which capture (discrete) moments of time. The set of hypernodes can be seen as a partitioning of the set of action nodes such that all action nodes belonging to the same hypernode are simultaneous; (iii) **quality edges** which model time-dependent properties which span action nodes. For a given quality edge $q = (a, b)$, we interpret the action node a as the stimulus responsible for *creating* (or introducing) the quality q. Similarly, b is seen as the action node that ceases (destroys) q.

Evolution graphs capture the dynamics of a given domain. In order to provide with a domain-dependent semantics, action nodes and quality edges are labelled with first-order predicates. For a more detailed description of evolution graphs, as well an extended set of examples, we direct the reader to [20].

An example of an evolution graph, capturing the behaviour of (a small part of) a HPC system, can be seen in Figure 1. For simplicity, we have omitted labelling action nodes. Here, two nodes n and m sharing the same rack, experience network failures at different moments of time. This is modelled by the qualities *Net_fail(n)* and *Net_fail(m)*. In the time-slot when both these qualities do not exist, a *network communication* binary quality describes the successful communication between network nodes n and m.

HPC systems consist of a high number of nodes that are usually placed in a hierarchical architecture. For example, in BlueGene systems, nodes are gathered into midplanes and multiple midplanes form a rack. Certain errors in the system, such as networking faults, affect multiple nodes depending on their relative position within the architecture. In another study [11], it has been observed that propagation paths for different error types follow closely the way components are connected in the system. For example if a fan breaks, all nodes sharing the same rack will be affected. The topology of a system is usually not known in advance. This forces failure prediction algorithms to rely on heuristics for tracking the locations of the failure's effects in the system. In our experiments, we use the logs generated by the Blue Gene/L system. This system is one of the few large-scale machines that offer a detailed view of its topology. This information is useful in having a better understanding of the prediction topologies we obtain with our method. Also, the Blue Gene systems are widely used machines in HPC and are representative for today's large-scale systems. For more details on the system-architecture see [1].

In this paper, we focus on the computational properties of the language $L_{\mathcal{H}}$, used for reasoning about evolution graphs, and on the implementation of a topology extraction system. In Section 2, we formally introduce evolution graphs, and in Section 3 we describe the language $L_{\mathcal{H}}$ and its semantics. In Section 4 we introduce the CTL language, and use it for proving some complexity results as

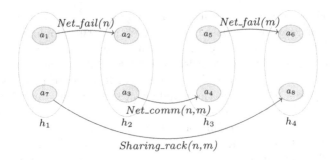

Fig. 1. A simple evolution graph

well as for gaining a better understanding on why $L_{\mathcal{H}}$ is more suitable for topology extraction. In Section 6 we further explore the relationship between $L_{\mathcal{H}}$ and temporal logics in general, as well as look at other similar approaches. Finally, in Section 5, we use a fragment of $L_{\mathcal{H}}$ for the implementation of a topology extraction system for fault propagation in HPC large-scale systems, that optimizes the prediction model presented in [2].

2   The Evolution Graph

Definition 1 (evolution graph). *An evolution graph is defined as a structure* $\mathcal{H} = \langle H, A, \mathcal{T}, E \rangle$, *where:*

- *H is a set of hypernodes, and A is a set of nodes;*
- *$\mathcal{T} : A \to H$ is an onto (surjective) function, sending each node to the hypernode it belongs to;*
- *$E \subseteq A^2$ is a directed edge relation with the following restrictions: (i) for any $a \in A$, there is at most one $b \in A$ such that $(a, b) \in E$ or $(b, a) \in E$. (i.e. any node creates or destroys a unique edge) and (ii) $(a, b) \in E \implies \mathcal{T}(a) \neq \mathcal{T}(b)$;*

Let $\sigma = \{R_1, \ldots, R_n\}$ be a vocabulary. The elements R_i are relation symbols each having a certain arity designated by $arity(R_i)$. In general, we require that σ contains two types of relation symbols: **quality labels** and **action labels** ($\sigma = \sigma_Q \cup \sigma_A$).

Definition 2 (Label structure). *A labeling structure is a $\sigma_Q \cup \sigma_A$-structure* $\mathcal{A} = \langle I, R_1^I, \ldots, R_n^I \rangle$, *where:*

- *I is a set of individuals (the structure's universe);*
- *for each $R_k \in \sigma_Q$ and $\bar{i} \in R_k^I$, the pair $\langle R_k, \bar{i} \rangle$ is a **quality label**;*
- *for each $R_k \in \sigma_A$ and $\bar{i} \in R_k^I$, the pair $\langle R_k, \bar{i} \rangle$ is an **action label**;*

We designate a quality or an action label by $R_k^I(\bar{i})$, with R_k from the appropriate vocabulary. We make a slight abuse of notation and use R^I to designate the appropriate set of quality or action labels, viewed as pairs $\langle R, \bar{i} \rangle$, instead of a set of tuples $\bar{i}$.

A *path* in an evolution graph $\mathcal{H}$ is a finite sequence $\lambda = a_1, a_2, \ldots, a_n$ of nodes from $\mathcal{H}$ such that, for any two consecutive nodes a_i and a_{i+1}, either of the following is true: (i) $E(a_i, a_{i+1})$ (there is an edge between a_i and a_{i+1}) or (ii) $\mathcal{T}(a_i) = \mathcal{T}(a_{i+1})$ (there exists a hypernode that contains both a_i and a_{i+1}). Intuitively, each path is a temporally ordered sequence of events and properties. An example can be seen in Fig. 1, where $\lambda = a_1, a_2, a_3, a_4, a_5, a_6$ is such a path. An evolution graph $\mathcal{H}$ is *cycle-free*, if there is no pair of nodes $a, b \in A$, having a path from a to b, and one from b to a i.e. $\mathcal{H}$ contains no cycles. In the following, we discuss cycle-free evolution graphs only.

Definition 3 (labelled evolution graph). *An $\mathcal{A}$-labelled evolution graph is a structure $\mathcal{H}_\mathcal{A} = \langle \mathcal{H}, \mathcal{L}_A, \mathcal{L}_Q \rangle$ consisting of a evolution graph and two total labelling functions:*

- $\mathcal{L}_Q : E \to \cup_{R \in \sigma_Q} R^I$; *$\mathcal{L}_Q$ maps each edge to a quality label;*
- $\mathcal{L}_A : A \to \cup_{R \in \sigma_A} R^I$ *maps each node to an action label;*

We refer to labeled edges and nodes as **quality edges** and **action nodes**, respectively.

3   The Language $L_\mathcal{H}$

$L_\mathcal{H}$ is defined over a labelling structure $\mathcal{A}$ and expresses temporal relations between quality edges and action nodes from $\mathcal{A}$-labelled evolution graphs. $L_\mathcal{H}$ contains two types of formulae: *Q-formulae* and *A-formulae*. The former evaluate to quality edges, and the latter to action nodes. Each action node a and quality edge (a, b) designates a moment of time $\mathcal{T}(a)$ and an interval $[\mathcal{T}(a), \mathcal{T}(b)]$, respectively. Given two quality edges $q = (a, b)$, $q' = (a', b')$, and action nodes c, d we introduce the following temporal operators, which abbreviate the traditional interval relationships introduced by Allen [22].

- (before): q **b** q' iff b occurs before a';
- (just before): q **jb** q' iff a occurs before a' but b does not occur before a';
- (starts same): q **s** q' iff a coincides with a';
- (ends same): q **e** q' iff b coincides with b';
- (meets): q **m** q' iff b coincides with a';
- (included): q **i** q' iff a occurs after a' and b occurs before b';
- $c \succ d$ iff c occurs before d;
- $c \equiv d$ iff c and d share the same hypernode;
- (creates/created by): c **c_A** q and q **c_Q** c iff $c = a$;
- (destroys/destroyed by): c **d_A** q and q **d_Q** c iff $c = b$;

For instance q **b** q' is true if q's interval occurs *before* q''s, and they do not overlap. An example of this relation can be found in Fig. 1, between qualities *Net_fail(n)* and *Net_fail(m)*. q **jb** q' is true if q's interval occurs *before* q''s and they overlap. We say q is *just before* q'. In the same figure *Sharing_rack(n,m)* occurs just before *Net_fail(m)*. **s** and **e** abbreviate *starts at the same time with* and *ends at the same time with*, respectively. **m** abbreviates *meets*, thus designating qualities that end at the same time other qualities start. **i** abbreviates inclusion. **c** and **d** refer to the creation and destruction of qualities, respectively. The inverse relations are defined in a similar manner. Notice that $\succ$ is only a *partial* order over action nodes, since if, for instance, $\mathcal{H}$ contains disconnected components, one could say nothing about the temporal order between elements from distinct components.

Let $\mathbb{V}$ars be a set of variables, $\mathcal{A}$ be a labelling structure over vocabulary $\sigma = \sigma_Q \cup \sigma_A$, and $\mathcal{H}_\mathcal{A}$ be a $\mathcal{A}$-labelled evolution graph. We designate by $\propto$ any connective for qualities in $\mathfrak{C}_Q = \{\, \mathbf{b}\, , \, \mathbf{jb}\, , \, \mathbf{s}\, , \, \mathbf{e}\, , \, \mathbf{m}\, , \, \mathbf{i}\, \}$, by $\triangleright$ any connective for actions in $\mathfrak{C}_A = \{\succ, \equiv\}$.

Definition 4 ($L_\mathcal{H}$ syntax). *Let $\mathbb{V}$ars be a set of variables, $\mathcal{A}$ be a $\sigma_Q \cup \sigma_A$-structure and $\mathcal{H}_\mathcal{A}$ be a $\mathcal{A}$-labelled evolution graph. Also, let $X \in \{Q, A\}$, and $\dagger_Q \in \mathfrak{C}_Q$ and $\dagger_A \in \mathfrak{C}_A$.*

The syntax of a X-formula is recursively defined with respect to $\mathcal{A}$, as follows:

1. *if $R \in \sigma_X$ with $\mathrm{arity}(R) = n$ and $\bar{x} \in \mathbb{V}\mathrm{ars}^n$, then $R(\bar{x})$ is an **atomic** X-formula (or an atom).*
2. *if ϕ is a X-formula then (ϕ) is also a X-formula;*
3. *if ϕ, ψ are X-formulae then $\phi \dagger_X \psi$ and $\phi\neg \dagger_X \psi$ are also X-formulae. We call $\dagger_X$ a **positive** connective and $\neg\dagger_X$ a **negative/negated** connective.*
4. *Let $R \in \sigma_X$, ϕ, ψ, ω be X-formulae and $\dagger_X$ designate either a positive or negated connective. If ϕ has any of the following forms: (i) $\phi = R(\bar{x})$, (ii) $\phi = R(\bar{x}) \dagger_X \psi$ or (iii) $\phi = (R(\bar{x}) \dagger \omega) \dagger_X \psi$, then it is R-**compatible**. Moreover, if ϕ and ψ are both R-compatible, then $\phi \wedge \psi$ and $\phi \vee \psi$ are X-formulae, and R-compatible as well.*

Negation in $L_\mathcal{H}$ has a restricted use. For instance:

$$(a)\ \mathrm{Net\_fail(x)}\ \neg\mathbf{b}\ \mathrm{Net\_comm(x,y)} \qquad (b)\ \neg\mathrm{Net\_fail(x)} \qquad (1)$$

the formula from Equation 1 (a) is well-formed, however Equation 1 (b) is not well-formed. The intuition is the following: we are interested in identifying classes of properties of a certain type (i.e. being labelled with a quality label of a distinct relational symbol in σ_Q). For instance, Equation 1 (a) characterizes the set of properties *of the type Net_fail*, such that they do not occur before some qualities *of the type Net_comm*. If we choose to interpret $\neg\mathrm{Net\_fail(x)}$ as the complement of the edge relation E from $\mathcal{H}$, with respect to all edges labelled $\mathrm{Net\_fail}(i)$ (with $i \in I$), then $L_\mathcal{H}$-formulae could characterize edges with arbitrary labels.

The restrictions for the usage of the traditional connectives $\wedge$ and $\vee$ have the same motivation as in the case of negation, i.e. to preserve *property types*.

$L_\mathcal{H}$ formulae are evaluated over *paths* from labelled evolution graphs $\mathcal{H}$. We assume there is no prior information regarding the temporal order of hypernodes. In the absence of such information, a partial ordering of hypernodes can be inferred only by inspecting sequences of quality edges. We lift this assumption in Section 5, where we consider evolution graphs with temporally ordered hypernodes. The evaluation of $L_{\mathcal{H}}$-formulae is defined by the mappings $\|\cdot\|_{\mathcal{H}}^{Q} : L_{\mathcal{H}} \to 2^{E}$ and $\|\cdot\|_{\mathcal{H}}^{A} : L_{\mathcal{H}} \to 2^{A}$. If ϕ is a Q or A formula, then $\|\phi\|_{\mathcal{H}}^{Q}$ and $\|\psi\|_{\mathcal{H}}^{A}$ are the set of quality edges or action nodes satisfying ϕ and ψ, respectively. Each temporal connective $\propto \in \mathfrak{C}_Q$ requires the existence (or absence) of paths between nodes belonging to the corresponding qualities. For instance, in Fig. 1, given $q = (a_1, a_2)$ and $q' = (a_5, a_6)$, for q **b** q' to be true, there must be (at least) one path between a_2 and a_5. Such a path exists: $\lambda = a_2, a_3, a_4, a_5$. Inclusion (**i**) requires two paths. In the same figure (a_3, a_4) **i** (a_7, a_8) is true because there is a path from a_1 to a_3, and one from a_4 to a_6. We further note that the temporal ordering of hypernodes (e.g. $h_1, \ldots h_4$) is not generally known in advance, but can be deduced based on the existing quality edges (in our example, the *Net_fail* and *Net_comm* quality edges).

Given two quality edges q, q' and a temporal connective $\propto$, we write $\lambda_{\propto}(q, q')$ to refer to the path conditions required by $\propto$ between q and q'. These are straightforward from the introduction of temporal operators from Section 3. We use a similar notation $(\lambda_{\triangleright}(a, a'))$, for path conditions between actions.

Definition 5 (Semantics). *The semantics of Q and A-formulae are defined as follows. Let $\bar{i}$ be a set of individuals from the universe of a labelling structure $\mathcal{A}$, a, a' denote action nodes, and q, q' denote quality edges from a $\mathcal{A}$-labelled evolution graph $\mathcal{H}_{\mathcal{A}}$. The tuple $\bar{\alpha}$ and $X \in \{Q, A\}$ are used in the following way: whenever $X = Q$, $\bar{\alpha}$ designates a quality edge, and whenever $X = A$, $\bar{\alpha}$ designates an action node. Finally, by $\phi_{[\bar{x} \setminus \bar{i}]}$, we refer to the formula obtained from ϕ by replacing all variables from $\bar{x}$ with individuals from $\bar{i}$.*

1. $\|\phi(\bar{x})\|_{\mathcal{H}}^{X} = \bigcup_{\bar{i}} \{\bar{\alpha} \in \|\phi_{[\bar{x} \setminus \bar{i}]}\|_{\mathcal{H}}^{X}\}$;
2. $\|R(\bar{i})\|_{\mathcal{H}}^{X} = \{\bar{\alpha} : \mathcal{L}_X(\bar{\alpha}) = R(\bar{i})\}$;
3. $\|(\phi) \propto \psi\|_{\mathcal{H}}^{Q} = \{q \in \|\phi\|_{\mathcal{H}}^{Q} : \exists q' \in \|\psi\|_{\mathcal{H}}^{Q} \text{ and } \lambda_{\propto}(q, q')\}$
4. $\|(\phi) \triangleright \psi\|_{\mathcal{H}}^{A} = \{a \in \|\phi\|_{\mathcal{H}}^{A} : \exists a' \in \|\psi\|_{\mathcal{H}}^{A} \text{ and } \lambda_{\triangleright}(a, a')\}$
5. $\|\phi \neg \dagger \psi\|_{\mathcal{H}}^{X} = \|\phi\|_{\mathcal{H}}^{X} \setminus \|\phi \dagger \psi\|_{\mathcal{H}}^{X}$;
6. $\|\phi \dagger (\psi)\|_{\mathcal{H}}^{X} = \|\phi \dagger \psi\|_{\mathcal{H}}^{X}$
7. $\|R(\bar{i}) \dagger \psi\|_{\mathcal{H}}^{X} = \|(R(\bar{i})) \dagger \psi\|_{\mathcal{H}}^{X}$;
8. $\|\phi \vee \psi\|_{\mathcal{H}}^{X} = \|\phi\|_{\mathcal{H}}^{X} \cup \|\psi\|_{\mathcal{H}}^{X}$;
9. $\|\phi \wedge \psi\|_{\mathcal{H}}^{X} = \|\phi\|_{\mathcal{H}}^{X} \cap \|\psi\|_{\mathcal{H}}^{X}$;
10. $\|\phi \ \mathbf{c_Q} \ \psi\|_{\mathcal{H}}^{Q} = \{(a, b) \in \|\phi\|_{\mathcal{H}}^{Q} : a \in \|\psi\|_{\mathcal{H}}^{A}\}$
11. $\|\phi \ \mathbf{d_Q} \ \psi\|_{\mathcal{H}}^{Q} = \{(a, b) \in \|\phi\|_{\mathcal{H}}^{Q} : b \in \|\psi\|_{\mathcal{H}}^{A}\}$
12. $\|\phi \ \mathbf{c_A} \ \psi\|_{\mathcal{H}}^{A} = \{a \in \|\phi\|_{\mathcal{H}}^{A} : \exists (a, b) \in \|\psi\|_{\mathcal{H}}^{Q}\}$
13. $\|\phi \ \mathbf{d_A} \ \psi\|_{\mathcal{H}}^{A} = \{b \in \|\phi\|_{\mathcal{H}}^{A} : \exists (a, b) \in \|\psi\|_{\mathcal{H}}^{Q}\}$

Rule 1 states that evaluating a formula with parameters reduces to the evaluation of formulae obtained by all possible substitutions of variables from $\mathbb{V}$ars with individuals from the labelling structure universe, I. Notice that in rules 2 to 9 the evaluation order of formulae matters. The parentheses and negation enforce the evaluation of the left-side formula. In the absence of parentheses, formulae evaluate from right to left. For instance, in the evolution graph from Fig. 1, let us designate $Q_1 = \mathrm{Net\_fail}(n)$, $Q_2 = \mathrm{Net\_comm}(n,m)$ and $Q_3 = \mathrm{Net\_fail}(m)$. Then, we have that $\|(Q_1\ \mathbf{b}\ Q_2)\ \mathbf{m}\ Q_3\|_{\mathcal{H}}^{Q} = \{(a,b)\}$ while $\|Q_1\ \mathbf{b}\ Q_2\ \mathbf{m}\ Q_3\|_{\mathcal{H}}^{Q} = \emptyset$.

Also, negation should not be seen as interpreting inverse relations. Consider the evolution graph from Fig. 1, but with the quality edge (a_1, a_2) removed. Then, $\|Q_3\ \neg\mathbf{b}\ Q_1\|_{\mathcal{H}}^{Q} = \{(a_5, a_6)\}$, whereas Q_3 *after* Q_1 would evaluate to the empty set. The main difference is that negation requires the **absence** of a relation, whereas an inverse relation requires the **presence** of an opposite relation.

Definition 6 (Model checking). *Let $\mathcal{H}$ be a $\mathcal{A}$-labelled evolution graph, and ϕ an X-formula in $L_{\mathcal{H}}$ ($X \in \{Q, A\}$). We write $\mathcal{H}, \overline{\alpha} \models_X \phi$ iff $\overline{\alpha} \in \|\phi\|_{\mathcal{H}}^{X}$. The problem whether $\mathcal{H}, \overline{\alpha} \models_X \phi$ is the X-model checking problem for $L_{\mathcal{H}}$.*

4 $L_{\mathcal{H}}$ and Computation Tree Logic

The path conditions described in the semantics of $L_{\mathcal{H}}$ can also be expressed in the well-known temporal logic CTL (Computation Tree Logic). CTL is strictly less expressive than $L_{\mathcal{H}}$, since it doesn't allow first-order predicates. Nevertheless, the language $L_{\mathcal{H}}^{*}$, obtained by restricting the labelling structure from $L_{\mathcal{H}}$ to propositional symbols, can be embedded into CTL, over a particular type of labelled transition systems. This result has a twofold utility: (i) it provides a means of comparing the efficiency of $L_{\mathcal{H}}^{*}$ and CTL, and (ii) it is useful for obtaining complexity results for both $L_{\mathcal{H}}^{*}$ and the full $L_{\mathcal{H}}$.

In the following, we give a brief introduction to the syntax and semantics of CTL. For a detailed description see [24].

Let $\mathcal{P}$ be a set of propositional symbols and $\mathcal{L}$ be a finite set of labels. Given $p \in \mathcal{P}$, $a \in \mathcal{L}$, the language CTL consists of formulae generated by the following grammar:

$$\varphi ::= p \mid \neg\varphi \mid \mathsf{E}\langle a \rangle \varphi \mid \varphi \wedge \varphi \mid \mathsf{E}(\varphi\ \mathcal{U}\ \varphi) \tag{2}$$

The other traditional connectives are introduced as abbreviations. For instance: $\varphi_1 \vee \varphi_2 \equiv \neg(\neg\varphi_1 \wedge \neg\varphi_2)$, $\mathsf{E}\langle a \rangle \varphi \equiv \neg\mathsf{E}\langle a \rangle \neg\varphi$.

Traditionally, CTL formulae are interpreted over *Kripke structures*. Here, we shall use *labelled transition systems* (LTS) instead. For details on evaluating CTL formulae over LTSs, see [8].

A LTS is a structure $\mathcal{M} = \langle S, (R_i)_{i \in \mathcal{L}}, \pi \rangle$ here S is a set of states, each $R_i \subseteq S \times S$ is an i-labelled transition relation, one for each label $i \in \mathcal{L}$, and $\pi : S \to 2^{\mathcal{P}}$ is an *interpretation function* associating for each state s a set $\pi(s)$ consisting of the propositional symbols that hold in s. The size of a LTS $\mathcal{M}$ is the sum of the state-space and the number of transitions of each type: $|\mathcal{M}| = \sum_{s \in S} |\pi(s)| + \sum_{i \in \mathcal{L}} |R_i|$.

A *path* in a LTS is a possibly infinite sequence $\theta = s_1, s_2, \ldots s_n, \ldots$ of states such that, for any s_i, s_{i+1} there is some transition from s_i to s_{i+1}. We use $\theta[i]$ to denote the i-th state in the sequence θ and $\theta[i, \infty]$ to denote the subpath of θ starting from i: $\theta[i]\theta[i+1]\ldots$. For a state $s \in S$ in some LTS $\mathcal{M}$, we write $\Theta_{\mathcal{M}}(s)$ to designate the set of paths in $\mathcal{M}$ that start in s.

Given a LTS $\mathcal{M} = \langle S, (R_i)_{i \in \mathcal{L}}, \pi \rangle$, a state $s \in \mathcal{S}$, and an interpretation function π, the semantics for CTL is defined as follows:

- $\mathcal{M}, s \models_{\text{CTL}} p$ iff $q \in \pi(s)$;
- $\mathcal{M}, s \models_{\text{CTL}} \neg\varphi$ iff $\mathcal{M}, s \not\models_{\text{CTL}}\varphi$;
- $\mathcal{M}, s \models_{\text{CTL}} \varphi_2 \wedge \varphi_2$ iff $\mathcal{M}, s \models_{\text{CTL}} \varphi_1$ and $\mathcal{M}, s \models_{\text{CTL}} \varphi_2$
- $\mathcal{M}, s \models_{\text{CTL}} \mathsf{E}\langle a \rangle \varphi$ iff there is a path $\theta \in \Theta_{\mathcal{M}}(s)$ such that $R_a(\theta[0], \theta[1])$ and $\mathcal{M}, \theta[1] \models_{\text{CTL}} \varphi$;
- $\mathcal{M}, s \models_{\text{CTL}} \mathsf{E}(\varphi_1 \, \mathcal{U} \, \varphi_2)$ iff there is a path $\theta \in \Theta_{\mathcal{M}}(s)$ such that $\mathcal{M}, \theta[i] \models_{\text{CTL}} \varphi_2$, for some $i \geq 0$ and $\mathcal{M}, \theta[j] \models_{\text{CTL}} \varphi_1$ for all j such that $0 \leq j < i$;

We also introduce some ad-hoc notations. Given a set of labels L:

- $\mathsf{E}\langle L \rangle \phi \equiv \bigvee_{i \in L} \mathsf{E}\langle i \rangle \phi$;
- $\mathsf{E}(\varphi_1 \, \mathcal{U}_L \, \varphi_2) \equiv \mathsf{E}((\varphi_1 \wedge \langle L \rangle \top) \, \mathcal{U} \, (\varphi_1 \wedge \langle L \rangle \varphi_2))$;

For instance $\mathsf{E}\langle a, b \rangle p$ is true in those states s that have access to states s' where p is true, via either a or b-transitions, and $(\neg q) \, \mathcal{U}_{\{a,b\}} \, p$ is true if there is a path consisting of either a or b transitions on which q is false in each state (at least) until p becomes true.

Proposition 1 (CTL model checking [7]). *Given a LTS $\mathcal{M}$, a state s and a CTL formula φ, checking whether $\mathcal{M}, s \models_{CTL} \varphi$ is PTIME-complete.*

4.1   The Language $L_{\mathcal{H}}^*$ and CTL

In this section, we describe a fragment of $L_{\mathcal{H}}$ having as labels propositional symbols only, and show that this fragment can be embedded in CTL. Let $\mathcal{A}^* = \langle I, R_1^I, \ldots, R_n^I \rangle$ be any labelling structure over a vocabulary with *unary* relation symbols, where $I = \{i_1, i_2, \ldots, i_n\}$ and for each $1 \leq k \leq n$ we have $R_k^I = \{i_k\}$. Under these restrictions, $\mathcal{A}^*$ becomes nothing more than a set of propositional symbols: $\mathcal{A}^* = \{p_k \equiv R_k^I(i_k) : 1 \leq k \leq n\}$. Let $L_{\mathcal{H}}^*$ denote the subset of the language $L_{\mathcal{H}}$, that is built over $\mathcal{A}^*$, and whose formulae contain no variables.

Starting from an $\mathcal{A}^*$-labelled evolution graph $\mathcal{H}$ we build a LTS $\mathcal{M}^{\mathcal{H}}$ in the following way: (i) the set of labels is $\mathcal{L} = \{h, c, d, c^{-1}, d^{-1}\}$, the set of propositional symbols is $\mathcal{P} = \mathcal{A}^*$ (ii) for each action node $a \in A$ and for each quality edge $q \in E$, we build states s_a and s_q, respectively. The interpretation function π is built as follows: if $\mathcal{L}_Q(q) = p_k$, then $p_k \in \pi(s_q)$ and if $\mathcal{L}_A(a) = p_k$, then $p_k \in \pi(s_a)$. Thus, quality edges and action nodes are transformed into states, and their labels become propositional symbols that hold in these states. (iii) transitions are built in the following way: for any two simultaneous action nodes $(\mathcal{T}(a) = \mathcal{T}(b))$, we build a h-transition between the corresponding states: $R_h(s_a, s_b)$. By this construction simultaneous action nodes form h-labelled cliques in $\mathcal{M}^{\mathcal{H}}$. For any quality edge $q = (a, b) \in E$, we build $R_c(s_a, s_q)$, $R_{c^{-1}}(s_q, s_a)$, $R_d(s_q, s_b)$ and $R_{d^{-1}}(s_b, s_q)$. Thus, c-labelled transitions bind action states to the quality states they introduce, and d-labelled transitions bind quality states to the action states that destroy them. c^{-1} and d^{-1}-labelled transitions make the inverse bindings. The entire construction of $\mathcal{M}^{\mathcal{H}}$ can be done in deterministic polynomial time, with respect to the size of $\mathcal{H}$.

Definition 7 (Embedding $L_{\mathcal{H}}^*$ in CTL). *Let ϕ, ψ be formulae in $L_{\mathcal{H}}^*$. We build equivalent CTL formulae, by applying a transformation procedure $\mathfrak{T} : L_{\mathcal{H}}^* \to CTL$, recursively defined as follows:*

1. *for* $p_k \in L_{\mathcal{H}}^*$, $\mathfrak{T}(p_k) = p_k$;
2. $\mathfrak{T}(\phi \mathbf{\ b\ } \psi) = \mathfrak{T}(\phi) \wedge \mathsf{E}(\top \, \mathcal{U}_{\{c,h,d\}} \, \mathfrak{T}(\psi))$;
3. $\mathfrak{T}(\phi \mathbf{\ s\ } \psi) = \mathfrak{T}(\phi) \wedge \mathsf{E}\langle c^{-1} \rangle \mathsf{E}\langle h \rangle \mathsf{E}\langle c \rangle \mathfrak{T}(\psi)$;
4. $\mathfrak{T}(\phi \mathbf{\ c}_Q \psi) = \mathfrak{T}(\phi) \wedge \mathsf{E}\langle c \rangle \mathfrak{T}(\psi)$;
5. $\mathfrak{T}(\phi \neg \dagger \psi) = \mathfrak{T}(\phi) \wedge \neg \mathfrak{T}(\phi \dagger \psi)$;
6. $\mathfrak{T}((\phi \dagger_1 \phi') \dagger_2 \psi) = \mathfrak{T}(\phi \dagger_1 \phi') \wedge \mathfrak{T}(\phi \dagger_2 \psi)$;
7. $\mathfrak{T}(\phi \wedge \psi) = \mathfrak{T}(\phi) \wedge \mathfrak{T}(\psi)$;
8. $\mathfrak{T}(\phi \vee \psi) = \mathfrak{T}(\phi) \vee \mathfrak{T}(\psi)$;

The relation between *action* states and *quality* states can be expressed in CTL using modalities. For instance $\mathsf{E}\langle c \rangle p_k$ is true in all action states that *create* a quality state *labelled* p_k. $\mathsf{E}\langle h \rangle p_k$ is true in all action states which are simultaneous with an action state labelled p_k. The transformation rule 2 gives us a formula that is true in a state where $\mathfrak{T}(\phi)$ is true, and there is a path consisting of c,h or d-labelled edges on which $\mathfrak{T}(\psi)$ will eventually become true.

Intuitively, all *local* relations such as *starts same* or *meets* are described using the *in the next state* operators $\langle a \rangle$ (and other boolean connectives), and those expressing *non-local* relations (i.e. arbitrary path conditions) such as *before* or *includes* are described using the CTL $\mathcal{U}$ (Until).

The translations for other temporal connectives for Q-formulae: $\mathbf{e}$, $\mathbf{jb}$, $\mathbf{m}$, $\mathbf{i}$ and $\mathbf{d}_Q$ and those for A-formulae: $\succ$, $\prec$, $\equiv$ and $\mathbf{d}_A$ are purely technical, and follow the same intuition. Due to limited space, we omit these definitions.

Proposition 2. *Let $\mathcal{H}$ be a $\mathcal{A}^*$-labelled evolution graph, $\phi \in L_{\mathcal{H}}^*$, $q \in E$ and $a \in A$. Then $\mathcal{H}, q \models_Q \phi$ iff $\mathcal{M}_{\mathcal{H}}, s_q \models_{CTL} \mathfrak{T}(\phi)$ and $\mathcal{H}, a \models_A \phi$ iff $\mathcal{M}_{\mathcal{H}}, s_a \models_{CTL} \mathfrak{T}(\phi)$.*

Proof (Sketch): In the following, we discuss Q-formulae only. The case for A-formulae is analogous. The property we prove is:

$$\mathcal{H}, (a,b) \models_Q \phi \iff \mathcal{M}_{\mathcal{H}}, s_{(a,b)} \models_{CTL} \mathfrak{T}(\phi)$$

The proof is done by structural induction over the construction of formulae ϕ. The basis case is for $\phi = p_k$. Since $\mathfrak{T}(p_k) = p_k$, $\mathcal{H}, q \models_Q p_k \iff \mathcal{M}_{\mathcal{H}}, s_q \models_{CTL} p_k$ trivially holds, from the construction of $\mathcal{M}_{\mathcal{H}}$. For each of the semantic rules 3...13 described in Definition 5, an induction step is required. Here, we will confine ourselves to rule 2, where $\propto = \mathbf{b}$. The remaining cases can be treated in a similar way.

Assume $\mathcal{H}, (a,b) \models_Q p_k \mathbf{\ b\ } \psi$, for some $p_k \in \mathcal{A}^*$. Therefore: (i) $\mathcal{H}, (a,b) \models_Q p_k$ and (ii) there is a quality edge $(a',b') \in \|\psi\|_{\mathcal{H}}^Q$ and (iii) a path λ, such that λ connects action nodes b and a': $\lambda = c_1, c_2, \ldots, c_n$, where $c_1 = b$ and $c_n = a'$. From (i), (ii) and the induction hypotheses, it follows that $\mathcal{M}_{\mathcal{H}}, s_{(a,b)} \models_{CTL} p_k$ and $\mathcal{M}_{\mathcal{H}}, s_{(a',b')} \models_{CTL} \mathfrak{T}(\phi)$. For each c_i, c_{i+1} in λ, we have either $E(c_i, c_{i+1})$

or $\mathcal{T}(c_i) = \mathcal{T}(c_{i+1})$. Therefore, in $\mathcal{M}_{\mathcal{H}}$, between s_{c_i} and $s_{c_{i+1}}$ there is either a quality state s_q such that $R_c(s_{c_i}, s_q)$ and $R_d(s_q, s_{c_{i+1}})$ or there is a h-transition: $R_h(c_i, c_{i+1})$. It immediately follows that, in $\mathcal{M}_{\mathcal{H}}$, there is a path θ from s_b to $s_{a'}$, consisting of c, d, or h-transitions. Since $\mathcal{H}, s_{(a,b)} \models_{\text{CTL}} p_k$ and $\mathcal{H}, s_{(a',b')} \models_{\text{CTL}} \mathfrak{T}(\psi)$, the existence of θ between s_b to $s_{a'}$ makes $\mathcal{H}, s_{(a,b)} \models_{\text{CTL}} p_k \wedge \mathsf{E}(\top \, \mathcal{U}_{\{c,h,d\}} \, \mathfrak{T}(\phi))$ true. Therefore $\mathcal{H}, s_{(a,b)} \models_{\text{CTL}} \mathfrak{T}(p_k \, \mathbf{b} \, \psi)$. The second part of the implication is shown similarly. □

Proposition 3 ($L_{\mathcal{H}}^*$-model checking). *The Q and A-model checking problems for $L_{\mathcal{H}}^*$ are in PTIME.*

Proof (Sketch): Given a evolution graph $\mathcal{H}$, a Q (or A) formula $\phi \in L_{\mathcal{H}}^*$, and $\overline{\alpha} \in E$ (or $\overline{\alpha} \in A$), we build a LTS $\mathcal{M}_{\mathcal{H}}$, and the transformed formula $\mathfrak{T}(\phi)$. The total construction is done in deterministic polynomial time. Finally, we solve $\mathcal{M}_{\mathcal{H}}, s_{\overline{\alpha}} \models_{\text{CTL}} \mathfrak{T}(\phi)$. Proposition 2 guarantees that the answer to the above problem is also an answer for the problem $\mathcal{H}, \overline{\alpha} \models_X \phi$. □

Proposition 3 does not imply completeness for PTIME, nor does it provide with an efficient mechanism for $L_{\mathcal{H}}^*$ model checking. Indeed, the transformation from Section 4.1 provides a solution for $L_{\mathcal{H}}^*$ model checking via CTL model checking, but this approach is not necessarily optimal, since the CTL formulae we model check, might depend in size to the size of the LTS. As we will further see, a more precise bound on $L_{\mathcal{H}}^*$ is unnecessary as the model checking problem for the full $L_{\mathcal{H}}$ is much harder. In order to obtain a hardness result, we use a reduction to the conjunctive query satisfaction problem. For details on conjunctive queries, see [15].

Definition 8 (Conjunctive sentences). *Let σ be an arbitrary vocabulary. A sentence φ over σ is conjunctive if it has the following form: $\varphi = \exists \overline{x} \bigwedge_{i=1}^{k} C_k(\overline{y_k})$ where each C_k is in σ and each $\overline{y_k}$ is a tuple consisting of variables from $\overline{x}$ and constant symbols from σ.*

Proposition 4 (Solving conjunctive queries [6]). *Given a σ-structure $\mathcal{S}$ and a conjunctive sentence φ, the decision problem $\mathcal{S} \models \varphi$ is NP-complete.*

Proposition 5 (Model checking the full $L_{\mathcal{H}}$). *The Q and A-model checking problems for the full $L_{\mathcal{H}}$ are NP-complete.*

Proof (Sketch): Let $\mathcal{H}$ be a $\mathcal{A}$-labelled evolution graph, $\overline{\alpha}$ be an edge (or action) from $\mathcal{H}$, and $\phi(\overline{x})$ be a $L_{\mathcal{H}}$ formula.

Membership: Membership is established by the following procedure: non-deterministically choose a tuple $\overline{i}$, and then solve the problem $\mathcal{H}, \overline{\alpha} \models_X \phi(\overline{i})$, in the following way: replace each occurrence of any $C_k(\overline{i_k})$ in $\mathcal{A}$ with a symbol $p_{C_k(\overline{i_k})}$. Thus, we get a labelling structure $\mathcal{A}^*$ consisting of propositional symbols only. By operating the same replacement in $\mathcal{H}$ and $\phi(\overline{i})$, we get $\mathcal{H}^*$ and ϕ^*, and our problem reduces to the model checking problem for $L_{\mathcal{H}}^*$, which is in PTIME.

Hardness: Hardness is shown for Q-formulae. Let σ be a vocabulary, $\mathcal{S}$ be a σ-structure, and $\varphi = \exists \overline{x} \bigwedge_{k=1}^{n} C_k(\overline{y_k})$ be a conjunctive sentence over σ. We build

$\sigma_Q = \sigma$ and $\sigma_A = \{N\}$ with $arity(N) = 1$. The set of individuals I consists of all elements from the universe of $\mathcal{S}$, and two distinguished elements $\{s, e\}$. The labelling structure $\mathcal{A}$, with the universe I is $\langle \mathcal{S}, N^I \rangle$ where $N^I = \{s, e\}$. The evolution graph is built as follows. First, we create an (initial) hypernode h_0. Assume we have m predicate symbols in $\mathcal{S}$. For each $1 \leq k \leq m$, we do the following: (i) create a new hypernode h_k; (ii) for each tuple $\bar{c} \in C_k^I$, we create two action nodes $a_{\bar{c}}^k$ and $b_{\bar{c}}^k$, as well as a quality edge $(a_{\bar{c}}^k, b_{\bar{c}}^k)$. All action nodes $a_{\bar{c}}^k$ and $b_{\bar{c}}^k$ are in hypernodes h_{k-1} and h_k, respectively ($\mathcal{T}(a_{\bar{c}}^k) = h_{k-1}$ and $\mathcal{T}(b_{\bar{c}}^k) = h_k$). They are labeled as follows: $\mathcal{L}_A(a_{\bar{c}}^k) = N(s)$, $\mathcal{L}_A(b_{\bar{c}}^k) = N(e)$ and $\mathcal{L}_Q(a_{\bar{c}}^k, b_{\bar{c}}^k) = C_k(\bar{c})$. The evolution graph obtained this way is a multi-link *chain*, where all qualities labelled by the same C_k span the same time intervals. Let q be some arbitrary quality edge labelled with a predicate symbol C_1. Now, build a $L_{\mathcal{H}}$-formula $\phi = C_1(\overline{y_1}) \; \mathbf{b} \; C_2(\overline{y_2}) \ldots \mathbf{b} \; C_n(\overline{y_n})$. It is straightforward that $\mathcal{H}, q \models_Q \phi$ iff $\mathcal{S} \models \varphi$. Hardness for A formulae is shown using a similar chain construction. $\qquad \square$

Proposition 5 shows us that, in terms of computational complexity, $L_{\mathcal{H}}$ pays much more for allowing first-order predicates than for exploring the temporal structure it is defined on. Restricting the arity of our predicates also brings no improvement. The proof of Proposition 4 makes this obvious since, even for predicates with arity 2, model checking a conjunctive sentence is NP-complete. It would seem unjustified to explore other fragments of $L_{\mathcal{H}}$ that do allow first-order predicate. As it turns out, there are practical cases where such fragments are interesting.

5 $L_{\mathcal{H}}$ in HPC Systems

In the following, we consider evolution graphs where the set of hypernodes has a total order: $\langle H, < \rangle$. This is motivated by the fact that, in practical applications such as ours, the moment when an action occurs is known in advance. The restriction has no impact on the model checking complexity, since, as seen previously, the source of complexity is in the usage of first-order predicates as labels.

In order to deploy $L_{\mathcal{H}}$ for the extraction of topology information in large-scale systems, we use evolution graphs as a means for the storage of events and event-related properties generated by such systems. For each event recorded in the HPC system log, the following information is given: the moment of occurrence (given as a Unix timestamp), the event type (e.g. network interface card error, memory error, etc.), and the machine that generated the message. An example can be seen in Fig. 2 a. We model the occurrence of an event as an action node, and use the node labelling to encode all event-dependent information. For instance, the record shown in Fig. 2 a, is described by an action node a, such that $\mathcal{L}_A(a) = Event(1244192545, abem5, 1130)$, where 1244192545 indicates the timestamp, $abem5$ indicates the device where the event was signalled and 1130 encodes the event type.

1244192545 abem5 1130   1004 1045 20
                a   b

Fig. 2. Log entries and correlations

Hypernodes are built by considering a certain interval δi as time unit. For practical reasons, the δi value used in our experiments was 5 seconds. The entire duration covered by the log is split into intervals of size δi, and a hypernode is created for each such interval. All action nodes having a timestamp falling in some interval of size δi is associated to the corresponding hypernode.

Based on the analysis model presented in [2], a list of correlated event types is built. An example of a simplified correlation record is shown in Fig. 2 b. We model a correlation between two actual events a and b as a quality edge (a, b) labelled *Correlation*$(1004, 1045, 20)$, where 1004 and 1045 are the correlated event types, and 20 indicates the approximate delay between events.

After the evolution graph is built in the manner described above, $L_{\mathcal{H}}$-model checking is used for extracting correlation patterns and statistical information about the system. An interpreter for $L_{\mathcal{H}}$ was implemented in Java and Jess. The Jess engine was responsible for storing the evolution graph as a knowledge base, and for the pattern matching process involved in $L_{\mathcal{H}}$-model checking. We use $L_{\mathcal{H}}$ to express correlations between events, and the locations where they occur. For instance, the formula from Fig. 3 identifies correlated error events between machines m_1 and m_2. If the set of quality edges satisfying the formula has a considerable size, then it can be assumed that the error event et_1 from m_1 will propagate as et_2 on m_2. By looking at the most frequent occurrences of correlated locations, a set of propagation paths for faults can be built. We call this structure a *propagation topology* and we further use it to get some insight of the behaviour of faults in large HPC systems.

Our results highlighted previous observations regarding error propagation and brought new insights. Firstly, our experiments show that, for fault messages, 98% of the correlations are between locations in the same midplane and rack, the 2% representing unknown locations. For informational messages the percentage is a little lower, around 90%. However, this still confirms our initial finding that messages tend to propagate following the architecture topology of the system. This is an important result since it highlights a possible optimization for the prediction method by distributing its execution independently on each rack.

Secondly, we found that only around 20% of the nodes in the system appear in the extracted topology. This was surprising and it shows that the propagation topology does not follow the exact architecture but only a subset of it. As a result,

$Correlation(et_1, et_2, x)$ $\mathbf{c}_Q$ $Event(t, m_1, et_1) \wedge$
$Correlation(et_1, et_2, x)$ $\mathbf{d}_Q$ $Event(t, m_2, et_2)$

Fig. 3. Inferring correlated locations

whenever attempting to predict failures, it is not always necessary to explore the entire system architecture. Another observation is that informational messages propagate less than faults and on a smaller number of locations. Therefore, these two types tend to behave differently and any prediction system needs to analyse them separately.

We have also investigated the distribution of identified correlations on different locations in the system, depending on how much of the log is analysed. We observed a logarithmic growth of the number of correlations found when analysing different number of months. After 6 months the number of correlations is almost identical with what we found after analysing the entire lifespan of the system, the difference being of only 0.71%. Therefore, 6 months of log data prove sufficient for building accurate prediction topologies.

An application running on a HPC machine usually uses only a subset of computing nodes, so not all node crashes influence its execution. It is important that prediction includes not only the time, but also the location of the next failure in order for current fault tolerance mechanisms to be able to take proactive measures. By extracting topology information, our implementation is able to identify the set of nodes that are potential threats to the application execution.

6   Related Work

Current knowledge representation methods have limitations with respect to modelling dynamic domains. They focus more on providing a static description of a modelled universe and less on capturing time and change. Approaches such as DL (Description Logics) [4] are suitable for describing snapshots of an application domain, but fail in describing its evolution. Although, in many cases, temporal concepts can be embedded, either as modelling primitives (Temporal Extensions of Description Logics (TEDL) [3]), or as pre-defined concepts (see OWLTime [17]), this approach is rather impractical since many TEDL's are either undecidable or have very high complexity bounds.

Temporal logics such as Linear Temporal Logics (LTL) [19], Computation Tree Logic (CTL and CTL*)[7] and the Mu Calculus [9] would seem appropriate for this task. Indeed, the model checking problem is in PTIME for interesting fragments of these logics. However, there is an important difference between Kripke Structures and evolution graphs. The first are *computational structures*[24] that encode all possible states of a deterministic system. Temporal reasoning (i.e. model checking) relies on unfolding the computational structure, and establishing whether certain properties hold. Unlike Kripke Structures, evolution graphs are models of behaviour, and thus can be compared to paths or computation trees. An evolution graph encodes an unique evolution of a system which is not necessarily deterministic. This means that there is no structure able to encode all possible configurations of a system, and which unfolded, can produce an evolution graph. This is the case for error message generation in HPC computing. Also, any system in which actions can occur arbitrarily (but which have foreseeable effects, i.e. the introduction or ceasing of qualities), fall in the same category. As a result, unlike temporal logics, $L_\mathcal{H}$ can only be used to *look into the past*. Based on the domain's history, one can make assumptions about the future evolution of the system, as is the case in HPC error message prediction.

As shown in Section 4.1, the information captured by evolution graphs could be embedded in Kripke Structures, and CTL-model checking could be used to verify temporal relations. However, there is a scalability issue. Computational structures are expected to have limited size. However, the logs used in our analysis had a number of 1,969,710 messages, and future systems are expected to produce much larger logs. Even with symbolic model checking, using such large Kripke Structures can become unfeasible.

Also, using Kripke Structures for storing temporal information in a way different from that shown in Section 4.1 may be inefficient. Conventionally, if a property p holds over a number of n states, all n states must be labelled with p. If there are two such properties in the system, then this will result in $2n$ labelings, whereas in evolution graphs (and in the particular type of Kripke Structures discussed in Section 4.1), such a property is represented as an edge (or a quality state), irrespective of it's lifespan. An exponential growth in the number of states can also be found in other approaches for encoding temporal intervals such as the one presented in [8].

Finally, evolution graphs and $L_\mathcal{H}$ provide with more expressiveness in describing the possible properties of the system. This is achieved by using relations for labelling, instead of just sets of propositional symbols.

7   Conclusions

Evolution graphs and $L_\mathcal{H}$ provide a straightforward way for representing and reasoning about domains that are constantly changing. While model checking is not as fast as in temporal logics, $L_\mathcal{H}$ provides an acceptable trade-off between efficiency and an increased flexibility in describing domain-dependent properties. The $L_\mathcal{H}$ connectives offer a simple way for expressing temporal patterns. The same task is not always as easy in temporal logics such as CTL. Also, evolution graphs and $L_\mathcal{H}$ prove useful. The $L_\mathcal{H}$ model checking mechanism provides with an accurate analysis method for HPC logs that highlights a couple of optimization solutions for fault prediction systems: (i) prediction algorithms can be parallelised, since errors propagate only locally (ii) the entire system architecture is not always relevant for fault prediction and (iii) for the building of a precise propagation topology, 6 months of logs suffice.

Also, we would like to note that the usage of $L_\mathcal{H}$ is not limited to the HPC setting. The implementation of our $L_\mathcal{H}$-model checker can be naturally extended to a language that allows the specification of time-dependent behaviour in Multi-Agent Systems. Rule-based languages such as Jason [5], SOAR [13], and even CLIPS [21], do not incorporate primitives for expressing temporal relations between entities in an application-dependent domain. As shown in our previous work [20], a language equipped with temporal primitives allows for more flexibility in describing time-dependent domains. Therefore, a temporally-flat knowledge base of an agent can be replaced by an evolution graph. Thus, $L_\mathcal{H}$ can be used to add a temporal dimension to the reasoning process in Multi-Agent Systems.

Acknowledgements. The work has been funded by Project 264207, ERRIC-Empowering Romanian Research on Intelligent Information Technologies/FP7-REGPOT-2010-1 and by the Sectoral Operational Programme Human Resources Development 2007-2013 of the Romanian Ministry of Labour, Family and Social Protection through the Financial Agreement POSDRU/88/1.5/S/61178.

References

1. Almási, G.S., Bellofatto, R., Brunheroto, J.R., Caşcaval, C., Castaños, J.G., Ceze, L., Crumley, P., Erway, C.C., Gagliano, J., Lieber, D., Martorell, X., Moreira, J.E., Sanomiya, A., Strauss, K.: An Overview of the Blue Gene/L System Software Organization. In: Kosch, H., Böszörményi, L., Hellwagner, H. (eds.) Euro-Par 2003. LNCS, vol. 2790, pp. 543–555. Springer, Heidelberg (2003)
2. Gainaru, A., Franck Cappello, W.K.: Taming of the shrew: Modeling the normal and faulty behavior of large-scale hpc systems. In: Proceedings of the International Parallel and Distributed Processing Symposium (IPDPS), pp. 24–35 (to appear, 2012)
3. Artale, A., Franconi, E.: A survey of temporal extensions of description logics. Annals of Mathematics and Artificial Intelligence 30, 171–210 (2001)
4. Baader, F., Calvanese, D., McGuinness, D.L., Nardi, D., Patel-Schneider, P.F. (eds.): The Description Logic Handbook: Theory, Implementation, and Applications. Cambridge University Press (2003)
5. Bordini, R.H., Wooldridge, M., Hübner, J.F.: Programming Multi-Agent Systems in AgentSpeak using Jason (Wiley Series in Agent Technology). John Wiley & Sons (2007)
6. Chandra, A.K., Merlin, P.M.: Optimal implementation of conjunctive queries in relational data bases. In: Proceedings of the Ninth Annual ACM Symposium on Theory of Computing, STOC 1977, pp. 77–90. ACM, New York (1977), http://doi.acm.org/10.1145/800105.803397
7. Clarke, E.M., Emerson, E.A., Sistla, A.P.: Automatic verification of finite-state concurrent systems using temporal logic specifications. ACM Trans. Program. Lang. Syst. 8(2), 244–263 (1986)
8. De Nicola, R., Vaandrager, F.: Action versus state based logics for transition systems. In: Proceedings of the LITP Spring School on Theoretical Computer Science on Semantics of Systems of Concurrent Processes, pp. 407–419. Springer-Verlag New York, Inc., New York (1990), http://dl.acm.org/citation.cfm?id=111693.111710
9. Emerson, E.A.: Model checking and the mu-calculus. In: Descriptive Complexity and Finite Models, pp. 185–214 (1996)
10. Capello, F., Geist, A., Gropp, B., Kale, S., Kramer, B., Snir, M.: Toward exascale resilience. International Journal of High Performance Computing Applications 23 (2009)
11. Gainaru, A., Cappello, F., Trausan-Matu, S., Kramer, B.: Event Log Mining Tool for Large Scale HPC Systems. In: Jeannot, E., Namyst, R., Roman, J. (eds.) Euro-Par 2011, Part I. LNCS, vol. 6852, pp. 52–64. Springer, Heidelberg (2011)

12. Gallet, M., Yigitbasi, N., Javadi, B., Kondo, D., Iosup, A., Epema, D.: A Model for Space-Correlated Failures in Large-Scale Distributed Systems. In: D'Ambra, P., Guarracino, M., Talia, D. (eds.) Euro-Par 2010, Part I. LNCS, vol. 6271, pp. 88–100. Springer, Heidelberg (2010),
    http://dl.acm.org/citation.cfm?id=1887695.1887707
13. Laird, J.E., Newell, A., Rosenbloom, P.S.: Soar: an architecture for general intelligence. Artif. Intell. 33(1), 1–64 (1987),
    http://dx.doi.org/10.1016/0004-3702(87)90050-6
14. Lan, Z., Zheng, Z., Li, Y.: Toward automated anomaly identification in large-scale systems. IEEE Trans. on Parallel and Distributed Systems 21(2), 174–187 (2010)
15. Libkin, L.: Elements Of Finite Model Theory. Texts in Theoretical Computer Science. An Eatcs Series. Springer (2004)
16. Oldfield, R.A., Arunagiri, S., Teller, P.J., Seelam, S., Varela, M.R., Riesen, R., Roth, P.C.: Modeling the impact of checkpoints on next-generation systems. In: Proceedings of the 24th IEEE Conference on Mass Storage Systems and Technologies, MSST 2007, pp. 30–46. IEEE Computer Society, Washington, DC (2007)
17. Pan, F.: An Ontology of Time: Representing Complex Temporal Phenomena for the Semantic Web and Natural Language. VDM Verlag, Saarbrucken (2009)
18. Park, Geist, A.: System log pre-processing to improve failure prediction. In: DSN 2009, pp. 572–577 (June 2009)
19. Pnueli, A.: The temporal logic of programs. In: Proceedings of the 18th Annual Symposium on Foundations of Computer Science, SFCS 1977, pp. 46–57. IEEE Computer Society, Washington, DC (1977)
20. Popovici, M., Muraru, M., Agache, A., Giumale, C., Negreanu, L., Dobre, C.: A Modeling Method and Declarative Language for Temporal Reasoning Based on Fluid Qualities. In: Andrews, S., Polovina, S., Hill, R., Akhgar, B. (eds.) ICCS-ConceptStruct 2011. LNCS, vol. 6828, pp. 215–228. Springer, Heidelberg (2011)
21. Riley, G.: NASA Clips: A Tool for Building Expert Systems (June 2006),
    http://www.ghg.net/clips/CLIPS.html
22. Roşu, G., Bensalem, S.: Allen Linear (Interval) Temporal Logic – Translation to LTL and Monitor Synthesis. In: Ball, T., Jones, R.B. (eds.) CAV 2006. LNCS, vol. 4144, pp. 263–277. Springer, Heidelberg (2006)
23. Salfner, F., Lenk, M., Malek, M.: A survey of online failure prediction methods. ACM Comput. Surv. 42(3), 10:1–10:42 (2010)
24. Schnoebelen, P.: The complexity of temporal logic model checking. In: Proceedings of Advances in Modal Logics AiML 2002. World Scientific (2003)

Enhancing Goal-Based Requirements Consistency: An Argumentation-Based Approach

Isabelle Mirbel[1] and Serena Villata[2]

[1] Université de Nice Sophia Antipolis
Isabelle.Mirbel@unice.fr
[2] INRIA Sophia Antipolis
serena.villata@inria.fr

Abstract. Requirements engineering research has for long recognized the leading role of goals as requirement artifacts during the requirements engineering specification processes. Given the large number of artifacts created during the requirements specification and the continuous evolution of these artifacts, reasoning about them remains a challenging task. Moreover, the rising complexity of the target domain under consideration during the requirements engineering process as well as the growth of geographically distributed projects explain why the number of collected requirements as well as their complexity also increase. In this context, providing support to stakeholders in achieving a common understanding of a set of goal-based requirements, in consolidating them and keeping them consistent over time is another challenging task. In this paper, we propose an approach to detect consistent sets of goal-based requirements and maintain their consistency over time. Our approach relies on argumentation theory which allows to detect the conflicts among elements called arguments. In particular, we rely on meta-argumentation, which instantiates abstract argumentation frameworks, where requirements are represented as arguments and the standard Dung-like argumentation framework is extended with additional relations between goal-based requirements.

1 Introduction

Requirements engineering (RE) research has for long recognized the leading role of goals during the requirements engineering processes. Several goal-oriented requirements engineering approaches have been proposed in the literature [26,10,2,23]. Goals have shown to be useful for achieving requirements completeness, avoiding irrelevant requirements, explaining requirements to stakeholders, structuring complex requirements documents through goal refinement, supporting decision making through alternative goal refinements, managing conflicts among multiple viewpoints, separating stable from more volatile information and driving requirements identification [19].

As it has been highlighted in Pohl [22], given the large number of artifacts created during the requirements engineering process and the continuous evolution of these artifacts, managing and organizing requirements artifacts is a

M. Fisher et al. (Eds.): CLIMA XIII 2012, LNAI 7486, pp. 110–127, 2012.
© Springer-Verlag Berlin Heidelberg 2012

challenging task. The rising complexity of the target domain under consideration during the requirements engineering process also increases the number of collected requirements as well as their inter-dependencies and it makes this task much more challenging. Dedicated tools are required to support stakeholders in achieving a common understanding of a set of requirements, in consolidating it and in keeping it consistent over the whole project life cycle. As it has been highlighted in the literature [19], even if inconsistencies may be desirable, for instance to allow further elicitation of requirements that would have been missed otherwise, their resolution is necessary at some point. Tools are required to highlight inconsistencies and to support stakeholders who will handle the resolution process. Requirements are usually provided by different groups of stakeholders. This means that we cannot just consider a set of requirements as correct or not. When a requirement is suitable for a group of stakeholders, this leads to the removal of other requirements in order to keep the full requirements set consistent. If this requirement is discovered as not so important for another group of stakeholders, it is therefore removed from the full requirements set to insure consistency from their point of view.

Different kinds of relationships hold between goals [22]. For instance, goal decomposition relationships are distinguished from goal dependencies, i.e., two kinds of decomposition are possible depending on the fact that all subgoals are required to satisfy a super-goal (*AND-decomposition*) or at least one subgoal (*OR-decomposition*). The following dependencies have been identified [22]: *equivalence, conflict,* and *require.*

This paper focuses on the modeling of goal-based requirements with the aim to support the stakeholders, i.e., the agents, in detecting inconsistent sets of requirements and solving these inconsistencies. We propose to use well-known Dung-like abstract argumentation [13] to reason about the consistency of a set of goal-oriented requirements. Dung-like abstract argumentation models the information as abstract elements called *arguments*. The arguments are linked to each others by an *attack* relation. Therefore, we present a way to model additional goal-based relations, to detect the inconsistencies among goals, and provide a decision support system for their resolution.

Following the idea proposed by Bagheri and Ensan [3], we propose an approach in which consistent subsets of requirements are provided to the stakeholders to allow them to understand the different units of consistent requirements. As it has been highlighted in Bagheri and Ensan [3], the use of abstract argumentation is reasonable because it does not need the requirements to be formally defined and only needs the relationships between the requirements to be defined. With respect to the work of Bagheri and Ensan [3], which concentrates on the conflict relation, in our approach we take into consideration all the relations required to organize goals, i.e., AND/OR-decomposition, conflict, require and equivalence dependencies. Therefore, we rely on meta-argumentation [7,8] which has been proposed as a general methodology to handle the introduction of new relations among the arguments by reusing Dung's theory and results.

Alternative approaches to argumentation theory are for instance Answer Set Programming, and first-order logic [15]. As underlined by Bagheri and Ensan [3], a drawback of pure logical formalisms for dealing with inconsistency in requirement specifications is that they identify and solve the inconsistency in pure syntactic form without taking into account the semantical information required to solve inconsistency. The advantage of using argumentation theory is twofold: first, argumentation theory provides a formal but intuitive technique to reason over inconsistency allowing the detection of the implicit relationships among the arguments and their inconsistencies, and second it allows the stakeholders to choose among different sets of consistent requirements using acceptability semantics [13] with the possibility of specifying whether the choice of the consistent set of requirements has to be guided by skeptical or credulous semantics.

The paper is organized as follows. In Section 2, we discuss why and how argumentation is helpful to check the consistency in requirements engineering. In Section 3, we detail how the different goals decomposition relationships and goals dependencies are modeled in our framework. In Section 4, we illustrate our proposal with an example. Section 5 compares the proposed approach to the related work. Finally, we conclude and give some perspectives.

2   Meta-argumentation: Overview

We provide the basic concepts of Dung's abstract argumentation [13]. A Dung-style argumentation framework [13] aims at representing conflicts among elements called *arguments*. It allows to reason about these conflicts in order to detect, starting by a set of arguments and the conflicts among them, which are the accepted arguments. The accepted arguments are those arguments which are considered as believable by an external evaluator, who has a full knowledge of the argumentation framework. A Dung-style framework is based on a binary *attack* relation among arguments, whose role is determined only by their relation to other arguments. Dung [13] presents several acceptability semantics that produce zero, one, or several sets of accepted arguments. The set of accepted arguments of an argumentation framework consists of a set of arguments that does not contain an argument attacking another argument in the set. Roughly, an argument is accepted if all the arguments attacking it are rejected and it is rejected if it has at least an argument attacking it which is accepted. The (possibly multiple) set of accepted arguments computed using one of the acceptability semantics are called *extensions*.

Definition 1 (Argumentation framework AF). *An argumentation framework is a tuple $\langle A, \rightarrow \rangle$ where A is a finite set of elements called arguments and $\rightarrow$ is a binary relation called attack defined on A.*

A semantics of an argumentation theory consists of a *conflict free* set of arguments $cf(\mathcal{S})$, i.e., a set of arguments that does not contain an argument attacking another argument in the set. Like Baroni and Giacomin [4], we use a function $\mathcal{E}$ called *acceptance function* mapping an argumentation framework $\langle A, \rightarrow \rangle$ to its set of extensions, i.e., to a set of sets of arguments.

Definition 2 (Acceptance function). *Let $\mathcal{U}$ be the universe of arguments. An acceptance function $\mathcal{E} : 2^{\mathcal{U}} \times 2^{\mathcal{U} \times \mathcal{U}} \to 2^{2^{\mathcal{U}}}$ is a partial function which is defined for each argumentation framework $\langle A, \to \rangle$ with finite $A \subseteq \mathcal{U}$ and $\to \subseteq A \times A$, and maps an argumentation framework $\langle A, \to \rangle$ to sets of subsets of A: $\mathcal{E}(\langle A, \to \rangle) \subseteq 2^A$.*

The following definition summarizes the most widely used acceptability semantics of arguments [13].

Definition 3 (Acceptability semantics). *Let $AF = \langle A, \to \rangle$ be an argumentation framework. Let $S \subseteq A$. S defends a if $\forall b \in A$ such that $b \to a$, $\exists c \in S$ such that $c \to b$. Let $D(S) = \{a \mid S$ defends $a\}$.*

- *$S \in \mathcal{E}_{admiss}(AF)$ iff $cf(S)$ and $S \subseteq D(S)$.*
- *$S \in \mathcal{E}_{compl}(AF)$ iff $cf(S)$ and $S = D(S)$.*
- *$S \in \mathcal{E}_{ground}(AF)$ iff S is smallest in $\mathcal{E}_{compl}(AF)$.*
- *$S \in \mathcal{E}_{pref}(AF)$ iff S is maximal in $\mathcal{E}_{admiss}(AF)$.*
- *$S \in \mathcal{E}_{stable}(AF)$ iff $cf(S)$ and $\forall b \in A \backslash S$ $\exists a \in S : a \to b$.*

2.1 Meta-argumentation

Meta-level argumentation has been proposed in several works [17,5,11,21] and further developed with different goals. Boella and colleagues [7,8], in particular, proposed the meta-argumentation methodology where extended argumentation frameworks are instantiated with meta-arguments, and reasoning in the meta-level is allowed without the need to extend Dung-like abstract framework. Meta-argumentation instantiates Dung's theory with meta-arguments, such that *Dung's theory is used to reason about itself* [8,21]. Meta-argumentation is a particular way to define mappings from argumentation frameworks to extended argumentation frameworks: arguments are interpreted as meta-arguments, of which some are mapped to "argument a is accepted", $acc(a)$, where a is an abstract argument from the extended argumentation framework EAF. Moreover, auxiliary arguments are introduced to represent, for example, attacks, so that, by being arguments themselves, they can be attacked or attack other arguments.

The function f assigns to each argument a in the EAF, a meta-argument "argument a is accepted" in the basic argumentation framework. The function f^{-1} instantiates an AF with an EAF. We use Dung's acceptance functions $\mathcal{E}$ to find functions $\mathcal{E}'$ between EAFs and the acceptable arguments AA' they return. The accepted arguments of the meta-argumentation framework are a function of the EAF $AA' = \mathcal{E}'(EAF)$. The transformation function consists of two parts: the function f^{-1}, transforming an AF to an EAF, and a function g which transforms the acceptable arguments of the AF into acceptable arguments of the EAF. Summarizing $\mathcal{E}' = \{(f^{-1}(a), g(b)) \mid (a, b) \in \mathcal{E}\}$ and $AA' = \mathcal{E}'(EAF) = g(AA) = g(\mathcal{E}(AF)) = g(\mathcal{E}(f(EAF)))$.

The first step of the meta-argumentation approach is to define the set of EAFs. The second step consists of defining flattening algorithms as a function

from this set of $EAFs$ to the set of all basic AF: $f : EAF \to AF$. The inverse
of the flattening is the instantiation of the AF. See [8] for further details.

Definition 4. *An extended argumentation framework EAF is a tuple $\langle A, \to \rangle$
where $A \subseteq \mathcal{U}$ is a set of arguments, and $\to$ is a binary attack relation on A. The
universe of meta-arguments is $MU = \{acc(a) \mid a \in \mathcal{U}\} \cup \{X_{a,b}, Y_{a,b} \mid a, b \in \mathcal{U}\}$,
where $X_{a,b}, Y_{a,b}$ are the meta-arguments corresponding to the attack $a \to b$. The
flattening function f is given by $f(EAF) = \langle MA, \longmapsto \rangle$, where MA is the set
of meta-arguments and $\longmapsto$ is the meta-attack relation. For a set of arguments
$B \subseteq MU$, the unflattening function g is given by $g(B) = \{a \mid acc(a) \in B\}$, and
for sets of subsets of arguments $AA \subseteq 2^{MU}$, it is given by $g(AA) = \{g(B) \mid B \in AA\}$.*

*Given an acceptance function $\mathcal{E}$ for an AF, the extensions of accepted argu-
ments of an EAF are given by $\mathcal{E}'(EAF) = g(\mathcal{E}(f(EAF)))$. The derived acceptance function $\mathcal{E}'$ of the EAF is thus $\mathcal{E}' = \{(f^{-1}(a), g(b)) \mid (a, b) \in \mathcal{E}\}$.*

Definition 5 presents the instantiation of a basic AF using meta-argumentation.

Definition 5. *Given an $EAF = \langle A, \to \rangle$ where $A \subseteq \mathcal{U}$ is a set of arguments,
and $\to \subseteq A \times A$. $MA \subseteq MU$ is $\{acc(a) \mid a \in U\} \cup \{X_{a,b}, Y_{a,b} \mid a, b \in \mathcal{U}\}$, and
$\longmapsto \subseteq MA \times MA$ is a binary relation on MA such that: $acc(a) \longmapsto X_{a,b}, X_{a,b} \longmapsto
Y_{a,b}, Y_{a,b} \longmapsto acc(b)$ if and only if $a, b \in A$ and $a \to b \in \to$.*

Intuitively, the $X_{a,b}$ auxiliary argument means that the attack $a \to b$ is "inac-
tive", and the $Y_{a,b}$ auxiliary argument means that the attack is "active". An
argument of an EAF is accepted iff it is accepted in the flattened AF.

In our approach, we propose to model decomposition relationships and dependencies as a meta-argumentation framework dedicated to goal-based requirements engineering. Goals are modeled as meta-arguments and decomposition relationships and dependencies as relations among them. Thanks to the semantics
assigned to each of the decomposition relationships and dependencies introduced,
mappings to the argumentation framework are possible as well as reasoning to
find consistent subsets of goals, i.e., extensions of the argumentation framework.
In the next sections, we illustrate our proposal with the help of an example
extracted from Pohl [22].

3   Goal Decomposition and Dependencies

Requirements engineering is generally viewed as a process consisting of four core
activities: *elicitation, analysis, negotiation* and *validation*. Each activity produces
information which must be made persistent by documenting it in the right way. In
order to facilitate communication, to support negotiation or to provide basis for a
contract, for deriving manuals or for project planning for instance, requirements
are traditionally defined in a requirement document or database. Requirements
artifacts can be documented using natural language or a conceptual modeling language. Goals [19] are proposed for this purpose. Goals aim at capturing the rationale of the software systems and document agents' intentions. Regardless of the
chosen means to document requirements, they appear closely related to each other.

According to the literature review presented in Pohl [22], different kinds of relationships hold between goals. Goal decomposition relationships are distinguished from goal dependencies. Two kinds of decomposition are possible depending on the fact that all subgoals are required to satisfy a super-goal (*AND-decomposition*) or at least one sub-goal (*OR-decomposition*). With regards to dependencies, *equivalence*, *conflict*, *obstruction*, *support* and *require* relationships have been identified. *Obstruction* and *support* aim at eliciting *partial* dependencies between goals. Therefore we do not take them into account in our current framework in which we only reason on crisp acceptance, and not on partial acceptance. This is left as future work.

In our approach, we rely on the meta-argumentation methodology to formally model the requirements and these main relationships among them. We choose the meta-argumentation methodology because it allows to model extended argumentation frameworks, i.e., argumentation frameworks where additional relations among the arguments are introduced, as Dung-like abstract frameworks in order to reuse Dung's properties and theorems. We define an extended argumentation framework for reasoning about requirements as follows:

Definition 6 (Requirement-based EAF). *A requirement-based extended argumentation framework $REAF$ is a tuple $\langle A, \rightarrow, CF, RQ, AND\text{-}dec, OR\text{-}dec, EQ \rangle$ where $A \subseteq \mathcal{U}$ is a set of requirements, $\rightarrow \subseteq A \times A$, CF is a binary conflict relation on A ($CF \subseteq A \times A$), RQ is a binary requires relation on A ($RQ \subseteq A \times A$), $AND - dec$ is a AND-decomposable relation on $2^A \times A$ ($AND - dec \subseteq 2^A \times A$), $OR - dec$ is a OR-decomposable relation on $2^A \times A$ ($OR - dec \subseteq 2^A \times A$), and EQ is a binary equivalence relation on A ($EQ \subseteq A \times A$). The universe of meta-requirements is $MU = \{acc(a) \mid a \in \mathcal{U}\} \cup \{X_{a,b}, Y_{a,b} \mid a, b \in \mathcal{U}\} \cup \{Z_{a,b} \mid a, b \in \mathcal{U}\} \cup \{R_{a,b} \mid a, b \in \mathcal{U}\} \cup \{T_{a,b} \mid a, b \in \mathcal{U}\}$, where $X_{a,b}, Y_{a,b}$ are the meta-requirements corresponding to the conflict relation ($a\ CF\ b$), $Z_{a,b}$ is the meta-requirement corresponding to the requires relation ($a\ RQ\ b$), $R_{a,b}$ is the meta-requirement corresponding to the OR-decomposable relation ($a\ OR - dec\ b$), and $T_{a,b}$ is the meta-requirement corresponding to the AND-decomposable relation ($a\ AND - dec\ b$). The flattening function f is given by $f(EAF) = \langle MA, \longmapsto \rangle$, where MA is the set of meta-requirements and $\longmapsto$ is the meta-conflict relation. For a set of requirements $B \subseteq MU$, the unflattening function g is given by $g(B) = \{a \mid acc(a) \in B\}$, and for sets of subsets of requirements $AA \subseteq 2^{MU}$, it is given by $g(AA) = \{g(B) \mid B \in AA\}$.*

Roughly, the extensions of the $REAF$ contain the set of requirements that do not conflict with each other and that satisfy the constraints posed by the other relations.

3.1   Goal Decomposition

Two kinds of goal decomposition have been identified in the literature [22]. In the following we explain how we model them in our meta-argumentation framework.

AND-Decomposition. Pohl [22] defines the AND-decomposition in the following way: The decomposition of a super-goal into a set of sub-goals is an AND-decomposition if and only if all sub-goals must be satisfied in order to satisfy the super-goal.

We model the AND-decomposition relationship in meta-argumentation as follows: a super-goal to be accepted has to have all its sub-goals accepted. The idea is that all the sub-goals are represented as meta-requirements in the meta-level. They attack meta-requirement T which attacks the meta-requirement representing the super-goal. Meta-requirement T is not connected to a real requirement in the object level, but as previously noticed for X and Y, it is just used to reason in the meta-level. The formalization of the AND-decomposition relation is presented in Definition 7.

Definition 7. *Given a $REAF = \langle A, \rightarrow, CF, RQ, AND-dec, OR-dec, EQ \rangle$, the set of meta-arguments $MA \subseteq MU$ is $\{acc(a) \mid a \in \mathcal{U}\} \cup \{X_{a,b}, Y_{a,b} \mid a, b \in \mathcal{U}\} \cup \{Z_{a,b} \mid a, b \in \mathcal{U}\} \cup \{R_{a,b} \mid a, b \in \mathcal{U}\} \cup \{T_{a,b} \mid a, b \in \mathcal{U}\}$ and $\longmapsto \subseteq MA \times MA$ is a binary relation on MA such that:*

- $acc(r_1) \longmapsto T_{r_1,a}$ *iff* $a \; AND-dec \; r_1, \ldots, r_n$, *and*
- $\ldots$
- $acc(r_n) \longmapsto T_{r_n,a}$ *iff* $a \; AND-dec \; r_1, \ldots, r_n$, *and*
- $T_{r_1,a} \longmapsto acc(a)$ *iff* $a \; AND-dec \; r_1, \ldots, r_n$, *and*
- $\ldots$
- $T_{r_n,a} \longmapsto acc(a)$ *iff* $a \; AND-dec \; r_1, \ldots, r_n$.

This is similar to the representation of a conjunctive pattern of arguments, as discussed by Villata et al. [24]. In this way, we have that the goal G is accepted only if all the sub-goals are accepted too. If one (or more) sub-goal is not accepted, then the respective meta-requirement T_i is accepted, and given the attack of this meta-requirement against the super-goal, the super-goal is made unacceptable. An example of *AND-decomposition* is shown in Figure 1, where both goals $G1$ and $G2$ need to be accepted to have goal $G3$ accepted.

Proposition 1 (Semantics of *AND-dec*). *Given a REAF, if it holds that $a_1, \ldots, a_n AND-dec \; b$ and all goals $a_1, \ldots, a_n$ are accepted then goal b is accepted too.*

Proof. We prove the contrapositive. If it holds that $a_1, \ldots, a_n AND-dec \; b$ and goal b is rejected, then goals $a_1, \ldots, a_n$ are rejected too. Assume $a_1, \ldots, a_n AND-dec \; b$ and assume that meta-requirement $acc(b)$ is rejected, then there exists at least one meta-requirement $T_{a_1}, \ldots, T_{a_n}$ that is accepted. Consequently, at least one meta-requirement $acc(a_1), \ldots, acc(a_n)$ is rejected.

OR-Decomposition. Pohl [22] defines the OR-decomposition in the following way: The decomposition of a super-goal into a set of sub-goals is an OR-decomposition if and only if satisfying one of the sub-goals is sufficient for satisfying the super-goal.

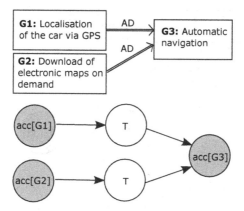

Fig. 1. Example of AND-decomposition. Accepted meta-requirements are represented in grey and rejected meta-requirements in white.

We model the OR-decomposition relationship in meta-argumentation as follows: a super-goal to be accepted needs to have at least one of its sub-goals accepted. The idea is that all the sub-goals in the meta-level attack the same meta-requirement R which attacks the meta-requirement representing the super-goal. In this way, we have that the goal G is accepted when at least one of its sub-goals is accepted too. If no sub-goal is accepted, then the meta-requirement R is accepted, and given the attack of this meta-requirement against the super-goal, the super-goal is made unacceptable. The formalization of the OR-decomposition relation is presented in Definition 8.

Definition 8. *Given a $REAF = \langle A, \rightarrow, CF, RQ, AND - dec, OR - dec, EQ \rangle$, the set of meta-arguments $MA \subseteq MU$ is $\{acc(a) \mid a \in \mathcal{U}\} \cup \{X_{a,b}, Y_{a,b} \mid a, b \in \mathcal{U}\} \cup \{Z_{a,b} \mid a, b \in \mathcal{U}\} \cup \{R_{a,b} \mid a, b \in \mathcal{U}\} \cup \{T_{a,b} \mid a, b \in \mathcal{U}\}$ and $\longmapsto \subseteq MA \times MA$ is a binary relation on MA such that:*

- *$acc(r_1) \longmapsto R_{r,a}$ iff a OR $- dec$ $r_1, \ldots, r_n$, and*
- *$\ldots$*
- *$acc(r_n) \longmapsto R_{r,a}$ iff a OR $- dec$ $r_1, \ldots, r_n$, and*
- *$R_{r,a} \longmapsto acc(a)$ iff a OR $- dec$ $r_1, \ldots, r_n$.*

An example of *OR-decomposition* is shown in Figure 2, where either goal $G1$ or goal $G2$ need to be accepted to have goal $G3$ accepted.

3.2   Goal Dependencies

Different kinds of dependencies between goals have been identified in the literature [22]. In the following, we explain how we model the *conflict*, *requires* and *equivalence* dependencies in our extended argumentation framework.

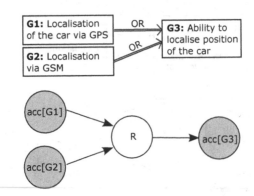

Fig. 2. Example of OR-decomposition

Conflict Dependency. Pohl [22] defines the *conflict* dependency in the following way: a *conflict* dependency exists between two goals if the satisfaction of one goal entirely excludes the satisfaction of the other goal, and vice versa.

In Definition 9, we present how to model the conflicts among requirements.

Definition 9. *Given a requirement-based extended argumentation framework* $REAF = \langle A, \rightarrow, CF, RQ, AND - dec, OR - dec, EQ \rangle$, *the set of meta-requirements* $MA \subseteq MU$ *is* $\{acc(a) \mid a \in \mathcal{U}\} \cup \{X_{a,b}, Y_{a,b} \mid a, b \in \mathcal{U}\} \cup \{Z_{a,b} \mid a, b \in \mathcal{U}\} \cup \{R_{a,b} \mid a, b \in \mathcal{U}\} \cup \{T_{a,b} \mid a, b \in \mathcal{U}\}$ *and* $\longmapsto \subseteq MA \times MA$ *is a binary relation on* MA *such that:*

- $acc(a) \longmapsto X_{a,b}$ *iff a CF b and*
- $X_{a,b} \longmapsto Y_{a,b}$ *iff a CF b and*
- $Y_{a,b} \longmapsto acc(b)$ *iff a CF b and*
- $acc(b) \longmapsto X_{b,a}$ *iff a CF b and*
- $X_{b,a} \longmapsto Y_{b,a}$ *iff a CF b and*
- $Y_{b,a} \longmapsto acc(a)$ *iff a CF b.*

The two meta-requirements X and Y are used to model the conflict relation in the meta-level as well as the attack relation. The semantics of the conflict dependency is similar to the semantics of the attack relation in Dung-style abstract argumentation. The difference is that the attack relation is directed from an argument to another argument while the conflict dependency leads to a cycle of attacks, i.e., the two arguments attack each other. An example of *conflict* dependency is shown in Figure 3, where goal $G1$ cannot be accepted if goal $G2$ is accepted and vice versa. In particular, the three extensions using complete semantics are $\{G1\}$, $\{G2\}$, and $\emptyset$.

Require Dependency. Pohl [22] defines the *require* dependency in the following way: a goal G_1 is related to a goal G_2 by a *requires* dependency if the satisfaction of the goal G_2 is a prerequisite for satisfying goal G_1.

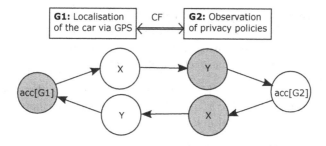

Fig. 3. Example of conflict dependency where the extension $\{G1\}$ is shown

We model the *requires* relation as a relation such that, given that G_1 requires G_2, G_1 is accepted only if G_2 is accepted too. This means that if G_2 is not accepted, then G_1 is not accepted either. We formalize the *requires* relation using meta-argumentation in Definition 10.

Definition 10. *Given a $REAF = \langle A, \rightarrow, CF, RQ, AND-dec, OR-dec, EQ \rangle$, the set of meta-arguments $MA \subseteq MU$ is $\{acc(a) \mid a \in \mathcal{U}\} \cup \{X_{a,b}, Y_{a,b} \mid a, b \in \mathcal{U}\} \cup \{Z_{a,b} \mid a, b \in \mathcal{U}\} \cup \{R_{a,b} \mid a, b \in \mathcal{U}\} \cup \{T_{a,b} \mid a, b \in \mathcal{U}\}$ and $\longmapsto \subseteq MA \times MA$ is a binary relation on MA such that:*

- *$acc(b) \longmapsto Z_{a,b}$ iff $a\ RQ\ b$, and*
- *$Z_{a,b} \longmapsto acc(a)$ iff $a\ RQ\ b$.*

Definition 10 highlights that goals cannot only conflict with each other but can also require the acceptability of other goals to be themselves accepted. The *requires* relation is defined following the example of the modeling in meta-argumentation of the support relation [9]. An example of *requires* dependency is shown in Figure 4, where the goal $G1$ needs goal $G2$ accepted to be accepted too.

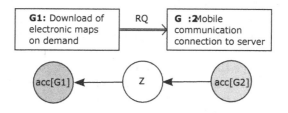

Fig. 4. Example of *requires* dependency

Proposition 2 (Semantics of *requires*). *Given a REAF, if it holds that $a\ RQ\ b$ and goal a is accepted, then goal b is accepted too.*

Proof. We prove the contrapositive. If it holds that a RQ b and goal b is not accepted, then goal a is not accepted. Assume that a RQ b and assume that meta-requirement $acc(b)$ is not accepted, then meta-requirement $Z_{a,b}$ is accepted. Consequently, meta-requirement $acc(a)$ is not accepted.

Proposition 3. *Given a REAF with goals a, b and c, if there is an attack such that $a \to c$ if a RQ b and $b \to c$, then the extensions do not change, using our meta-argumentation model and one of Dung's semantics.*

Proof. We use reasoning by cases. Case 1: $acc(a)$ is accepted, then also $acc(b)$ is accepted following Proposition 2, and given $b \to c$, $a \to c$ can be deleted without changing the extension. Case 2: $acc(a)$ is not accepted, then $a \to c$ can be deleted.

Our representation of the *requires* relation is based on the fact that a requires b is modeled by the flattening function with a path from $acc(b)$ to $acc(a)$, i.e. $acc(a)$ is accepted only if $acc(b)$ is accepted. Notice that, given a RQ b, in meta-argumentation we condense all the attacks which are both on b and thus on a (both from b and thus from a) using only meta-requirement $Z_{a,b}$, as we show in Proposition 4.

Proposition 4. *Given a REAF, if there is an attack such that $c \to a$ if a RQ b and $c \to b$, then the extensions do not change, using our meta-argumentation model and one of Dung's semantics.*

Proof. We use reasoning by cases. Case 1: $acc(c)$ is accepted, then $acc(a)$ is not accepted, follows from Proposition 2, and given $c \to b$, $c \to a$ can be deleted without changing the extension. Case 2: $acc(c)$ is not accepted, then $acc(a)$ is accepted, and the attack relation $c \to a$ can be avoided.

Goal Equivalence. Pohl [22] defines the goal *equivalence* in the following way: An *equivalence* dependency exists between two goals if the satisfaction of one goal implies the satisfaction of the other goal. We model the *equivalence* dependency in the following way: given that $G1$ is equivalent to $G2$ then if G_1 is in conflict with other goals, then G_2 is in conflict with these other goals too, and if goal G_2 is in conflict with other goals, then goal G_1 conflicts with these goals too. In order to maintain the semantics of the *equivalence* dependency, we have to consider how to manage the conflicts addressed against goal B when goal A is equivalent to B. In this case, we want to model the situation such that every time goal B is in conflict with another goal, then this new goal is in conflict also with A and vice-versa. We achieve it by introducing an additional kind of conflict among the goals called *equivalence* attacks.

An example of *equivalence* dependency is shown in Figure 5. In this example, G_1 is conflicting with G_3 then G_3 is also conflicting with G_2 as it is shown by the dashed lines. And if a conflict involving G_2 would exist, then G_1 would also be in conflict with this goal. We do not include this case in the figure for clarity purpose.

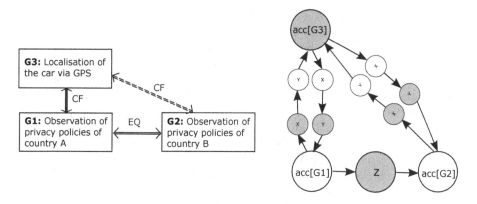

Fig. 5. Example of equivalence

In the following section, we introduce an example including the different kinds of decomposition and dependency relationships previously discussed to show the effectiveness of our approach.

4   Example

To show how the translations of the different relationships existing between goals are combined into our extended argumentation framework, an example of goal-oriented requirements modeling is presented in Figure 6.

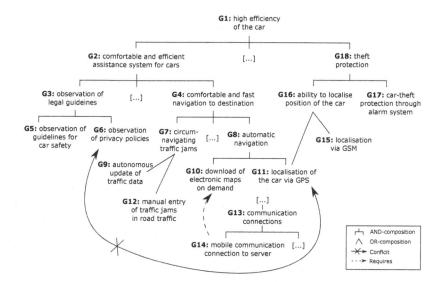

Fig. 6. Example of goal oriented requirement modeling

In this example, there is a conflict between G_6 and G_{11}. Therefore the mapping to our meta-argumentation framework leads to 2 extensions in complete semantics: the former in which G_6 is accepted and G_{11} not accepted; and the latter in which G_{11} is accepted and G_6 is not accepted[1].

Figure 7 shows the representation in the meta-level of the example from Figure 6. In this framework, we show the first extension, where G_6 is accepted and G_{11} is rejected. For clarity of the figure, we duplicated the meta-requirement *acc[G11]*. The set of goals in grey corresponds to a coherent set of goals. No goal represented in white can be added to this set without making it inconsistent. Note that only meta-requirements representing the goals are requirements in the object level. Figure 8 shows the set of accepted goals on the goal hierarchy corresponding to this first extension.

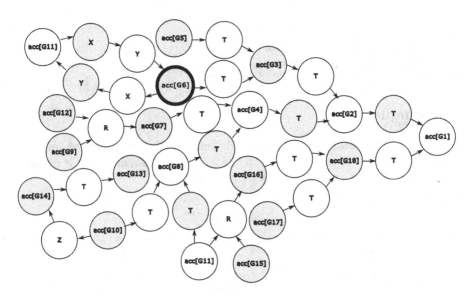

Fig. 7. The meta-argumentation framework and the extension where goal G_6 is accepted

The second extension starting from the goal-oriented requirement modeling of Figure 6 is shown in Figure 9. In this extension, G_{11} is accepted and G_6 is not accepted. Again, meta-requirement *acc[G11]* is duplicated for clarity reasons. No goal represented in white can be added to the set without making it inconsistent. Figure 10 shows the set of accepted goals on the goal hierarchy corresponding to the second extension.

As it is shown by this running example, we propose an approach in which consistent subsets of an initial goals set are provided to the stakeholders to

---

[1] We do not consider here the third extension ∅ because we want to provide the stakeholders with alternatives where the two conflicting goals are included.

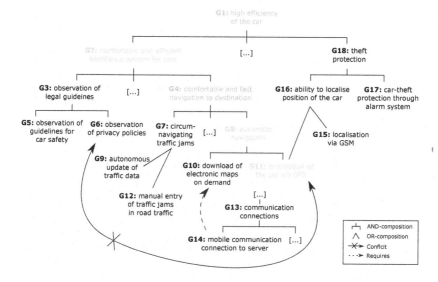

Fig. 8. The object level of the example with the goals accepted in the first extension

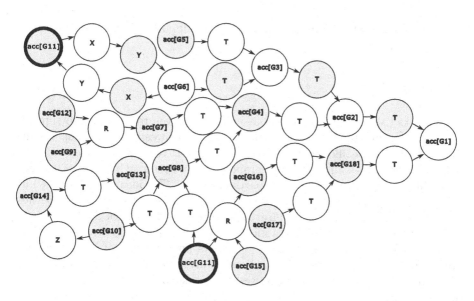

Fig. 9. The meta-argumentation framework and the extension where goal G_{11} is accepted

allow them to understand the different units of consistent goals. This is particularly useful when the number of collected requirements as well as the number of inter-dependencies are big. In this context, our approach aims at supporting stakeholders in achieving a common understanding of a set of goal-based

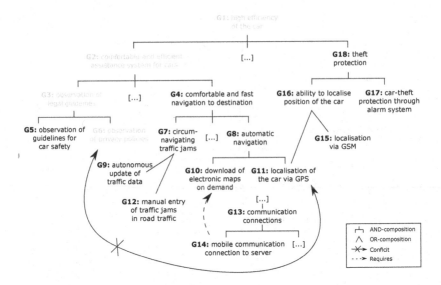

Fig. 10. The object level of the example with the goals accepted in the second extension

requirements and at providing them a decision support system for inconsistencies resolution.

5   Related Work

Frameworks to reason about goals have already proven to be useful to support goal-based requirements management. In van Lamsweerde et al. [20], for instance, goals are specified in a formal way to support reasoning on their content. In Giorgini et al. [14], an approach is proposed to analyze goal hierarchies in order to establish goals satisfiability (full, partial or none). The idea is to show the impact of the adoption of some goals on the other goals of the system. Approaches relaying on argumentation have already been proposed to check the consistency of a requirement set [6,3]. Our approach relies on meta-argumentation while the proposal of Bagheri and Ensan [3] adopts an extension of Dung's framework with preferences over the arguments. Jureta et al. [18] present a formal model to analyze the discussions between the stakeholders about the validity of the requirements engineering artifacts using argumentation theory. In particular, they introduce the Acceptability Evaluation framework (ACE) which is a propositional reasoning framework. In this framework, an acceptability condition is proposed on an artifact such that if the condition holds then it means that the relative validity for the artifact is verified. They use argumentation theory to model the discussions among stakeholders where inference, attack and preference relationships are used. There are several points which distinguish our approach from the work of Jureta et al. [18]: first, we rely on abstract argumentation theory and on its notion of acceptability semantics to assess which are the acceptable requirements, instead of introducing a new framework; second, we reason at the pure abstract level as done by Bagheri and Ensan [3] starting from the set of goal-based requirements and their relationships, we are not interested in modeling the discussions of the stakeholders to verify the validity of an artifact using a propositional language; third, we do not consider only the conflict and the preference relationships among the requirements, but we consider goal-based requirements and their additional relationships (AND/OR-decomposition, and require, conflict and equivalence goal dependencies) provided by the stakeholders to detect the (possibly multiple) consistent sets of requirements, showing in addition how the inconsistencies may be resolved. Ingolfo et al. [16] use the ACE framework to deal with the compliance of software requirements. In Goknil et al. [15], a meta model is proposed to reason about requirements consistency. In their approach, some well-known relationships between requirements are formalized by relying on first-order logic. Thanks to this meta model, implicit relations and inconsistencies are detected. We propose to address this issue by using abstract argumentation theory in order to put in evidence consistent sets of requirements.

6   Conclusion

In this paper we present an approach to support consistency checking in goal-based requirements engineering. Our approach aims at detecting implicit relationships between the requirements and checking the possible inconsistencies among them.

Our proposal uses argumentation theory to formalize the requirement and their relationships, and to detect the inconsistencies. We represent requirements as abstract arguments and the conflicts among the requirements are the conflicts among the arguments. In particular, we rely on the meta-argumentation methodology to formally model the decomposition and dependencies which may exist between goals. We choose the meta-argumentation methodology because it allows to model argumentation frameworks with additional relations among the arguments as Dung-like abstract frameworks thus reusing Dung's properties and algorithms.

Several open challenges will be addressed as future works. First, we are developing a tool which asks the stakeholders to enter the set of requirements and the relationships among them, and it returns a graphical visualization of the requirements, as shown in Figure 6 and 7. The tool highlights the set of consistent requirements, and provides the stakeholder with the possible alternatives. These alternatives depend on the chosen acceptability semantics. Second, we plan to introduce into the framework also the relationships between agents and the requirements they propose. This has to be done to be able to reason about trust, allowing the expression of different evaluations of the acceptability of the arguments depending on the stakeholder who is proposing them [25]. Third, we plan to use fuzzy values expressing the degree of acceptability of the arguments to take into account partially satisfied goals [12], as it is necessary to model the obstruction and support relationships. Moreover, we plan to address dynamical issues such as changes in the set of requirements and goals, which are common in most engineering projects. Finally, we will investigate the cost associated with argumentation-based approaches to software engineering.

References

1. Ab Aziz, R., Zowghi, D., McBride, T.: Towards a Classification of Requirements Relationships. In: 21st International Conference on Software Engineering and Knowledge Engineering, pp. 26–32 (2009)
2. Amyot, D., Mussbacher, G.: User Requirements Notation: The First Ten Years, The Next Ten Years. Journal of Software 6(5), 747–768 (2011)
3. Bagheri, E., Ensan, F.: Consolidating multiple requirement specifications through argumentation. In: 26th Symposium on Applied Computing, pp. 659–666 (2011)
4. Baroni, P., Giacomin, M.: On principle-based evaluation of extension-based argumentation semantics. Artif. Intell. 171(10-15), 675–700 (2007)
5. Baroni, P., Cerutti, F., Giacomin, M., Guida, G.: Afra: Argumentation framework with recursive attacks. Int. J. Approx. Reasoning 52(1), 19–37 (2011)
6. Besnard, P., Hunter, A.: Elements of argumentation. MIT Press (2008)
7. Boella, G., van der Torre, L., Villata, S.: On the Acceptability of Meta-arguments. In: International Conference on Intelligent Agent Technology, pp. 259–262 (2009)
8. Boella, G., Gabbay, D.-M., van der Torre, L., Villata, S.: Meta-Argumentation Modelling I: Methodology and Techniques. Studia Logica 93(2-3), 297–355 (2009)
9. Boella, G., Gabbay, D.M., van der Torre, L., Villata, S.: Support in abstract argumentation. In: 3rd International Conference Computational Models of Argument, pp. 40–51. IOS Press (2010)
10. Bresciani, P., Perini, A., Giorgini, P., Giunchiglia, F., Mylopoulos, J.: Modeling Early Requirements in Tropos: A Transformation Based Approach. In: Wooldridge, M.J., Weiß, G., Ciancarini, P. (eds.) AOSE 2001. LNCS, vol. 2222, pp. 151–168. Springer, Heidelberg (2002)
11. Cayrol, C., Lagasquie-Schiex, M.-C.: Coalitions of arguments: A tool for handling bipolar argumentation frameworks. Int. J. Intell. Syst. 25(1), 83–109 (2010)
12. da Costa Pereira, C., Tettamanzi, A., Villata, S.: Changing ones mind: Erase or rewind? In: 22nd International Joint Conference Artificial Intelligence, pp. 164–171 (2011)
13. Dung, P.-M.: On the acceptability of arguments and its fundamental role in nonmonotonic reasoning, logic programming and n-person games. Artif. Intell. 77(2), 321–357 (1995)
14. Giorgini, P., Mylopoulos, J., Sebastiani, R.: Goal-oriented requirements analysis and reasoning in the Tropos methodology. In: Agent-oriented Software Development, vol. 18(2), pp. 159–171 (2005)
15. Goknil, A., Kurtev, I., van den Berg, K., Veldhuis, J.-W.: Semantics of trace relations in requirements models for consistency checking and inferencing. Software and System Modeling 10(1), 31–54 (2011)
16. Ingolfo, S., Siena, A., Mylopoulos, J.: Establishing Regulatory Compliance for Software Requirements. In: 30th IEEE International Requirements Engineering Conference, pp. 47–61 (2011)
17. Jakobovits, H., Vermeir, D.: Robust semantics for argumentation frameworks. J. Log. Comput. 9(2), 215–261 (1999)

18. Jureta, I., Mylopoulos, J., Faulkner, S.: Analysis of Multi-Party Agreement in Requirements Validation. In: 17th IEEE International Requirements Engineering Conference, pp. 57–66 (2009)
19. van Lamsweerde, A.: Goal-Oriented Requirements Engineering: A Guided Tour. In: Fifth IEEE International Symposium on Requirements Engineering, vol. 249 (2001)
20. van Lamsweerde, A., Darimont, R., Letier, E.: Managing conflicts in goal-driven requirements engineering. IEEE Transactions on Software Engineering 24(11), 908–926 (1998)
21. Modgil, S., Bench-Capon, T.J.M.: Metalevel argumentation. J. Log. Comput. 21(6), 959–1003 (2011)
22. Pohl, K.: Requirements Engineering. Fundamentals, Principles, and Techniques. Springer (2010)
23. Rolland, C., Prakash, N., Benjamen, A.: A Multi-Model View of Process Modelling. Requirement Engineering 4(4), 169–187 (1999)
24. Villata, S., Boella, G., van der Torre, L.: Argumentation Patterns. In: 8th International Workshop on Argumentation in Multi-Agent Systems, pp. 133–150 (2011)
25. Villata, S., Boella, G., Gabbay, D.M., van der Torre, L.: Arguing about the Trustworthiness of the Information Sources. In: Liu, W. (ed.) ECSQARU 2011. LNCS, vol. 6717, pp. 74–85. Springer, Heidelberg (2011)
26. Yu, E.: Towards Modelling and Reasoning Support for Early-Phase Requirements Engineering. In: 3rd IEEE Int. Symp. on Requirements Engineering, pp. 226–235 (1997)

A Game Theoretic Approach for Optimal Network Topologies in Opportunistic Networks

Nils Bulling[1], Michael Köster[1], and Matei Popovici[2]

[1] Clausthal University of Technology
Institute for Informatics, Clausthal-Zellerfeld, Germany
`bulling@in.tu-clausthal.de, michael.koester@tu-clausthal.de`
[2] POLITEHNICA University of Bucharest
Splaiul Independentei nr. 313, Bucharest, Romania, Postal Code 060042
`matei.popovici@cs.pub.ro`

Abstract. *Opportunistic networks* (ON) are particular types of delay-tolerant networks in which users/network entities participate in order to propagate information. Besides the advantages of these networks (e.g. decentralization, independence of communication infrastructure) they raise new problems regarding for example effectiveness, message routing, message delivery, security issues, and trust. In this paper we introduce a formal description of an ON and of optimal communication topologies, for the non-cooperative and cooperative settings. We follow a game theoretic approach and allow users to express properties about how their messages should be handled in the network by means of a logical language (for instance, message privacy may be achieved by requiring that network nodes with internet access should be avoided on the communication path). We determine the complexity of associated verification and synthesis problems of network topologies.

1 Introduction

The ever increasing use of online social networking services together with the popularity of new generation smartphones and of other smart mobile devices are causing mobile networks to be overloaded. In order to solve this problem, novel communication methods and new types of network architectures, such as *delay-tolerant* [3] and *opportunistic networks* [12,10] have emerged. Traditionally, delays are seen as networking problems caused by connectivity interruptions. In the conventional setting they are the exception. However, in *delay-tolerant networks* they are the rule: messages are (deliberately) delayed, and offloaded to alternative communication routes, in order to relieve wireless and mobile networks of data traffic [7,9].

An *opportunistic network* is a particular type of delay-tolerant network in which participants are mobile and able to communicate at limited range (e.g. humans carrying wireless communication devices). It is assumed that: (i) global Internet access is not available, (ii) end-to-end connectivity between any two participants is not generally possible and (iii) the entire network might be disconnected, i.e. certain groups of participants might be outside the communication range of other groups from the network. In this setting, communication occurs *opportunistically*: whenever two devices are in

M. Fisher et al. (Eds.): CLIMA XIII 2012, LNAI 7486, pp. 128–145, 2012.

proximity, they will consider this as an *opportunity* to exchange messages. Moreover, the participants' mobility is exploited in order to transmit messages between disconnected groups of users. According to this *store-carry-and-forward* mechanism [1], a message is *stored* in user A's buffer and is *carried* around until A is in communication range with another user B. When this happens, the message is forwarded to user B and the process is repeated until the final destination is reached, or the message is outdated.

One of the main advantages of opportunistic networks is the fact that they are: (i) decentralized, (ii) independent of any communication infrastructure and (iii) inexpensive. Opportunistic networks also raise new problems regarding for example effectiveness, message routing in such a dynamic environment, maximizing message delivery, security issues, and trust. Moreover, not all network topologies are desirable nor stable because (i) users may wish to avoid specific routes/users and (ii) users lack incentives to provide services (e.g. message forwarding) to other users.

In this paper we address these two problems and propose a game-theoretic communication model for opportunistic networks, in which each user (or each group of users) has certain communication preferences which express the users' goals and also restrictions on the network. Instead of using rankings or other community-dependent metrics, we use the temporal logic **CTL** for expressing these preferences. The advantage of this approach is that it allows a flexible description of various preferences like reachability or avoidance properties.

The contributions of this paper are a game-theoretic analysis of *optimal network topologies* for message forwarding and related complexity results. The optimal topology should minimize communication costs, while satisfying the players' goals. We model a network topology as the outcome of a strategic game in which the actions of each player consist of establishing communication channels. Then, optimal topologies correspond to game theoretic solution concepts. In this paper, we consider individual and group rationality, each leading to a different notion of optimality and stability.

We consider both a cooperative and a non-cooperative setting. Often cooperation is required as players are usually not able to achieve their goals by themselves. Apart from the game theoretic modelling approach, the complexity results regarding verification and synthesis problems of optimal topologies form the main technical results of this paper. Finally, we would like to note that a lot of work in this area has focused on game theoretic methods for package forwarding and routing strategies. Our work should not only be understood as yet another analysis but in particular as a pre-processing step. We propose a way for finding an optimal network topology and once it has been found existing methods for package routing and forwarding can be applied on top of it.

The paper is structured as follows: In Section 2 we introduce the basic ingredients of an *opportunistic network* (ON), motivate our game theoretic approach, define the *opportunistic network game*, and put game theoretic solution concepts in the context of optimal topologies. In Section 3 we propose a computational setting based on the temporal logic **CTL**. In Section 4 we analyze the complexity of verification and synthesis problems. Finally, in Section 5 and 6 we discuss related work and conclude, respectively.

2 Optimal Opportunistic Networks

In this section we introduce an *opportunistic network* (ON), motivate our game theoretic approach, define the *opportunistic network game* which is used to determine
optimal topologies. The concept of optimality depends on the specific solution concept at hand and reflects different stability conditions of a topology. An ON is defined
over an *opportunistic network frame (ONF)* which models the participants of an ON (to
which will henceforth also refer as *players*), the locations they can reach, the possible
connections (or channels) they can establish, and a cost for each such channel. Players have the intention to send messages to one or several locations, but are interested
in enforcing restrictions on the way messages are delivered. These restrictions include
prohibiting specific players (or rather characteristics of players) on the message delivery path, requiring the existence of several paths towards destination, or restricting the
path's length.

2.1 Opportunistic Networks

An *opportunistic network frame* (ONF) essentially defines a set of players $\mathcal{P}$ and their
abilities to communicate with each other. We use a neighborhood function $N : \mathcal{P} \to 2^{\mathcal{P}}$
to model the players to whom a (communication) channel can be established; that is,
$N(i)$ is the possibly empty set of players with whom i can set up a channel. We require
that $i \notin N(i)$. The establishment of a channel from player i to player j has cost $c(i,j)$.
The cost function c can aggregate a number of internal and external factors related to
players such as bandwidth consumption, trust level, resource usage etc. Finally, each
player i attempts to satisfy a certain goal ϕ_i. Goals give players the ability to enforce
restrictions on how messages are forwarded. One such restriction could be that any path
to destination must not include certain players (or group of players).

The *value* function v quantifies the value of a player's goal. The values are subjective
to the agents and can be of various origin. In this paper, we do not discuss this issue in
more detail.

Definition 1 (Opportunistic Network Frame). *An opportunistic network frame (ONF)
is given by* $\mathcal{F} = (P, N, \mathcal{P}rops, c, \mathcal{I}, (\phi_i)_{i \in \mathcal{P}}, v)$ *where*

- $\mathcal{P}$ *is a finite set of players;*
- $N : \mathcal{P} \to 2^P$ *is a neighborhood function. $N(i)$ is the set of neighbors with which
  i can establish channels. We require that $i \notin N(i)$, i.e. players cannot establish
  channels with themselves.*
- $\mathcal{P}rops$ *is a set of propositional symbols that represent different user properties.*
- $\mathcal{I} : \mathcal{P} \to 2^{\mathcal{P}rops}$ *is a valuation function assigning, for each player i, a set of
  propositions which are true for player i.*
- *A partial cost function $c : \mathcal{P} \times \mathcal{P} \to \mathbb{R}^{\geq 0}$. $c(i,j)$ is the cost for player i of establishing a channel with player j. The value $c(i,j) \geq 0$ must be defined for any two
  players $i \neq j$ provided that $j \in N(i)$. Moreover, $c(i,i) = 0$ for all players i.*
- ϕ_i *is the goal for player i.*
- *A value function $v : \mathcal{P} \to \mathbb{R}$ models the value of a player's goal when the goal
  becomes satisfied.*

A proposition $p \in Props$ can for instance represent certain real world locations or a *communication channel* (e.g. a wifi hotspot, a mobile connection, etc.) which a player can access. A possible goal of a player could be the following: *Player 1 wants to access a specific communication channel*. In particular, goals can also be understood as restrictions on communication paths and network topologies.

Remark 1 (Player goals). In ONF each player has a single goal. It is rather straight forward to extend the setting to a set of goals, one for each player, and to assign different values to each goal. However, for a clearer presentation, we do only consider the single goal setting in this paper.

In our particular setting, goals are expressed using the language of *computation tree logic* (**CTL**). **CTL** is, in our opinion, a natural choice since model checking **CTL**-formulae can be done in polynomial time. Thus, it brings no significant overhead to the computational complexity of our solution concepts, described in Section 4. However, the general framework is not dependent on **CTL** and can be used with other suitable languages for specifying goals. For this reason, we defer the introduction of **CTL** and the formal definition of goal satisfaction to Section 3.

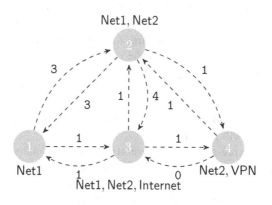

Fig. 1. A simple opportunistic network frame

Example 1 (Simple ONF). Consider the ON with 4 players shown in Figure 1. The scenario describes two partially disconnected networks modeled by the propositions Net1 and Net2, respectively. Player 1, which is a member of Net1 is unable to communicate directly with player 4, which is a member of Net2. Players 2 and 3 are members of both Net1 and Net2 and thus can communicate with any other player. Player 3 has access to Internet, and player 4 to a virtual private network, denoted as VPN. We model this scenario as a ONF where the set of propositions $Props =$ {Net1, VPN, Net2, Internet} describes all existing networks and the valuation function defined as $\mathcal{I}(1) = \{\text{Net1}\}, \mathcal{I}(2) = \{\text{Net1}, \text{Net2}\}, \mathcal{I}(3) = \{\text{Net1}, \text{Net2}, \text{Internet}\}$ and $\mathcal{I}(4) = \{\text{Net2}, \text{VPN}\}$ describes what networks are accessible for each player.

The dashed arrows describe all possible communication channels which can be established, and they are labeled with their corresponding costs. Therefore: $N(1) =$

$N(4) = \{2,3\}, N(2) = \{1,3,4\}$ and $N(3) = \{1,2,4\}$. The costs are $c(1,2) = c(2,1) = 3, c(1,3) = c(2,4) = c(3,1) = c(3,4) = c(4,2) = c(3,2) = 1, c(4,3) = 0$ and $c(2,3) = 4$.

Let us assume that player 1 wants to send a message to the VPN. In order to do so, one possible path is $(1,3,4)$, i.e. to send the message from player 1 over player 3 to player 4. However, let us moreover assume that player 1 requires that its message must not pass through any node which has access to Internet. We will refer to this goal as ϕ_1. The single path that obeys this restriction is $(1,2,4)$.

Similarly, player 2 has the goal–to which we refer to as ϕ_2–of sending a message to the Internet. Players 3 and 4 have no communication goals. The goal values for the players are, $v(1) = 10, v(2) = 5$ and $v(3) = 0, v(4) = 0$, respectively.

As seen in Example 1, the *optimality* of a certain *network topology* dependents on several issues. We may, for instance, call a topology optimal if all the players' goals are satisfied, or if the costs are minimal and the goal of a particular player is satisfied. We discuss optimality in more detail in Section 2.2. In what follows, we describe *topologies* as *structures* which depend on a certain ONF. We assume players have the intention of sending messages to one or several other players. Furthermore, we expect that destinations are not (always) directly reachable, and that messages must be routed via intermediate players. Whenever this is the case, a message will cross a sequence of players, from source to destination. A *transition* $i \xrightarrow{k} j$ in a *topology* represents a directed communication channel in which player i forwards one (or several) messages generated by or on behalf of player k, to player j. j is the next-hop (as in relay networks) on the message delivery path. It might be the case that $i = k$, if j is the first hop on the message path. The cost of setting a channel is captured by $c(i,j)$, and it has to be put up by the sender, i.e. player i in this very case. Since we assume players are self-interested, setting up communication links and relaying messages for other players requires some kind of incentive, as we will further see.

Each player's goal expresses one (or several) destinations that should be reached, or can also enforce certain restrictions on how these destinations are reached. The expressiveness of the goals depends on the concrete goal language used. Possible restrictions/goals include, for example, *channel P should be accessible via at most two hops* or *channel P should be accessible via a path that doesn't pass through node/player i* (i.e. player i should not be able to receive the message sent), etc. We note however that a player k can only formulate goals that involve forwarding its own messages, i.e. it can only express preferences regarding edges of the form $i \xrightarrow{k} j$ in the topology.

In the remainder of this paper we assume that $\mathcal{F} = (P, N, \mathit{Props}, c, \mathcal{I}, (\phi_i)_{i \in \mathcal{P}}, v)$ is an opportunistic network frame, as described by Definition 1.

Definition 2 (*$\mathcal{F}$-topology, $\mathcal{T}ops(\mathcal{F})$*). *An $\mathcal{F}$-topology is a labeled transition system $\mathcal{T}_{\mathcal{F}} = (\mathcal{P}, \rightarrow, \mathit{Props}, \mathcal{I})$ where $\mathcal{P}$ is the set of nodes and $\rightarrow \subseteq \mathcal{P} \times \mathcal{P} \times \mathcal{P}$ where we require that $(i,i,i) \in \rightarrow$ for all $i \in \mathcal{P}$ and that $c \in N(a)$ if $(a,b,c) \in \rightarrow$ and $a \neq c$. The elements Props and $\mathcal{I}$ are taken from $\mathcal{F}$. We write $a \xrightarrow{b} c$ for $(a,b,c) \in \rightarrow$. The relation $a \xrightarrow{b} c$ models a b-labeled transition from a to c.*

The set of all $\mathcal{F}$-topologies is denoted $\mathcal{T}ops(\mathcal{F})$. We write $\mathcal{T}$ instead of $\mathcal{T}_{\mathcal{F}}$ if $\mathcal{F}$ is clear from context.

The reflexive loops $i \overset{i}{\rightarrow} i$ are due to technical reasons. They model a player's possibility to do nothing.

Remark 2 ($\mathcal{F}$-topologies and labeled transition systems). Labeled transition system are often used to describe the states of a certain system, and labeled transitions represent possible actions which can be taken, in order to reach some state from another. We would like to emphasize that in our setting, nodes in a $\mathcal{F}$-topologies represent players and their properties. Edges correspond to the possible communication channels they can establish.

Proposition 1. *We have $|\mathcal{T}ops(\mathcal{F})| \leq 2^{|\mathcal{P}|^3}$.*

Definition 3 (Opportunistic Network). *An opportunistic network (ON) is a tuple $\mathcal{O} = (\mathcal{F}, \mathcal{T})$ consisting of an opportunistic network frame $\mathcal{F}$ and an $\mathcal{F}$-topology $\mathcal{T} \in \mathcal{T}ops(\mathcal{F})$.*

Intuitively, an opportunistic network $\mathcal{O}$ is obtained by taking one possible instantiation of the opportunistic frame $\mathcal{F}$. Such an instantiation consists of labeled transitions between players. The label stands for the player on whose behalf the message is forwarded.

Example 2. (Simple ON) We continue Example 1. Figure 2 shows an ON in which the goal ϕ_1 (we recall that ϕ_1 expresses the goal of reaching VPN without ever visiting a node in which Internet holds) of player 1 is violated. The violation is caused by the labeled transition $1 \overset{1}{\rightarrow} 3$ which causes player 1's messages to be forwarded to player 3 who has access to Internet. Also, we would like to emphasize that player 1 sets two channels to player 3: one for itself and one on behalf of player 2.

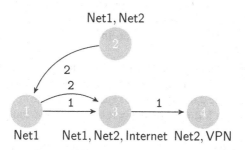

Fig. 2. A simple opportunistic network. The reflexive edges (i.e. $i \overset{i}{\rightarrow} i$ for all players i) are omitted to improve the readability.

In the usual cases we are interested in economical networks. For this purpose, we need to introduce the *cost of a network*. We define it as the sum of all established channel costs.

Definition 4 (Cost). *Let $\mathcal{O} = (\mathcal{F}, \mathcal{T})$ be an ON. The cost of player i in $\mathcal{O}$ is defined as the costs of all outgoing edges from player i, i.e. $cost_i(\mathcal{T}) = \sum_{(i,k,j)\in\rightarrow} c(i,j)$ where i is fixed. The total cost of ON $\mathcal{O}$ is defined as $cost(\mathcal{O}) = \sum_{i\in\mathcal{P}} cost_i(\mathcal{T})$.*

Given this definition we can ask what is the best ON? Is it the one with the minimal costs? This depends on the behavior of the players, e.g. whether they are social, strictly self-interested, cooperative, or non-cooperative. Notice that a player may not unconditionally follow the satisfaction of its goal. If the player's costs exceed the value of its goal the player may be better off not establishing a link at all. Players often reason strategically. In particular, this is the case if costs are involved and network nodes belong to different organizations, which often is a realistic scenario in opportunistic nets and relay networks.

Example 3 (Cost of an ON). In our example (Figure 2), the individual costs $cost_i(\mathcal{O})$ and the overall costs $cost(\mathcal{O})$ are given as follows: $cost_1(\mathcal{O}) = 2$, $cost_2(\mathcal{O}) = 3$, $cost_3(\mathcal{O}) = 1$, $cost_4(\mathcal{O}) = 0$ and $cost(\mathcal{O}) = 5$. The channel costs are included in the definition of the ONF shown in Figure 1.

2.2 How Does an Optimal Solution Look?

In this section we informally discuss properties of optimal ONs. It is straightforward that optimality is highly affected by: (i) the goal fulfillment of each player, (ii) the goal value, and (iii) the players' costs. Given a player i which participates in creating a topology $\mathcal{T}$ by setting up channels, we require a measure of its profit in $\mathcal{T}$, i.e. a *utility value*, which takes into account the properties (i), (ii) and (iii).

Rational players usually prefer topologies in which they get higher utility over those in which they get less utility. However, they can only set up a channel with their (directly accessible) neighbours and thus depend on the other players' actions in most of the cases. Therefore, it might be the case that achieving an optimal topology requires the contribution of other players and a certain deal of *compromise*. For instance, players might be required to accept higher costs, in order for their goals to become satisfied at all. As a result, finding optimal topologies amounts to finding the optimal compromises, the ones that are acceptable by each player. In other words, players act in a *highly strategic* manner.

Game theory offers a framework for analysing such strategic interactions. Therefore, one natural solution is to make use of game theoretic solution concepts for non-cooperative and cooperative games to analyse and to determine optimal topologies. This approach has already been followed by many researchers. We compare their work with ours in Section 5.

In the non-cooperative setting we model strictly selfish players which always prefer the topology awarding them the greatest utility. The first solution concept we study, the *Nash equilibrium*, describes ON optimality in terms of *individual* stability. The question we ask is whether a player will accept setting (some of) its channels given the set of channels set by all the other players.

We then turn to a stronger solution concept, the *strong Nash equilibrium*, to address *group deviations*. In contrast to the Nash equilibrium solution concept we ask whether a *group* can deviate to increase its payoff. The intuition is that players can partly communicate to find solutions in which *each* of the deviating group members is better off. This is quite a strong assumption and is relaxed by the last optimality concept we consider: the *core*.

The *core*, which is rather a cooperative concept, is used to examine group deviations which allows for the *transfer of utility* between players. In our opinion, this concept is more sensible than the strong Nash equilibrium: if players are already assumed to jointly deviate, why should they not be able to agree on a payoff division which is beneficial for all members? We would like to note that we are not concerned with the actual payoff distribution here. An ON which does not satisfy the requirements of the *core* describes an unstable network. The instability is caused by a group of (deviating) players which can achieve a strictly higher group utility than the sum of the utilities of each individual member in the ON. In this paper we are only considering whether such a group utility can be achieved and do not discuss the construction of a fair payoff distribution.

2.3   The Opportunistic Network Game

In Section 2.2 we motivated the use of game theory to give a characterisation of optimal ONs, that is, optimal topologies for an ONF. If we assume no cooperation between players, in particular no payoff distribution, the utility of a player is given by the value of its goal, if satisfied, minus the costs of the channels established by this very player. Formally, we have:

Definition 5 (Utility $u_i(\mathcal{O})$). *The utility of player i in the ON $\mathcal{O}$ is defined as*

$$u_i(\mathcal{O}) = \begin{cases} v(i) - cost_i(\mathcal{O}) & \text{if } \phi_i \text{ is satisfied in } \mathcal{O}, \\ -cost_i(\mathcal{O}) & \text{otherwise.} \end{cases}$$

We say that a player i (strictly) prefers $\mathcal{O}$ over $\mathcal{O}'$ iff $u_i(\mathcal{O}) > u_i(\mathcal{O}')$; then, we write $\mathcal{O} \succ_i \mathcal{O}'$. Analogously, we define $\succeq_i$ with respect to $\geq$. (We would like to note that in Section 4 we will be concrete about what "satisfaction" means wrt. to a specific language to express goals.)

The costs of a player depend on the channels it creates. From a game theoretic perspective these are the actions of the player, i.e. an action of a player is a *set* of transition/channels.

Definition 6 (Actions). *The $\mathcal{F}$-actions of player i in an ONF $\mathcal{F}$ are given by:* $Actions_i = 2^{\{i \xrightarrow{j} k \mid j \in \mathcal{P} \text{ and } k \in N(i)\}}$. *We define $Actions = \times_{i \in \mathcal{P}} Actions_i$. An element $a \in Actions$ is called $\mathcal{F}$-action profile. We omit $\mathcal{F}$ if clear from context.*

It is easy to see that each action tuple gives rise to an $\mathcal{F}$-topology and thus to an ON.

Definition 7 ($\mathcal{F}(a)$). *Given an $\mathcal{F}$-action profile $a = (a_1, \ldots, a_{|\mathcal{P}|})$ we use $\mathcal{F}(a)$ to refer to the ON $(\mathcal{F}, \mathcal{T})$ where $\mathcal{T} = (\mathcal{P}, (\bigcup_{i \in \mathcal{P}} a_i) \cup \{i \xrightarrow{i} i \mid i \in \mathcal{P}\}, Props, \mathcal{I})$.*

Now it is easy to see that for each ON $\mathcal{O} = (\mathcal{F}, \mathcal{T})$ there is an $\mathcal{F}$-action a such that $\mathcal{O} = \mathcal{F}(a)$ and vice versa. Hence, we define the utility for player i for an $\mathcal{F}$-action profile a as the utility of i in $\mathcal{F}(a)$:

$$(\star) \qquad u_i(a) := u_i(\mathcal{F}(a)).$$

We are ready to associate an ONF with a strategic game:

Definition 8 (Opportunistic Network Game). *Let $\mathcal{F}$ be an ONF. The $\mathcal{F}$-opportunistic network game (ONG), is given by the tuple $\mathcal{G}_{\mathcal{F}} = (\mathcal{F}, Actions, u)$ where:*

- *Actions is the set of $\mathcal{F}$-action profiles defined in Def. 6 and*
- *$u : \mathcal{P} \times Actions \rightarrow \mathbb{R}$ is the payoff function defined in $(\star)$.*

We do also lift the preference relations $\succ$ from Definition 5 to action profiles: $a \succ_i^{\mathcal{F}} a'$ iff $\mathcal{F}(a) \succ_i \mathcal{F}(a')$. Relation $\succeq_i^{\mathcal{F}}$ is defined analogously.

Example 4 (Simple ONG). The scenario from Example 1 formulated as an ONG $\mathcal{G}_{\mathcal{F}} = (\mathcal{F}, Actions, u)$ looks as follows:

- $\mathcal{F}$ is defined as in Example 1,
- $Actions_1 = 2^{\{1 \xrightarrow{j} 2, 1 \xrightarrow{j} 3 | j \in \mathcal{P}\}}$, $Actions_2 = 2^{\{2 \xrightarrow{j} 1, 2 \xrightarrow{j} 3, 2 \xrightarrow{j} 4 | j \in \mathcal{P}\}}$, $Actions_3 = 2^{\{3 \xrightarrow{j} 1, 3 \xrightarrow{j} 2, 3 \xrightarrow{j} 4 | j \in \mathcal{P}\}}$, $Actions_4 = 2^{\{4 \xrightarrow{j} 2, 4 \xrightarrow{j} 3 | j \in \mathcal{P}\}}$.
- The following action profile $a \in Actions$ results in the ON from Fig. 2:
  $a = (\{1 \xrightarrow{1} 3, 1 \xrightarrow{2} 3\}, \{2 \xrightarrow{2} 1\}, \{3 \xrightarrow{1} 4\})$. The utility of this action profile is given by: $u(1, a) = -2$, $u(2, a) = 2$, $u(3, a) = -1$ and $u(4, a) = 0$.

In the following section we discuss how we can use ONGs to find optimal ONs.

2.4 Optimal Solutions for Non-cooperative Players

In this section we discuss classic solution concepts of non-cooperative game theory. That is, players chose their actions independently from each other and no payoff division takes place.

Definition 9 (Nash equilibrium). *A Nash equilibrium of an ONG $\mathcal{G}$ is an action profile $a^* \in Actions$ such that, for each player $i \in \mathcal{P}$ and all actions $a_i \in Actions_i$ we have that $(a^*_{-i}, a^*_i) \succeq_i (a^*_{-i}, a_i)$.*

Intuitively, a Nash equilibrium is a stable action profile, i.e., given the actions of the other players, no player can deviate and increase its payoff.

Example 5 (Nash solution). We continue Example 4. First of all, notice that for Player 4 the cost of setting any channel to Player 3 is zero, therefore Player 4 has no incentive to deviate from the choice of setting (or not setting) such a channel, no matter what other players do. Additionally, Player 4 will not establish a channel to Player 2 because it would decrease its utility. Thus, we have two distinct scenarios: (i) Player 4's action contains $4 \xrightarrow{2} 3$ (which is convenient for Player 2) or (ii) Player 4's action is an arbitrary member of $O = 2^{\{4 \xrightarrow{i} 3 | i \in \{1,3,4\}\}}$.

The Nash equilibria of our example are given by $S_1 \cup \{NE_2\} \cup S_3$ where: $S_1 = \{(\emptyset, \{2 \xrightarrow{2} 3\}, \emptyset, X) \mid X \in O\}$, $NE_2 = (\emptyset, \{2 \xrightarrow{2} 4\}, \emptyset, \{4 \xrightarrow{2} 3\})$, and $S_3 = \{(\{1 \xrightarrow{1} 2, 1 \xrightarrow{2} 3\}, \{2 \xrightarrow{2} 1, 2 \xrightarrow{1} 4\}, \emptyset, X) \mid X \in O\}$. Let us refer to $(\{1 \xrightarrow{1} 2, 1 \xrightarrow{2} 3\}, \{2 \xrightarrow{2} 1, 2 \xrightarrow{1} 4\}), \emptyset, \emptyset)$ as NE_3. Figure 3 shows NE_2 and NE_3. To increase readability, we have omitted all propositions except Internet and VPN. If Player 4's choice is to set the channel $4 \xrightarrow{2} 3$, then Player 2 would prefer to set $2 \xrightarrow{2} 4$ thus satisfying its goal with utility 4 (which is maximal). This scenario emerging from NE_2 leaves Player 1 with its goal unsatisfied, however the player has no better alternative, given the actions of the other players.

In any Nash Equilibrium from S_1 and S_3, Player 4 takes no action helping player 2 to satisfy its goal. As a result, it may be the case that Player 2 sets the channel $2 \xrightarrow{2} 3$ to player 3, and thus satisfies its goal with utility 1 (as is the case with all Nash Equilibria from S_1), or that Players 2 and 3 set channels one on behalf of each other (S_3).

We note that $(\{1 \xrightarrow{1} 2\}, \{2 \xrightarrow{1} 4, 2 \xrightarrow{2} 4\}, \{4 \xrightarrow{2} 3\})$ is *not* a Nash equilibrium but it offers a higher utility than any Nash equilibrium. In Example 8 we will see that this profile is contained in the core of the same game.

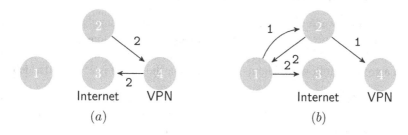

Fig. 3. Figure (a) shows Nash Equilibrium NE_2; and Figure (b) the Nash equilibrium NE_3. Again, we omit the reflexive edges in the interpretation as ON, cf. Definition 7.

It is easy to see that players may not behave very cooperative in the case of Nash equilibria. If a player's goal cannot be satisfied, the player has no incentive to establish any non-cost free channels:

Proposition 2. *Suppose a^* is a Nash equilibrium such that player i's goal is not satisfied in $\mathcal{F}(a^*)$; then for all communication channels $i \xrightarrow{j} k \in a_i^*$ the following is true:* $c(i, k) = 0$.

Proposition 2 captures the intuition that players are not expected to exhibit altruism. If it was the case that $c(i, k) > 0$, for some channel $i \xrightarrow{j} k$, then player i would be better of by not setting such a channel, and therefore a^* is not a Nash equilibrium.

Definition 10 (Strong Nash equilibrium). *A strong Nash equilibrium of an ONG $\mathcal{G}$ is an action profile $a^* \in \mathcal{A}ctions$ such that, for each coalition $C \subseteq \mathcal{P}$ and all actions $a_C \in \times_{i \in C} \mathcal{A}ctions_i$ we have that $(a_{-C}^*, a_C^*) \succeq_i (a_{-C}^*, a_C)$ for all $i \in C$.*

The strong Nash equilibrium a^* is a Nash equilibrium where no coalition can be formed that can cooperatively deviate from the action profile such that *all* of the members of the coalition get a payoff at least as high as in a^* and at least one deviating player gets a strictly better payoff. The difference between a Nash and a strong Nash equilibrium is that in order to ensure the property, in the latter case we have to take all possible coalition deviations into account while for the former only single player deviations have to be considered. This means that strong Nash equilibria are more stable then Nash equilibria but also more restrictive. Concerning the ONG a drawback of the (strong) Nash equilibrium is that as soon as a player's goal is not satisfied it only executes actions without negative costs, i.e., the player becomes passive. This is a direct consequence of Proposition 2.

Example 6 (Strong Nash equilibrium). There is a unique strong Nash Equilibrium in the previous example: $\text{NE}_2 = (\emptyset, \{2 \xrightarrow{2} 3\}, \emptyset, \{4 \xrightarrow{2} 3\})$. The Nash Equilibria from S_1 and S_3 are not strong, since the coalition $C = \{2, 4\}$ will always prefer the action profile $(\emptyset, \{2 \xrightarrow{2} 3\}, \emptyset, \{4 \xrightarrow{2} 3\})$.

2.5   Optimal Solutions for Cooperative Players

From Proposition 2 we know that a player does not establish channels with costs greater than 0 if its goal is not satisfied (given the other players' actions). What if players cooperate and are allowed to transfer utility, to set up side payments? We define the utility of a group as follows (without explaining *how* the payoff is actually divided).

Definition 11 (Group utility). *Let $X \subseteq \mathcal{P}$ be a group of players and $\mathcal{O}$ be an ON. We define $u_X(\mathcal{O}) = \sum_{i \in X} u_i(\mathcal{O})$. As before we define the group utility of action profiles $a \in \text{Actions}$ as $u_X(a) = u_X(\mathcal{F}(a))$. Similarly, we also lift the preference relations $\succ_i$ $\succeq_i$ to groups of players, $\succ_X$ and $\succeq_X$, respectively.*

Example 7 (Group utility). The group utility of the ON shown in Fig. 3(b) is: $u(\mathcal{O}) = u(1, a) + u(2, a) + u(3, a) + u(4, a) = (10 - 4) + (5 - 4) + 0 + 0 = 7$ where $a = (\{1 \xrightarrow{1} 2, 1 \xrightarrow{2} 3\}, \{2 \xrightarrow{2} 1, 2 \xrightarrow{1} 4\}, \emptyset, \emptyset)$. Similarly, the group utility of the ON shown in Fig. 3(a) is 4.

Finally, we lift the strong Nash equilibrium concept to the setting in which players can transfer payoff. Now, a player may establish channels even if its goal is *not* satisfied.

Definition 12 (Core). *The core of an ONG consists of the set of all action profiles a such that there is no coalition $X \subseteq \mathcal{P}$ and no action profile a' which agrees with a for all players $\mathcal{P} \setminus X$ such that $a' \succ_X a$.*

Example 8 (Core). We continue Example 7. The action profile $(\{1 \xrightarrow{1} 2\}, \{2 \xrightarrow{1} 4, 2 \xrightarrow{2} 4\}, \{4 \xrightarrow{2} 3\})$ yields a utility of $11 = (10 - 3) + (5 - 1) + 0$ and is the only member of the core.

Intuitively, the core provides the best topology $\mathcal{T}$ in $\mathcal{T}ops(\mathcal{G})$ regarding the (social) payoff of all players.

3   Computational Setting

In the following, we introduce the temporal logic **CTL** for expressing players' goals in an ON.

3.1 Preferences as Temporal Formulae

In this section we define a goal of an player to be expressed as a **CTL**-formula. In the following, we review the syntax and semantics of the logic.

The *language of* **CTL** [2] is given by all formulae generated by the grammar:

$$\varphi ::= \mathsf{p} \mid \neg\varphi \mid \varphi \wedge \varphi \mid \mathsf{E}(\varphi\,\mathcal{U}\,\varphi) \mid \mathsf{E}\bigcirc\varphi \mid \mathsf{E}\square\varphi.$$

where $\mathsf{p} \in \mathit{Props}$ is a proposition. The Boolean connectives are given by their usual abbreviations. The basic temporal operators are $\mathcal{U}$ *(until)* and $\bigcirc$ *(in the next state)*. The path quantifier E *(there is a path)* allows to existentially quantify over possible system behaviors; that is, in our case, over communication paths. The dual universal path quantifier A *(for all paths)* and the additional temporal operators $\Diamond$ *(eventually)* and $\square$ *(always from now on)* can be defined as macros: $\Diamond\varphi \equiv \top\,\mathcal{U}\,\varphi$, $\mathsf{A}\bigcirc\varphi \equiv \neg\mathsf{E}\bigcirc\neg\varphi$, $\mathsf{A}\square\varphi \equiv \neg\mathsf{E}\Diamond\neg\varphi$, and $\mathsf{A}\varphi\,\mathcal{U}\,\psi \equiv \neg\mathsf{E}((\neg\psi)\,\mathcal{U}\,(\neg\varphi \wedge \neg\psi)) \wedge \neg\mathsf{E}\square\neg\psi$.

Example 9 (Goals). The goals of Example 1 can be expressed as **CTL**-formulae as follows: $\phi_1 = \mathsf{E}(\neg\mathsf{Internet}\,\mathcal{U}\,(\mathsf{VPN} \wedge \mathsf{A}\square\neg\mathsf{Internet}))$, $\phi_2 = \mathsf{E}\Diamond\mathsf{Internet}$, and $\phi_3 = \phi_4 = \top$. We would like to note that one could imagine other formalizations capturing the informal (and ambiguous) description of goal ϕ_1. Here, we actually express that no node with internet access is visited until VPN is true and then, that on all possible extensions it is not possible to visit a node with internet access via a channel established on behalf of player 1.

The standard semantics of **CTL** is defined over Kripke structures. Given a $\mathcal{F}$-topology $\mathcal{T}$ we simply ignore the labels and interpret the resulting structure as Kripke structure. This is done by adjusting the definition of a path.

Definition 13 (Communication path). *A communication path* $\lambda = i_0, i_1, \cdots \in \mathcal{P}^\omega$ *in* $\mathcal{T}$ *is an infinite sequence of players/nodes that are interconnected by channels; that is, for all* $j = 0, 1, 2, \ldots$, *there exists some* $k \in \mathcal{P}$ *(not necessary the same, for all* j*) such that* $i_j \xrightarrow{k} i_{j+1}$. *We use* $\lambda[j]$ *to denote the jth player* (i_j) *on path* λ *(starting from* $j = 0$*) and* $\lambda[j,\infty]$ *to denote the subpath of* λ *starting from* j *(i.e.* $\lambda[j,\infty] = \lambda[j]\lambda[j+1]\ldots$*). We write* $\Lambda(i)$ *to refer to the set of all paths that start with player* i.

Let $\mathcal{T}$ be a $\mathcal{F}$-topology and $i \in \mathcal{P}$ be a player/node in $\mathcal{T}$. The semantics of **CTL**-formulae is given by the satisfaction relation $\models^{\mathbf{CTL}}$ defined below:

$\mathcal{T}, i \models^{\mathbf{CTL}} \mathsf{p}$ iff $\mathsf{p} \in \mathcal{I}(i)$ and $\mathsf{p} \in \mathit{Props}$;

$\mathcal{T}, i \models^{\mathbf{CTL}} \neg\varphi$ iff $\mathcal{T}, i \not\models^{\mathbf{CTL}} \varphi$;

$\mathcal{T}, i \models^{\mathbf{CTL}} \varphi \wedge \psi$ iff $\mathcal{T}, i \models^{\mathbf{CTL}} \varphi$ and $\mathcal{T}, i \models^{\mathbf{CTL}} \psi$;

$\mathcal{T}, i \models^{\mathbf{CTL}} \mathsf{E}\bigcirc\varphi$ iff there is a path $\lambda \in \Lambda(i)$ such that $\mathcal{T}, \lambda[1] \models^{\mathbf{CTL}} \varphi$;

$\mathcal{T}, i \models^{\mathbf{CTL}} \mathsf{E}\square\varphi$ iff there is a path $\lambda \in \Lambda(i)$ such that $\mathcal{T}, \lambda[j] \models^{\mathbf{CTL}} \varphi$ for every $j \geq 0$;

$\mathcal{T}, i \models^{\mathbf{CTL}} \mathsf{E}\varphi\,\mathcal{U}\,\psi$ iff there is a path $\lambda \in \Lambda(i)$ such that $\mathcal{T}, \lambda[j] \models^{\mathbf{CTL}} \psi$ for some $j \geq 0$, and $\mathcal{T}, \lambda[k,\infty] \models^{\mathbf{CTL}} \varphi$ for all $0 \leq k < j$.

Finally, we define the satisfaction of goals in an ON. The idea is that player i's goal is satisfied if the underlying topology in which only channels intended for i are considered satisfies its goal. We also note that the goal formula is interpreted in a communication path starting from player i. (Note that the definition of satisfaction is also used within an ONG.)

Definition 14 (Satisfaction in ON). *Let $\mathcal{O} = (\mathcal{F}, \mathcal{T})$ be an ON. For a player $i \in \mathcal{P}$ we write $\mathcal{T}|_i$ to refer to the $\mathcal{F}$-topology in which each transition $(k, l, m) \in \rightarrow$ with $l \neq i$ is removed. The goal ϕ_i of player i is satisfied in $\mathcal{O}$, denoted by $\mathcal{O} \models \phi_i$, iff $\mathcal{T}|_i, i \models^{\textbf{CTL}} \phi_i$.*

In the following we give some examples to illustrate the usefulness of **CTL** for expressing goals. Subsequently, in Section 4 we show that **CTL** has good computational properties regarding ONs, cf. Proposition 3.

Example 10. Notice that goals ϕ_1 and ϕ_2 described in Example 9 are both satisfied in the topology $\mathcal{T}$ from Fig. 3 (b). $\mathcal{T}|_1, 1 \models^{\textbf{CTL}} \phi_1$ since there exists the communication path $\lambda = 1, 2, 4, 4, \ldots$ on which Internet is not true until (i) VPN is true and (ii) Internet can never be true (on any path) further on. Similarly, the communication path $\lambda = 2, 1, 3, 3, \ldots$ is a witness for $\mathcal{T}|_2, 2 \models^{\textbf{CTL}} \phi_2$. For illustration we consider a few other goals:

- A◇VPN requires that on all paths (set for player 1) VPN must be accessible. This is not true in Fig. 3(b), but is true if the channel $3 \xrightarrow{1} 4$ would have been established.
- E□(VPN ∨ E○Internet) expresses that on all paths from player 1 and at each hop-node, VPN is true or Internet is accessible via a direct neighbour. This goal is satisfied in $\mathcal{T}|_1$ if the path $\lambda = 1, 2, \ldots$ would exist in $\mathcal{T}|_1$.

4   Complexity of Finding Optimal Solutions

In the following we analyze the complexity of finding optimal opportunistic networks. Throughout this section we assume that we are given the ONF $\mathcal{F} = (\mathcal{P}, N, \mathcal{P}rops, c, \mathcal{I}, (\phi_i)_{i \in \mathcal{P}}, v)$ with goals given as **CTL**-formulae, the $\mathcal{F}$-topology $\mathcal{T}$ and that $\mathcal{O} = (\mathcal{F}, \mathcal{T})$ is an ON. Moreover, we use $\mathcal{G}_{\mathcal{F}}$ to refer to the $\mathcal{F}$-opportunistic network game.

Complexity results are always with respect to the size of the input. As input we take an ON or an ONF. We measure the size of both objects in terms of the number of players and the sum of the lengths of the goal formulae.

Definition 15 (Size). *We use $|\phi_i|$ to denote the length of the formula. The size of $\mathcal{O}$ and of $\mathcal{F}$ is defined as $|\mathcal{P}| + \sum_{i \in \mathcal{P}} |\phi_i|$ (i.e. the sizes are given by the number of players and the sum of the lengths of all goal formulae).*

We note that the number of transitions in $\mathcal{T}$ is polynomial in the number of players (more precisely, $\leq |\mathcal{P}|^3$, also cf. Proposition 1). This justifies that we base the size of the input solely on the number of players and lengths of the formulae.

Definition 16 (Optimal opportunistic networks). *Given an ON $\mathcal{O} = (\mathcal{F}, \mathcal{T})$ we say that $\mathcal{O}$ is Nash-optimal (resp. strong Nash-optimal, core-optimal) if the action profile $a \in \mathcal{A}ctions$ with $\mathcal{F}(a) = \mathcal{T}$ is a Nash equilibrium (resp. a strong Nash equilibrium, in the core) of the $\mathcal{F}$-opportunistic network game $\mathcal{G}_{\mathcal{F}}$.*

4.1   Verification of Optimal Solutions

The following result follows immediately from [2]:

Proposition 3 ([2]). *For any player $i \in \mathcal{P}$, checking whether $\mathcal{O} \models \phi_i$ is P-complete with respect to the size of $\mathcal{O}$.*

Now we turn to checking whether a given opportunistic network is Nash-optimal.

Proposition 4 (Checking Nash optimality). *Checking whether $\mathcal{O}$ is Nash-optimal is coNP-complete.*

Proof. Membership: We show that the complement is in NP. Let $\mathcal{O}$ be the given ON and let a be the action profile with $\mathcal{F}(a) = \mathcal{O}$. We guess a player and an action a_i of i, i.e. a set of channels. Let a' be the action profile a with ith action replaced by a_i. We then check whether $\mathcal{F}(a')$ is preferred by the current player to $\mathcal{O}$. If so, $\mathcal{O}$ is not Nash-optimal. By Proposition 3 the latter can be done in deterministic polynomial time.

Hardness: We reduce the *Minimum Cover Problem*[1] to the complement of our problem. Given a set S, the subsets $S_1, \ldots S_n \subseteq S$, and a value $m \leq n$, we introduce a propositional symbol $p_u \in Props$ exactly for each element $u \in S$. We note that $Props$ is finite as S is finite. For each subset S_k, we introduce a player i_k such that $p_u \in \mathcal{I}(i_k)$ iff $u \in S_k$. These players all have the same goal: $\top$. We define a special player i^* having as goal $\phi^* = \wedge_{p \in Props} \mathsf{E} \bigcirc p$ (this is a finite conjunction because $Props$ is finite). The player can establish a channel with all other players. $v(i^*)$ has value $m + 1$ and $c(i^*, i) = 1$, for all $i \neq i^*$. All other costs and values are set to zero. We denote by a the action profile in which each player sets no edge, and by $\mathcal{O}$ the resulting ON. Then, there is a covering of the universe U with m subsets from $S_1, \ldots S_n$ iff $\mathcal{O}$ is not Nash-optimal. Now we have: there is a covering of S iff i^* can satisfy its goal with positive utility (by setting channels to all players/elements in the covering) iff $\mathcal{O}$ is not Nash-optimal. □

The proof for the next proposition is done in the very same way with the only difference that one guesses a set of players and their actions (instead of a player and an action).

Proposition 5 (Checking strong Nash optimality). *Checking whether $\mathcal{O}$ is strong Nash-optimal is coNP-complete.*

Proposition 6 (Checking core optimality). *Checking whether $\mathcal{O}$ is core-optimal is coNP-complete.*

Proof. Membership: We show that non-membership is in NP. We guess a tuple (C, a'_C) where $C \subseteq \mathcal{P}$ is a set of players and $a'_C \in \times_{i \in C} Actions_i$ an action profile of C. Let a be the action profile with $\mathcal{F}(a) = \mathcal{O}$ and let a'' be a with C's actions replaced by a'_C, i.e. $a'' = (a_{-C}, a'_C)$. Now, we can construct $\mathcal{F}(a'')$ and check whether $a'' \succ^{\mathcal{F}}_C a$ in deterministic polynomial time. So, we have shown that the problem of core-optimality is in coNP. *Hardness*: The same construction as in the proof of Proposition 4 works. □

---

[1] Minimum cover [5] takes as input a finite set S and subsets $S_1, \ldots S_n$ of S as well as an integer $m \leq n$. The question is wether there are $S_{i_1}, \ldots, S_{i_m}$ such that $\bigcup_{j=1, \ldots m} S_{i_j} = S$. This is an NP-complete problem. Note that S_{i_j} and S_{i_k} may be equal for some $1 \leq j, k \leq m$.

4.2 Synthesis of Optimal Solutions

In the last section, we have shown that the *verification problems* are all coNP-complete. The *synthesis problem* refers to the problem of *constructing* an optimal solution and not to just checking wether we are given one. Formally, we are given an ONF $\mathcal{F}$, one of the three optimality concepts C (i.e. Nash, strong Nash, core) and would like to construct a $\mathcal{F}$-topology $\mathcal{T}$ such that $\mathcal{O} = (\mathcal{F}, \mathcal{T})$ is C-optimal.

Firstly, we introduce the associated *decision problem* to each of the three synthesis problems: Does there exist a $\mathcal{F}$-topology such that $\mathcal{O} = (\mathcal{F}, \mathcal{T})$ is C-optimal?

It is easy to see that the synthesis problem is at least as hard as the associated decision problem. Formally, we have the following result:

Theorem 1 (Synthesis problems). *Let $\mathcal{F}$ be an ONF. The decision problem whether there is a $\mathcal{F}$-topology $\mathcal{T}$ such that $(\mathcal{F}, \mathcal{T})$ is Nash-optimal (resp. strong Nash-optimal, core-optimal) is in Σ_2^P.*

Moreover, if such a $\mathcal{F}$-topology $\mathcal{T}$ exists it can be synthesized by a non-deterministic Turing machine which runs in polynomial time and which has access to a NP-oracle.

Proof. We show that all decision problems are in Σ_2^P: We guess a $\mathcal{F}$-topology in non-deterministic polynomial time and check whether it is optimal wrt. one of the three optimality notions (cf. Propositions 3-5). This shows that the problem is in $\mathrm{NP}^{\mathrm{coNP}} = \mathrm{NP}^{\mathrm{NP}} = \Sigma_2^P$. Now it is also obvious that the synthesis problem can be implemented by a non-deterministic Turing machine which runs in polynomial time and which has access to an NP-oracle.   □

Finally, we also claim hardness for the decision problems:

Claim. : The decision problem whether there is a $\mathcal{F}$-topology $\mathcal{T}$ such that $(\mathcal{F}, \mathcal{T})$ is Nash-optimal (resp. strong Nash-optimal, core-optimal) is Σ_2^P-complete.

Remark 3 (Discussion on the complexity). The complexity results justify our choice of **CTL** to express goals. The verification problem is only P-complete and the expressiveness of the language is still sufficient to express interesting properties. Richer languages like **CTL*** and **LTL** do already have a $PSPACE$-complete model checking problem. Also the complexities of the optimality checks and decision problems are in line with complexity results for finding Nash equilibria etc. in strategic games and one cannot hope for better worst-case complexity results [6]. (Note that in our setting the number of actions is exponential in the size of an opportunistic network frame $\mathcal{F}$.)

5 Related Work

In this section we discuss related work. In [13] routing and forwarding protocols in wireless ad-hoc networks are considered. Similar to our approach, strategic games are used as models. The authors show that there is no forwarding-dominant protocol and propose cooperation-optimal protocols as solution for non-cooperative selfish players. Similarly, the authors in [4] analyze Nash equilibria of packet forwarding strategies in a fixed network topology. Unlike other existing game-theoretic approaches, which are aimed at describing how communication can be established in ad-hoc (or opportunistic) networks, our work is not focused on defining routing schemes or forwarding strategies. We consider such information to be known: the neighbourhood function N describes all possible channels, and the cost function may encapsulate measurable channel parameters such as throughput, required emitting power, etc.

Our method is focused on taking player preferences into account, when establishing routes in any particular type of ad-hoc network. As already seen, using languages such as **CTL**, players have the ability to enforce certain restrictions on how messages should be forwarded. Depending on the particular network at hand, our framework can be used as a standalone tool for establishing a communication network, or as a complement to existing routing and forwarding strategies which can now be defined on top of our established (optimal) topologies.

The impact of offloading mobile data traffic from 3G networks is discussed in [7] and efficient algorithms are proposed. Next, in [9] the routing problem in a delay-tolerant network with path failures is considered. The authors introduce a framework for studying the effectiveness of sending the same message over different paths in order to maximise the delivery rate. In this approach, the expected failure of a path is governed by a certain probability distribution. The work from [8] extends this setting. Path failures are replaced by a mobility model, which takes into account the players' social relationships, and assigns metrics such as *popularity ranking* or *centrality* (the importance of a node in a metric). Using this mobility model, routing performance and efficiency are improved [8]. An alternative approach, based on a Markovian model of mobility, is discussed in [1].

Quality of service (QoS) is considered in [11], from the perspective of individual selfishness: players may often be reluctant to participate in an opportunistic network, either for personal security issues, or for avoiding the consumption of battery power or computational resources. The model from [11] uses competitive markets in order to enforce optimal player QoS in an opportunistic network.

The results from [8,11,7] show that the behaviour of an opportunistic network is heavily dependent on the human factor. The algorithms from [8] exploit social structures within a community, whereas [11] exploits the idea of a self-interested player which is willing to compromise, in order to achieve some benefit (QoS). It is expected that humans' involvement in the way communication occurs in an opportunistic network will increase, and the player's choice in the way messages are routed will be equally important as other performance factors.

Differently to [8,1], our modeling approach does not attempt to build a mobility model. We rather assume that the set of locations which are reachable by a player are known. As a result, our setting relies on existing methods such as [1,9], for detecting these locations (or selecting the most likely reachable ones).

6 Conclusions

As opportunistic networks become more popular, players would like to have more control over the way their messages are delivered to the destination. As a result, routing methods that maximise delivery should also be complemented by preference-based routing mechanisms. Our approach exploits the *expressiveness of* **CTL** for formulating routing preferences, and uses standard game-theoretic tools in order to characterize *stable/optimal topologies*. The solution concepts we study explore different sides of stability: against individual deviation and group deviation. For the latter, we also consider the case when groups might decide to exchange payoff.

Future work: A distinctive feature of our setting, is that it captures a snapshot of the evolution of an opportunistic network: the number of players, and the way they can communicate is fixed. It would be interesting to see how a dynamically changing set of players affect the stability, and also whether computing new equilibria/network topologies can make use of previously computed ones. Currently, goals are evaluated with respect to the player's position and can only express properties of the player's message deliver path. It would be interesting to explore games in which this restriction is removed, and thus giving players the ability to specify properties of other player's message delivery paths; that is, a player's preferences can take into account other players' communication. Finally, it is important to consider the implementation of our solution concepts, and to assess the impact they have, both in terms of computational complexity and practical use.

Acknowledgements. The work has been funded by the Sectoral Operational Programme Human Resources Development 2007-2013 of the Romanian Ministry of Labour, Family and Social Protection through the Financial Agreement POSDRU/88/1.5/S/61178 and by the NTH Focused Research School for IT Ecosystems. NTH (Niedersächsische Technische Hochschule) is a joint university consisting of Technische Universität Braunschweig, Technische Universität Clausthal, and Leibniz Universität Hannover.

References

1. Becchetti, L., Clementi, A.E.F., Pasquale, F., Resta, G., Santi, P., Silvestri, R.: Information spreading in opportunistic networks is fast. CoRR abs/1107.5241 (2011)
2. Clarke, E., Emerson, E.: Design and Synthesis of Synchronization Skeletons Using Branching Time Temporal Logic. In: Engeler, E. (ed.) Logic of Programs 1979. LNCS, vol. 125, pp. 52–71. Springer, Heidelberg (1981)
3. Fall, K.: A delay-tolerant network architecture for challenged internets. In: Proceedings of the 2003 Conference on Applications, Technologies, Architectures, and Protocols for Computer Communications, SIGCOMM 2003, pp. 27–34. ACM, New York (2003), http://doi.acm.org/10.1145/863955.863960
4. Felegyhazi, M., Hubaux, J.P., Buttyan, L.: Nash equilibria of packet forwarding strategies in wireless ad hoc networks. IEEE Transactions on Mobile Computing 5(5), 463–476 (2006), http://dx.doi.org/10.1109/TMC.2006.68
5. Garey, M.R., Johnson, D.S.: Computers and Intractability: A Guide to the Theory of NP-completeness. W. H. Freeman, San Francisco (1979)
6. Gottlob, G., Greco, G., Scarcello, F.: Pure nash equilibria: hard and easy games. Journal of Artificial Intelligence Research, 215–230 (2003)
7. Han, B., Hui, P., Kumar, V.A., Marathe, M.V., Shao, J., Srinivasan, A.: Mobile data offloading through opportunistic communications and social participation. IEEE Transactions on Mobile Computing 99 (PrePrints) (2011)

8. Hui, P., Crowcroft, J., Yoneki, E.: Bubble rap: social-based forwarding in delay toler-ant networks. In: Proceedings of the 9th ACM International Symposium on Mobile ad Hoc Networking and Computing, MobiHoc 2008, pp. 241–250. ACM, New York (2008), http://doi.acm.org/10.1145/1374618.1374652

9. Jain, S., Demmer, M., Patra, R., Fall, K.: Using redundancy to cope with failures in a delay tolerant network. SIGCOMM Comput. Commun. Rev. 35, 109–120 (2005), http://doi.acm.org/10.1145/1090191.1080106

10. Lilien, L., Kamal, Z., Bhuse, V., Gupta, A.: The concept of opportunistic networks and their research challenges in privacy and security. In: Makki, S., Reiher, P., Makki, K., Pissinou, N., Makki, S. (eds.) Mobile and Wireless Network Security and Privacy, pp. 85–117. Springer US (2007), http://dx.doi.org/10.1007/978-0-387-71058-7_5

11. Pal, R., Kosta, S., Hui, P.: Settling for less – a qos compromise mechanism for opportunistic mobile networks. In: Proceeding of the Thirteenth Workshop on MAthematical Performance Modeling and Analysis, MAMA (2011)

12. Pelusi, L., Passarella, A., Conti, M.: Opportunistic Networking: Data Forwarding in Discon-nected Mobile Ad Hoc Networks. IEEE Communications Magazine 44(11), 134–141 (2006), http://dx.doi.org/10.1109/MCOM.2006.248176

13. Zhong, S., Li, L.E., Liu, Y.G., Yang, Y.R.: On designing incentive-compatible rout-ing and forwarding protocols in wireless ad-hoc networks: an integrated approach us-ing game theoretic and cryptographic techniques. Wirel. Netw. 13(6), 799–816 (2007), http://dx.doi.org/10.1007/s11276-006-9855-1

MKNF Knowledge Bases in Multi-Context Systems

Martin Homola[1], Matthias Knorr[2], João Leite[2], and Martin Slota[2]

[1] Faculty of Mathematics, Physics and Informatics, Comenius University
[2] CENTRIA & Departamento de Informática, Universidade Nova de Lisboa

Abstract. In this paper we investigate the relationship between Multi-Context Systems and Hybrid MKNF Knowledge Bases. Multi-Context Systems provide an effective and modular way to integrate knowledge from different heterogeneous sources (contexts) through so-called bridge rules. Hybrid MKNF Knowledge Bases, based on the logic of minimal knowledge and negation as failure (MKNF), allow for a seamless combination of description logic ontology languages with non-monotonic logic programming rules. In this paper, we not only show that Hybrid MKNF Knowledge Bases can be used as particular contexts in Multi-Context Systems, but we also provide transformations from the former into the latter, without the need for an explicit Hybrid MKNF context, hence providing a way for agents to reason with Hybrid MKNF Knowledge Bases within Multi-Context Systems without the need for specialized Hybrid MKNF reasoners.

1   Introduction

In *Open Multi-Agent Systems*, interaction and cooperation is increasingly being governed by *institutions* that regulate agents' behaviour and promote desirable properties. In such systems, it is crucial for agents and institutions to make sense of knowledge obtained from different sources, not only to increase the chance of individually making the right choice, but also to potentiate the chance of agreement in negotiations.

These sources of knowledge include the increasing number of available ontologies and rule sets, to a large extent developed within initiatives such as Semantic Web and Linked Open Data, as well as the norms and policies published by the *institutions*, the information communicated by other agents, to name only a few. With such diverse sources of knowledge to deal with, agent developers have turned their attention to Multi-Context Systems (MCS) [7,8,4,5,16,17]. Within MCSs, knowledge is modularly composed of contexts, each of which possibly encapsulating a source of knowledge of a different type, while bridge rules provide effective means for integration [12,11]. With the equilibria semantics of Brewka and Eiter [6], MCSs provide an effective and modular way to integrate knowledge from different heterogeneous sources, for example, different ontologies written in some Description Logic based ontology language, such as OWL, a rule set written in Answer-Set Programming representing some business policies, or some facts written in propositional logic representing the agent's model of some other agent, to name only a few. MCSs are simple enough to allow this heterogeneous knowledge to be bridged and integrated, while keeping their distinct provenance.

M. Fisher et al. (Eds.): CLIMA XIII 2012, LNAI 7486, pp. 146–162, 2012.
© Springer-Verlag Berlin Heidelberg 2012

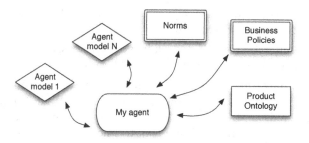

Fig. 1. Schematic depiction of a MCS representing agent's view of the system

For example, consider an open multi-agent system in which agents participate in online trading. In such a system, an agent may need to represent knowledge and reason about an ontology of products that can be purchased, models of the other existing agents (e.g. their perceived intentions based on communicated information and observed behaviour), its own business policies as well as those of the system in which it is integrated, together with existing norms. Such a system can be modelled as MCS, as depicted in Fig. 1. In such an MCS, ontologies can be modelled with DL contexts, the business policies and norms could be modelled with rule-based contexts, e.g., using logic programs, and other agents with separate contexts using propositional facts or additional rules in a more complex case. To propagate logical consequences across contexts, contexts are connected with bridge rules, illustrated by arrows in Fig. 1.

Recently, it has been shown in [2,1] that realistic norms and policies that mimic the real world require a more complex knowledge representation formalism, such as Hybrid MKNF [15] – based on the Logic of Minimal Knowledge and Negation as Failure (MKNF) [14] – that tightly combines Logic Programming (LP) and Description Logic (DL). In such scenarios, the Closed-World Assumption provided by LP rules is used e.g. to deal with defeasible knowledge, such as exceptions, while the Open-World Assumption provided by DL axioms is employed e.g. to deal with ontological knowledge and features such as reasoning with unknown individuals.

If norms and policies are to be published in such a language, it is crucial to relate them to MCSs, so that agent's imbued with the ability to deal with MCSs can also reason with them.

To this purpose, in this technical paper we investigate the relationship between MCSs and Hybrid MKNF. Taking the two-valued semantics of Hybrid MKNF [15], which is based on the Stable Model Semantics [9], we provide transformations from Hybrid MKNF into MCSs without the need for an explicit Hybrid MKNF context. This provides a way for agents to reason with Knowledge Bases written in Hybrid MKNF within MCSs, with additional contexts and bridge rules, *without the need for specialized Hybrid MKNF reasoners*.

The main contributions of this paper are three distinct ways to deal with MKNF Knowledge bases within MCSs, namely by:

– using Hybrid MKNF in the form of an MKNF context, which can then be bridged to other contexts;

- translating each Hybrid MKNF context into a First-Order context together with additional *non-monotonic* bridge rules;
- translating each Hybrid MKNF context into two contexts, a DL context and a fact base context, together with *non-monotonic* bridge rules.

The remainder of this paper is structured as follows: in Sect. 2, we review Description Logics, Logic Programs, Multi-Context Systems, and MKNF Knowledge Bases. In Sect. 3, we introduce MKNF contexts, present the two transformations into other kinds of contexts, and illustrate their use with fragments of the running example. We conclude in Sect. 4 and point to future directions.

2   Preliminaries

2.1   Description Logics

We first briefly summarise the syntax and semantics of standard function-free first-order logic with equality which forms the basis for representing both ontological and rule-based knowledge.

We assume the standard syntax of first-order *atoms, formulas* and *sentences*, defined inductively over disjoint sets of *constant* and *predicate symbols* $\mathbf{C}$ and $\mathbf{P}$. A first-order formula is *ground* if it contains no variables. The set of all first-order sentences is denoted by Φ. A *first-order theory* is a set of first-order sentences.

The satisfaction of a first-order sentence ϕ in a standard first-order interpretation I is denoted by $I \models \phi$; we also say that I is a *model of* ϕ if $I \models \phi$.

Description Logics (DLs) [3] are fragments of first-order logic whose reasoning tasks are usually decidable. Throughout the paper we assume that some first-order fragment is used to describe an *ontology*, i.e. to specify a shared conceptualisation of a domain of interest. Unless stated otherwise, we do not constrain ourselves to a specific DL for representing ontologies. The only assumption taken in the theoretical developments is that the ontology language is a syntactic variant of a fragment of first-order logic, covering also cases when this fragment would normally not be considered a DL. We assume that for any ontology axiom ϕ and ontology $\mathcal{O}$, $\kappa(\phi)$ and $\kappa(\mathcal{O})$ denote a first-order sentence that semantically correspond to ϕ and $\mathcal{O}$, respectively. Such translations are known for most DLs [3]. Given a first-order sentence ϕ, we say that an ontology $\mathcal{O}$ *entails* ϕ, denoted by $\mathcal{O} \models \phi$, if and only if every first-order model of $\kappa(\mathcal{O})$ is also a first-order model of ϕ.

2.2   Logic Programs

Like Description Logics, Logic Programming has its roots in classical first-order logic. However, logic programs diverge from first-order semantics by adopting the Closed World Assumption and allowing for non-monotonic inferences. In what follows, we introduce the syntax of extended normal logic programs and define the *stable models* [9] for such programs.

Syntactically, logic programs are built from *atoms* consisting of first-order atoms without equality. An *objective literal* is an atom p or its (strong) negation $\neg p$. We denote the set of all objective literals by $\mathbf{L}$ and the set of ground objective literals by $\mathbf{L_G}$. A *default literal* is an objective literal preceded by $\sim$ denoting *default negation*. A *literal* is either an objective literal or a default literal. Given a set of literals S, we introduce the following notation: $S^+ = \{\, l \in \mathbf{L} \mid l \in S \,\}$, $S^- = \{\, l \in \mathbf{L} \mid \sim l \in S \,\}$, $\sim S = \{\, \sim L \mid L \in S \,\}$.

A *rule* is a pair $\pi = (H(\pi), B(\pi))$ where $H(\pi)$ is an objective literal, referred to as *head of* π and $B(\pi)$ is a set of literals, referred to as *body of* π. Usually, for convenience, we write π as $(H(\pi) \leftarrow B(\pi)^+, \sim B(\pi)^-.)$ We also say that $B(\pi)^+$ is the *positive body of* π and $B(\pi)^-$ the *negative body of* π. A rule is called *ground* if it does not contain variables and *definite* if it does not contain any default literal. The *grounding* of a rule π is the set of rules $gr(\pi)$ obtained by replacing in π all variables with constant symbols from $\mathbf{C}$ in all possible ways. A *program* is a set of rules. A program is *ground* if all its rules are ground; *definite* if all its rules are definite. The grounding of a program $\mathcal{P}$ is defined as $gr(\mathcal{P}) = \bigcup_{\pi \in \mathcal{P}} gr(\pi)$.

The stable models of a program are determined by considering its first-order models in which all constant symbols are interpreted by themselves, and every ground atom p is interpreted separately of (though still consistently with) its strong negation $\neg p$. An interpretation thus corresponds to a subset of $\mathbf{L_G}$ that does not contain both p and $\neg p$ for any ground atom p and *models of programs* are determined by treating rules as classical implications. A stable model is then a model of the program that can be fully derived using rules of the program assuming that literals not present in it are false by default.[1]

Definition 1 (Stable Model). *Let $\mathcal{P}$ be a ground program. An interpretation J is a stable model of $\mathcal{P}$ if and only if J is a subset-minimal model of the reduct of $\mathcal{P}$ relative to J: $\mathcal{P}^J = \{\, H(\pi) \leftarrow B(\pi)^+. \mid \pi \in \mathcal{P} \wedge J \models \sim B(\pi)^- \,\}$.*

The stable models of a non-ground program $\mathcal{P}$ are the stable models of $gr(\mathcal{P})$. The set of all stable models of a program $\mathcal{P}$ is denoted by $[\![\mathcal{P}]\!]_{\mathsf{SM}}$.

2.3 Multi-Context Systems

Syntax of Multi-Context Systems. Following [6], a multi-context system consists of a collection of components, each of which contains knowledge represented in some logic. Abstractly, a *logic* is a triple $L = (\mathbf{KB}, \mathbf{BS}, \mathbf{ACC})$ where $\mathbf{KB}$ is the set of well-formed knowledge bases of L, $\mathbf{BS}$ is the set of possible belief sets[2] and $\mathbf{ACC}$: $\mathbf{KB} \to 2^{\mathbf{BS}}$ is a function describing the semantics of L by assigning to each knowledge base a set of acceptable belief sets.

In addition to the knowledge base in each component, *bridge rules* are used to interconnect the components, specifying what knowledge to assert in one component given certain beliefs held in the other components. Formally, for a collection of logics $L = \langle L_1, \ldots, L_n \rangle$, an L_i-*bridge rule* σ over L, $1 \leq i \leq n$, is of the form $(H(\sigma) \leftarrow B(\sigma).)$, where $B(\sigma)$ is a set of *bridge literals* of the forms $(r : p)$ and $\mathbf{not}\,(r : p)$ where $1 \leq r \leq n$ and p is an element of some belief set of L_r, and for each $kb \in \mathbf{KB}_i : kb \cup \{\, H(\sigma) \,\} \in \mathbf{KB}_i$.

---

[1] Note that, unlike in [10], we do not allow a program without a model to have a stable model.

[2] We assume that each element of $\mathbf{KB}$ and $\mathbf{BS}$ is a set.

Thus, putting these concepts together, a *multi-context system* (MCS) is a collection of contexts $M = \langle C_1, \ldots, C_n \rangle$ where $C_i = (L_i, kb_i, br_i)$, $L_i = (\mathbf{KB}_i, \mathbf{BS}_i, \mathbf{ACC}_i)$ is a logic, $kb_i \in \mathbf{KB}_i$ a knowledge base, and br_i is a set of L_i-bridge rules over $\langle L_1, \ldots, L_n \rangle$.

In the following we present the *grounded equilibria* semantics [6], which is motivated by the stable models semantics for logic programs.

Grounded Equilibria. Given an MCS $M = \langle C_1, \ldots, C_n \rangle$, a *belief state of M* is a sequence $S = \langle S_1, \ldots, S_n \rangle$ such that each S_i is an element of $\mathbf{BS}_i$. For every bridge literal $(r : p)$ we write $S \models (r : p)$ if $p \in S_r$ and $S \models \mathbf{not}\,(r : p)$ if $p \notin S_r$; for a set of bridge literals S, $S \models S$ if $S \models L$ for every $L \in S$.

A belief state $S = \langle S_1, \ldots, S_n \rangle$ of M is an *equilibrium* if, for all i with $1 \leq i \leq n$, the following condition holds:

$$S_i \in \mathbf{ACC}_i(kb_i \cup \{\, H(\sigma) \mid \sigma \in br_i \wedge S \models B(\sigma) \,\}) \ .$$

We say that an equilibrium S is *minimal* if there is no equilibrium $S' = \langle S'_1, \ldots, S'_n \rangle$ such that $S'_i \subseteq S_i$ for all i with $1 \leq i \leq n$ and $S'_j \subsetneq S_j$ for some j with $1 \leq j \leq n$.

Now we formalise the conditions under which the minimal equilibrium is *unique*, in which case we assign it as the *grounded equilibrium* of the MCS. This can be guaranteed if the contexts can be *reduced*, using a reduction function, to monotonic ones. Formally, a logic $L = (\mathbf{KB}, \mathbf{BS}, \mathbf{ACC})$ is *monotonic* if

1. $\mathbf{ACC}(kb)$ is a singleton set for each $kb \in \mathbf{KB}$, and

2. $S \subseteq S'$ whenever $kb \subseteq kb'$, $\mathbf{ACC}(kb) = \{S\}$ and $\mathbf{ACC}(kb') = \{S'\}$.

Furthermore, $L = (\mathbf{KB}, \mathbf{BS}, \mathbf{ACC})$ is *reducible* if

1. there is $\mathbf{KB}^* \subseteq \mathbf{KB}$ such that the restriction of L to $\mathbf{KB}^*$ is monotonic,

2. there is a reduction function $red : \mathbf{KB} \times \mathbf{BS} \to \mathbf{KB}^*$ such that for each $kb \in \mathbf{KB}$ and $S, S' \in \mathbf{BS}$:
   - $red(kb, S) = kb$ whenever $kb \in \mathbf{KB}^*$,
   - red is antimonotone in the second argument, that is $red(kb, S) \subseteq red(kb, S')$ whenever $S' \subseteq S$,
   - $S \in \mathbf{ACC}(kb)$ if and only if $\mathbf{ACC}(red(kb, S)) = \{S\}$.

A context $C = (L, kb, br)$ is *reducible* if its logic L is reducible and, for all $H \subseteq \{\, H(\sigma) \mid \sigma \in br \,\}$ and all belief sets S, $red(kb \cup H, S) = red(kb, S) \cup H$.

An MCS is *reducible* if all of its contexts are. Note that a context is reducible whenever its logic L is monotonic. In this case $\mathbf{KB}^*$ coincides with $\mathbf{KB}$ and red is identity with respect to the first argument. A reducible MCS $M = \langle C_1, \ldots, C_n \rangle$ is *definite* if

1. none of the bridge rules in any context contains $\mathbf{not}$,

2. for all i and all $S \in \mathbf{BS}_i$, $kb_i = red_i(kb_i, S)$.

In a definite MCS bridge rules are monotonic, and knowledge bases are already in reduced form. Inference is thus monotonic and a unique minimal equilibrium exists. We take this equilibrium to be the grounded equilibrium:

Definition 2 (Grounded Equilibrium of a Definite MCS). *Let* $M = \langle C_1, \ldots, C_n \rangle$ *be a definite MCS.* $S = \langle S_1, \ldots, S_n \rangle$ *is the* grounded equilibrium *of* M, *denoted by* $\mathbf{GE}(M)$, *if* S *is the unique minimal equilibrium of* M.

Grounded equilibria for general MCSs are defined based on a reduct which generalises the Gelfond-Lifschitz reduct to the multi-context case:

Definition 3 (Reduct of a Reducible MCS). *Let* $M = \langle C_1, \ldots, C_n \rangle$ *be a reducible MCS and* $S = \langle S_1, \ldots, S_n \rangle$ *a belief state of* M. *The* S-*reduct of* M *is*

$$M^S = \langle C_1^S, \ldots, C_n^S \rangle$$

where, for each $C_i = (L_i, kb_i, br_i)$, *we define* $C_i^S = (L_i, red_i(kb_i, S_i), br_i^S)$. *Here* br_i^S *results from* br_i *by deleting*

1. *every rule with some* **not** $(r : p)$ *in the body such that* $S \models (r : p)$, *and*
2. *all* **not** *literals from the bodies of remaining rules.*

For each MCS M and each belief set S, we have that the S-reduct of M is definite. We can thus check whether S is a grounded equilibrium in the usual manner:

Definition 4 (Grounded Equilibrium). *Let* $M = \langle C_1, \ldots, C_n \rangle$ *be a reducible MCS and* $S = \langle S_1, \ldots, S_n \rangle$ *a belief state of* M. S *is a* grounded equilibrium *of* M *if* S *is the grounded equilibrium of* M^S, *that is* $S = \mathbf{GE}(M^S)$.

For example, let us model a multi-agent system in which the agent b_1 aims to purchase product item i_1. For simplicity assume that there are only two agents, s_1 and s_2, offering products for sale. Agent s_1 readily offers i_1 for 30 credits and agent s_2 also currently offers i_1, but for 35 credits. Agent b_1 may model this by the following two contexts:

$$s_1 : \quad \mathsf{available}(i_1) \leftarrow . \qquad\qquad s_2 : \quad \mathsf{available}(i_1) \leftarrow .$$
$$\mathsf{price}(i_1, 30) \leftarrow . \qquad\qquad\qquad \mathsf{price}(i_1, 35) \leftarrow .$$

Agent b_1 represents its business rules as context b_1. First, it imports information from s_1 and s_2 using bridge rules:[3]

$$b_1 : \quad \mathsf{offers}(A, I, P) \leftarrow A : \mathsf{available}(I), A : \mathsf{price}(I, P).$$
$$\mathsf{best\_price}(I, X) \leftarrow s_1 : \mathsf{price}(I, X), s_2 : \mathsf{price}(I, Y), X \leq Y.$$
$$\mathsf{best\_price}(I, Y) \leftarrow s_1 : \mathsf{price}(I, X), s_2 : \mathsf{price}(I, Y), X > Y.$$

Finally, agent b_1 uses additional rules to implement its own business logic. For instance, it can be a good strategy to go for the best price unless there is a very good reason to buy from some other agent. This is implemented by adding the rule into b_1:

$$\mathsf{purchase}(I, A) \leftarrow \mathsf{offers}(A, I, P), \mathsf{best\_price}(I, P), {\sim}\mathsf{worth\_buy}(B). \qquad (1)$$

---

[3] A bridge rule with a variable (A) in place of the context identifier stands for the set of ground instances obtained by replacing A with context identifiers in all possible ways. The predicates $<, \leq$ and the function $+$ (meaning less, less or equal relations and addition on numeric domains) can be formalized in logic programming and we abstract from this for space reasons. Also, due to space reasons the computation of best price is slightly simplified given the case of two selling agents, which can be easily extended in case of multiple agents.

Indeed, sometimes it might be worth not to buy for the best price in the long term. If b_1 has long standing business relations with some supplier, it may be worth purchasing some items even for a slightly higher price assuming that later on it may be rewarded with a discount or other value. Hence assuming that s_2 is the valuable supplier we add the following rules into b_1:

$$\text{worth\_buy}(A) \leftarrow \text{best\_price}(I,P), \text{offers}(A,I,Q), \text{good\_supplier}(A), Q \leq P+5. \quad (2)$$
$$\text{purchase}(I,A) \leftarrow \text{offers}(A,I,P), \text{worth\_buy}(A). \quad (3)$$
$$\text{good\_supplier}(s_2) \leftarrow . \quad (4)$$

The MCS $M = \langle b_1, s_1, s_2 \rangle$ has a single grounded equilibrium $S = \langle B_1, S_1, S_2 \rangle$ such that $\text{purchase}(i_1, s_2) \in B_1$ and $\text{purchase}(i_1, s_1) \notin B_1$. So the agent actually reasons according to the business strategy that we described.

2.4 MKNF Knowledge Bases

MKNF Knowledge Bases [15] are based on the logic of Minimal Knowledge and Negation as Failure (MKNF) [14], an extension of first-order logic with two modal operators: $\mathbf{K}$ and $\mathbf{not}$. We use the variant of this logic introduced in [15]. *MKNF sentences* and *theories* are defined by extending function-free first-order syntax by the mentioned modal operators in a natural way.

As in [15], we assume that the set of constant symbols $\mathbf{C}$ is infinite and consider only *Herbrand interpretations* that interpret the equality predicate $\approx$ as a congruence relation on $\mathbf{C}$. The set of all such interpretations is denoted by $\mathbf{I}$. An *MKNF structure* is a triple $(I, \mathcal{M}, \mathcal{N})$ where $I \in \mathbf{I}$ and $\mathcal{M}, \mathcal{N} \subseteq \mathbf{I}$.[4] Intuitively, the first component is used to interpret the first-order parts of an MKNF sentence while the other two components interpret the $\mathbf{K}$ and $\mathbf{not}$ modalities, respectively. By $\phi[a/x]$ we denote the formula obtained from ϕ by replacing every unbound occurrence of variable x with the constant symbol a. The satisfaction of an MKNF sentence and an MKNF theory $\mathcal{T}$ in an MKNF structure $(I, \mathcal{M}, \mathcal{N})$ is defined as follows:

$$
\begin{aligned}
(I,\mathcal{M},\mathcal{N}) &\models p & &\text{iff} & &I \models p \\
(I,\mathcal{M},\mathcal{N}) &\models \neg\phi & &\text{iff} & &(I,\mathcal{M},\mathcal{N}) \not\models \phi \\
(I,\mathcal{M},\mathcal{N}) &\models \phi_1 \wedge \phi_2 & &\text{iff} & &(I,\mathcal{M},\mathcal{N}) \models \phi_1 \text{ and } (I,\mathcal{M},\mathcal{N}) \models \phi_2 \\
(I,\mathcal{M},\mathcal{N}) &\models \exists x : \phi & &\text{iff} & &(I,\mathcal{M},\mathcal{N}) \models \phi[a/x] \text{ for some } a \in \mathbf{C} \\
(I,\mathcal{M},\mathcal{N}) &\models \mathbf{K}\phi & &\text{iff} & &(J,\mathcal{M},\mathcal{N}) \models \phi \text{ for all } J \in \mathcal{M} \\
(I,\mathcal{M},\mathcal{N}) &\models \mathbf{not}\,\phi & &\text{iff} & &(J,\mathcal{M},\mathcal{N}) \not\models \phi \text{ for some } J \in \mathcal{N} \\
(I,\mathcal{M},\mathcal{N}) &\models \mathcal{T} & &\text{iff} & &(I,\mathcal{M},\mathcal{N}) \models \phi \text{ for all } \phi \in \mathcal{T}
\end{aligned}
$$

The symbols $\top$, $\bot$, $\vee$, $\forall$ and $\supset$ are interpreted accordingly. Also, for any $\mathcal{M} \subseteq \mathbf{I}$ we write $\mathcal{M} \models \mathcal{T}$ if $(I, \mathcal{M}, \mathcal{M}) \models \mathcal{T}$ for all $I \in \mathcal{M}$. An *MKNF interpretation* $\mathcal{M}$ is a

---

[4] Differently from [15], we allow for empty $\mathcal{M}, \mathcal{N}$ in this definition as later on it will be useful to have satisfaction defined for this marginal case.

non-empty subset of $\mathbf{I}$.[5] By $\mathbf{M} = 2^{\mathbf{I}}$ we denote the set of all MKNF interpretations together with the empty set. The semantics of MKNF theories is defined as follows:

Definition 5 (MKNF Semantics). *Let $\mathcal{T}$ be an MKNF theory. We say that an MKNF interpretation $\mathcal{M}$ is*

- *an S5 model of $\mathcal{T}$ if $\mathcal{M} \models \mathcal{T}$;*
- *an MKNF model of $\mathcal{T}$ if $\mathcal{M}$ is an S5 model of $\mathcal{T}$ and for every MKNF interpretation $\mathcal{M}' \supsetneq \mathcal{M}$ there is some $I' \in \mathcal{M}'$ such that $(I', \mathcal{M}', \mathcal{M}) \not\models \mathcal{T}$.*

MKNF knowledge bases [15] consist of two components – an ontology $\mathcal{O}$ and a program $\mathcal{P}$ – and their semantics is given by translation to an MKNF theory. In the following we introduce the syntax and semantics of MKNF knowledge bases in which we constrain the program component to a normal logic program.[6]

An *MKNF knowledge base* is a set $\mathcal{K} = \mathcal{O} \cup \mathcal{P}$ where $\mathcal{O}$ is an ontology and $\mathcal{P}$ is a logic program. An MKNF knowledge base is *ground* if $\mathcal{P}$ is ground; *definite* if $\mathcal{P}$ is definite. The grounding of an MKNF knowledge base $\mathcal{K}$ is defined as $\mathrm{gr}(\mathcal{K}) = \mathcal{O} \cup \mathrm{gr}(\mathcal{P})$.

The translation function κ is defined for all literals l, default literals $\sim l$, sets of literals S, rules π with vector of free variables x, programs $\mathcal{P}$ and MKNF knowledge bases $\mathcal{K} = \mathcal{O} \cup \mathcal{P}$ as follows: $\kappa(l) = \mathbf{K}\, l$, $\kappa(\sim l) = \mathbf{not}\, l$, $\kappa(S) = \bigwedge \{\, \kappa(L) \mid L \in S \,\}$, $\kappa(\pi) = (\kappa(B(\pi)) \supset \kappa(H(\pi)))$, $\kappa(\mathcal{P}) = \{\, \kappa(\pi) \mid \pi \in \mathcal{P} \,\}$, $\kappa(\mathcal{K}) = \{\, \kappa(\mathcal{O}) \,\} \cup \kappa(\mathcal{P})$.

The semantics of MKNF knowledge bases is thus defined as follows:

Definition 6 (Semantics of MKNF Knowledge Bases). *Let $\mathcal{K}$ be an MKNF knowledge base. We say that an MKNF interpretation $\mathcal{M}$ is an S5 model of $\mathcal{K}$ if $\mathcal{M}$ is an S5 model of $\kappa(\mathcal{K})$. Similarly, $\mathcal{M}$ is an MKNF model of $\mathcal{K}$ if $\mathcal{M}$ is an MKNF model of $\kappa(\mathcal{K})$.*

In the normative part of our running example, DL axioms could be used to classify different products depending on their availability on the market into available and unavailable, but also into products that can be directly purchased and special products for which licitation is required. Then, rules will be used to evaluate if a particular product can be purchased by some agent or not (e.g., normally the product can be purchased whenever it is available, but in the exceptional case when licitation is required additional conditions must be satisfied). Note that while DL axioms are required to encode the classification, non-monotonic rules are required to express exceptions. This can be encoded in the MKNF knowledge base n composed of the ontology $\mathcal{O}_n$ and the rule set $\mathcal{P}_n$:

---

[5] Notice that if $\mathcal{M}$ is empty, then it vacuously holds that $\mathcal{M} \models \phi$ for all sentences ϕ. For this reason, and in accordance with [15], $\emptyset$ is not considered an MKNF interpretation.

[6] Note that we do not directly include the $\mathbf{K}$ and $\mathbf{not}$ modalities in rules of the MKNF knowledge base; instead, they are introduced by the translation function κ (denoted by π in [15]) upon translation to an MKNF theory. Also, unlike in [15], κ is overridden to accept atoms, literals and sets of literals and produces an MKNF theory instead of an MKNF sentence. Thus we do not need to assume that the program is finite and can deal with infinite ground programs that result from grounding a finite but non-ground program (the same is actually done in [15] from Section 4 onwards).

$\mathcal{O}_n$: $\leqslant 0$ offered_by.supplier $\sqsubseteq$ unavailable_product

$\quad$ $=1$ offered_by.supplier $\sqsubseteq$ purchasable_product

$\quad$ $\geqslant 2$ offered_by.supplier $\sqsubseteq$ licitable_product

$\mathcal{P}_n$: purchase_allowed(I, A) $\leftarrow$ offered_by(I, A), $\sim$licitable_product(I)

$\quad$ purchase_allowed(I, A). $\leftarrow$ licitable_product(I), offered_by(I, A), best_price(I, A).

3   Reducing an MKNF Context

MKNF knowledge bases can be used within Multi-Context Systems by specifying an *MKNF context* that uses the *MKNF logic*. We formalise these notions below. Subsequently, we show that every MKNF context can be transformed into a *first-order context*. The transformed MCS has the same grounded equilibria as the original one, showing that instead of a specialised MKNF reasoner, a first-order reasoner can be used to obtain equivalent results. Subsequently, we show that this result can be strengthened even further, resulting in a multi-context system that requires only a DL reasoner instead of an MKNF reasoner provided all bridge literals referring to that context are expressible in the DL in consideration. In this case, a DL reasoner is basically all that is necessary to handle reasoning with MKNF contexts within a multi-context system.

3.1   MKNF Contexts and First-Order Contexts

We start by formalising what an *MKNF context* actually is. The *MKNF logic* is the logic $L_{\mathrm{MKNF}} = (\mathbf{KB}_{\mathrm{MKNF}}, \mathbf{BS}_{\mathrm{MKNF}}, \mathbf{ACC}_{\mathrm{MKNF}})$ where

- $\mathbf{KB}_{\mathrm{MKNF}}$ is the set of MKNF knowledge bases,
- $\mathbf{BS}_{\mathrm{MKNF}}$ is the set of deductively closed sets of first-order sentences,
- $\mathbf{ACC}_{\mathrm{MKNF}}(\mathcal{K})$ contains $\{\phi \in \Phi \mid \mathcal{M} \models \phi\}$ for every MKNF model $\mathcal{M}$ of $\mathcal{K}$ and also the inconsistent belief set Φ in case $\mathcal{K}'$, obtained from $\mathcal{K}$ by removing all rules with default negation, has no MKNF model.

The latter condition is required to adhere to the formal framework of multi-context systems. An *MKNF context* can now be established as follows:

Definition 7 (MKNF Context). *A context* $C = (L, kb, br)$ *is an* MKNF *context if* $L = L_{\mathrm{MKNF}}$, *kb is an MKNF knowledge base, and, for every* $\sigma \in br$, $H(\sigma)$ *is either an ontology axiom or a definite rule. We also say that such* σ *is an* MKNF *bridge rule.*

$\quad$ *An MKNF context* $C = (L_{\mathrm{MKNF}}, \mathcal{K}, br)$ *is ground if* $\mathcal{K}$ *is ground and all rules in heads of MKNF bridge rules from br are ground; finite if both* $\mathcal{K}$ *and br are finite.*

In order to talk about grounded equilibria of multi-context systems with MKNF contexts, their reducibility must be guaranteed. Given our definition above, this is indeed the case:

Proposition 8. *Every MKNF context is reducible.*

We are now able to plug the normative MKNF KB n into our example MCS using the bridge rule set br_n:

$$br_n : \mathsf{supplier}(A) \leftarrow A : \mathsf{available}(I).$$
$$\mathsf{offered\_by}(I, A) \leftarrow A : \mathsf{available}(I).$$
$$\mathsf{best\_price}(I, s_1) \leftarrow s_1 : \mathsf{price}(I, X), s_2 : \mathsf{price}(I, Y), X \leq Y.$$
$$\mathsf{best\_price}(I, s_2) \leftarrow s_1 : \mathsf{price}(I, X), s_2 : \mathsf{price}(I, Y), X > Y.$$

Agent b_1 is now required to reason with the norms. To implement this, the following bridge rule is added to b_1:

$$\mathsf{allowed}(I, A) \leftarrow n : \mathsf{purchase\_allowed}(I, A).$$

Additionally, the business rules (1) and (3) need to be altered (in the respective order):

$$\mathsf{purchase}(I, A) \leftarrow \mathsf{offers}(A, I, P), \mathsf{allowed}(I, A), \mathsf{best\_price}(I, P), \sim\!\mathsf{worth\_buy}(B). \quad (5)$$
$$\mathsf{purchase}(I, A) \leftarrow \mathsf{offers}(A, I, P), \mathsf{allowed}(I, A), \mathsf{worth\_buy}(A). \quad (6)$$

The agent will now take the norms into account during reasoning. The updated MCS $M^n = \langle b_1, s_1, s_2, n \rangle$ has a single grounded equilibrium $S^n = \langle B_1^n, S_1^n, S_2^n, N^n \rangle$, however, neither $\mathsf{purchase}(i_1, s_1)$ nor $\mathsf{purchase}(i_1, s_2)$ belong to B_1^n. Indeed the agent's business strategy is now in conflict with the norms, it cannot favour the valuable supplier any longer if there is a better momentary offer.

To fully accommodate the norms while keeping the agent operational, we would have to drop $\sim\!\mathsf{worth\_buy}(B)$ from the rule (5) and completely drop the rule (6) which is now obsolete, it represents an invalid strategy. Or if in turn we chose to ignore the norms (and bear eventual consequences) we might drop $\mathsf{allowed}(I, A)$ from both rules and return to the previous purchasing strategy.

To reduce an MKNF context to a simpler one, we define *first-order contexts*. The *first-order logic* is the logic $L_{\mathrm{FO}} = (\mathbf{KB}_{\mathrm{FO}}, \mathbf{BS}_{\mathrm{FO}}, \mathbf{ACC}_{\mathrm{FO}})$ where

– $\mathbf{KB}_{\mathrm{FO}}$ is the set of first-order theories,

– $\mathbf{BS}_{\mathrm{FO}}$ is the set of deductively closed sets of first-order sentences,

– $\mathbf{ACC}_{\mathrm{FO}}(\mathcal{T}) = \{ \phi \in \Phi \mid \mathcal{T} \models \phi \}$.

A *first-order context* is henceforth defined as follows:

Definition 9 (First-Order Context). *A context $C = (L, kb, br)$ is a* first-order context *if $L = L_{\mathrm{FO}}$, kb is a first-order theory, and, for every $\sigma \in br$, $H(\sigma)$ is a first-order sentence. We also say that such σ is a* first-order bridge rule.

The first-order logic is monotonic, so every first-order context is reducible.

Proposition 10. *Every first-order context is reducible.*

3.2 Reduction to a First-Order Context

We are now ready to introduce a transformation of an MKNF context to a corresponding first-order context. This transformation is based on transforming the rules from

the MKNF knowledge base to bridge rules, leaving us with only the ontology component which can already be handled by a first-order context. For example, if the MKNF
knowledge base in the MKNF context C_j contains the rule

$$p \leftarrow q, \sim r.$$

the corresponding first-order bridge rule is of the form

$$p \leftarrow (j : q), \mathbf{not}\, (j : r).$$

Furthermore, since bridge rules in an MKNF context may have definite rules in their
heads, we also need to transform them in some way so that the resulting bridge rules
are compatible with the first-order context. This is done by moving the body of the
definite rule π in the head of a bridge rule σ to the body of σ. For example, if the
MKNF context C_j contains the MKNF bridge rule

$$(p \leftarrow q.) \leftarrow (i_1 : q), \mathbf{not}\, (i_2 : r).$$

then the transformed first-order bridge rule will be

$$p \leftarrow (j : q), (i_1 : q), \mathbf{not}\, (i_2 : r).$$

In case of MKNF bridge rules that have an ontology axiom ϕ in their head, this axiom
needs to be translated to its first-order counterpart $\kappa(\phi)$. For all ground rules these
transformations can be formalised as follows:

Definition 11 (Transformation to First-Order Bridge Rules). *Let j be an integer.
We introduce the following notation for every $l \in \mathbf{L_G}$ and $S \subseteq \mathbf{L_G}$: $\beta_j(l) = (j : l)$,
$\beta_j(\sim l) = \mathbf{not}\, (j : l)$, $\beta_j(S) = \{ \beta_j(L) \mid L \in S \}$.*
*Let $C = (L_{\mathrm{MKNF}}, \mathcal{O} \cup \mathcal{P}, br)$ be a ground MKNF context. For every rule $\pi \in \mathcal{P}$,
$\beta_j(\pi)$ denotes the first-order bridge rule*

$$H(\pi) \leftarrow \beta_j(B(\pi)).$$

*Furthermore, for every MKNF bridge rule $\sigma \in br$ of the form $(\pi \leftarrow B(\sigma).)$, where π
is a definite rule, $\beta_j(\sigma)$ denotes the first-order bridge rule*

$$H(\pi) \leftarrow \beta_j(B(\pi)) \cup B(\sigma).$$

*and for every MKNF bridge rule $\sigma \in br$ of the form $(\phi \leftarrow B(\sigma).)$, where ϕ is an
ontology axiom, $\beta_j(\sigma)$ denotes the first-order bridge rule*

$$\kappa(\phi) \leftarrow B(\sigma).$$

Also, for any set of rules or MKNF bridge rules S, $\beta_j(S) = \{ \beta_j(\pi) \mid \pi \in S \}$.

The definition of the first-order context that corresponds to an MKNF context is now
straightforward – it suffices to apply the above transformation β_j to all rules and MKNF
bridge rules of the MKNF context:

Definition 12 (First-Order Context Corresponding to MKNF Context). *Let* $C_j = (L_{\text{MKNF}}, \mathcal{O} \cup \mathcal{P}, br_j)$ *be a ground MKNF context. The* first-order context corresponding *to* C_j *is* $C_j^{\text{FO}} = (L_{\text{FO}}, \{\kappa(\mathcal{O})\}, \beta_j(br_j) \cup \beta_j(\mathcal{P}))$.

Due to the properties of the MKNF semantics, when we consider a finite ground MKNF context, which is usually the most interesting case in applications, we find that it can be substituted by the corresponding first-order context without affecting the grounded equilibria of the multi-context system. Formally:

Theorem 13 (Reduction Into First-Order Context). *Let* $M = \langle C_1, \ldots, C_n \rangle$ *be a multi-context system such that for some j with $1 \leq j \leq n$, C_j is a finite ground MKNF context and put*

$$M' = \langle C_1, \ldots, C_{j-1}, C_j^{\text{FO}}, C_{j+1}, \ldots, C_n \rangle \ .$$

The grounded equilibria of M and M' coincide.

This transformation can be repeated for all MKNF contexts in the multi-context system, yielding an equivalent system that does not require to use the MKNF logic. Formally:

Corollary 14. *For every multi-context system M with some finite ground MKNF contexts there exists a multi-context system M' such that the grounded equilibria of M and M' coincide and M' uses first-order contexts instead of the original MKNF contexts.*

Revisiting our running example, the MCS M^n is reduced into $M^{n'} = \langle b_1, s_1, s_2, n^{\text{FO}} \rangle$ where $n^{\text{FO}} = (L_{\text{FO}}, \{\kappa(\mathcal{O}_n)\}, \beta_n(br_n) \cup \beta_n(\mathcal{P}_n))$:

$\kappa(\mathcal{O}_n):$ $\forall X \forall Y \neg\text{offered\_by}(X, Y) \vee \neg\text{supplier}(Y) \implies \text{unavailable\_product}(X)$

$\forall X \exists Y \text{offered\_by}(X, Y) \wedge \text{supplier}(Y) \wedge (\forall Z(Z = Y) \vee \neg\text{offered\_by}(X, Z)$

$\vee \neg\text{supplier}(Z)) \implies \text{purchasable\_product}(X)$

$\forall X \exists Y \exists Z(Y \neq Z) \wedge \text{offered\_by}(X, Y) \wedge \text{supplier}(Y) \wedge \text{offered\_by}(X, Z)$

$\wedge \text{supplier}(Z) \implies \text{licitable\_product}(X)$

$\beta_n(\mathcal{P}_n):$ $\text{purchase\_allowed}(I, A) \leftarrow n : \text{offered\_by}(I, A), \textbf{not}\ (n : \text{licitable\_product}(I)).$

$\text{purchase\_allowed}(I, A) \leftarrow n : \text{licitable\_product}(I), n : \text{offered\_by}(I, A),$

$n : \text{best\_price}(I, A).$

and $\beta_n(br_n) = br_n$.

3.3 Translation Into Two Contexts

To be able to translate an MKNF context into a *DL context* we need to define DL contexts first. The *DL logic* is the logic $L_{\text{DL}} = (\textbf{KB}_{\text{DL}}, \textbf{BS}_{\text{DL}}, \textbf{ACC}_{\text{DL}})$ where

- $\textbf{KB}_{\text{DL}}$ is the set of all ontologies;
- $\textbf{BS}_{\text{DL}}$ is the set of all deductively closed sets of first-order sentences;
- $\textbf{ACC}_{\text{DL}}(\mathcal{O})$ returns the set of first-order sentences ϕ such that $\mathcal{O} \models \phi$.

A *DL context* is obtained as follows:

Definition 15 (DL Context). *A context $C = (L, kb, br)$ is a DL context if $L = L_{DL}$, kb is an ontology $\mathcal{O}$, and, for every $\sigma \in br$, $H(\sigma)$ is a DL-axiom. We also say that such σ is a DL bridge rule.*

DLs as fragments of first-order logic are monotonic, so DL contexts are reducible.

Proposition 16. *Every DL context is reducible.*

Since DLs only make use of unary and binary predicates, and an MKNF context is not limited to these due to the presence of atoms over predicates whose arity is greater than 2, we need an additional context here that serves as a means to store and retrieve facts. For simplicity, we introduce an abstract *fact base context* and its associated logic. The *fact base logic* is the logic $L_{FB} = (\mathbf{KB}_{FB}, \mathbf{BS}_{FB}, \mathbf{ACC}_{FB})$ where

- $\mathbf{KB}_{FB}$ is the set of subsets of $\mathbf{L_G}$;
- $\mathbf{BS}_{FB}$ is the set of subsets of $\mathbf{L_G}$;
- $\mathbf{ACC}_{FB}(kb)$ is the identity function.

A *fact base context* is established as follows:

Definition 17 (Fact Base Context). *A context $C = (L, kb, br)$ is a fact base context if $L = L_{FB}$, kb is a subset of $\mathbf{L_G}$, and, for every $\sigma \in br$, $H(\sigma)$ is $l \in \mathbf{L_G}$. We also say that such σ is a fact base bridge rule.*

A fact base context is obviously reducible.

Proposition 18. *Every fact base context is reducible.*

Essentially, the idea is to translate an MKNF context C_j into a pair of contexts, namely a DL context and a fact base context, which is possible under certain restrictions as specified below. This can be achieved by first considering the reduction into a first-order context, which contains only bridge rules and $\kappa(\mathcal{O})$. The bridge rules can be divided between the two contexts depending on whether the literal in the head appears only in the rules or not. In the former case such a head can never be used for reasoning in the DL context, hence, all these rules are added to the fact base context, while in the latter case, they are added to the DL context. Additionally, in all bridge literals that do not appear in $\mathcal{O}$, the pointer is changed to the fact base context.

We formalize this, by first defining this division of literals appearing in the MKNF context, i.e. in the corresponding MKNF KB. Given an MKNF knowledge base $\mathcal{K} = \mathcal{O} \cup \mathcal{P}$, we define that $l \in \mathbf{L_G}$ is a DL-literal if the predicate of l appears in $\mathcal{O}$. Otherwise, l is a non-DL literal.

Now we can define an abstract function that can be used to transform the bridge literals in a given first-order context, with the intention that bridge rules with a non-DL-atom in the head point to a different context k.

Definition 19 (Transformation to Two-Context Bridge Rules). *Let j and k be integers and S a set of bridge rules. We define $\beta_j^k(S) = \{\, \beta_j^k(\pi) \mid \pi \in S \,\}$. For every $\pi \in S$ $\beta_j(\pi)$ denotes the bridge rule $H(\pi) \leftarrow \beta_j^k(B(\pi))$. We define for sets of bridge literals S that $\beta_j^k(S) = \{\, \beta_j^k(L) \mid L \in S \,\}$. Moreover, we define for single bridge literals $(j : l)$ and $\mathbf{not}\,(j : l)$:*

- $\beta_j^k((j:l)) = (k:l)$ and $\beta_j^k(\text{not } (j:l)) = \text{not } (k:l)$ if l is a non-DL-atom;
- $\beta_j^k((j:l)) = (j:l)$ and $\beta_j^k(\text{not } (j:l)) = \text{not } (j:l)$ otherwise.

Finally, $\beta_j^k((i:l)) = (i:l)$ and $\beta_j^k((i:l)) = (i:l)$ for $1 \le i \ne j \le n$.

Note that the second case not only handles DL-atoms, but also arbitrary first-order sentences, which also covers translations of DL axioms.

We define the two-context DL MCS corresponding to an MKNF context.

Definition 20 (Two-Context DL MCS Corresponding to an MKNF Context). *Let* $C_j = (L_{\text{MKNF}}, \mathcal{O} \cup \mathcal{P}, br_j)$ *be a ground MKNF context. The* two-context DL MCS *corresponding to* C_j, $\langle C_j^{\text{DL}}, C_k^{\text{FB}} \rangle$, *is defined as follows:*

- $C_j^{\text{DL}} = (L_{\text{DL}}, \mathcal{O}, br_j)$;
- $br_j = \{H(\pi) \leftarrow \beta_j^k(B(\pi)) \mid \pi \in (\beta_j(br_j) \cup \beta_j(\mathcal{P})) \land H(\pi) \text{ is a DL-atom}$
  $fact\} \cup \{\phi \leftarrow \beta_j^k(B(\pi)) \mid \pi \in br_j \land H(\pi) \text{ is an ontology axiom } \phi\}$;
- $C_k^{\text{FB}} = (L_{\text{FB}}, \emptyset, br_k)$;
- $br_k = \{H(\pi) \leftarrow \beta_j^k(B(\pi)) \mid \pi \in (\beta_j(br_j) \cup \beta_j(\mathcal{P})) \land H(\pi) \text{ is a non-DL-atom}$
  $fact\}$.

Bridge rules in $(\beta_j(br_j) \cup \beta_j(\mathcal{P}))$ are divided between the two contexts as outlined. The only exception are bridge rules in br_j with an ontology axiom in the head. These are added to the DL context. Note that the index k for the fact base context allows us to add C_k^{FB} to an MCS with n contexts at a position of choice, which is $n + 1$.

Given a belief set S, S^* denotes the deductive closure of S. We can substitute a finite, ground MKNF context with a two-context MCS without affecting the grounded equilibria provided that certain conditions hold.

Theorem 21 (Translation Two-Context DL MCS). *Let* $M = \langle C_1, \ldots, C_n \rangle$ *be a reducible multi-context system such that, for some* j *with* $1 \le j \le n$, C_j *is a finite ground MKNF context, and, for all* i *with* $1 \le i \le n$, *all* $\pi \in br_i$, *and each* $(j:l) \in \pi$ *and* $\text{not } (j:l) \in \pi$, l *is an objective literal. Let* k *be* $n + 1$, *and set*

$$M' = \langle C_1', \ldots, C_{j-1}', C_j^{\text{DL}}, C_{j+1}', \ldots, C_n', C_{n+1}^{\text{FB}} \rangle$$

where, for all i *with* $1 \le j \ne i \le n$, C_i' *results from* C_i *by applying* β_j^{n+1} *to* br_i.

The grounded equilibria of M *and* M' *are equivalent, i.e., for all* i *with* $1 \le i \ne j \le n$, $S_i = S_i'$, *and* $S_j = (S_j^{\text{DL}} \cup S_{n+1}^{\text{FB}})^*$.

The restriction on bridge literals in MCS given in Theorem 21 could be seen as being too severe, i.e. it is possible to come up with a less restrictive result that only limits these bridge literals to a degree such that they are not arbitrary first-order sentences, but either non-DL atoms or formulas that are in the belief set of the DL in consideration. We claim that these more restrictive conditions are sufficient here, in particular in light of the kind of rules we allow in MKNF knowledge bases, and leave lifting the result to more expressive MKNF knowledge bases (and more expressive bridge rules) for future work.

Again, this transformation can be repeated for all MKNF contexts in the multi-context system, yielding an equivalent system that does not require to use the MKNF logic if the bridge literals to the MKNF context are appropriately restricted. Formally:

Corollary 22. *For every multi-context system M with some finite ground MKNF contexts such that all bridge literals to these contexts are objective literals, there exists a multi-context system M' such that the grounded equilibria of M and M' are equivalent (in the sense of Theorem 21) and M' uses pairs of DL contexts and fact base contexts instead of the original MKNF contexts.*

Turning again to our running example, if we choose the two-context translation instead of the previous one, Translating M^n is reduced into $M^{n''} = \langle b_1, s_1, s_2, n^{\mathrm{DL}}, m^{\mathrm{FB}} \rangle$ where $n^{\mathrm{DL}} = (L_{\mathrm{DL}}, \mathcal{O}_n, br_n)$ and $m^{\mathrm{FB}} = (L_{\mathrm{FB}}, \emptyset, br_m)$ where $\mathcal{O}_n$ is as defined above and br_n and br_m are as follows:

br_n: supplier$(A) \leftarrow A :$ available(I).

   offered_by$(I, A) \leftarrow A :$ available(I).

br_m: best_price$(I, s_1) \leftarrow s_1 :$ price$(I, X), s_2 :$ price$(I, Y), X \le Y$.

   best_price$(I, s_2) \leftarrow s_1 :$ price$(I, X), s_2 :$ price$(I, Y), X > Y$.

   purchase_allowed$(I, A) \leftarrow n :$ offered_by$(I, A),$ **not** $(n :$ licitable_product$(I))$.

   purchase_allowed$(I, A) \leftarrow n :$ licitable_product$(I), n :$ offered_by$(I, A),$

$$m :$$ best_price(I, A).

4 Conclusions

Open multi agent systems can be modelled in MCSs, and we have considered MKNF knowledge bases as one such context, which allows the usage of a highly expressive knowledge representation and reasoning formalism in such MCSs. One immediate result of our work is that the Hybrid MKNF [15] can indeed be used in MCSs, namely in the form of MKNF contexts, which can then be interlinked with other contexts in the MCS.

Since not all agents may necessarily be able to reason with such a context, we investigated the possibility of using the expressiveness of MKNF knowledge bases without having to use an actual MKNF context. We showed that an MKNF context can be reduced to an associated first-order context without any effects on the semantics, i.e. the grounded equilibria of the considered MCS. Hence, a first order reasoner can be used instead. Moreover, restricting the form of bridge literals to objective literals, we have shown that we can even use a combination of a DL reasoner and a simple store for (rule) facts to achieve the same result. In the former case, the resulting MCS is more general, while in the latter case we are enabled to use a decidable and faster reasoner.

Future work includes loosening the restriction in Theorem 21 such that bridge literals may contain more expressive formulas w.r.t. the DL context. In line with this lies the extension of the results to more general MKNF KBs, i.e. where objective literals in MKNF rules may not just be atoms and their (classical) negations. Another line of work would be to consider substituting an MKNF context with two contexts where one context is a DL-context and the other one in ASP. In this case, contrary to our translation into two contexts, the treatment of non-monotonic rules would be literally hidden in the context and it would be interesting to compare these different two-context translations. In [6], also a well-founded semantics is defined for MCSs and considering this semantics and investigating its correlation with the well-founded semantics for Hybrid MKNF [13] would also be interesting possibly enabling us to use a semantics in MCSs that is, due to its nature, of a lower computational complexity.

Acknowledgments. Matthias Knorr, João Leite and Martin Slota were partially supported by Fundação para a Ciência e a Tecnologia under project "ERRO – Efficient Reasoning with Rules and Ontologies" (PTDC/EIA-CCO/121823/2010). Martin Homola was partially supported by the Slovak national project VEGA no. 1/1333/12. The collaboration between the co-authors resulted from the Slovak–Portuguese bilateral project "ReDIK – Reasoning with Dynamic Inconsistent Knowledge", supported by the APVV agency under SK-PT0-0028-10 and by Fundação para a Ciência e a Tecnologia (FCT/2487/3/6/2011/S).

References

1. Alberti, M., Gomes, A.S., Gonçalves, R., Knorr, M., Leite, J., Slota, M.: Normative systems require hybrid knowledge bases (extended abstract). In: Conitzer, V., Winikoff, M., Padgham, L., van der Hoek, W. (eds.) Proceedings of the 11th International Conference on Autonomous Agents and Multiagent Systems (AAMAS 2012), June 4-8. IFAAMAS, Valencia, Spain (2012)
2. Alberti, M., Gomes, A.S., Gonçalves, R., Leite, J., Slota, M.: Normative Systems Represented as Hybrid Knowledge Bases. In: Leite, J., Torroni, P., Ågotnes, T., Boella, G., van der Torre, L. (eds.) CLIMA XII 2011. LNCS, vol. 6814, pp. 330–346. Springer, Heidelberg (2011)
3. Baader, F., Calvanese, D., McGuinness, D.L., Nardi, D., Patel-Schneider, P.F. (eds.): The Description Logic Handbook: Theory, Implementation, and Applications, 2nd edn. Cambridge University Press (2007)
4. Benerecetti, M., Cimatti, A., Giunchiglia, E., Giunchiglia, F., Serafini, L.: Formal Specification of Beliefs in Multi-Agent Systems. In: Jennings, N.R., Wooldridge, M.J., Müller, J.P. (eds.) ECAI-WS 1996 and ATAL 1996. LNCS, vol. 1193, pp. 117–130. Springer, Heidelberg (1997)
5. Benerecetti, M., Giunchiglia, F., Serafini, L.: Model checking multiagent systems. Journal of Logic and Computation 8(3), 401–423 (1998)
6. Brewka, G., Eiter, T.: Equilibria in heterogeneous nonmonotonic multi-context systems. In: Proceedings of the 22nd AAAI Conference on Artificial Intelligence, July 22-26, pp. 385–390. AAAI Press, Vancouver (2007)
7. Casali, A., Godo, L., Sierra, C.: Graded BDI Models for Agent Architectures. In: Leite, J., Torroni, P. (eds.) CLIMA 2004. LNCS (LNAI), vol. 3487, pp. 126–143. Springer, Heidelberg (2005)
8. Cimatti, A., Serafini, L.: Multi-Agent Reasoning with Belief Contexts: The Approach and a Case Study. In: Wooldridge, M.J., Jennings, N.R. (eds.) ECAI 1994 and ATAL 1994. LNCS, vol. 890, pp. 71–85. Springer, Heidelberg (1995)
9. Gelfond, M., Lifschitz, V.: The stable model semantics for logic programming. In: Kowalski, R.A., Bowen, K.A. (eds.) Proceedings of the 5th International Conference and Symposium on Logic Programming (ICLP/SLP 1988), August 15-19, pp. 1070–1080. MIT Press, Seattle (1988)
10. Gelfond, M., Lifschitz, V.: Classical negation in logic programs and disjunctive databases. New Generation Computing 9(3-4), 365–385 (1991)

11. Ghidini, C., Giunchiglia, F.: Local models semantics, or contextual reasoning=locality+compatibility. Artificial Intelligence 127(2), 221–259 (2001)
12. Giunchiglia, F.: Contextual reasoning. Epistemologia - Special Issue on I Linguaggi e le Macchine XVI, 345–364 (1993)
13. Knorr, M., Alferes, J.J., Hitzler, P.: Local closed world reasoning with description logics under the well-founded semantics. Artificial Intelligence 175(9-10), 1528–1554 (2011)
14. Lifschitz, V.: Nonmonotonic databases and epistemic queries. In: Mylopoulos, J., Reiter, R. (eds.) Proceedings of the 12th International Joint Conference on Artificial Intelligence (IJCAI 1991), pp. 381–386. Morgan Kaufmann, Sydney, Australia (1991)
15. Motik, B., Rosati, R.: Reconciling description logics and rules. Journal of the ACM 57(5), 93–154 (2010)
16. Parsons, S., Sierra, C., Jennings, N.R.: Agents that reason and negotiate by arguing. Journal of Logic and Computation 8(3), 261–292 (1998)
17. Sabater, J., Sierra, C., Parsons, S., Jennings, N.R.: Engineering executable agents using multi-context systems. Journal of Logic and Computation 12(3), 413–442 (2002)

Implementing Reversible Processes in Multi-agent Action Languages Using Answer Set Planning

Ben Wright*, Enrico Pontelli, and Tran Cao Son

New Mexico State University,
Department of Computer Science,
Las Cruces, New Mexico, USA
{bwright,epontell,tson}@cs.nmsu.edu

Abstract. This paper presents an implementation of the action language $\mathcal{L}^{mt}$ in answer set programming. The novelty of this language comes from the use of processes to execute delayed effects for actions. In addition, the ability to reverse, or cancel, the processes is available. A simple example is introduced to show when reversing actions are useable - even by other agents in the domain. These processes are the base foundation for future implementation of commitments in planning for multi-agent domains.

Keywords: Knowledge Representation, Action Languages, Multi-agent systems, Answer Set Programming.

1 Introduction

In the study of representing actions and change, actions with delayed effects have been considered for some time [7,19]. The ability to reason about actions that have a non-deterministic endpoint is quite fascinating. However, to fully represent this idea, one should also consider the idea that the agent (or other agents) may potentially want to stop the effect before it has time to occur.

This idea can be seen in many examples. For instance, take the following scenario, "It is the end of a tied soccer match and the game is down to the final penalty kick. The player kicks the ball towards the goal. Before it arrives, the goalkeeper has the ability to *stop* the incoming ball from reaching the goal". Another example could be, "A consumer just purchased some goods from a merchant by putting the check in the mail. However, when he inspected the goods he found them to be of low quality and wished to cancel his check prior to it arriving."

In order to study these types of actions, we developed an implementation in Answer Set Programming of the language $\mathcal{L}^{mt}$ first presented in [26]. To show

---

* This research has been partially supported by NSF grants DGE-0947465 and IIS-0812267.

M. Fisher et al. (Eds.): CLIMA XIII 2012, LNAI 7486, pp. 163–180, 2012.

the utility of the language and implementation we use two examples, Penalty Kick and Merchant/Consumer.

The rest of this paper is structured as follows. In the rest of this section we give some background information about action languages and answer set programming as well as mention some related works. In Section 2 we define the action language $\mathcal{L}^{mt}$ and provide two examples using the action language. In Section 3 we actually define the translation of the action language into ASP rules. Following this, we evaluate our results in Section 4 and then discuss some of the issues we noticed in Section 5. Finally, we conclude and offer some future directions in Section 6.

1.1   Action Languages and Answer Set Programming

Action languages, like $\mathcal{A}$, $\mathcal{B}$, and $\mathcal{C}$ [18], use transition function based semantics and English like syntax to approach the area of representing and reasoning about actions and change. Recently, there have been several attempts at developing action languages for multi-agent environments [25,26,5].

The transition-function based semantics offer straight forward semantics that can be viewed as directed graphs and can easily be extended for various additional features desired for the action language. By using english-like syntax, the language provides a clear and declarative syntax that avoids ambiguity or complicated functions. With these semantics and syntax, action languages provide a quick, simple, and efficient way to reason and represent actions and change.

Answer set programming (ASP) is a logic programming paradigm built on the concept of stable model semantics [17]. These stable models, or answer sets, are generated from a list of rules and constraints given as a logic program. For instance simple rules such as, "Penguins are birds." can be represented by:

$$penguin(P) \leftarrow bird(P). \tag{1}$$

Additionally, we can represent constraints like, "Two nodes that share an edge should not be the same color" by:

$$\leftarrow node(X), node(Y), edge(X, Y), color(C, X), color(C, Y). \tag{2}$$

A logic program is said to have a stable model if one of the conditions below holds:

1. The program does not contain any 'negation as failure' literals (naf-literal). A naf-literal is a literal of the form: **not** a, where a is an atom. Without any naf-literals, the set of atoms given is the smallest set that satisfy the rules from the program. That is, it is already a reduced answer set.
2. If naf-literals are present, then this is an answer set if the reduction of this program with respect to a set of ground atoms is also an answer set. That is, if we remove all of the naf-literals we can still reach a stable model.

If a stable model results, then that is a 'valid' or *satisfiable* model. In addition, the program is said to be *consistent*, while a program without a stable model is *inconsistent*.

An interest in ASP has been seen by some in the planning community by some researchers [21,22,27]. In Answer Set Planning, logics of answer sets are mapped to planning problems such that *plans*, or sequences of actions, arise from stable models.

1.2 Related Work

There is a great deal of previous work in the area of encoding action theories and multi-agent action languages. Other action languages have dealt with delayed and continuous effects [7]. However, this was the theory and not the implementation. There have been other action languages that have looked into temporal actions as well [19]. In addition, these action languages only dealt with single agents, while we focus on the multi-agent aspect of delayed effects.

Many encodings of Action Languages in ASP exist: [12] encodes ε, [11] encodes $CCALC$, [13,14] encode versions of $\mathcal{B}$, [10] applies Definite Agent Logic Programs (definite ALPs) to answer sets, and [16] offers a compiler for many Action Languages into ASP. Other implementations of multi-agent action languages exist [25,5]. However, they do not use the concept of processes or address delayed or continuous effects.

In addition to action languages, another large body of related work is that of the planning language PDDL 2.1 and its various successors [15]. While PDDL 2.1 does provide a system for durative actions, it does not use a transition function base for its semantics. In addition, PDDL 2.1 does not focus on ir/reversible processes or multiple agents. MAPL [9], is an extension of PDDL 2.1 that does take into account multiple agents. However, it also does not use a transition function base semantics or focus on ir/reversible processes.

Other agent languages exist for multi-agent systems (MAS) as well. One in particular is AgentSpeak [23], which has been implemented in the interpreter JASON [8], using Java. JASON provides a good implementation for logical singular agent encoding with AgentSpeak and also for setting up dynamic environments easily in Java. However, this set up has a more "online" feel to its planning procedures and would also require more coordination to encode actions between agents. [3] presents an action language, Dylog, and [2] further shows how to use this as a means to program many web agents. [4] also shows an implementation of an agent language based on logics and actions. [20] defines the agent language LPS based on Abductive Logic Programming which provides both operational and model-theoretic semantics.

2 Representing Delayed Effects in Action Languages

The delayed effects implemented in this paper are one part of the action language $\mathcal{L}^{mt}$. Other parts of the language include situational reasoning for narratives, temporal fluents, and the use of commitments to form complex protocols [26].

$\mathcal{L}^{mt}$ is first fully defined in [26] and sets up delayed effects as the basis for future work reasoning about *narratives* and *commitments*. The language is built up from the language $\mathcal{L}$ defined in [6]. We do not go in depth in covering the actions from that language, we only focus on the extensions implemented for $\mathcal{L}^{mt}$.

2.1   Syntax of $\mathcal{L}^{mt}$

The syntax of action languages are very simple. Action theories are tuples $(\mathcal{I}_D, D)$ where $\mathcal{I}_D$ is the *initial world* of the domain D and D is the domain of the problem which holds the fluents, actions, agents, and processes of the problem. Fluents, $\mathcal{F}$, are propositional variables and all the agents in the domain are in $\mathcal{AG}$. The list of action names is given by $\mathcal{A}$. Additionally, sometimes fluents and actions are partitioned to the scope of one agent. When this occurs, they are defined by $\mathcal{F}_a$ and $\mathcal{A}_a$ respectively when $a \in \mathcal{AG}$.

The above definitions have been used in previous multi-agent action theories [5,25]. Additionally, as actions occur, more than one action can occur at a time as long as each agent only performs one action. To view this idea, the concept of *action snapshots*, denoted by α, is used. An action snapshot contains a set of actions performed by all agents in one time step. It is also assumed that all agents have the ability to perform the action *noop* which does not cause any effects and does not have any preconditions.

A *plan* would then consist of a sequence of action snapshots such that some fluent formula would hold after those actions occurred. This is expressed by the following rule, which is further defined in [26,5]:

$$\varphi \textbf{ after } Plan \tag{3}$$

From this, the formula φ is referred to as the *goal* and *Plan* is the sequence of action snapshots α that should be taken from the initial world $\mathcal{I}_D$ to allow φ to hold.

[26] introduced one last concept as well, that of an *annotated fluent*. An annotated fluent appears like, f^t, where $f \in \mathcal{F}$ and t is a time step. Then this annotated fluent f is said to have its effect produced in t time steps.

In order to use delayed effects as actions, *processes* are used and a list of the processes, $\mathcal{P}$, is given to the domain D. By itself, the idea of delayed effects is rather simple to grasp and the following action rules set them up:

$$action \textbf{ starts } process\_irrev \textbf{ irreversible } fluent\_effect \textbf{ in } x \textbf{ to } y \tag{4}$$

$$action \textbf{ starts } process\_rev \textbf{ reversible } fluent\_effect \textbf{ in } x \textbf{ to } y \tag{5}$$

Where $action \in \mathcal{A}$, $process\_irrev$, $process\_rev \in \mathcal{P}$, $fluent\_effect \in \mathcal{F}$, and x,y are time steps. The *action* is the trigger to the process starting which will attempt to make the fluent *fluent_effect* true in x to y time steps.
Canceling effects is rather straight forward as well:

$$stopAction \textbf{ stops } process\_rev \tag{6}$$

$$\textbf{impossible } stopAction \textbf{ if } fluent\_effect \qquad (7)$$

Here $stopAction \in \mathcal{A}$, $process\_rev \in \mathcal{P}$, and $fluent\_effect \in \mathcal{F}$. The $stopAction$ wishes to undo the process, $process\_rev$, before the fluent the process is attempting completes. Therefore there is an executability rule stating not to perform a stop action if the process has already made the fluent hold.

2.2   Semantics of $\mathcal{L}^{mt}$

The transition functions are changed slightly in order to correctly work with delayed effects. In order to effectively keep track of processes, [26] introduces the idea of an *extended state*. This extended state is a triple (s, IR, RE) where s is a state, or a possible world of the fluent literals in $\mathcal{F}$ from the domain D, and IR and RE are a set of pairs $(x : l^t)$ where x is a process name and l^t an annotated fluent. Ideally, s is the current state and IR and RE hold the active irreversible and reversible processes respectively.

Using these *extended* states, how do we transition to a new extended state? With the addition of delayed effects, states can now change even if an action has not occurred in the previous time step. For instance, in a new time step the annotated fluent p^2 would go to p^1. Then on the following time step, p would then hold in the extended state $(s\backslash\{\neg p\} \cup \{p\})$. However, if an action were to occur in addition, causing let us say q to hold as well then the state transition would be $s\backslash\{\neg p, \neg q\} \cup \{p, q\}$.

In order to find the future extended states, an *update* function was created. This functions as the first part above where we are not dealing with any new action occurrences. The update function works by 'ticking off' time steps on annotated fluents and actualizing fluents that have been reduced to time 0, as they can no longer be delayed.

For the new extended state, $\hat{s}$, the update function needs to keep track of both the annotated fluents time steps in IR and RE as well as updating the state if any fluents have actualized. Given this clarification, the following is used to minimize the number of literals to use in updating $\hat{s}$:

$$\tau(\hat{s}) = \{l \mid (x : l^1) \in IR\} \cup \{l \mid (x : l^1) \in RE \text{ such that } \not\exists (z : \bar{l}^1) \in IR\} \qquad (8)$$

Using $\tau(\hat{s})$, then we only look at the literals l that have 1 time step left. As you can see in (8), priority is taken on the irreversible processes. Now that we know what fluents might affect our updated state $\hat{s}$, we need to look at the processes in IR and RE as well. These function in about the same way, except that we also have to keep track of *stopped* processes. So let $IR_1(s) = \{(process\_id : l^{\hat{t}}) \mid$ there exists a law of the form (4)\} be the set of irreversible processes started in s. A difference in the presentation of the laws (4,5,6) from [26] has slightly altered this equation, however it remains the same semantically (the above rules would be assumed to have 'if *true*' on the end). Likewise, $RE_1(s)$ can be defined with law (5). However, let us define $P_2(s)$ as the set of stopped processes, which can be formed as well using the same ideas with law (6).

Using these formulas, we can come to the formulation of the update function for $\hat{s}$:

$$update(\hat{s}) = \{(s', I(IR, s'), R(ER, s')|s' = Cl_D(\tau(\hat{s}) \cup (s \cap s')) \text{ and } s' \text{ is a state}\} \quad (9)$$

where, $I(IR, s') = (IR-1) \cup IR_1(s')$ and $R(ER, s') = ((RE-1) \cup RE_1(s')) \backslash P_2(s')$. s' is intuitively a state where the effects are satisfied one step from now. $(IR-1)$ reduces the annotated fluents time by one step in IR and Cl_D is the closure in domain D of equivalent states.

With the idea of future effects handled, let us look back at the overall transition function. For an action snapshot, $\alpha = \{a_i\}_{i \in AG}$, there are only two possible types: the direct effect from a basic action and the processes that are created by the action. The direct effects must be satisfied in the next step, however the effects of the processes are different.

Let us define the effects of the processes started by α in s, denoted by $procs_\alpha(s)$ as a set of pairs (IR', RE') where:

- For each law (4) in D, with $a_i \in \alpha$ we have that IR' contains $(p_{id} : l^t)$ for some t s.t. $t_1 \le t \le t_2$.
- For each law (5) in D, with $a_i \in \alpha$ we have that RE' contains $(p_{id} : l^t)$ for some t s.t. $t_1 \le t \le t_2$.

In addition to this though, we need to pay attention to the stopped processes. The stopped processes by α are denoted by $stop_\alpha(s)$ and contains the names of the processes stopped by law (6). Now we have (IR', RE') which encodes a possible set of effects that α can create and $stop_\alpha(s)$ which lists the processes needed to stop. Now we can begin to organize our transition function. One additional notation is needed. We use $\top$ as a special process name and for a set of literals L we define the following: $\oplus(L) = \{(\top : l^1)|l \in L\}$.

The transition function $\phi_D^t(\alpha, \hat{s})$ is defined as follows:

$$\phi_D^t(\alpha, \hat{s}) = \bigcup_{(I,R) \in procs_\alpha(s)} update((s, IR \cup I \cup \oplus(e_\alpha(s)), (RE \cup R) \backslash stop_\alpha(s))) \quad (10)$$

2.3   Example Domains

In order to model the delayed and reversible effects we used two different examples. One was taken from the original paper describing $\mathcal{L}^{mt}$ - the Merchant/Consumer example. However, when developing and implementing this example, it was found to be overly intricate with multiple processes running. A second, simpler, example was created - the penalty kick example. Both are described below.

Penalty Kick. In this example, there are two agents: a kicker and a goalie. The objective is for the kicker to kick the ball into the goal and the goalie then has the option to block the ball before it arrives in the goal. We can define a rather simple domain, D_{goal}, for this example in the following manner.

- Agents = {kicker, goalie}.
- Fluents = {ball_in_goal}
- Actions$_{kicker}$ = {kick_ball}
- Actions$_{goalie}$ = {block_ball}
- Processes$_{rev}$ = {ball_in_air}
- Actions for the kicker:

$$\text{\textit{kick\_ball}} \textbf{ starts } \textit{ball\_in\_air} \textbf{ reversible } \textit{ball\_in\_goal} \textbf{ in } \textit{3} \textbf{ to } \textit{5} \qquad (11)$$

- Actions for the goalie:

$$\text{\textit{block\_ball}} \textbf{ stops } \textit{ball\_in\_air} \qquad (12)$$

$$\textbf{impossible } \textit{block\_ball} \textbf{ if } \textit{ball\_in\_goal} \qquad (13)$$

Where the goal formulae can be either $ball\_in\_goal$ or $\neg ball\_in\_goal \wedge pcomp(ball\_in\_air)$. Which stands for a) the ball getting into the goal and b) the ball not going in the goal, but still being kicked. $pcomp()$, which stands for 'process completed', is defined below in Section 3.3.

The *executability rule* for *block_ball* is used to specify that you can not 'stop' the process of *ball_in_air* if it has already completed its effect. Let the above rules be the domain, D_{goal}, and the following to be the initial world, $\mathcal{I}_{goal}$: $\{\neg ball\_in\_goal\}$.

Now we can walk through the transition function:

- The initial state $s_0 = \{\neg ball\_in\_air\}$ and with the extended state as $\hat{s}_0 = (s_0, \emptyset, \emptyset)$
- Let $\alpha_1 = \{kick\_ball, noop\}$.
- $\phi^t_{D_{goal}}(\alpha_1, \hat{s}_0) = \{update((s_0, \emptyset, \{ball\_in\_air : ball\_in\_goal^i\}))|i = 3, 4, 5\}$

From here, we can see that the fluent annotation for $ball\_in\_goal$ will become true in at most 5 time steps, assuming that $block\_ball$ is not added to the action snapshot in future time steps.

Merchant / Consumer. This example was used in the originating paper, but further defined in [24]. In this example, the merchant and consumer try to sell/buy some goods from each other. As the negotiation continues, the consumer has the option to cancel his payment before it arrives. The following exchange between a consumer and a merchant is supposed to work as follows:

- A consumer *requests* a quote from a merchant pertaining to a good it sells.
- The merchant sends the *quote* to the consumer.
- After receiving the quote, the consumer may *accept* the quote for the goods.
- Upon receiving confirmation of acceptance, the merchant sends the *goods* to the consumer.
- After the goods arrive for the consumer, *payment* is sent.
- With payment received, the merchant sends confirmation with a *receipt*.

This example uses two different delayed actions, *sendQuote* and *sendPayment*. *sendQuote* is an *irreversible* action. That is, it can not be interrupted by a **stop** action. On the other hand, *sendPayment* is a *reversible* action and does have an action that can reverse it. Here is the domain, $D_{payment}$, for the example:

- Agents = {merchant, consumer}.
- Fluents = {request, pay, goods, receipt, quote, accept}.
- Actions$_m$ = {sendQuote, sendGoods, sendReceipt}.
- Actions$_c$ = {sendRequest, sendAccept, sendPayment, cancelPayment}.
- Processes$_{irrev}$ = {quote_process}.
- Processes$_{rev}$ = {payment_process}.
- Actions for the merchant:

$$sendQuote \textbf{ starts } quote\_process \textbf{ irreversible } quote \textbf{ in } 2 \textbf{ to } 2 \qquad (14)$$

$$\textbf{impossible } sendQuote \textbf{ if } \neg request \qquad (15)$$

$$sendGoods \textbf{ causes } goods \qquad (16)$$

$$\textbf{impossible } sendGoods \textbf{ if } \neg accept \qquad (17)$$

$$sendReceipt \textbf{ causes } receipt \qquad (18)$$

$$\textbf{impossible } sendReceipt \textbf{ if } \neg pay \qquad (19)$$

- Actions for consumer:

$$sendRequest \textbf{ causes } request \qquad (20)$$

$$sendAccept \textbf{ causes } accept \qquad (21)$$

$$\textbf{impossible } sendAccept \textbf{ if } \neg quote \qquad (22)$$

$$sendPayment \textbf{ starts } payment\_process \textbf{ reversible } pay \textbf{ in } 3 \textbf{ to } 5 \qquad (23)$$

$$cancelPayment \textbf{ stops } payment\_process. \qquad (24)$$

$$\textbf{impossible } cancelPayment \textbf{ if } pay \qquad (25)$$

Let the above rules be the domain, $D_{payment}$, and the following to be the initial world $\mathcal{I}_{payment}$: {¬request, ¬pay, ¬goods, ¬receipt, ¬quote, ¬accept}.

Where the goal formulae would be either *pay ∧ receipt* or *pcomp(payment_process) ∧ ¬payment*.

3   Implementation

3.1   Design Concept

For the most part, a lot of ideas are taken from the traditional planning techniques used in ASP already. To that end, some of the assumptions taken is that there is a defined *goal state*, or *goal formulae*, which the agents are attempting to attain and there is also a defined *initial state* where the fluents used are defined. We leave further talk about goal states until the discussion in Section 5. In addition, the type of planner we will use in ASP works on an iterative step. So, as part of the input for each run, there will be a known *finite horizon* of a plan to check for. As such, there will be a variable known as *length* in the code which will function as the end point for time steps.

On its own, delayed effects can actually be implemented using a regression type method to anchor the effect in time, and then work backwards to find when the action occurred. However, this method proved difficult to use when including the ability to cancel the effect of the action.

From that original idea however, the concept of 'anchoring' the resulting effect stayed, and that has become the foundation of setting up the rest of the delayed action in this implementation.

3.2   ASP Representation of Basic Features

The backbone of this ASP representation takes its ideas from planning techniques. Therefore, all domains should have a well defined *initial state* along with a definable *goal* to achieve.

As goals are currently static in this implementation, the model is either trying to cancel the process or complete it. It is possible to have returned models that have both canceled or completed processes. This was not pursued heavily in our examples as we were looking for specific deterministic outcomes.

Basic actions use the traditional causal rule in ASP such as for the rule "*action* **causes** f **if** g":

$$holds(f, T + 1) \leftarrow holds(g, T), occ(action, T, agent) \qquad (26)$$

where T is a time step between 0 and the *finite horizon* which is generally set at runtime.

In addition, the ASP program works by finding correct models which satisfy the following choice rule:

$$1\{occ(A, T, Ag) : action(A, Ag)\}1 \leftarrow agent(Ag), time(T), T < length. \qquad (27)$$

Which states that "Each agent executes one action per time step". Here the $occ/3$ variable stands for 'occurs' so it can be read as 'Action A is performed by agent Ag at time T.

3.3   ASP Representation of Delayed Effects

The method used to implement delayed effects makes use of the *choice rule* in ASP to decide one time in the window of the timeframe to complete the process. Once this timeframe is chosen, everything else is built around it using basic ideas from traditional approaches to planning in ASP.

As an example, we will show the implementation of the Penalty Kick scenario. As defined above, the Penalty Kick example has one process: *ball_in_air* (*bna*). This process is started by the action *kick_ball* (*kb*), the agent *kicker* (*k*), and has a time window to complete of 3 to 5 time steps. Given this, however, we know that the process will only complete once in this time frame. This idea serves as the main idea for our rule:

$$1\{pcomp(bna, B + W) : time(B) : pwin(bna, W)\}1 \leftarrow occ(kb, B, k). \qquad (28)$$

The predicate *pcomp()*, or *process completes*, serves as the main idea as mentioned above. The above *choice rule* states that the process (*bna* in this case) completes at time step $B + W$ where B is the originating time-step where the action starting the process occurred and W is the point in the process window which is chosen. W is chosen from options of the following rule:

$$pwin(bna, W). \qquad (29)$$

pwin(), or *process window*, is defined for each process and for each possible time delay. For instance, in the above rule where the process completes in 3 to 5, there will be a rule where W is equal to each time delay 3,4, and 5.

While finding the source of the process is good, it does not actually map the intended 'effect' into the state space yet. Since the action does not directly cause the effect, as it is delayed for a period of time steps, we use the time of the process completing from *pcomp()* to anchor the effect of the overall process and action. Which we show below:

$$h(bng, T) \leftarrow time(T), pcomp(bna, T). \qquad (30)$$

In addition to the above rules, some house-keeping constraints were also introduced. These included:

$$\leftarrow pcomp(Pid, T1), pcomp(Pid, T2), T1! = T2. \qquad (31)$$

Which states that processes only occur once in a run. This was needed for keeping the process together with the cancelled process (defined below) as well as removing any 'zombie processes'.

$$\leftarrow occ(kb, T, k), occ(kb, BT, k), h(neg(bng), T), pcomp(bna, GT), GT > T > BT. \qquad (32)$$

This is a particularly helpful constraint which would be for each delayed action which states that while the time step is less than when the process completes *and* the effect of the process is not true do not try and do the action again. This was the source of much aggravation in testing.

3.4   ASP Representation of Cancellation

Stopping a delayed effect is rather easy. We introduced a special fluent for each *reversible* process. This fluent serves as a flag or toggle for when the effect should or should not happen. For example in the Penalty Kick example, this fluent could be *proc_reverse_ball_in_air* (abbreviated to *prevbna*). In order to function later on, we set the fluent to false in the initial world (time step 0) as the process has not been reversed yet.

$$fluent(prevbna). \tag{33}$$

$$holds(neg(prevbna), 0) \tag{34}$$

This fluent will then serve as a flag which shows whether or not the process was actually reversed. In addition to adding the fluent, we should specify in the initial world that the flag is not triggered. We can then add our new fluent into the checks for our action effects. Below is the continued example for the *kick_ball* reversible action.

$$h(bng, T) \leftarrow pcomp(bna, T), h(neg(prevbna), T). \tag{35}$$

$$h(neg(bng), T) \leftarrow pcomp(bna, T), h(prevbna, T). \tag{36}$$

The first one holds when the process behaves as normal and performs its intended action. The second is to show that "nothing" happens, even though an action of *kicking the ball* did occur. One should note that in both cases, the process still *completes*. This is used later as a way to check that the originating action occurred.

The next step however, is to actually figure out when the *flag* fluent is triggered. This is with the **stop** action. Such as with the Penalty Kick example action: *block_ball* (abbrv. *bb*).

$$h(prevbna, T + 1) \leftarrow occ(bb, T, g). \tag{37}$$

Here we can see that this **stop** action actually performs just like any standard action - just on the special *flag fluent*. As you might have noticed, one odd side effect of this setup is the fact that you can give a goal for "reversing" the action or "not reversing" the action, however allowing for both to happen in the same action sequence can not occur. That feature is not currently implemented, although could be if in addition to "starting" processes, the delayed effect action also "reset" the *flag* fluent.

Along with these rules, a few *constraint* rules are needed as well. While in the domain, an *executability rule* is defined for the action - saying do not stop an action if it has already performed its effect. We need to also 'attach' the stop action to the process started from the originating action. We give the example using the Penalty Kick domain as follows:

$$\leftarrow occ(bb, T, g), occ(kb, AT, kicker), AT > T. \tag{38}$$

Which simply states "Do not let *block_ball* occur before *kick_ball*".

4   Evaluation

4.1   Implementation versus Theory

While the encoding for ASP above is given with examples, generalizing these actions to other uses would be simple following the same action rules defined above. Replacement of the actions and annotated fluents are simple as long as they follow the rules 4, 5, and 6.

There are two main issues that need to be shown when comparing the implementation to the theory, and that is that the irreversible processes and non-reversed processes complete as they should in the correct extended state of the transition function (defined in Section 2.2) and that the reversed processes behave similarly in their respective extended state.

Proposition 1. *Let (I_D, D) be a complete and consistent action theory of $\mathcal{L}^{mt}$ and Π to be a consistent program. For every answer set Ω of Π we will show that there is an equivalent extended state $\hat{s}$.*

Base Case: There are no processes in Ω, in this case this follows previous works encoding Action Theories and ASP and the extended state $\hat{s}$ is only the state s.

Completed Process: In the case of *irreversible* processes and completed *reversible* processes, we will have to use extended states. Let s be the state of the extended state and s' and $\hat{s}'$ be a previous state and extended state respectively. Let the process in question be $p \in \mathcal{P}$, its effect be $f \in \mathcal{F}$, $a \in \mathcal{A}$ the originating action, and its time window be between x and y:

- Ω will contain $occ(a, t)$, $proc\_comp(p, t1)$, $holds(f, t1)$, $holds(neg(proc\_rev\_p, t1)$. $t1$ will be between times $t + x$ and $t + y$
- $\hat{s}'$ will contain $(p : f^t) \in IR$ or $(p : f^t) \in RE$ depending on which type of process completed where $x <= t <= y$.
- $\hat{s}$ is an *update()* of $\hat{s}'$ or a successor of $\phi_D^t(\alpha, \hat{s}')$ for some sequence of actions α.
- $\hat{s}$ will contain $f \in s$ and $(p : f) \notin IR \cup RE$.

As the process p completes only once in Ω and in $\hat{s}$ and is started only by the action a we can see that there is an equivalent beginning and ending state for both the encoding and the theory.

Reversed Process: For reserving processes we use most of the setup from the Completed Process case above, but we introduce a few new things as well. Let s be the state of the extended state and s' and $\hat{s}'$ be a previous state and extended state respectively. Additionally, there will be an extended state $\hat{s}''$ in between $\hat{s}'$ and $\hat{s}$ such that $\phi_D^t(b, \hat{s}') = \hat{s}''$. Let the process in question be $p \in P$, its effect be $f \in F$, $a \in A$ the originating action, $b \in A$ be the canceling action, and the process time window be between x and y:

- Ω will contain $occ(a, t)$, $occ(b, t1)$, $proc\_comp(p, t2)$, $holds(neg(f), t2)$, $holds(proc\_rev\_p, t2)$ where $t + x <= t1 < t2 <= t + y$
- $\hat{s}'$ will contain $(p : f^t) \in RE$ where $x <= t <= y$
- $\hat{s}''$ will contain $(p : f^t) \in RE$ and $p \in stop_{s''}$
- $\hat{s}$ will contain $\neg f \in s$ and $(p : f) \notin RE$ and $p \notin stop_s$

As the process is created, both Ω and the extended states behave the same as they did in the previous case. The difference comes with $\hat{s}''$ and the occurrence of the *cancel* process action b. This is reflected in the additional extended state making use of the *stop* set in the transition function and Ω containing the occurrence of the stop action b and having the *flag* fluent 'flipped' for the process. At the end, we can see that both have finished the process, Ω with $proc\_comp()$ and $\hat{s}$ with $p \notin RE$ and $\neg f$ holding for both. We can now see that the beginning and end points of both Ω and the extended states are equivalent as both change due to the originating and reversing actions.

From the original theory laid down in [26] to the implementation just shown, a few differences are apparent. One of these differences is how the implementation executes the direct effect actions. While the transition function creates a default irreversible process of 1 time step to perform the transition, the implementation just treats them as basic direct effects and does not do anything additional. Another big difference is the idea behind the **stop** action law. In the implementation above, this functions very similar to the idea of an *interrupt* from basic process / OS management. The transition function uses it more as a barrier or wall to ensure that the process completed.

A smaller issue that is different is the idea of '*annotated fluents*'. As the action language is using simple English statements, it is hard to superscript time variables onto any kind of literal. Therefore, in the implementation the timed steps are only given as part of the action — rather than as part of the fluent input.

4.2   Quality of Models

The quality of the solutions given the goal of reversing the reversible process are fairly good, resulting in only differences in the permutations of when the process can start and finish. By quality, we refer to the resulting atoms in the answer set describing the desired goal. There are some repeats in model actions however, for instance given the Merchant/Consumer example and the *payment_process* window of 3 to 5 time steps. Let us say three of the models decide the process completes on the third, fourth, and fifth time step respectfully. Now we have 3 'different' models, however if all three have the process stopped on the 3rd time step — they are effectively the same model even though they will show in the results as different.

4.3   Resulting Models

The actual ASP code was run using clasp [1]. Both of the examples defined above were tested and the goals for both examples were to *cancel* all reversible actions.

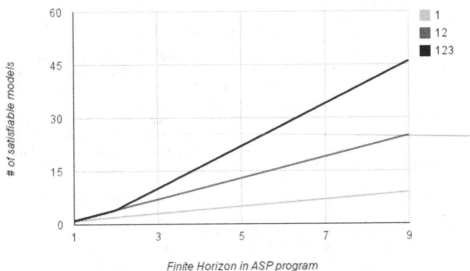

Fig. 1. Various times the ball kicked could arrive at the goal. The times signify the options available for the action 'kick_ball'. Either 1, 1 or 2, or 1, 2 or 3 time steps.

Figure 1 shows some simple results from the Penalty Kick example. In this example, the *ball_in_air* process was allowed to be active for either 1, 1 or 2, or 1, 2 or 3 time steps. The path lengths tested were between 1 and 9 time steps.

Figure 2 shows some of the more interesting results from the Merchant/ Consumer example. In this example, the action *sendQuote* was an irreversible action that took one time step to finish. The reversible action *sendPayment* could have optionally taken 1 or 2 time steps, 1,2 or 3 time steps, 2,3, or 4 time steps, or 3,4,or 5 time steps (which was the original time window given in the example from [26]). The horizontal line on the chart shows how long the plan length was that we tested, which we tested plan lengths ranging from 6 to 18 time steps.

5   Discussion

During our testing, one thing became clear. The goal specification for canceling actions is odd. How does one 'plan' to cancel an action half way through reaching a goal? It seems to be very awkward to use as a goal 'complete the process but do not let its effect hold', which is the type of goals used to perform the cancellation. Finding an example domain that used such explicit cancellation in its plan could not be found, however we are optimistic that one may be found.

On the other hand, if we were only concerned with the possibility of what might happen when a reversible process completes this implementation works

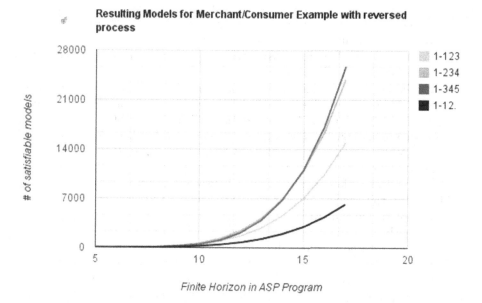

Fig. 2. Various options for delayed actions for the Merchant/Consumer example. The different options show the different options in the delayed actions. The labeling is based on [Quote Times] - [Payment Times] so the option '1-123' stands for the instance where the 'sendQuote' process competes in 1 time step and 'sendPayment' completes in 1,2, or 3 time steps.

well. If the goal was changed to only having the process complete, rather than also wanting the effect to hold, then models would show up where the process is both reversed and where it is not reversed. This has more of the *non-deterministic* feel for computing models. This was not pursued much above in Section 4 as we were interested in testing cases when the action **stop** always occurred.

Another large area that has a great impact on our evaluations in Section 4 is the scope of our fluents. Everything done was used with all agents having full knowledge of all fluents. While this feature is nice and allows for the ability for non-originating agents to cancel processes, such as the goalie blocking the ball before it reaches the goal, it can lead to an overabundance of fluent options to take care of and variances in the fluents which may not actually matter to the overall model's goal.

While our tests were only with two agents, if there were examples with more agents it is our belief these models would increase even more drastically as the options for processes increases at each time. For instance, let us take the *penalty kick* domain. What would happen if we increased that to a full sized soccer match and gave the goal to be "One team should win by two goals"? The amount of variance would be enormous!

This example leads to another issue that has been mentioned in previous sections, and that is the current implementation does not allow for an action process to be run multiple times. That is, there is no *reset* mechanism to undo the *proc_comp()* rule. For that reason, the above suggestion could not be tested to see how many models were possible.

One thing to note is that these implemented delayed processes model an *existential temporal operator* quite well. In the sense that the delayed process complies with the following temporal notion, "There is a point of time between 3 and 5 steps from now in which *pay* becomes true". That being said, we do not attempt a similar version for a *universal temporal operator*. However, we think this can be easily done through the use of *static causal laws* and other constraints for the temporal notion of, "For all time between 3 and 5 steps from now, *pay* holds". Also, the concept of *scenarios* described in the originating paper [26] may address this idea as well.

Along with the same concept as the *universal temporal operator*, is the idea of having an *un-timed* window for the process. This idea might prove rather difficult to implement. As we saw in Section 4 the number of returned models increases dramatically the more time steps the process runs. So ideas like, "Anytime between now and the end of the plan *pay* will become true" would be quite difficult to model in this implementation.

6   Conclusion and Future Direction

In this paper, we introduced a simple example of reversible processes using $\mathcal{L}^{mt}$ with the Penalty Kick example and gave an encoding for it and the Merchant/Consumer example in Answer Set Programming.

This is the first stage in implementing fully functional *narratives* and complex *commitments* in a declarative fashion like ASP. As the originating paper for $\mathcal{L}^{mt}$ alluded to, implementing more complex examples of negotiation protocols and ways to facilitate *maintenance* of commitments (that is identifying violated or breached commitments) will be pursued in addition to using planning techniques to find ways to *satisfy* possibly violated or breached commitments.

Besides encoding more complicated extensions of $\mathcal{L}^{mt}$, we will also pursue adding in *belief* or *epistemic* states to this implementation. This will eventually lead to the pursuit of *epistemic commitments* that agents may have which may be very similar to belief revision in MAS.

While not mentioned in the original description of $\mathcal{L}^{mt}$, the idea of 'stopping a process' poses an interesting question for exogenous actions. While we currently have it used as a pseudo-*interrupt*, an investigation into its use as a way to model failed actions in a similar fashion to some *contingency planning* may prove fruitful.

One last avenue of possible future direction is to pursue implementing this in a more 'on-line' fashion. As the current implementation works entirely off-line and in an iterative fashion (one checks each possible plan length at a time).

References

1. Potassco - the potsdam answer set solving collection,
   `http://potassco.sourceforge.net/`
2. Baldoni, M., Baroglio, C., Chiarotto, A., Patti, V.: Programming Goal-Driven Web
   Sites Using an Agent Logic Language. In: Ramakrishnan, I.V. (ed.) PADL 2001.
   LNCS, vol. 1990, pp. 60–75. Springer, Heidelberg (2001),
   `http://www.springerlink.com/index/labcg2d7yjdcjrjc.pdf`
3. Baldoni, M., Giordano, L., Martelli, A., Patti, V.: Modeling Agents in a Logic
   Action Language. In: Proc. of Workshop on Practical Reasoning Agents, FAPR
   2000 (2000)
4. Baldoni, M., Martelli, A., Patti, V., Giordano, L.: Programming Rational Agents
   in a Modal Action Logic. Annals of Mathematics and Artificial Intelligence 41(2-4),
   207–257 (2004),
   `http://www.springerlink.com/openurl.asp?`
   `id=doi:10.1023/B:AMAI.0000031196.24935.b5`
5. Baral, C., Gelfond, G., Pontelli, E., Son, T.C.: Logic programming for finding
   models in the logics of knowledge and its applications: A case study. TPLP 10(4-
   6), 675–690 (2010)
6. Baral, C., Gelfond, M., Provetti, A.: Representing actions: Laws, observations and
   hypotheses. J. Log. Program. 31(1-3), 201–243 (1997)
7. Baral, C., Son, T.C., Tuan, L.C.: A transition function based characterization of
   actions with delayed and continuous effects. In: Proceedings of the Eighth International Conference on Principles of Knowledge and Representation and Reasoning
   (KR 2000), pp. 291–302 (2002)
8. Bordini, R.H., Wooldridge, M., Hübner, J.F.: Programming Multi-Agent Systems
   in AgentSpeak using Jason (Wiley Series in Agent Technology). John Wiley &
   Sons (2007)
9. Brenner, M.: A Multiagent Planning Language. In: Proc. of ICAPS 2003 Workshop
   on PDDL (2003)
10. Brewka, G., Strass, H., Thielscher, M.: Declarative strategies for agents with incom-
    plete knowledge. In: NMR 2012: 14th International Workshop on Non-Monotonic
    Reasoning (2012)
11. Casolary, M., Lee, J.: Representing the language of the causal calculator in answer
    set programming. In: Gallagher, J.P., Gelfond, M. (eds.) ICLP (Technical Com-
    munications). LIPIcs, vol. 11, pp. 51–61. Schloss Dagstuhl - Leibniz-Zentrum fuer
    Informatik (2011)
12. Dimopoulos, Y., Kakas, A.C., Michael, L.: Reasoning About Actions and
    Change in Answer Set Programming. In: Lifschitz, V., Niemelä, I. (eds.) LP-
    NMR 2004. LNCS (LNAI), vol. 2923, pp. 61–73. Springer, Heidelberg (2003),
    `http://dblp.uni-trier.de/db/conf/lpnmr/lpnmr2004.html#DimopoulosKM04`
13. Dovier, A., Formisano, A., Pontelli, E.: Planning with action languages: Perspec-
    tives using clp(fd) and asp. In: CILC 2006: Convegno Italiano di Logica Com-
    putazionale (2006)
14. Dovier, A., Formisano, A., Pontelli, E.: Perspectives on Logic-Based Approaches
    for Reasoning About Actions and Change. In: Logic Programming, Knowledge
    Representation, and Nonmonotonic Reasoning, pp. 259–279. Springer, Heidelberg
    (2011), `http://dl.acm.org/citation.cfm?id=2001078.2001096`
15. Fox, M., Long, D.: PDDL2.1: An Extension to PDDL for Expressing Temporal
    Planning Domains. Journal of Artificial Intelligence Research 20, 61–124 (2003)

16. Gebser, M., Grote, T., Schaub, T.: Coala: A Compiler from Action Languages to ASP. In: Janhunen, T., Niemelä, I. (eds.) JELIA 2010. LNCS, vol. 6341, pp. 360–364. Springer, Heidelberg (2010)
17. Gelfond, M., Lifschitz, V.: The stable model semantics for logic programming, pp. 1070–1080. MIT Press (1988)
18. Gelfond, M., Lifschitz, V.: Action languages. Electronic Transactions on AI 3 (1998)
19. Giunchiglia, E., Lifschitz, V.: Action languages, temporal action logics and the situation calculus. In: Working Notes of the IJCAI 1999 Workshop on Nonmonotonic Reasoning, Action, and Change (1999),
    http://citeseerx.ist.psu.edu/viewdoc/download?
    doi=10.1.1.25.2280&rep=rep1&type=pdf
20. Kowalski, R., Sadri, F.: An Agent Language with Destructive Assignment and Model-Theoretic Semantics. In: Dix, J., Leite, J., Governatori, G., Jamroga, W. (eds.) CLIMA XI. LNCS, vol. 6245, pp. 200–218. Springer, Heidelberg (2010),
    http://dl.acm.org/citation.cfm?id=1893859.1893877
21. Lifschitz, V.: Action languages, answer sets and planning. In: The Logic Programming Paradigm: a 25-Year Perspective, pp. 357–373. Springer (1999)
22. Lifschitz, V.: Answer set programming and plan generation. Artif. Intell. 138(1-2), 39–54 (2002), http://dx.doi.org/10.1016/S0004-3702(02)00186-8
23. Rao, A.: Agentspeak(l): Bdi Agents Speak Out in a Logical Computable Language. In: Perram, J., Van de Velde, W. (eds.) MAAMAW 1996. LNCS, vol. 1038, pp. 42–55. Springer, Heidelberg (1996), http://dx.doi.org/10.1007/BFb0031845
24. Sirbu, M.: Credits and debits on the internet. In: Huhns, M., Singh, M.P. (eds.) Readings in Agents, pp. 299–305. Morgan Kaufmann (1998)
25. Son, T.C., Pontelli, E., Nguyen, N.-H.: Planning for Multiagent Using ASP-Prolog. In: Dix, J., Fisher, M., Novák, P. (eds.) CLIMA X. LNCS, vol. 6214, pp. 1–21. Springer, Heidelberg (2010),
    http://dx.doi.org/10.1007/978-3-642-16867-3_1, 10.1007, doi:10.1007/978-3-642-16867-3_1
26. Son, T.C., Pontelli, E., Sakama, C.: Formalizing Commitments Using Action Languages. In: Sakama, C., Sardina, S., Vasconcelos, W., Winikoff, M. (eds.) DALT 2011. LNCS, vol. 7169, pp. 67–83. Springer, Heidelberg (2012)
27. Subrahmanian, V.S., Zaniolo, C.: Relating stable models and ai planning domains. In: Proc. ICLP 1995, pp. 233–247. MIT Press (1995)

Full Hybrid μ-Calculus, Its Bisimulation Invariance and Application to Argumentation

Cristian Gratie[1], Adina Magda Florea[1], and John-Jules Ch. Meyer[2]

[1] AI-MAS Laboratory, Computer Science Department
University "Politehnica" of Bucharest, Romania
cristian.gratie@cs.pub.ro, adina.florea@cs.pub.ro
[2] Intelligent Systems Group, Computer Science Department
Utrecht University, The Netherlands
J.J.C.Meyer@uu.nl

Abstract. Previous research has shown that argumentation semantics can be described with Monadic Second Order Logic. While certain less expressive, modal, logics can also capture some of the semantics, the general issue of finding minimal modal logics that are able to describe certain argumentation semantics has not received a lot of attention in the literature so far. In this paper we show that full hybrid μ-calculus cannot describe the preferred semantics, thus providing a negative answer to an open question. We show that the same holds for the skeptical and credulous versions of the preferred semantics. Our result relies on the invariance of full hybrid μ-calculus with respect to a suitable notion of bisimulation. We provide a complete proof of this invariance in the paper.

Keywords: full hybrid mu-calculus, argumentation, bisimulation.

1 Introduction

Modal logic was first used for describing argumentation semantics by Grossi in [1]. He also showed in [2] that many argumentation semantics can be described using Monadic Second Order Logic ($MSOL$). However, for most semantics, it is still not known whether the full expressive power of $MSOL$ is indeed required.

In this paper we focus on full hybrid μ-calculus [3,4], a modal logic combining hybrid logics [5], μ-calculus [6], global modality and the converse operator. We define a suitable notion of bisimilarity for this logic and prove an invariance result with respect to it. The proof is not very intricate, but it avoids a second induction on fixpoint approximants, the approach suggested in [6], where bisimulation invariance of μ-calculus is discussed.

We use the invariance result in order to anwer an open question in [1] concerning the use of hybrid logics in addition to fixpoint operators in order to describe the preferred semantics of abstract argumentation frameworks [7]. We show that this logic is not expressive enough for this task, not even if the preferred extensions are aggregated by taking their intersection or their union.

M. Fisher et al. (Eds.): CLIMA XIII 2012, LNAI 7486, pp. 181–194, 2012.

The paper also discusses the standard translation of full hybrid μ-calculus ($L\mu(\mathbf{E}, @, ^{-})$) into Monadic Second Order Logic ($MSOL$). We leave the problem of whether $L\mu(\mathbf{E}, @, ^{-})$ is the full hybrid bisimulation invariant fragment of $MSOL$ open, but point out that Janin and Walukiewicz's proof for the case of μ-calculus [8] is not applicable without significant changes because of the fact that $L\mu(\mathbf{E}, @, ^{-})$ does not have the tree model property.

We introduce full hybrid mu-calculus and the corresponding bisimulation in Section 2, where we also prove the invariance result. The standard translation to $MSOL$ is covered in Section 3. The application of our result to argumentation is presented in Section 4, together with a basic background on abstract argumentation. The paper ends with conclusions and ideas for future work in Section 5.

2   Full Hybrid μ-Calculus and Its Bisimulation

We start by introducing full hybrid μ-calculus, which will also be denoted by $L\mu(\mathbf{E}, @, ^{-})$. For more details, the reader may see [3,4]. The notations that we use are more in the spirit of Blackburn et al [9].

Definition 1. *Let $\mathcal{P}rop$ be a set of **atomic propositions**, $\mathcal{R}el$ a set of **relation names**, $\mathcal{N}om$ a set of **nominals** and $\mathcal{V}ar$ a set of **proposition variables**. A **full hybrid μ-calculus formula** is recursively defined as follows:*

(a) *$\bot$ is a formula*
(b) *any atomic proposition $p \in \mathcal{P}rop$ is a formula*
(c) *any nominal $i \in \mathcal{N}om$ is a formula*
(d) *any variable $X \in \mathcal{V}ar$ is a formula*
(e) *if ϕ is a formula, then $\neg\phi$ is a formula – negation*
(f) *if ϕ and ψ are formulas, then $\phi \vee \psi$ is a formula – disjunction*
(g) *if ϕ is a formula and $r \in \mathcal{R}el$ is a relation, then $\langle r \rangle \phi$ is a formula – diamond*
(h) *if ϕ is a formula and $r \in \mathcal{R}el$ is a relation, then $\langle r^{-} \rangle \phi$ is a formula – (diamond of the) converse of a relation*
(i) *if ϕ is a formula then $\mathbf{E}\phi$ is a formula – global diamond (existential modality)*
(j) *if ϕ is a formula and $i \in \mathcal{N}om$ is a nominal, then $@_i\phi$ is a formula – satisfaction (formula true at a nominal)*
(k) *if $X \in \mathcal{V}ar$ is a variable and $\phi(X)$ is a formula where all free occurrences of X are positive (within the scope of an even number of negations), then $\nu X.\phi(X)$ is a formula – maximal fixpoint*

Note that we have not included the dual operators in the definition, in order to simplify both the proofs and the definitions that follow. These operators can be defined as follows:

- conjunction: $\phi \wedge \psi := \neg(\neg\phi \vee \neg\psi)$
- box: $[r]\phi := \neg\langle r \rangle \neg\phi$
- global box (universal modality): $\mathbf{A}\phi := \neg\mathbf{E}\neg\phi$

- minimal fixpoint: $\mu X.\phi := \neg\nu X.\neg\phi(\neg X)$; note that we need three negations in order to ensure that the free occurrences of X are still under the scope of an even number of negations.

Note also that the @ operator can be defined with the help of the global modalities as either $@_i\phi := \mathbf{E}(i \wedge \phi)$ or $@_i\phi := \mathbf{A}(\neg i \vee \phi)$. Note that the two formulas are not equivalent in general, but only when the valuation of i is a single world, which does hold for nominals. We chose to include @ in the definition because the satisfaction operator can also be part of modal logics that do not have the global modalities.

In fact, the whole definition might have been written in a more compact form, but we wanted to make explicit reference to individual items so that the logics that are subsumed by full hybrid μ-calculus can be easily described. Indeed, let us note that propositional logic PL is defined by items (a), (b), (e) and (f). Basic modal logic ML (with multiple modalities) can be obtained by adding (g) to PL, while for the global modal logic $ML(\mathbf{E})$ we also need to add the global modality, item (i).

The simple μ-calculus $L\mu$ is defined by ML plus (d) and (k), whereas the hybrid modal logic $\mathcal{H}(@)$ is defined by ML plus (c) and (j). The full hybrid μ-calculus $L\mu(\mathbf{E}, @, ^-)$ subsumes all the aforementioned logics and contains, in addition, the converse operator for relations, item (h) of Definition 1.

Satisfiability of modal formulas is generally defined with respect to Kripke models. In what follows we will assume that the sets $\mathcal{P}rop$, $\mathcal{R}el$, $\mathcal{N}om$ and $\mathcal{V}ar$ are fixed and we will define the elements of a model with respect to them.

Definition 2. *A **Kripke model** is defined as a tuple $\mathfrak{M} = (W, R, V)$, where W is a set of **worlds** (or **states**), $R : \mathcal{R}el \to W \times W$ is a function that returns, for each relation symbol $r \in \mathcal{R}el$, an **accessibility relation** $R(r) \subseteq W \times W$, and $V : \mathcal{P}rop \cup \mathcal{N}om \cup \mathcal{V}ar \to \mathcal{P}(W)$ is a **valuation function** that returns the set of worlds for which a certain proposition, nominal or variable holds. The valuation function V must satisfy $|V(i)| = 1$ for all nominals $i \in \mathcal{N}om$ i. e. exactly one world is designated by a nominal.*

Examples of such models can be seen in Figure 1 and Figure 2. Note that we have drawn the model as a labeled transition system, with the names of the corresponding relations on the arrows. For the valuation, we have put the atomic propositions and nominals next to each world where they hold. Note that nominals act as names for certain worlds, since there is exactly one world in the valuation of each nominal.

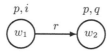

Fig. 1. Simple Kripke model

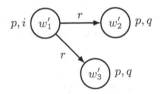

Fig. 2. Kripke model that is bisimilar to the one in Figure 1

The valuation function gives us the worlds where atomic formulas (propositions, nominals or variables) are true. We can use this information in order to decide whether more complex formulas are true at a given world in a model. This leads to the definition of modal satisfaction. We will use *and* instead of ∧ and *or* instead of ∨ in the meta-language, so that there is a clear distinction with respect to the object language. Furthermore, implication (⇒) and equivalence (⇔), as well as the existential (∃) and the universal (∀) quantifiers, are only part of the meta-language.

Definition 3. *Let* $\mathfrak{M} = (W, R, V)$ *be a Kripke model.* ***Modal satisfaction*** *of a* $L\mu(\mathbf{E}, @, ^-)$ *formula is recursively defined as follows:*

- $\mathfrak{M}, w \not\Vdash \bot$
- $\mathfrak{M}, w \Vdash t \Leftrightarrow w \in V(t)$, *for all* $t \in \mathcal{P}rop \cup \mathcal{N}om \cup \mathcal{V}ar$
- $\mathfrak{M}, w \Vdash \neg\phi \Leftrightarrow \mathfrak{M}, w \not\Vdash \phi$
- $\mathfrak{M}, w \Vdash \phi \vee \psi \Leftrightarrow \mathfrak{M}, w \Vdash \phi$ *or* $\mathfrak{M}, w \Vdash \psi$
- $\mathfrak{M}, w \Vdash \langle r \rangle\phi \Leftrightarrow \exists v.(w, v) \in R(r)$ *and* $\mathfrak{M}, v \Vdash \phi$
- $\mathfrak{M}, w \Vdash \langle r^- \rangle\phi \Leftrightarrow \exists v.(v, w) \in R(r)$ *and* $\mathfrak{M}, v \Vdash \phi$
- $\mathfrak{M}, w \Vdash \mathbf{E}\phi \Leftrightarrow \exists v.\mathfrak{M}, v \Vdash \phi$
- $\mathfrak{M}, w \Vdash @_i\phi \Leftrightarrow \forall v.V(i) = \{v\} \Rightarrow \mathfrak{M}, v \Vdash \phi$
- $\mathfrak{M}, w \Vdash \nu X.\phi(X) \Leftrightarrow \exists T.T \subseteq W$ *and* $T \subseteq \{v \in W \mid \mathfrak{M}_{[X:=T]}, v \Vdash \phi(X)\}$ *and* $w \in T$, *where* $\mathfrak{M}_{[X:=T]}$ *stands for the model that keeps all elements of the original model, excpet for the valuation of variable* X, *which is changed to* T.

It is easy to see for example that $\mathfrak{M}_1, w_1 \Vdash p$ and $\mathfrak{M}_1, w_1 \Vdash [r]q$, where $\mathfrak{M}_1$ is the model in Figure 1. We can see that we also have that $\mathfrak{M}_2, w'_1 \Vdash p$ and $\mathfrak{M}_2, w'_1 \Vdash [r]q$ for the model $\mathfrak{M}_2$ from Figure 2. In fact, no formula from ML can distinguish $\mathfrak{M}_1, w_1$ from $\mathfrak{M}_2, w'_1$. This happens because the two models are alike in some sense, more precisely they are bisimilar. We introduce full hybrid bisimulation below, then discuss its meaning.

Definition 4. *Let* $\mathfrak{M}_1 = (W_1, R_1, V_1)$ *and* $\mathfrak{M}_2 = (W_2, R_2, V_2)$ *be two models. A relation* $Z \subseteq W_1 \times W_2$ *is said to be a full hybrid bisimulation iff it satisfies the following constraints:*

(i) *if* $(w_1, w_2) \in Z$ *then* $w_1 \in V_1(t) \Leftrightarrow w_2 \in V_2(t)$, *for any* $t \in \mathcal{P}rop \cup \mathcal{N}om \cup \mathcal{V}ar$ *(agreement on atomic propositions, nominals and proposition variables)*

(ii) for any nominal $i \in \mathcal{N}om$, if $V_1(i) = \{w_1\}$ and $V_2(i) = \{w_2\}$ then $(w_1, w_2) \in Z$ (nominals)

(iii) for any $w_1, w_1' \in W_1$ and $w_2 \in W_2$, if $(w_1, w_2) \in Z$ and $(w_1, w_1') \in R_1(r)$ for some $r \in \mathcal{R}el$ then there is a world $w_2' \in W_2$ such that $(w_2, w_2') \in R_2(r)$ and $(w_1', w_2') \in Z$ (zig for relations)

(iv) for any $w_1 \in W_1$ and $w_2, w_2' \in W_2$, if $(w_1, w_2) \in Z$ and $(w_2, w_2') \in R_2(r)$ for some $r \in \mathcal{R}el$ then there is a world $w_1' \in W_1$ such that $(w_1, w_1') \in R_1(r)$ and $(w_1', w_2') \in Z$ (zag for relations)

(v) for any $w_1, w_1' \in W_1$ and $w_2' \in W_2$, if $(w_1', w_2') \in Z$ and $(w_1, w_1') \in R_1(r)$ for some $r \in \mathcal{R}el$ then there is a world $w_2 \in W_2$ such that $(w_2, w_2') \in R_2(r)$ and $(w_1, w_2) \in Z$ (zig for converse)

(vi) for any $w_1' \in W_1$ and $w_2, w_2' \in W_2$, if $(w_1', w_2') \in Z$ and $(w_2, w_2') \in R_2(r)$ for some $r \in \mathcal{R}el$ then there is a world $w_1 \in W_1$ such that $(w_1, w_1') \in R_1(r)$ and $(w_1, w_2) \in Z$ (zag for converse)

(vii) for any world $w_1 \in W_1$ there is a world $w_2 \in W_2$ such that $(w_1, w_2) \in Z$ (zig for the global modality)

(viii) for any world $w_2 \in W_2$ there is a world $w_1 \in W_1$ such that $(w_1, w_2) \in Z$ (zag for the global modality)

If there is a full hybrid bisimulation Z between two models $\mathfrak{M}_1$ and $\mathfrak{M}_2$ we say that the models are full hybrid bisimilar and write this as $\mathfrak{M}_1 \underline{\leftrightarrow}_{fh} \mathfrak{M}_2$. If w_1 is a world in $\mathfrak{M}_1$ and w_2 is a world in $\mathfrak{M}_2$ such that $(w_1, w_2) \in Z$, we say that the two worlds are full hybrid bisimilar and we write this as $\mathfrak{M}_1, w_1 \underline{\leftrightarrow}_{fh} \mathfrak{M}_2, w_2$.

Note that we have subscripted the bisimulation relation with its type (full hybrid) in order to distinguish it from the usual bisimulation relation $\underline{\leftrightarrow}$, which only requires conditions (i), (iii) and (iv). It is a known result that ML formulas cannot distinguish between bisimilar models, in the sense that, if $\mathfrak{M}_1, w_1 \underline{\leftrightarrow} \mathfrak{M}_2, w_2$ then for any modal formula $\phi \in ML$ we have that $\mathfrak{M}_1, w_1 \Vdash \phi \Leftrightarrow \mathfrak{M}_2, w_2 \Vdash \phi$. For more information about bisimulations see [9].

The original notion of bisimulation can be extended for other modal logics. Total bisimulation, for example, adds the zig-zag constraints for the global modalities, items (vii) and (viii) from Definition 4. It also holds that any $ML(\mathbf{E})$ formula is invariant under total bisimulations. Hybrid bisimulation [5] adds the rule for nominals, item (ii), and it has been shown that hybrid formulas in $\mathcal{H}(@)$ are invariant under hybrid bisimulations.

In what follows, we will show that full hybrid μ-calculus formulas $\phi \in L\mu(\mathbf{E}, @, ^-)$ are invariant under full hybrid bisimulations.

Theorem 1. *Let $\mathfrak{M}_1 = (W_1, R_1, V_1)$ and $\mathfrak{M}_2 = (W_2, R_2, V_2)$ be two full hybrid bisimilar models and let $w_1 \in W_1$ and $w_2 \in W_2$ be two bisimilar worlds. In other words, we have $\mathfrak{M}_1, w_1 \underline{\leftrightarrow}_{fh} \mathfrak{M}_2, w_2$. Then, for any formula $\phi \in L\mu(\mathbf{E}, @, ^-)$, we have that:*

$$\mathfrak{M}_1, w_1 \Vdash \phi \Leftrightarrow \mathfrak{M}_2, w_2 \Vdash \phi$$

Proof. First, let us denote by $Z \subseteq W_1 \times W_2$ a full hybrid bisimulation between $\mathfrak{M}_1, w_1$ and $\mathfrak{M}_2, w_2$.

The base cases consist in $\bot$ and the atomic formulas $t \in \mathcal{P}rop \cup \mathcal{N}om \cup \mathcal{V}ar$. The $\bot$ case is trivial (since no model satisfies it) while for the atomic formulas the claim follows from constraint (i) of full hybrid bisimulation.

For the negation we have that $\mathfrak{M}_1, w_1 \Vdash \neg\phi \Leftrightarrow \mathfrak{M}_1, w_1 \nVdash \phi$, which, by the induction hypothesis, is equivalent to $\mathfrak{M}_2, w_2 \nVdash \phi \Leftrightarrow \mathfrak{M}_2, w_2 \Vdash \neg\phi$.

For disjunction we have: $\mathfrak{M}_1, w_1 \Vdash \phi \vee \psi \Leftrightarrow \mathfrak{M}_1, w_1 \Vdash \phi \ \underline{or} \ \mathfrak{M}_1, w_1 \Vdash \psi \Leftrightarrow \mathfrak{M}_2, w_2 \Vdash \phi \ \underline{or} \ \mathfrak{M}_2, w_2 \Vdash \psi \Leftrightarrow \mathfrak{M}_2, w_2 \Vdash \phi \vee \psi$, where we have used the induction hypothesis for ϕ and ψ.

For the modal operators we have $\mathfrak{M}_1, w_1 \Vdash \langle r \rangle \phi \Leftrightarrow \exists w_1'.(w_1, w_1') \in R_1(r) \ \underline{and}$ $\mathfrak{M}_1, w_1' \Vdash \phi \Leftrightarrow \exists w_2'.(w_2, w_2') \in R_2(r) \ \underline{and} \ \mathfrak{M}_2, w_2' \Vdash \phi \Leftrightarrow \mathfrak{M}_2, w_2 \Vdash \langle r \rangle \phi$, where we have used the induction hypothesis for ϕ and also the zig-zag constraints for relations.

For the converse operator and the global modality we use the same approach, but based on the corresponding zig-zag constraints.

For the satisfaction operator, we have: $\mathfrak{M}_1, w_1 \Vdash @_i\phi \Leftrightarrow \forall w_1'.V_1(i) = \{w_1'\} \Rightarrow \mathfrak{M}_1, w_1' \Vdash \phi \Leftrightarrow \forall w_2'.V_2(i) = \{w_2'\} \Rightarrow \mathfrak{M}_2, w_2' \Vdash \phi \Leftrightarrow \mathfrak{M}_2, w_2 \Vdash @_i\phi$. Here, we relied on the fact that the nominals constraint of full hybrid bisimulations ensures that the worlds named by the same nominal in the two models are bisimilar and we have also used the induction hypothesis.

The last remaining operator is the fixpoint ν. We have $\mathfrak{M}_1, w_1 \Vdash \nu X.\phi(X) \Leftrightarrow \exists T.(T \subseteq W_1 \ \underline{and} \ T \subseteq \{w_1' \in W_1 \mid \mathfrak{M}_{1[X:=T]}, w_1' \Vdash \phi(X)\} \ \underline{and} \ w_1 \in T)$. Let us consider the following relation $\rho \subseteq W_1 \times W_1$, given by $(u, v) \in \rho \Leftrightarrow \exists x.x \in W_2 \ \underline{and} \ (u, x) \in Z \ \underline{and} \ (v, x) \in Z$. Clearly, we have $\mathfrak{M}_1, u \Vdash \phi \Leftrightarrow \mathfrak{M}_2, x \Vdash \phi \Leftrightarrow \mathfrak{M}_1, v \Vdash \phi$, using the induction hypothesis. Let us denote by $\approx$ the reflexive and transitive closure of ρ. It is easy to see that $\approx$ is an equivalence relation. Furthermore, we have that if $u \approx v$ then $\mathfrak{M}_1, u \Vdash \phi \Leftrightarrow \mathfrak{M}_1, v \Vdash \phi$. Clearly, we can define a similar equivalence relation for $\mathfrak{M}_2$ as well. We will not use a different notation, since the worlds from the two models cannot be mixed anyway, so there is no possibility for confusion.

Now, let us take $T_1 = \{w \in W_1 \mid \exists w'.w' \in T \ \underline{and} \ w \approx w'\}$. Clearly we have $T \subseteq T_1$ and, thus, $w_1 \in T_1$. Since all occurrences of X in $\phi(X)$ are positive, we have that $\phi(X)$ is upward monotone, which means that $\{w \in W_1 \mid \mathfrak{M}_{1[X:=T]}, w \Vdash \phi(X)\} \subseteq \{w \in W_1 \mid \mathfrak{M}_{1[X:=T_1]}, w \Vdash \phi(X)\}$. So we also have $T \subseteq \{w \in W_1 \mid \mathfrak{M}_{1[X:=T_1]}, w \Vdash \phi(X)\}$. Now, let us take an arbitrary world $u \in T_1$. Then there is a world $v \in T$ such that $u \approx v$. Since $v \in T$, we have that $v \in \{w \in W_1 \mid \mathfrak{M}_{1[X:=T_1]}, w \Vdash \phi(X)\}$. But then, since $u \approx v$, we have $\mathfrak{M}_1, u \Vdash \phi(X) \Leftrightarrow \mathfrak{M}_1, v \Vdash \phi(X)$, which leads to $u \in \{w \in W_1 \mid \mathfrak{M}_{1[X:=T_1]}, w \Vdash \phi(X)\}$. Thus, we have shown that $T_1 \subseteq \{w \in W_1 \mid \mathfrak{M}_{1[X:=T_1]}, w \Vdash \phi(X)\}$.

Let us now show that for this T_1 we can find a corresponding $T_2 \subseteq W_2$ such that $\mathfrak{M}_{1[X:=T_1]} \underline{\leftrightarrow}_{fh} \mathfrak{M}_{2[X:=T_2]}$. We take $T_2 = \{w \in W_2 \mid \exists x.x \in T_1 \ \underline{and} \ (x, w) \in Z\}$. Since the only change to the original models is the valuation of X, the only constraint that might be violated by Z is (i). From the choice of T_2 we clearly have $u_1 \in T_1 \Rightarrow u_2 \in T_2$ for all $(u_1, u_2) \in Z$. Let us show that the converse holds as well. Indeed, take $u_2 \in T_2$. Then there is $x \in T_1$ such that $(x, u_2) \in Z$. Since we also have $(u_1, u_2) \in Z$, it follows that $u_1 \approx x$, so $u_1 \in T_1$, which concludes our proof.

Based on the considerations above, this also concludes the proof for the fixpoint operator and ends the induction proof of the theorem.   □

To see the intuition behind the ρ relation used in the proof, suppose we can find $T' \subseteq W_2$ such that $\mathfrak{M}_{1[X:=T]} \underline{\leftrightarrow}^Z_{fh} \mathfrak{M}_{2[X:=T']}$. Then, for any $v_2 \in T'$, from constraint (viii) of the bisimulation (zag for the global modality) we have $\exists v_1.(v_1, v_2) \in Z$, which, coupled with constraint (i) leads to $v_1 \in T$ (because $T = V_1(X)$ and $T' = V_2(X)$). But then $\mathfrak{M}_{1[X:=T]}, v_1 \Vdash \phi(X) \Leftrightarrow \mathfrak{M}_{2[X:=T']}, v_2 \Vdash \phi(X)$, using the choice of T' and the induction hypothesis. But this means that $T' \subseteq \{w'_2 \in W_2 \mid \mathfrak{M}_{2[X:=T']}, w'_2 \Vdash \phi(X)\}$. Since we have used the same bisimulation Z, we also have w_1 bisimilar with w_2, so we must have $w_2 \in T'$, which would complete the proof for the fixpoint operator.

However, it might be impossible to find an appropriate T' in order to maintain bisimilarity. To see why, consider two worlds $u_1, u'_1 \in W_1$ that are both bisimilar with a world $u_2 \in W_2$ and also satisfy $u_1 \in T$ and $u'_1 \notin T$. Since u_1 and u_2 are bisimilar, we must have $u_2 \in T'$. But then, u'_1 and u_2 being bisimilar as well, we should also have $u'_1 \in T$, which contradicts the hypothesis. Of course, we might be able to add u'_1 to T and be lucky to have the new T satisfy the same properties required for the fixpoint operator, but other changes might be necessary based on other pairs of worlds in one model that are bisimilar to the same world in the other model. The ρ relation helps to overcome this problems.

Note that the proof for the fixpoint case is different from the one suggested (but not included) in [6], which would need a second induction on the approximants of the fixpoint operator.

We end this section with a few words about what makes $L\mu(\mathbf{E}, @, ^{-})$ particularly interesting for us. First of all, it is easy to see that full hybrid μ-calculus has an impressive set of operators, which means a high expressivity. Furthermore, it is shown in [4] that it is decidable.

There are other operators that are missing, but whose addition would lead to undecidable logics. Graded modalities can be added to μ-calculus instead of nominals or the converse in order to get other powerful decidable logics [4].

Other important operators are the complement and the intersection of relations, but these two lead to undecidability rather quickly: add one of them and the global modalities to ML and the obtained logic is already undecidable [9].

A very strong operator from hybrid logics is the down arrow binder $\downarrow$, which allows one to talk about "here and now" in modal logic. However, in the presence of both nominals and the global modality, this operator provides full first-order expressive power, so it implicitly leads to undecidable logics.

This particular enrichment of $L\mu$ is interesting for us because it features appealing operators from an argumentation perspective. More precisely, μ-calculus has already been used in [1] for describing the grounded semantics and the global modality has been used for describing several others. The converse can also have an important use in argumentation for determining mutual conflict, whereas

graded modalities seem unrelated to the notions used in argumentation. We will
see more about the argumentation applications of Theorem 1 in Section 4.

3   Considerations about Expressivity with Respect to MSOL

It is well known that modal logic formulas can be translated into first-order
logic formulas with a single free variable (and many bound variables). Atomic
propositions are translated into unary (monadic) predicates, whereas the usual
modalities (boxes and diamonds – unary operators) translate into binary relations. If modalities of arity n are allowed, as in [9], then the translation language
will contain predicates of arity $n + 1$. It is shown in [9] that it is even possible
to translate ML to a first order language with only two variables.

Whenever such a translation goes both ways, in the sense that any formula
from the translation language (possibly satisfying some constraints) is equivalent to the translation of some modal formula, it is said that the corresponding
modal logic is the fragment of the translation language that satisfies the given
constraints. For example, it is known that the basic modal logic is the bisimulation invariant fragment of first order logic.

A similar translation is possible for hybrid logics as well, by providing constants and equality in the translation language. It is shown in [5] that the hybrid
logic $H(@)$ is the hybrid bisimulation invariant fragment of first order logic.

The fixpoint operators, on the other hand, go beyond first order logic. However, they can be translated into second order formulas. It was shown in [6] that
μ-calculus is the bisimulation invariant fragment of Monadic Second Order Logic
($MSOL$), where second order quantification is only allowed for subsets of the domain. The proof of this fact, due to Janin and Walukiewicz [8], is rather intricate
and uses alternating automatons that accept infinite trees. While we feel that a
similar result should hold for full hybrid μ-calculus as well, we acknowledge that
their proof cannot be directly applied for this language. The main reason for this
is the fact that full hybrid μ-calculus does not have the tree model property.

Indeed, a key element of Janin and Walukiewicz's proof relies on unraveling
models of μ-calculus into bisimilar (possibly infinite) trees. However, the nominals make such an unraveling sometimes impossible. Let us consider for example
the formula $\phi = i \wedge \langle r \rangle (j \wedge \langle r \rangle i)$, satisfied by the model in Figure 3. It is obvious that this formula cannot be satisfied by any tree model, since it actually
describes a cycle of length 2. Thus, one should either work with automatons

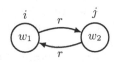

Fig. 3. A model satisfying a hybrid formula that cannot be satisfied by tree models

that accept cyclic graphs as well, or devise a completely different proof. The forest model property discussed in [3] may also be useful. We leave this part for future work, but we continue this paper with an application of the bisimulation invariance of $L\mu(\mathbf{E}, @, ^-)$ to abstract argumentation.

4 Application for the Preferred Argumentation Semantics

Argumentation frameworks are defined as directed graphs where the edges convey the attack relation between arguments. It is natural to establish a link between argumentation frameworks and the models of modal logic and this has already been done by Grossi [1]. We start with a basic argumentation background, based on [7], but with slightly different notations.

Definition 5. *An **argumentation framework** is a pair $F = (\mathcal{A}, \mathcal{R})$, where $\mathcal{A}$ is a set of arguments and $\mathcal{R} \subseteq \mathcal{A} \times \mathcal{A}$ is an attack relation on $\mathcal{A}$. We say that an argument a **attacks** an argument b and we write this as $a \to b$ iff $(a, b) \in \mathcal{R}$. In this case, we say that a is an **attacker** of b. A set of arguments S (**set-)attacks** an argument a iff S contains an attacker of a. A set S **defends** an argument a iff S attacks all the attackers of a.*

Given such an argumentation framework, there are several methods for selecting arguments that are acceptable together. Such methods are known in the argumentation literature as semantics. We will only introduce here the ones that are needed for a good understanding of the rest of the paper. The definitions are adapted from [7].

Definition 6. *Let $F = (\mathcal{A}, \mathcal{R})$ be an argumentation framework.*

(a) *A set of arguments S is said to be **conflict-free** iff there are no arguments $a, b \in S$ such that $a \to b$. The set of all conflict-free sets of F is denoted by $\mathcal{E}_{\mathcal{CF}}(F)$.*

(b) *A conflict-free set of arguments S is said to be **admissible** iff S defends all the arguments it contains. The set of all admissible sets of F is denoted by $\mathcal{E}_{\mathcal{AS}}(F)$.*

(c) *An admissible set of arguments S is said to be a **complete** extension of F iff it contains all the arguments it defends. The set of all complete extensions of F is denoted by $\mathcal{E}_{\mathcal{CO}}(F)$.*

(d) *The **grounded** extension of F is defined as the minimal (with respect to set inclusion) complete extension. We will use $GR(F)$ to denote the grounded extension of F, but also we will write $\mathcal{E}_{\mathcal{GR}}(F) = \{GR(F)\}$, for uniformity.*

(e) *A **preferred** extension of F is a maximal (with respect to set inclusion) complete extension. The set of all preferred extensions of F is denoted by $\mathcal{E}_{\mathcal{PR}}(F)$.*

Note that several other argumentation semantics exist, but they are not very relevant for this work. The interested reader may see [10] for a survey.

We will ilustrate the argumentation semantics with an example. The argumentation framework in Figure 4, call it F, is given by $F = (\mathcal{A}, \mathcal{R})$ with $\mathcal{A} = \{a, b, c, d\}$ and $\mathcal{R} = \{(a, b), (b, a), (a, c), (b, c), (c, d)\}$. For this framework, we have:

$$\begin{aligned}
\mathcal{E}_{\mathcal{CF}}(F) &= \{\varnothing, \{a\}, \{b\}, \{c\}, \{d\}, \{a, d\}, \{b, d\}\} \\
\mathcal{E}_{\mathcal{AS}}(F) &= \{\varnothing, \{a\}, \{b\}, \{a, d\}, \{b, d\}\} \\
\mathcal{E}_{\mathcal{CO}}(F) &= \{\varnothing, \{a, d\}, \{b, d\}\} \\
\mathcal{E}_{\mathcal{GR}}(F) &= \{\varnothing\} \\
\mathcal{E}_{\mathcal{PR}}(F) &= \{\{a, d\}, \{b, d\}\}
\end{aligned} \tag{1}$$

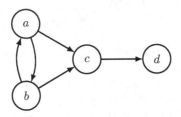

Fig. 4. A simple argumentation framework

It is not difficult to see that, at least from the representation point of view, argumentation frameworks are rather similar to Kripke models, all that they are missing is the valuation function. The link between the two domains was established by Grossi in [1], where it was shown that several argumentation semantics can be described using modal formulas. In order to give a good intuition of this link, we discuss several of Grossi's results. First, let us consider the following formulas, taken from [1] and adapted to our notation:

$$\begin{aligned}
\mathcal{CF}(x) &= \mathbf{A}(x \to \neg \langle r^- \rangle x) \\
\mathcal{AS}(x) &= \mathbf{A}(x \to ([r^-]\neg x \wedge [r^-]\langle r^- \rangle x)) \\
\mathcal{CO}(x) &= \mathbf{A}((x \to [r^-]\neg x) \wedge (x \leftrightarrow [r^-]\langle r^- \rangle x))
\end{aligned} \tag{2}$$

We will use the following extended valuation function:

$$V^*(\phi) = \{w \in W \mid \mathfrak{M}, w \Vdash \phi\} \tag{3}$$

If we read r as an attack relation and worlds as arguments, the first formula states that, for any argument a, if a is in $V_\bullet^*(x)$, then a is not attacked by an argument that is also in $V^*(x)$. In other words, $V^*(x)$ is a conflict-free set. The other formulas describe in a similar manner the corresponding extensions from argumentation:

$$\mathfrak{M}, w \Vdash \mathcal{S}em(\phi) \Leftrightarrow V^*(\phi) \in \mathcal{E}_{\mathcal{S}em}(W, R(r)) \tag{4}$$

where $\mathcal{S}em$ stands for the name of the argumentation semantics.

The following formula is provided in [1] for the grounded semantics:

$$\mathcal{G}R = \mu Z.[r^-]\langle r^-\rangle Z \tag{5}$$

We can also write this formula in a form that is similar to those in (2) and also follows the general intuition captured in (4):

$$\mathcal{G}R(x) = \mathbf{A}(x \leftrightarrow \mu Z.[r^-]\langle r^-\rangle Z) \tag{6}$$

As far as the preferred semantics is concerned, Grossi states in [1] that it cannot be described within μ-calculus, because preferred extensions are not bisimulation invariant. The example he provides relies on a model with a self-attacking argument and the unraveling of that model into an infinite chain of attacks. We will provide a different example.

Indeed, suppose that there exists a ML formula $\mathcal{PR}(x)$ that tests preferred extensions. Consider the models in Figure 5, call the one on the left $\mathfrak{M} = (W, R, V)$ and the one on the right $\mathfrak{M}' = (W', R', V')$. For model $\mathfrak{M}_1$ we have that $\mathcal{E}_{\mathcal{PR}}(W, R(r)) = \{\varnothing\}$, so $\mathfrak{M}, w \Vdash \mathcal{PR}(\bot)$ for any w, whereas for $\mathfrak{M}'$ we have $\mathcal{E}_{\mathcal{PR}}(W', R'(r)) = \{\{w_1'\}, \{w_2'\}\}$, so $\mathfrak{M}', w' \nVdash \mathcal{PR}(\bot)$, for all $w' \in W'$.

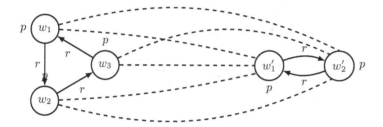

Fig. 5. Bisimilar models with different preferred extensions. Dashed lines show the full hybrid bisimulation between them.

So we have seen that $\mathcal{PR}(\bot)$ can distinguish the two models. However, note that the relation depicted in Figure 5 with dashed lines is a (simple) bisimulation, so a μ-calculus formula should not be able to distinguish the two models. We have reached our contradiction, so there is no μ-calculus formula for the preferred semantics. We prefer this example to that provided in [1] because it is not based on elements that are rather uncommon in argumentation (infinite frameworks, self-attacking arguments). Instead, it is a consequence of the fact that odd and even length cycles are handled differently by the preferred semantics, an aspect that has been discussed in the argumentation literature. Several counter-intuitive behaviors of the preferred semantics that are related to the odd vs even length cycles are presented in [11].

Furthermore, one can see that the relation from Figure 5 is in fact a full hybrid bisimulation, so we can use the same example and reasoning to get the stronger result that the added power of nominals, satisfaction operator, global modalities and converse is not enough for describing the preferred semantics. This provides a partial answer to the open question regarding the possibility of describing the preferred semantics with a combination of μ-calculus and hybrid logics [1]. The answer is just partial because $L\mu(\mathbf{E}, @,^-)$ does not contain the powerful down arrow binder $\downarrow$ pertaining to hybrid logics. Adding $\downarrow$ to μ-calculus (even without nominals) leads to an undecidable logic [5], because $\downarrow$ gives full first order expressive power. Whether $\downarrow$ is expressive enough for describing the preferred semantics remains an interesting open problem.

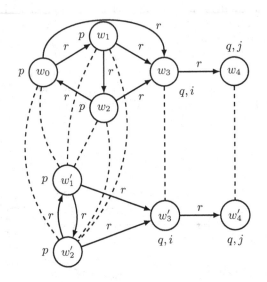

Fig. 6. Bisimilar models distinguished by the intersection of their preferred extensions. Dashed line shows the full hybrid bisimulation between them.

Let us see whether a weaker description of the preferred semantics is available within $L\mu(\mathbf{E}, @,^-)$. What we are looking for is a formula similar to (5). For this, we would have to aggregate the information contained within preferred extensions into a single set. We can do this by either intersection (skeptical approach) or union (credulous approach). We will show that full hybrid μ-calculus is still not expressive enough.

Let us assume that there exist $\mathcal{PR}_\cup$ and $\mathcal{PR}_\cap$ in $L\mu(\mathbf{E}, @,^-)$ such that, for any model $\mathfrak{M} = (W, R, V)$, we have:

$$\begin{aligned} \mathfrak{M}, w \Vdash \mathcal{PR}_\cup &\Leftrightarrow w \in \bigcup \mathcal{E}_{\mathcal{PR}}(W, R(r)) \\ \mathfrak{M}, w \Vdash \mathcal{PR}_\cap &\Leftrightarrow w \in \bigcap \mathcal{E}_{\mathcal{PR}}(W, R(r)) \end{aligned} \qquad (7)$$

We will use the models from Figure 6. Assume that $\mathfrak{M} = (W, R, V)$ is the model at the top and $\mathfrak{M}' = (W', R', V')$ is the one at the bottom. We have that the two models are bisimilar using the full hybrid bisimulation depicted in the figure.

Furthermore, let us see that their preferred extensions with respect to relation symbol r are $\mathcal{E}_{\mathcal{PR}}(W, R(r)) = \{\varnothing\}$ and $\mathcal{E}_{\mathcal{PR}}(W', R'(r)) = \{\{w'_1, w'_4\}, \{w'_2, w'_4\}\}$.

Thus, for the skeptical approach we get that $\bigcap \mathcal{E}_{\mathcal{PR}}(W, R(r)) = \varnothing$ and $\bigcap \mathcal{E}_{\mathcal{PR}}(W', R'(r)) = \{w'_4\}$. But then $\mathfrak{M}, w_4 \nVdash \mathcal{PR}_\cap$ and $\mathfrak{M}', w'_4 \Vdash \mathcal{PR}_\cap$, although w_4 and w'_4 are bisimilar. This contradicts the invariance of full hybrid μ-calculus with respect to full hybrid bisimulation. For the credulous approach we have $\bigcup \mathcal{E}_{\mathcal{PR}}(W, R(r)) = \varnothing$ and $\bigcup \mathcal{E}_{\mathcal{PR}}(W', R'(r)) = \{w'_1, w'_2, w'_4\}$. But then $\mathfrak{M}, w_4 \nVdash \mathcal{PR}_\cup$ and $\mathfrak{M}', w'_4 \Vdash \mathcal{PR}_\cup$, so again a contradiction. This shows that full hybrid μ-calculus is not expressive enough to describe $\mathcal{PR}_\cap$ or $\mathcal{PR}_\cup$.

Note that the example from Figure 5 hides an implicit requirement that the set of nominals is empty. Indeed, should there exist any nominal, the bisimulation depicted in the figure would violate condition (ii) of Definition 4 and, even more, it would be impossible to find a full hybrid bisimulation between the two models. The example from Figure 6, on the other hand, contains nominals and the preferred semantics distinguishes those two models as well, so our result does not rely on the assumption that there are no nominals.

5   Conclusions and Future Work

In this paper we proved that full hybrid μ-calculus is invariant with respect to full hybrid bisimulation. The definitions of both the logic and the corresponding bisimulation were presented in such a way as to emphasize the subsumed concepts. Our proof follows a different approach for the fixpoint operators than the one suggested in the literature for the simple μ-calculus.

Furthermore, we showed that the invariance result for the full hybrid μ-calculus helps answer an open question in the argumentation literature, namely whether a hybrid approach in addition to fixpoint operators is enough for capturing the preferred semantics. We provided a negative answer to this question and strengthened the result by showing that the intersection and the union of all preferred extensions corresponding to a model cannot be described either.

It may seem that there is no use for the converse operator in argumentation, in the sense that one can simply use the converse of the attack relation as an accessibility relation for the modal formulas and eliminate the need for the actual operator in the language. There are, however, argumentation concepts that require both the attack and its converse.[1]

We also discussed the standard translation of hybrid μ-calculus and showed that, while the translation to Monadic Second Order Logic follows easily from existing results in the literature, the reverse translation cannot benefit directly from the proof for μ-calculus because the logic does not have the tree model property, which is a key ingredient of that proof. Future work will focus on deciding whether full hybrid mu-calculus is indeed the fragment of $MSOL$ invariant to full hybrid bisimulations.

---

[1] For example, the $\mathcal{CF}$-reinstatement principle [12] requires that an extension E contains every argument a that is defended by E and is not in conflict with E (i.e. a does not attack E and E does not attack a). This principle can be formulated in full hybrid μ-calculus as $\mathbf{A}([r^-]\langle r^-\rangle x \wedge \neg\langle r^-\rangle x \wedge \neg\langle r\rangle x \to x)$.

Furthermore, it is interesting to note that writing the formal definition of the preferred semantics leads to a $MSOL$ formula. We have seen in this paper that full hybrid μ-calculus, which translates to a fragment of $MSOL$, is not expressive enough to describe the preferred semantics. On the other hand, it is not obvious whether the missing expressive power is of first order nature (and can be met by adding $\downarrow$ or possibly a weaker operator) or of second order nature. We will approach this open question in future work.

Acknowledgement. This work has been funded by the Sectoral Operational Programme Human Resources Development 2007-2013 of the Romanian Ministry of Labour, Family and Social Protection through the Financial Agreement POS-DRU/88/1.5/S/61178 and by project ERRIC (Empowering Romanian Research on Intelligent Information Technologies), number 264207/FP7-REGPOT-2010-1.

References

1. Grossi, D.: On the logic of argumentation theory. In: van der Hoek, W., Kaminka, G., Lesperance, Y., Luck, M., Sandip, S. (eds.) Proceedings of the 9th International Conference on Autonomous Agents and Multiagent Systems (AAMAS 2010), pp. 409–416. IFAAMAS (2010)
2. Grossi, D.: An Application of Model Checking Games to Abstract Argumentation. In: van Ditmarsch, H., Lang, J., Ju, S. (eds.) LORI 2011. LNCS (LNAI), vol. 6953, pp. 74–86. Springer, Heidelberg (2011)
3. Sattler, U., Vardi, M.Y.: The Hybrid μ-Calculus. In: Goré, R.P., Leitsch, A., Nipkow, T. (eds.) IJCAR 2001. LNCS (LNAI), vol. 2083, pp. 76–91. Springer, Heidelberg (2001)
4. Bonatti, P.A., Lutz, C., Murano, A., Vardi, M.Y.: The complexity of enriched μ-calculi. Logical Methods in Computer Science 4(3:11), 1–27 (2008)
5. Areces, C., ten Cate, B.: Hybrid logics. In: Handbook of Modal Logic. Studies in Logic and Practical Reasoning, vol. 3, pp. 821–868. Elsevier (2007)
6. Bradfield, J., Stirling, C.: Modal μ-calculi. In: Handbook of Modal Logic. Studies in Logic and Practical Reasoning, vol. 3, pp. 721–756. El (2007)
7. Dung, P.M.: On the acceptability of arguments and its fundamental role in nonmonotonic reasoning, logic programming and n-person games. Artificial Intelligence 77(2), 321–357 (1995)
8. Janin, D., Walukiewicz, I.: On the Expressive Completeness of the Propositional μ-Calculus with Respect to Monadic Second Order Logic. In: Sassone, V., Montanari, U. (eds.) CONCUR 1996. LNCS, vol. 1119, pp. 263–277. Springer, Heidelberg (1996)
9. Blackburn, P., de Rijke, M., Venema, Y.: Modal Logic. Cambridge Tracts in Theoretical Computer Science, vol. 27. Cambridge University Press (2001)
10. Baroni, P., Giacomin, M.: Semantics of abstract argument systems. In: Rahwan, I., Simari, G. (eds.) Argumentation in Artificial Intelligence, pp. 24–44. Springer (2009)
11. Baroni, P., Giacomin, M., Guida, G.: SCC-recursiveness: a general schema for argumentation semantics. Artificial Intelligence 168(1-2), 162–210 (2005)
12. Baroni, P., Giacomin, M.: On principle-based evaluation of extension-based argumentation semantics. Artificial Intelligence 171(10-15), 675–700 (2007)

A Numerical Approach to the Merging
of Argumentation Networks

Dov Gabbay[1] and Odinaldo Rodrigues[2]

[1] Bar Ilan University, Israel; Department of Informatics,
King's College London; and University of Luxembourg
dov.gabbay@kcl.ac.uk
[2] Department of Informatics, King's College London
odinaldo.rodrigues@kcl.ac.uk

Abstract. In this paper, we propose a numerical approach to the problem of merging of argumentation networks. The idea is to consider an augmented network containing the arguments and attacks of all networks to be merged and then associate a weight to each of its components based on how they are perceived by the agents associated with the local networks. The combined weighted network is then used to define a system of equations from which the overall strength of the arguments is calculated.

1   Introduction

An argumentation system is a tuple $\langle S, R \rangle$, where S is a non-empty set of *arguments* and R is a binary relation on S representing *attacks* between the arguments [12]. One may argue that the main objective of an argumentation system is to identify sets of *winning* arguments in S, based on the interactions represented by R and an appropriate semantics determining which subsets of S can be taken as a coherent view. Such subsets are called extensions.

This paper concerns the merging of argumentation systems. We imagine a family of k agents and a large set of possible arguments. Each agent a_i can see a subset S_i of these arguments and in her opinion, the attack relation should be $R_i \subseteq S_i^2$. Agent a_i further adopts a set of winning arguments $E_i \subseteq S_i$. The agents form a community and a consensus is required. Thus our problem is to merge these k systems $\langle S_i, R_i, E_i \rangle$ into a single system.

At first, one may think that the merging process can be done at the *meta level*, i.e., by considering only the winning arguments in each local system. However, this not only will sometimes produce unintuitive results [11], but will also fail to simultaneously satisfy well-known social choice properties [22]. The reasons have to do with the fact that attacks known only locally are not represented by the local extensions of winning arguments, but they may well be relevant during the collective decision as a whole. If we want to take both the local decisions and the local topologies of the various systems into account, we need a framework that can take all this information into account.

Our starting point is an augmented argumentation system containing the arguments and attacks of all individual networks. We approach the merging problem from a voting

M. Fisher et al. (Eds.): CLIMA XIII 2012, LNAI 7486, pp. 195–212, 2012.

perspective: agents put forward a vote on the components of the augmented system depending on how they perceive these components locally. However, the votes are not used as in an usual voting procedure such as majority voting, etc. For us, votes are used to support the idea of *reinforcement*: the more a component appears locally, the more it is represented collectivelly. We aggregate the votes of the components resulting in an augmented argumentation system in which both arguments and attacks have weights with values in the interval $U = [0, 1]$. Thus, we get a network of the form $\langle S, R, V \rangle$, where $\langle S, R \rangle$ is a traditional network and V is a function from $S \cup R$ into U. Such augmented systems can be seen a special case of *support and attack networks* [3]. We believe that the merging of argumentation systems is a scenario that naturally justifies the employment of weights in attacks and arguments.

We now have a situation whereby each agent has a traditional argumentation system, they all vote and get a merged combined numerically weighted argumentation system. This is a mismatch. So we need to explain how we understand the numerical weights and then extract/project from the merged system a set of winning arguments. Had we started working from the outset with numerical weighted systems, we would have more choice on how to perform the merging because we could use the original weights in the computation of the overall result, e.g., by constructing a new weighted argumentation system representing the group as a whole.

Given an augmented argumentation system with weights constructed as described above, we see the weights of the nodes as the overall initial level of support for the arguments in the community and the weights of the edges as the intensity with which the attacks between the arguments are carried out.

It is natural to expect that the overall support for an argument will decrease in proportion to the strength of its attacking arguments and the intensity with which these attacks are carried out. However, since the attacking arguments may themselves be attacked, we need to find a way to systematically propagate the values in the network and determine *equilibrium* values for the nodes based on their interactions, much in the spirit of an *interaction-based valuation* [8]. This is akin to finding the extensions in a traditional network. However, our work has two important differences: *1)* we allow both arguments and attacks to have weights; and *2)* we calculate the equilibrium values using the equational approach of [14,15]: we see the augmented system as a generator of numerical equations whose solutions correspond to the equilibrium values.

Argumentation systems in which weights are associated to arguments have been studied before. One of the first approaches was proposed in [4] where the weight of an argument is used to express its relative strength for a particular audience. Besnard and Hunter proposed a *categoriser* function that assigned a value to a tree of arguments [5]; Cayrol and Lagasquie-Schiex introduced the concept of *graduality* in the valuation of arguments in [8]; and other examples of systems using weights in one form or another include [3,13,2,6,23,19]. The novelty of our approach is in the use of the weights to represent the support of the community for both arguments and attacks and in the way that equilibrium values for these components are calculated using a system of equations.

The rest of the paper is structured as follows. In Section 2, we introduce some basic concepts and the equational approach. In Section 3, we show how the merging process is done. We then show how to calculate equilibrium values in Section 4 and illustrate the idea with some examples in Section 5. Some comparisons with related work are done in Section 6 and we finish with some discussions and conclusions in Section 7.

2 Background

As mentioned in the previous section, given an argumentation system $\langle S, R \rangle$, one is generally interested in finding the *winning* arguments in S according to a particular semantics.

One way of doing this is to look at subsets $E \subseteq S$ that are as large as possible and yet whose arguments are *compatible* with each other. Two common notions of compatibility require E to be *conflict-free*, i.e., $\forall X, Y \in E$, it is not the case that $(X, Y) \in R$; and that all arguments $X \in E$ are *acceptable*, i.e., $\forall Y \in S$, if $(Y, X) \in R$, then $\exists Z \in E$ such that $(Z, Y) \in R$. If E is conflict-free and only contains acceptable arguments, then we say that E is *admissible*. An admissible set $E \subseteq S$ that is also maximal with respect to set inclusion amongst all admissible sets is called a *preferred extension* of $\langle S, R \rangle$.

A preferred extension can be defined in terms of a complete labelling of the set of arguments that assigns in to arguments that are accepted; out to those that are rejected; and $undec$ to those that are neither [7, Theorem 2]. Such labelling is called a *Caminada labelling* [7, Definition 5] and has advantages over the extension approach, because the latter only identifies the set of arguments that are accepted. We will return to this type of labelling later in the section.

In traditional argumentation systems, there is no notion of weight associated to an argument or attack. However, there are scenarios in which this association seems natural. In the case of arguments, the weights may come, for instance, from an underlying many-valued logic; as the normalised result of a vote put to a community of agents; or as the result of interactions between the arguments in a network (as in [8]). In the first case, the values are intrinsic to the arguments whereas in the last two, the values are conceptually *external* to the argumentation framework. Mixed approaches are also possible. We may start with each agent assigning numerical values via considerations which are conceptually connected to the arguments and their meaning and end up with merged values obtained during a voting procedure. The application area can dictate the most appropriate approach.

For similar reasons, an attack between arguments X and Y may also be given varying degrees of strength rather than just 0 or 1. Again, the strength may have conceptually related, internal, argumentation meaning or may be conceptually external to the arguments themselves. For example, it may be obtained from the statistics about the correlation between X and Y; or calculated from the proportion of members of a community supporting the attack of X on Y (as in [9]). It may even come from considerations about the geometry of the network itself.

An even more compelling scenario for the use of extended values is because they arise naturally in formalisms that are concerned with the problem of *merging* of argumentation systems, which we consider here. The concept was introduced by Coste-Marquis et. al. in [11].

Because of these considerations, it may be wise when presenting a numerical argumentation network to provide not only the numerical values themselves but also to give their origin, internal or external, etc.

Now, given the numerical network $\langle S, R, V \rangle$ we need to somehow figure out what the various values mean. We can regard the values given by V as *start-up values* that we may want to adjust depending on how the components interact in the network. The adjustment corresponds to the *valuation step* in Cayrol and Lagasquie-Schiex's terminology [8]. However, in our case we want arguments to be *weakened* in proportion to the strength of the attacks and the intensity with which these attacks are carried out. Ideally, we want to find *equilibrium* values for all arguments.

One good option to calculate these values is by using the *equational approach* proposed in [14,15] which sees a numerical network as a generator of equations. Provided the equations respect the meaning of the weights of the arguments and attacks an "evaluation" of the network can be done according to the solutions found for the system of equations. For an argument X, the equilibrium value 1 means definitely "in"; 0 means definitely "out"; and any other value inbetween means how close to in (or out) X is. We may even decide on an appropriate threshold value for the acceptance of arguments.

An example of how such equations can be generated is given by the schema Eq_{max} below. The symbol $V_e(X)$ will be used to denote the *equilibrium* value of a node X. Now let $Att(Y)$ denote the set of all arguments attacking Y, i.e., $Att(Y) = \{X_i \in S \mid (X_i, Y) \in R\}$. We can define the equilibrium value of Y through the equation

$$(Eq_{max}) \qquad V_e(Y) = 1 - \max_{X_i \in Att(Y)}\{V_e(X_i)\}$$

Note that for a node Y, $V_e(Y) = 1$ if and only if $V_e(X) = 0$ for all $X \in Att(Y)$ and $V_e(Y) = 0$ if and only if $V_e(X) = 1$ for some $X \in Att(Y)$.

Thus, the network of Fig. 1. generates the following system of equations:

$$V_e(X) = 1$$
$$V_e(Z) = 1$$
$$V_e(W) = 1 - \max\{V_e(Z)\} \, (= 0)$$
$$V_e(Y) = 1 - \max\{V_e(X), V_e(W)\} \, (= 0)$$

If we set the threshold for acceptance of arguments at the value 1, we get that only the arguments X and Z are accepted as traditionally expected.

Generally speaking, Gabbay has shown that the totality of the solutions of the equations generated from a network using Eq_{max} corresponds to the totality of Caminada labellings of that network [15]. However, note that Eq_{max} does not take into account a node's initial value or the intensity with which the attacks to it have been carried out. We will consider a more sophisticated equation schema to take these into account in Section 4.

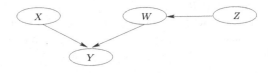

Fig. 1. A simple argumentation system

3   Merging Argumentation Networks

In this section, we provide some intuitions about our proposed method of merging argumentation networks. Our first goal is to show how to combine the networks into a single weighted argumentation network.

As discussed in Section 1, we start by associating each network with an agent who "votes" for its components. Obviously, in any interesting scenario, the networks being merged are distinct. Consider the networks in Fig. 2 and the chosen extensions of each network containing its winning arguments.

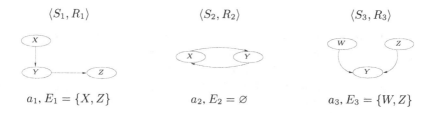

$\langle S_1, R_1 \rangle$ $\langle S_2, R_2 \rangle$ $\langle S_3, R_3 \rangle$

$a_1, E_1 = \{X, Z\}$ $a_2, E_2 = \varnothing$ $a_3, E_3 = \{W, Z\}$

Fig. 2. Argumentation networks of three different agents

We immediately notice that the three agents have different sets of arguments, and even in the case where the arguments coincide, the agents may disagree with respect to the attack relationships between them. For instance, argument W is only known to agent a_3, and in her network, Z attacks Y, whereas in the network of agent a_1, Y attacks Z.

There are many reasons why agents may have different argument systems. They may use different knowledge bases; they may have different deductive capabilities; they may use different inference systems; etc. These may also generate disagreements with respect to the direction of the attacks between arguments which are arguably akin to the existence of cycles in a single network. In fact, individual acyclic networks when combined into a single network may well end up containing cycles.

A simple way of harmonising the differences is to consider expansions to the networks. Unlike in [11], we do not expand each network individually, but rather we consider the single augmented network that includes the components of all other networks.

However, the augmented network alone is not sufficient to represent the community, because some components appear in more networks than others and we would like to reflect that by using weights. We first introduce the notion of a profile of (traditional) networks and then we define the notion of an augmented network with weights for a profile.

Definition 1. *A profile of argumentation systems is a tuple $P = \langle AN_1, \ldots, AN_k \rangle$ where each $AN_i = \langle S_i, R_i \rangle$ is an argumentation system. We assume each agent a_i has a procedure w_i for selecting a subset of S_i representing the winning arguments in S_i according to a_i's local semantics and we use E_i to denote this set, i.e., $w_i(S_i) = E_i$.*

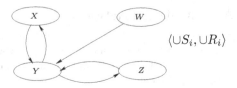

Fig. 3. Augmented network containing all components of $\langle S_1, R_1 \rangle$, $\langle S_2, R_2 \rangle$ and $\langle S_3, R_3 \rangle$

Definition 2. *Let* $P = \langle AN_1, \ldots, AN_k \rangle$ *be a profile of argumentation systems and let* $AN_i = \langle S_i, R_i \rangle$. *The weighted augmented network for* P *is a tuple* $AWN_P = \langle S, R, V_0, \xi \rangle$ *where*

- $S = \cup_i S_i$ *and* $R = \cup_i R_i$
- $V_0 : S \to [0,1]$ *represents the initial level of support for an argument* $X \in S$ *within* P, *as to be calculated/voted from all the* AN_i
- $\xi : R \to [0,1]$ *represents the intensity of an attack* $(X,Y) \in R$ *within* P, *as to be calculated/voted from all the* AN_i

Now we need to decide on a policy for representing each agent's perception of the arguments and attacks in AWN_P depending on the agent's original network. We shall see that these will later be used to define V_0 and ξ. For simplicity, we will refer generally to the arguments of these functions, i.e., arguments and attacks respectively, as the "components" of the network.

In agreement with [11] we believe that there is an intrinsic difference between supporting a component; rejecting it and being ignorant about its existence (in which case a decision for or against it is impossible). In order to distinguish these attitudes, we let agents vote for components by assigning to them one of the three values below.

    0: the agent does not know about the component
    1: the agent knows about the component and supports it
    −1: the agent knows about the component but does not support it

Definition 3. *Let* P *be a profile. The attitude of an agent* a_i *towards the component* c *of* AWN_P, *in symbols* $v_i(c)$, *is represented in the following way.*[1]

$v_i(X)$	$v_i((X,Y))$
0: if $X \notin S_i$	0: if either $X \notin S_i$ or $Y \notin S_i$ (or both)
1: if $X \in E_i$	1: if $(X,Y) \in R_i$
−1: if $X \in S_i - E_i$	−1: if $X,Y \in S_i$, but $(X,Y) \notin R_i$

That is, the agent a_i votes with 0 for *argument* X, if a_i has no knowledge about it; otherwise a_i will vote with 1 or −1 depending on whether X is amongst the winning arguments of S_i. The case of an attack from X to Y is similar but an attack may not exist because one or both arguments are not known. Hence, the agent a_i will vote with 0 if at least one of X and Y is not known (in which case a judicious decision about the

---

[1] To simplify notation we use the same function symbol v_i for nodes and edges.

attack is not possible). Otherwise, if both X and Y are known, the agent will vote with -1 if $(X, Y) \notin R_i$ and with 1 if $(X, Y) \in R_i$. Note that the vote 1 depends only on the existence of the attack in the agent's local network. Even if $Y \in E_i$ and $X \notin E_i$, the agent a_i must still vote with 1 if $(X, Y) \in R_i$, since she knows about it. The agent's choice for Y over X in spite of the attack of X on Y in this case is already taken into account in the agent's votes for X and Y.

The above voting strategy only requires that there is a local semantics for deciding the winning arguments in each network and does not make any assumptions on what it should be. In fact, the group as a whole may have several different local semantics.

If the local networks are themselves numerical, then a number of alternatives arise. One could compute each network individually, decide on the winning arguments and apply the same technique given above; or one could feed the equilibrium values of each network into the augmented one, normalise the values as appropriate, generate the equations and then compute the overall equilibrium values as before; or one could choose a combination of these ideas.

We now need to generate the initial weights for the augmented network based on each agent's attitude to its components. Again, because some components are only known to some agents, the community may take two different approaches when considering the overall level of support for a component:

 - in the *credulous* approach, the weights are calculated based on the total number of agents *that know about a component*
 - in the *sceptical* approach, the weights are calculated taking into account the total number of agents in the profile P

We will associate the credulous approach with the superscript $^+$ and the sceptical one with the superscript $^-$ in the definitions of the initial values V_0 and ξ below. Whenever the distinction is not important we will simply omit the superscripts.

Definition 4. *Let* $P = \langle AN_1, \ldots, AN_k \rangle$ *be a profile of argumentation systems and* AWN_P *the weighted augmented network for* P. *Let* $v^+(c) = |\{i \mid v_i(c) = 1\}|$ *and* $v^-(c) = |\{i \mid v_i(c) = -1\}|$. *We define*

$$V_0^+(X) = \frac{v^+(X)}{v^+(X)+v^-(X)} \qquad\qquad V_0^-(X) = \frac{v^+(X)}{k}$$

$$\xi^+((X,Y)) = \frac{v^+((X,Y))}{v^+((X,Y))+v^-((X,Y))} \qquad \xi^-((X,Y)) = \frac{v^+((X,Y))}{k}$$

Note that we have purposefully excluded the agents who do not know about a component c in the definitions of $V_0^+(c)$ and $\xi^+(c)$ above. These agents vote with 0 for c according to Definition 3 and hence are not counted in either $v^+(c)$ or $v^-(c)$. $V_0^-(c)$ and $\xi^-(c)$ on the other hand look at the components more sceptically and consider their representation across all voters.

For the example in Fig. 2 we get the initial weights shown in Fig. 4 for the components of the augmented network under each approach. Given these weights, we then need to calculate equilibrium values for the nodes (this will be done in Section 4).

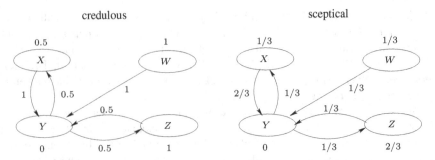

Fig. 4. Merged networks of Fig. 2 under the credulous and sceptical approaches

Note in Fig. 4 that under either approach, the initial weight of argument Y is 0. This is because Y is not a winning argument in any of the initial networks. Analogously, the initial value of Z is 1 only in the credulous approach. This is because Z is an winning argument in every network in which it is known, but it is not known in every network. Similarly, W's initial weight is 1 under the credulous approach, but $1/3$ under the sceptical one. This is reasonable, since it is only known by one out of the three agents, but for that agent (a_3) it is one of the winning arguments. The weights for the attacks follow the same pattern.

Generally speaking, we have the following.

Proposition 1. *Let* $P = \langle AN_1, \ldots, AN_k \rangle$ *be a profile of argumentation systems where each* $AN_i = \langle S_i, R_i \rangle$ *and* E_i *identifies the winning arguments in* S_i. *Let* $AWN_P = \langle S, R, V, \xi \rangle$ *be the weighted augmented network for* P *according to Definition 2. The following hold for all arguments* $X \in S$.

1. *if* $X \in \cap_i E_i$, *then* $V_0^+(X) = V_0^-(X) = 1$
2. *if* $X \notin \cup_i E_i$, *then* $V_0^+(X) = V_0^-(X) = 0$
3. *if* $X \in E_i$ *for all* i *such that* $X \in S_i$, *then* $V_0^+(X) = 1$

Proof. 1. and 2. follow directly from Definitions 3 and 4. For 3., note that if $X \in E_i$ *for all* i *such that* $X \in S_i$, *then* $v^-(X) = 0$, *and hence* $V_0^+(X) = 1$.

The situation with attacks is similar, but simpler.

Proposition 2. *For all attacks* $(X, Y) \in R$.

1. *if* $(X, Y) \in \cap_i R_i$, *then* $\xi^+\big((X, Y)\big) = 1$ *and* $\xi^-\big((X, Y)\big) = 1$.
2. *if* $(X, Y) \in \cup_i R_i$, *then* $\xi^+\big((X, Y)\big) > 0$ *and* $\xi^-\big((X, Y)\big) > 0$

Proof. These follow directly from Definitions 3 and 4.

We now turn to the problem of calculating equilibrium values for the arguments of a weighted augmented network.

4   Equilibrium Values in a Weighted Augmented Network

One important aspect in the calculation of the equilibrium values of the arguments in a weighted augmented network is the decision of how the attacks to an argument should affect its initial support value.

As in any usual argumentation system, arguments may be attacked by any number of arguments. Since we work with numerical values, we want to aggregate the strength of these attacks somehow in order to *weaken* the weight of the attacked node. The strength of an attack itself depends on the strength of the attacking node and the intensity with which the attack is carried out. The attacking nodes may be themselves attacked, so we need to perform the aggregation systematically. We start by analysing the effect of attacks in general.

Consider the network in Fig. 5, in which x, y and z are the initial weights of the arguments X, Y and Z, respectively. Let us for a moment ignore these initial weights.

Fig. 5. A typical weighted argument network

If we want to mimic the standard behaviour of the attacks in an argumentation system [12], we need to accept arguments X and Z and reject argument Y. The reasoning is as follows. Since no arguments attack X, it *persists*. X then attacks Y, which is *defeated*, and hence no persisting arguments attack Z, which then consequently also persists. In our numerical semantics, persistence is associated with the values $[t, 1]$ (for some $t > 0$) and defeat with the value 0. For us, "to be defeated" means to end up with equilibrium value 0 and "to persist" means to end up with a value equal or higher than a minimum acceptance level $t > 0$. If we want to be strict, we can set $t = 1$. Otherwise, we may settle for any value greater than 0 (up to 1).

Ideally, we would like to remain close to the basic semantics, taking care of the arguments' initial weights (which are all in the unit interval U) and the intensity with which the attacks between them are carried out. Hence, our objective is to calculate the values $V_e(X)$, $V_e(Y)$ and $V_e(Z)$, based on x, y, z, ξ_{XY} and ξ_{YZ}. Arguably, since X is not attacked by any node, its equilibrium value $V_e(X)$ can be calculated directly by some manipulation on the value x alone. The simplest procedure is to make $V_e(X) = x$, its initial value. On the other hand, the value of $V_e(Y)$ depends both on $V_e(X)$ and the *intensity* ξ_{XY} with which the attack from X to Y is carried out. Once $V_e(Y)$ is calculated, the equilibrium value for $V_e(Z)$ can be calculated using ξ_{YZ} in the same way. If there are cycles, the equations get more complex, but they are solvable, as long as the functions involved are all continuous.[2]

If we give initial value 1 to all arguments and consider all attacks being transmitted with full intensity, then since X has initial value 1 and it is not attacked by any other argument, its equilibrium value becomes 1. It then attacks Y with full intensity (i.e.,

---

[2] This and some other related issues will be explored in more detail in a forthcoming paper.

$\xi_{XY} = 1$), which means that the initial value of Y, $y = 1$, is weakened by 1 and its equilibrium value becomes 0. Effectively, this annihilates the attack on Z, which then gets as its equilibrium value the same value as its initial one, i.e., 1. As a result, we end up with the acceptance of X (because of its equilibrium value 1); the rejection of Y (because of its equilibrium value 0); and the acceptance of Z (also because of its equilibrium value 1).

We stress that, in general, we are free to decide on the minimum value we require for considering an argument as accepted. As we mentioned, we may decide this to be the value 1 itself, leaving all values $0 < x < 1$ to represent *undecided* arguments; or we may even do away with the notion of undecidedness altogether and divide the interval in two halves only: one with the values which we consider accepted and the other with the ones we consider rejected.

If we want to think in terms of the effect of the attacks on an argument X, our problem is to determine a factor $0 \le \pi(X) \le 1$ representing the combined strength of these attacks. The equilibrium value for X can be calculated by multiplying X's initial value by this factor, i.e., $V_e(X) = V_0(X) \cdot \pi(X)$.

When there are multiple attacks to an argument X, π must *aggregate* the value of these attacks. In order to remain close to the standard argumentation semantics, we want π to satisfy at least the three conditions below.

(SSC1) $\pi(X) = 1$, if $max_{Y \in Att(X)}\{\xi((Y,X))V_e(Y)\} = 0$
(SSC2) $\pi(X) = 0$, if $max_{Y \in Att(X)}\{\xi((Y,X))V_e(Y)\} = 1$
(SSC3) π is continuous

(SSC1) says that if all arguments attacking X are fully defeated or transmitted with null intensity, then X retains its initial value fully. (SSC2) says that if any argument that attacks X has full strength *and* the attack is carried out with full intensity, then X is fully defeated. (SSC3) ensures that the considerations about the interactions between the nodes are robust, i.e., that small changes in the initial values do not cause sudden variations in the equilibrium ones.

So the idea is that the stronger an attack is, the closer the attack gets to the value 1 and hence the closer we want π to get to 0 so that the equilibrium value of the attacked argument decreases proportionally (since its initial value is multiplied by π). In the case of a single attack of strength u to node X with transmission factor κ, one possibility is to make $\pi(X) = 1 - \kappa u$. In the network of Fig. 5 above, this would make $\pi(Y) = 1 - \xi((Y,X))V_e(X)$ and hence Y's equilibrium value would be $V_e(Y) = V(Y) \cdot (1 - V_e(X)) = 1 \cdot 0 = 0$, as expected.

Besnard and Hunter's *categoriser* [5] is an example of a function satisfying (SSC1)–(SSC3) (more on this in Section 6).

But what can we say about $\pi(X)$ when X is attacked by multiple arguments?

As usual, attacking arguments combine via *multiplication*, which is compatible with the behaviour of conjunction in Boolean logic and in probability. The equations for the equilibrium values of the nodes of a weighted augmented network are defined below.

Definition 5. Let $P = \langle AN_1, \dots, AN_k \rangle$ be a profile of argumentation systems and $AWN_P = \langle S, R, V, \xi \rangle$ the weighted augmented network for P as defined before. The equation for the equilibrium value of an argument $X \in S$ is defined as

(Eq_{inv}) $\qquad$ $V_e(X) = V_0(X) \cdot \prod_{Y_i \in Att(X)}(1 - \xi((Y_i, X))V_e(Y_i))$

One can choose V_0^+ and ξ^+ or V_0^- and ξ^- depending on whether a credulous or scepti-cal approach is desired (this will be explored further in Section 5). Note that the highest possible intensity of the attack by an argument Y is $V_0(Y)$ itself. This happens when the attack is carried out with full intensity and Y is not itself attacked by any node — in this case it retains its initial value fully, i.e., $V_e(Y) = V_0(Y)$. Because we take the com-plement of this attack to 1, in such circumstances the equilibrium value of the attacked argument would be 0.

Eq_{max} decreases the initial support value of an argument according to the value of the strongest attack. Eq_{inv} on the other hand is *cumulative*: it aggregates the strength of the attacking nodes. The intuition is that each challenge to an argument contributes to decrease the argument's overall credibility.

Henceforth, we formally set the value $\pi(X)$ to $\prod_{Y_i \in Att(X)}(1 - \xi((Y_i, X))V_e(Y_i))$.

Proposition 3. π *satisfies (SSC1)–(SSC3).*

Proof. If $\max_{Y \in Att(X)}\{\xi((Y, X))V_e(Y)\} = 0$, then by Definition 5, $\prod_{Y_i \in Att(X)}(1 - \xi((Y_i, X))V_e(Y_i)) = 1$. Therefore, (SSC1) is satisfied. If $\max_{Y \in Att(X)}\{\xi((Y, X)) V_e(Y)\} = 1$, then by Definition 5, for some $Y' \in Att(X)$, $1 - \xi((Y', X))V_e(Y') = 0$, and then $\prod_{Y_i \in Att(X)}(1 - \xi((Y_i, X))V_e(Y_i)) = 0$. Hence (SSC2) is also satisfied. (SSC3) is trivially satisfied.

Combining attacks in this way was initially proposed in [3].

It is easy to see that when all attacks are carried out with full intensity, $\pi(X)$ can be written simply as

$$\prod_{Y \in Att(X)} (1 - V_e(Y))$$

which is equivalent to

$$1 - \curlyvee_{Y \in Att(X)} V_e(Y) \qquad (1)$$

where $a \curlyvee b = a + b - a.b$ and for $\Delta = \{a_1, \ldots, a_k\}$, $\curlyvee\Delta = ((a_1 \curlyvee a_2) \curlyvee \ldots \curlyvee a_k)$. The expression in (1) is the complement of the probabilistic sum t-conorm used by Leite and Martins in [19]. In probability theory, the probabilistic sum expresses the probability of the occurrence of independent events. Since we want to weaken the value of the attacked node, we take the complement of this sum to 1.

It is worth emphasizing that the equilibrium value of a node can never be higher than its initial support value.

Proposition 4. *For arguments* X, $V_e(X) \leq V_0(X)$.

Proof. Straightforward. Note that $V_e(X) = V_0(X) \cdot \pi(X)$. By Definition 4, for all arguments Y, $0 \leq V_0(Y) \leq 1$. By Definition 5, $0 \leq \pi(X) \leq 1$ and hence $V_e(X) \leq V_0(X)$.

Proposition 5 (Unanimity of acceptance). *Let* $P = \langle AN_1, \ldots, AN_k \rangle$ *be a profile of argumentation systems where each* $AN_i = \langle S_i, R_i \rangle$ *and let* $AWN_P = \langle S, R, V, \xi \rangle$ *be* *the weighted augmented network for P. If each E_i is conflict-free and $X \in \cap_i E_i$, then $V_e(X) = 1$.*

Proof. By Proposition 1, if $X \in \cap_i E_i$, then $V_0^+(X) = V_0^-(X) = 1$. Suppose $(Y, X) \in R_i$, for some argumentation framework AN_i. Since each E_i is conflict-free, then $Y \notin E_i$ and hence $Y \notin \cup_i E_i$. By Proposition 4, $V_0^+(Y) = V_0^-(Y) = 0$ and by Proposition 4, $V_e(Y) = 0$. It follows that $\pi(X) = 1$ and hence $V_e(X) = 1$.

If each E_i is conflict-free and $V_e(X) = 1$, then $X \in \cap_i E_i$ only if V_e is calculated under the sceptical approach. The credulous approach is more lenient, because it gives initial support value 1 to an argument as long as it wins in every argumentation system *in which it is known* and this may be sufficient to make the argument's equilibrium value 1 too as long as the sets of winning arguments are conflict-free (see Example 2. in Section 5). It is worth emphasizing that the flip side of this is that attacks are treated in the same way and as a consequence the value of an argument may also decrease as a result. This is illustrated in Example 1. of Section 5, where the equilibrium value of the argument Y is lower in the credulous approach than in the sceptical one as the result of credulously accepting X which attacks Y.

Thresholds for Acceptance

The equilibrium values simply represent how the initial overall level of support for a component is affected by the interactions with the other components in the network. If one wants to make a decision on what arguments to accept overall, an appropriate threshold for acceptance for the network at hand must be decided. The value 1 represents the strongest possible level of acceptance, but setting this as the minimum acceptance level could prove too strict even under the credulous approach. One could base the minimum acceptance level on the maximum or minimum of the equilibrium values or simply take the average and accept the arguments whose equilibrium values are *above* it. Another possibility is to accept arguments with equilibrium value above 0.5. Although this may seem arbitrary, in fact values above 0.5 can be associated with the concept of *majority*, because acceptance of an argument by clear majority produces a initial support value strictly greater than 0.5.

However, in the examples that follow, we will simply use the average of the equilibrium values calculated. In more realistic scenarios an appropriate threshold value can be determined through a more sophisticated analysis of the networks in the profile in a similar way to how it is done in [2] (which is itself based on the notion of the "inconsistency degree" of a knowledge base). This investigation itself is quite complex and left for future work.

5   Worked Examples

We now illustrate our technique with a few examples. In each example, we show the networks to be merged on the left and the augmented (merged) network in the middle with its components annotated with the initial weights in the form "credulous : sceptical". The equilibrium values obtained are given on the right and the accepted arguments indicated with a shadowed box. Due to space limitations we cannot include the equations here, but they can be easily obtained using Definition 5.

1.

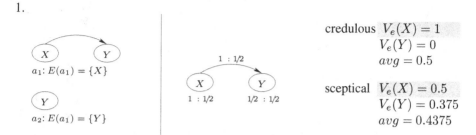

Under the credulous approach $V_0(X) = 1$ and hence $V_e(X) = 1$. Its attack on Y is transmitted with full intensity. $V_0(Y) = 0.5$. Therefore, $V_e(Y) = 0.5 \times (1-1) = 0$. Under the sceptical approach $V_0(X) = 0.5$ and hence $V_e(X) = 0.5$. Its attack on Y is transmitted with intensity 0.5. Therefore, $V_e(Y) = 0.5 \times (1-0.5 \times 0.5) = 0.375$. Note that the sceptical approach produces a higher equilibrium value for Y because under the credulous approach X is fully accepted and its attack on Y fully defeats it. The only argument with equilibrium value above the average of the values is X in both approaches.

2.

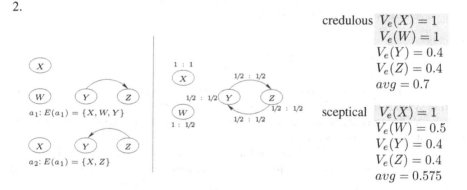

In this example both agents accept argument X and there are no attacks on it in any network. Thus, regardless of the approach, the equilibrium value of X is 1. In spite of there not being any attacks on W, it is only known by agent a_2. Under the credulous approach $V_e(W) = 1$, but under the sceptical approach $V_e(W) = 0.5$, since it is accepted by only half of the community. Y and Z are also accepted by half of the community, but in each case, the other half supports a complementary attack of one on the other. As a result, their equilibrium values are both reduced from 0.5 to 0.4. X and W have equilibrium values above the average under the credulous approach and are hence accepted, but under the sceptical approach only X is accepted.

3.

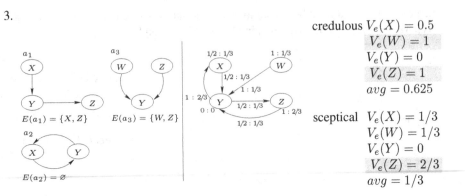

This is the example appearing in Fig. 2. Y does not feature in any of the agents' winning arguments. Its initial support value is 0 and hence its equilibrium value is also 0. This leaves X's initial support values unchanged. Under the credulous approach both W and Z get value 1. Under the sceptical approach Z's equilibrium value is the highest, because it is accepted by $2/3$ of the agents (as opposed to X and W which are accepted by only $1/3$ of them). Both W and Z have equilibrium values above the average under the credulous approach and are hence accepted, but only Z is accepted under the sceptical one (note that it is the only argument accepted by the majority of the agents).

6   Comparisons with other Work

As mentioned in Section 1, many frameworks consider extensions to Dung's argumentation systems that are capable of representing in one way or another the notion of the strength of arguments or attacks. In this section, we discuss the relationship between some of these approaches and ours.

In terms of numerical *merging*, the formalism that most resembles ours is the one proposed in [9], which uses a weighted argumentation system. The idea is also based on the combination of all networks into a single augmented one in which attacks are assigned weights that correspond to ours under the credulous approach. However, the similarities stop there. In particular, there is no notion of sceptical support; no mechanism to associate weights to arguments; and the concept of acceptance is based on the notion of "various-strength" defence: an argument X defends an argument Y against argument Z, if the weight of the attack of X on Z is greater than the weight of the attack of Z on Y. This is then used in the definition of admissibility. We believe that once we are prepared to evaluate the strength of the attacks based on the opinions of the agents, we should also be prepared to take these opinions into account in the evaluation of the support for the arguments as well.

Bistarelli and Santini also consider a numerical approach but, as in the above, their formalism only assigns weights to attacks [6]. Amgoud and Kaci take a different approach to merging by considering the merging of knowledge bases whose underlying formalism is a possibilitic logic [2]. This allows for the calculation of the *inconsistency degree* of a base, which in turn can be used to determine its "plausible" consequences. This notion of a degree of inconsistency is something we would like to investigate further to provide a more robust definition for the threshold of acceptance of arguments.

Other formalisms for merging not based on numerical approaches include [11,22].

If we have an adequate meaning for the initial weights, we can use the equational approach for a single weighted network independently of the merging process. Leaving considerations about merging aside, it is possible to compare our formalism with other weighted argumentation systems. In [5], the equilibrium value of an argument is calculated by a so-called *categoriser* function, an example of which is the **h-categoriser** h, which defined for an argument X as $h(X) = 1$, if $Att(Y) = \emptyset$; and $h(X) = 1/(1 + \sum_{Y \in Att(X)} h(Y))$, otherwise.

Let us now analyse what happens in a sequence of attacks like the one below. For comparison, we assume that all nodes have the same initial values v and consider the intensity with which all attacks are carried out to be 1.

Assuming initial value $v = 1$ in the example above, we would have that $h(X_1) = 1$; $h(X_2) = 0.5$; $h(X_3) = 0.66$; and so forth. This obviously does not agree with Dung's semantics. Using the equational approach, we get that $V_e(X_1) = v$, $V_e(X_2) = v(1-v)$, $V_e(X_3) = v(1-(v(1-v)))$, ... If $v = 1$, then $V_e(X_1) = 1$, $V_e(X_2) = 0$, $V_e(X_3) = 1$, and so forth, agreeing with Dung's semantics as expected. If $v = 0$, then $V_e(A_i) = 0$ for all i. This is as expected, since in this case no arguments have any initial support. In fact, for all nodes X, $V_e(X) \le V(X)$, since $\pi(X) = \prod_{Y \in Att(X)} (1 - \xi((Y, X))V_e(Y)) \le 1$. If $v = 0.5$, we get $V_e(X_1) = 0.5$, $V_e(X_2) = 0.25$, $V_e(X_3) = 0.375$, ...[3]

Leite and Martins proposed *social abstract argumentation frameworks* (SAAFs) which can be seen as an extension of Dung's abstract argumentation frameworks to allow the representation of information about votes to arguments. The motivation of these networks is to provide a means to calculate the result of the interaction between arguments using approval and disapproval ratings from users of news forums. The idea is that when a user sees an argument, she may approve it, disapprove it, or simply abstain from expressing an opinion. The 'weights' associated with the arguments in this case can also be seen as being generated by how the agents perceive the arguments. However, the initial support level for an argument is calculated differently in their formalism and there is no notion of strength of attack, even though, as in our case attacks are aggregated using the probabilistic sum t-conorm.

7 Conclusions and Future Work

In this paper, we showed how a profile of argumentation systems can be merged through the use of an augmented argumentation network provided with weights for the arguments and the attacks between them. The initial weights are calculated based on how

---

[3] We can think of an infinite sequence of this kind as a node with an attack on itself. In the limit $k \to \infty$, for $V_0(X_1) = 0.5$, $V_e(X_k) = \frac{1}{3}$.

representative each component features in the profile and are independent of the local semantics of each network. We proposed credulous and sceptical approaches for calculating the weights. The credulous approach calculates the overall representation based on how many agents "know" about a component whereas the sceptical approach looks at the total number of networks in the profile.

Weighted argumentation networks have been proposed before. Sometimes weights have been assigned to the arguments (e.g., as in [2,3,5,8,19]) and sometimes they have been assigned to the attacks (e.g., as in [3,6,13,23]). In our approach, both arguments and attacks have weights and the network is seen as a generator for equations. The idea is to calculate equilibrium values for the arguments based on their initial support value within the profile and the interactions with other arguments through the attack relation. These values can be calculated by solving a system of equations generated by the augmented network, following [14]. Once calculated, the notion of acceptance can be defined in terms of a threshold value for the equilibrium values, for which a strict interpretation is the value 1. However, the framework is flexible in the sense that a particular application is free to associate segments of the unit interval in different ways. For instance, one could associate 0 with rejection; 1 with acceptance and consider anything else inbetween as undecided.

We can see the initial values in our augmented network as coming from an extended form of approval voting in which voters can also express ignorance and rejection for some components. There are variations on this idea that are worth investigating, including giving varying degrees of preference to the components depending on the expertise level of the agents supporting them. Furthermore, there are interesting connections with several other areas of research. From the aggregation perspective, it is worth exploring similarities with other procedures for voting and formalisms for merging of knowledge bases as in [10,16,17,18]. Some similarities also appear in the spirit of the calculation of the interactions with the areas of network flows [1], belief propagation and Bayesian networks [20]. We will explore these issues in more detail in future work.

The merging of argumentation systems is an application that leads naturally to the employment of weights in a network. However, one need not restrict its use to such scenarios only. All that is required is a suitable interpretation for the weights; an adequate schema for generating the equations; and an interpretation for the equilibrium values. This paper paves the way for a new type of research in argumentation networks not only because its approach is numerical, but also because it is an initial study of *vector evaluations*. We can see this work as a preliminary investigation on how to aggregate many-dimensional values of the components of a network and propagate them through the network taking its attack relation into account.

To realise the potential, consider the very well developed area of many-dimensional temporal logics. In these logics, a formula is evaluated at several indices. As a complex formula is evaluated in the model we move from one set of indices to another. The analogous movement in the case of argumentation is that of an attack. One can move from one node to another evaluating and propagating the values.

The equational approach can also be used in a more general context. For instance, if the underlying representation is itself based on a fuzzy or possibilitic logic, the initial weights can be obtained from the computations in the logic themselves, in the spirit of Prakken [21] or Amgoud-Kaci's "force of an argument" [2]. The weights can then subsequently be combined taking the topology of the network into account as done here.

Acknowledgements. The authors would like to thank Sanjay Modgil and the referees for useful comments and suggestions to this paper. D. M. Gabbay was partially supported by the Israel Science Foundation Project 1321/10: Integrating logic and networks.

References

1. Ahuja, R.K., Magnanti, T.L., Orlin, J.B.: Network flows – Theory, algorithms and applications. Prentice-Hall (1993)
2. Amgoud, L., Kaci, S.: An argumentation framework for merging conflicting knowledge bases. Journal of Approximate Reasoning 45, 321–340 (2007)
3. Barringer, H., Gabbay, D.M., Woods, J.: Temporal Dynamics of Support and Attack Networks: From Argumentation to Zoology. In: Hutter, D., Stephan, W. (eds.) Mechanizing Mathematical Reasoning. LNCS (LNAI), vol. 2605, pp. 59–98. Springer, Heidelberg (2005)
4. Bench-Capon, T.J.M.: Persuasion in practical argument using value-based argumentation frameworks. Journal of Logic and Computation 13(3), 429–448 (2003)
5. Besnard, P., Hunter, A.: A logic-based theory of deductive arguments. Artificial Intelligence 128(1-2), 203–235 (2001)
6. Bistarelli, S., Santini, F.: A common computational framework for semiring-based argumentation systems. In: Proceedings of the 2010 conference on ECAI 2010: 19th European Conference on Artificial Intelligence, pp. 131–136. IOS Press, Amsterdam (2010)
7. Caminada, M., Gabbay, D.M.: A logical account of formal argumentation. Studia Logica 93(2-3), 109–145 (2009)
8. Cayrol, C., Lagasquie-Schiex, M.-C.: Graduality in argumentation. Journal of Artificial Intelligence Research 23, 245–297 (2005)
9. Cayrol, C., Lagasquie-Schiex, M.-C.: Merging argumentation systems with weighted argumentation systems: a preliminary study. Technical Report RR 2011-18 FR, IRIT (2011)
10. Chopra, S., Ghose, A., Meyer, T.: Social choice theory, belief merging, and strategy-proofness. Information Fusion 7(1), 61–79 (2006)
11. Coste-Marquis, S., Devred, C., Konieczny, S., Lagasquie-Schiex, M.-C., Marquis, P.: On the merging of Dung's argumentation systems. Artificial Intelligence 171, 730–753 (2007)
12. Dung, P.M.: On the acceptability of arguments and its fundamental role in nonmonotonic reasoning, logic programming and n-person games. Artificial Intelligence 77, 321–357 (1995)
13. Dunne, P.E., Hunter, A., McBurney, P., Parsons, S., Wooldridge, M.: Weighted argument systems: Basic definitions, algorithms, and complexity results. Artificial Intelligence 175(2), 457–486 (2011)
14. Gabbay, D.M.: Introducing Equational Semantics for Argumentation Networks. In: Liu, W. (ed.) ECSQARU 2011. LNCS, vol. 6717, pp. 19–35. Springer, Heidelberg (2011)
15. Gabbay, D.M.: An equational approach to argumentation networks. Argumentation and Computation 3 (2012)
16. Gabbay, D.M., Pigozzi, G., Rodrigues, O.: Belief revision, belief merging and voting. In: Proceedings of the Seventh Conference on Logic and the Foundations of Games and Decision Theory (LOFT 2006), pp. 71–78. University of Liverpool (2006)
17. Konieczny, S., Pino-Pérez, R.: On the logic of merging. In: Proceedings of KR 1998, pp. 488–498. Morgan Kaufmann (1998)

18. Konieczny, S., Pino-Pérez, R.: Logic based merging. Journal of Philosophical Logic 40(2), 239–270 (2011)
19. Leite, J., Martins, J.: Social abstract argumentation. In: Proceedings of the 22nd International Joint Conference on Artificial Intelligence, pp. 2287–2292 (2011)
20. Pearl, J.: Fusion, propagation, and structuring in belief networks. Artificial Intelligence 29(3), 241–288 (1986)
21. Prakken, H.: An abstract framework for argumentation with structured arguments. Argument and Computation 1, 93–124 (2010)
22. Rahwan, I., Tohmé, F.: Collective argument evaluation as judgement aggregation. In: Proceedings of the 9th International Conference on Autonomous Agents and Multiagent Systems, AAMAS 2010, vol. 1, pp. 417–424. International Foundation for Autonomous Agents and Multiagent Systems, Richland (2010)
23. Wang, J., Luo, G., Wang, B.: Argumentation framework with weighted argument structure. In: 10th IEEE International Conference on Cognitive Informatics Cognitive Computing (ICCI*CC), pp. 385–391 (2011)

Author Index